CIVIL SOCIL

Counter-terrorism Policy, Civil Society,
and Aid Post-9/11

CIVIL SOCIETY UNDER STRAIN

Counter-terrorism Policy, Civil Society, and Aid Post-9/11

Edited by

Jude Howell

and

Jeremy Lind

Kumarian Press
An Imprint of Stylus Publishing

Civil Society under Strain: Counter-terrorism Policy, Civil Society, and Aid Post-9/11
Published in 2010 in the United States of America by Kumarian Press
22883 Quicksilver Drive, Sterling, VA 20166-2012 USA

The text of this book is set in 10/12.5 Sabon

Proofread by Publication Services, Inc.
Index by Publication Services, Inc.
Production and design by Publication Services, Inc.

Printed in the United States of America by Thomson-Shore, Inc.
Text printed with vegetable oil-based ink.

∞ The paper used in this publication meets the minimum requirements of the American National Standard for Information Sciences-Permanence of Paper for printed Library Materials, ANSI Z39.48-1984

Library of Congress Cataloging-in-Publication Data

   Civil society under strain: counter-terrorism policy, civil society, and aid post-9/11 / edited by Jude Howell and Jeremy Lind.
      p. cm.
   Includes bibliographical references and index.
      ISBN 978-1-56549-297-4 (pbk. : alk. paper) — ISBN 978-1-56549-298-1 (cloth : alk. paper)
   1. War on Terrorism, 2001-. 2. Terrorism—Government policy—Case studies. 3. Terrorism—Prevention—Case studies. I. Howell, Jude. II. Lind, Jeremy.
   HV6431.C496 2010
   363.325'17—dc22
                                                          2009027447

TABLE OF CONTENTS

Acronyms

ACLU	American Civil Liberties Union
AEDPA	Antiterrorism and Effective Death Penalty Act
AFP	Australian Federal Police
AMCRAN	Australian Muslim Civil Rights Advocacy Network
APEC	Asia-Pacific Economic Cooperation
ASIO	Australian Security Intelligence Organisation
ATA	Anti-Terrorism Act (Uganda)
ATIME	Association of Immigrant Moroccan Workers in Spain
BJP	Bharatiya Janata Party (India)
CERD	United Nations Committee on the Elimination of Racial Discrimination
CIA	Central Intelligence Agency (US)
CJTF-HOA	Combined Joint Task Force—Horn of Africa
COIN	Counter-Insurgency
CSO	Civil society organization
CTC	Counter-Terrorism Committee (UN)
DFID	Department for International Development (UK)
DOD	Department of Defense
DRC	Democratic Republic of Congo
EBA	Effects based approach
EMP	Euro-Mediterranean Partnership
FATF	Financial Action Task Force
FCO	Foreign and Commonwealth Office
FDC	Forum for Democratic Change (Uganda)

FEERI	Federation of Islamic Religious Entities
GOSL	Government of Sri Lanka
HREOC	Human Rights and Equal Opportunity Commission (Australia)
ICC	International Criminal Court
ICRC	International Committee of the Red Cross
IEEPA	International Emergency Economic Powers Act (United States)
JVP	Janatha Vimukthi Peramuna
LRA	Lord's Resistance Army
LSSP	Lanka Sama Samaja Party
LTTE	Liberation Tigers of Tamil Eelam
MHRF	Muslim Human Rights Forum
MOD	Ministry of Defence
MOU	Memorandum of Understanding
NATO	North Atlantic Treaty Organization
NGO	Non-governmental organization
NRM	National Resistance Movement (Uganda)
OAU	Organization of African Unity
OFAC	Office of Foreign Assets Control (United States)
PJCIS	Parliamentary Joint Committee on Intelligence and Security (Australia)
PP	Popular Party (Spain)
PCRU	Post-Conflict Reconstruction Unit
POTA	Prevention of Terrorism Act (India)
POTO	Prevention of Terrorism Ordinance (India)
PRT	Provincial Reconstruction Team
PVS	Partner Vetting System
QIPs	Quick impact projects
RSS	Rashtriya Swayamsevak Sangh
SFLP	Sri Lanka Freedom Party
SDGT	Specially designated global terrorist
SLCLC	Senate Legal and Constitutional Legislation Committee (Australia)

SLCRC	Senate Legal and Constitutional References Committee (Australia)
SLRC	Security Legislation Review Committee (Australia)
SMA	Sher Mohammed Akhundzadha (former governor of Helmand province, Afghanistan)
TADA	Terrorist and Disruptive Activities (Prevention) Act (India)
TRO	Tamils Rehabilitation Organisation
UCIDE	Union of Islamic Communities in Spain
UNP	United National Party
UWT	Ummah Welfare Trust
UNPROFOR	United Nations Protection Force
UPDF	Uganda People's Defence Forces
US	United States
USAID	United States Agency for International Development
VHP	Vishwa Hindu Parishad

1

INTRODUCTION

Jude Howell and Jeremy Lind

In response to the 9/11 attacks on New York's Twin Towers and the Pentagon, President Bush launched the War on Terror. With his famous words, "You are either with us or against us," President Bush warned governments across the world of the potentially dire consequences of not allying with the United States in facing the perceived threat of global jihadist terrorism. In the aftermath of these rapid events, political leaders set about swiftly introducing counter-terrorist legislation, measures, and practices to demonstrate their commitment to countering this seemingly new brand of terrorism and their support for the United States. UN Security Resolutions 1373 and 1535 soon followed, endorsing the need for governments to institute counter-terrorist legislation and measures and act in concert to thwart terrorism. In a similar vein the Financial Action Task Force put pressure on governments to introduce and/or strengthen anti-money laundering legislation to tackle terrorist financing, drawing charities, foreign exchange bureaus, and money service businesses such as informal money transmittance services for the first time into its ambit.

The spate of counter-terrorist legislation, measures, and practices that ensued has aroused considerable alarm among human rights activists, lawyers, and scholars. Political leaders have skillfully deployed the climate of fear and insecurity generated by the global "War on Terror"[1] regime to justify the rapid introduction of extraordinary measures to secure their electorates from perceived terrorist threats. Concerned about civil liberties and human rights, human rights lawyers, activists, and scholars have challenged the necessity and details of counter-terrorist legislation, defended the rights of detained suspects, queried the legality of the US detention camp in Guantanamo Bay, Cuba, and opposed the practice of extraordinary renditions and the use of torture to extract evidence. Their

1

efforts have been significant in raising public awareness of the human rights and civil liberties costs of extraordinary counter-terrorist measures hastily conceived in the name of security.

Though much attention has rightly been given to the consequences of counter-terrorist practices for human rights and civil liberties, there has been much less focus on the effects of these on civil society or on aid policy—and particularly on how aid policy relates to civil society. There is an emerging body of literature that has begun to scrutinize the effects of post-9/11 counter-terrorist legislation on charities, on Muslim populations and organizations, on diasporic groups, and on the regulatory frameworks governing registered civil society groups.[2] There is also a smaller body of work that addresses the impacts of the global War on Terror regime for development and humanitarian aid policy and practice.[3]

Much of this literature has focused on the restrictive, punitive, and negative effects of counter-terrorist legislation. Given the degree of secrecy pertaining to counter-terrorist measures and operations, it has not been easy for researchers to obtain detailed, accurate, or reliable information. In the early years after 2001, much of this early writing on civil society and counter-terrorism relied on emerging, piecemeal, anecdotal evidence rather than systematic, sustained research. At this point the imperative was to raise awareness of these issues and to stimulate public debate rather than engage in long-term evidence-gathering, which necessarily requires time, resources, and access. The corollary of this emphasis on the restrictive effects of "hard" counter-terrorist measures is that there has been relatively little attention given to the impact of "soft" counter-terrorist measures such as de-radicalization initiatives, courting moderate Muslim groups, and manipulating the ideological battlefield to win "hearts and minds."[4] The UK and US governments have increasingly realized the importance of a dual-pronged approach to terrorism that draws on both hard and soft measures.

This book sets out to add to this emerging literature by bringing together recent research on a diversity of contexts. The book covers a range of countries affected by the global War on Terror regime, such as Sri Lanka and India in South Asia, Uzbekistan and Kyrgyzstan in Central Asia, the United Kingdom and Spain in Europe, Kenya and Uganda in Africa, and the United States. In this way the book adopts an international perspective on the global War on Terror regime. In doing so the book addresses a number of key themes, namely, the inter-weaving of the global War on Terror regime with domestic politics; the rendering of civil society as suspect in terrorism and its subsequent regulation and control; the selective targeting of parts of civil society for control and co-option; and the deployment of aid policy, and particularly its engagement with civil society, for security objectives. In this way it draws attention to the multiple strains that the War on Terror regime has placed on civil society.

Before proceeding further, it is important to clear some conceptual ground in relation to the terms "civil society" and "global War on Terror regime." As civil society is a much-contested concept, we use the term in this book to refer to the arena where people deliberate upon and organize around shared, collective purposes.[5] As an ideal-type it is distinct from government, market, and family, though in practice the boundaries between these spheres are blurred and interwoven to varying degrees. Civil society is populated by organizations that vary in their degree of formality and typically includes associational forms such as trade unions, social movements, virtual networks, campaigns, coalitions, faith groups, direct action groups, peace groups, human rights organizations, and so on. Whereas liberal democratic interpretations of civil society emphasize its plural and essentially harmonious nature, this book starts from the premise that civil society is as much a site of division as of unity, and of conflict as of consensus. In other words, it is a battlefield upon which different values, ideas, and political visions are debated, contended, and struggled over. As such it is also a site that is used instrumentally by different actors, whether within the civil society realm or without, for different ideological, political, and organizational purposes.

The concept of a global War on Terror regime comprises a set of interrelated constitutive elements. The concept expresses a mobilizing discourse that is used by political leaders to rally and justify public support for a range of political and military objectives. It outlines a crude, polarizing vision of the world, which pits civilization against barbarism, modernity against backwardness, good against evil, and freedom against oppression. It deploys militaristic language, as reflected in the very words of "war" and "terror" and is a shorthand justification for pre-emptive, unilateral military action, as occurred with the invasion of Iraq in 2003. It also depicts a new global, post-Cold War, political re-ordering that creates new alliances and divisions among states and non-state actors of varying stripes and hues. It constitutes a new set of global and national institutional arrangements— policy and legal instruments that seek to bind the inputs of otherwise discrete national governments and of otherwise compartmentalized agencies and departments around a counter-terrorist agenda. In doing so, it draws upon both "hard" security, intelligence, policing, and legislative measures as well as "soft" measures that seek to dominate the ideological ground. The regime nurtures a network of political actors stretching across the public and private, governmental and nongovernmental, the commercial and charitable, and the north and the south.

It is a "regime" rather than merely a political discourse or set of policies associated with a particular administration. As such, it implies that the policies, laws, bureaucratic regulations and practices, and institutional arrangements that have been formed in support of global counter-terrorism cooperation will endure beyond the political actors that hastened their emergence. The recent change in political administration in the United States, the subsequent abandonment of the term "War on Terror," and the various actions taken to address some of the excesses of the regime such as the closure of Guantanamo Bay are not in themselves sufficient to remove the regime. For this a much more concerted effort to overhaul the policy, regulatory, legal, and institutional constitutive elements of the regime would be needed.

Having cleared the conceptual ground, we now look more closely at the key themes explored in the book and the contributions of authors to each of these.

Key Themes

Interweaving of the Global War on Terror Regime with Domestic Politics

A key theme explored in the book is the intersection between the global War on Terror regime and regional and national politics. An assumption here is that the global War on Terror regime is not a blueprint that can be applied straightforwardly in any context, even though its originators may wish that to be the case. Rather, it is suggested that its effectiveness and how it unfolds varies considerably according to specific regional and national politics. Power is not a zero-sum game, whereby the United States and its allies can easily assert their objectives and policies; rather, it is constantly negotiated and contested to yield outcomes that its players may or may not have intended.

Stevens and Jailobeva's chapter on Uzbekistan and Kyrgyzstan illustrates well how political leaders can manipulate the language of terrorism to clamp down on dissidents and political opponents. The global circulation of the War on Terror discourse provides international legitimacy to actions taken by national leaders against groups and individuals they may choose to brand with the label of terrorist. In the case of Uzbekistan, however, its alliance in the War on Terror quickly backfired on the United States as the perceived terrorist threat from the Islamic Movement of Uzbekistan faded. President Karimov then constructed the United States as a key regime threat, insinuating that it was supporting terrorist activity to destabilize the government. President Akaev of Kyrgystan and his successor, President Bakiev, both manipulated the War on Terror discourse to justify a crackdown on religious groups in particular and civil society in general, though Kyrgyzstan's more liberal and open regime precluded as severe a clampdown on non-governmental organizations (NGOs) as had occurred in Uzbekistan.

In Uganda, the National Resistance Movement (NRM) under President Museveni, in power since 1986, has similarly played the terrorist card to target dissidents and crack down on some sections of civil society. Joshua Rubongoya explains how the NRM regime, faced with declining levels of domestic support and an insurgency in western and northern parts of the country, hastily passed an anti-terrorism law in the aftermath of the 9/11 attacks as well as created secret detention facilities in the capital to interrogate and torture terror suspects. The NRM government's counter-terrorism responses were part of its broader effort to restrict spaces for political debate and to promote a notion of "no-party democracy" that the regime favored. The Anti-Terrorism Act was used to bring charges against an opposition presidential candidate who was forced into exile. Intimidation of journalists and police raids on the offices of print and radio media houses that had broadcast critical stories of the government were justified on national security grounds.

Nisrine Mansour echoes this tale in her compelling account of the Lebanese government's contrasting response to the Israeli invasion of southern Lebanon in July 2006, which was in retaliation for Hezbollah's kidnapping of two Israeli soldiers, and to the robbery of a bank by Fateh Al Islam (FAI), which resulted in the death of twenty Lebanese soldiers. In the first case the government preserved the legitimacy of Hezbollah, despite historic controversy over its status and politics in Lebanon. For the Lebanese government, Israel was the greater threat, so it joined Hezbollah in denouncing Israel's state terrorism. Thus, Hezbollah was able to cement its legitimacy through controlling reconstruction assistance for populations affected by the Israeli military campaign and delivering assistance directly to the civilian population. In the second case it constructed the FAI as a terrorist organization that neither was representative of the Palestinian people nor bore any political significance in Lebanese or Palestinian politics. It thus attacked the FAI, which had taken refuge in the Palestinian Nahr Al Bared camp. What is thus evident in the Lebanon case is the intense battle to define civil society—the battle of perceptions regarding who is a terrorist and who is a victim, who is a militant and who is a civilian.

This is also seen in Sri Lanka, where the government of President Mahinda Rajapakse has repressed peace-building NGOs and Sinhalese ethno-nationalist opposition groups in the context of the ongoing war between the Sri Lankan government and the Liberation Tigers of Tamil

Eelam (LTTE). Kristian Stokke explains how the Rajapakse government has so fruitfully exploited the global discourses on the War on Terror to recast the conflict as part of the war against terrorism. By defining the conflict in these terms, the Rajapakse government has been able to pursue a hard strategy of defeating the LTTE militarily while seeking to control the political spaces for civil society to organize. The current authoritarian control of civil society is especially hard-felt for Tamil welfare organizations that are accused of channeling funds from the Tamil diaspora to the LTTE.

In the case of Spain, however, the interweaving of global and domestic politics took a different direction. Alex Colas suggests that the initial disinformation spread by the then-ruling Popular Party after the 2004 Madrid bombings—that the Basque movement was culpable—fed into the new socialist administration's decision to withdraw from Iraq on the grounds that the bombings were linked to Spain's foreign policy. However, he also points out that such a move was to some degree cosmetic and expedient, as Spain has continued to provide troops for Afghanistan. Colas also makes the interesting point that the maturity of Spain's political institutions and electorate were sufficient to prevent any over-reaction either to the 9/11 attacks or the Madrid bombings. Thus, unlike Australia and the United Kingdom, which responded to the events of September 11, 2001, with a spate of counter-terrorist legislation, Spain did not institute any new counter-terrorist legislation, relying instead on the criminal law and judicial system for prosecution of the Madrid bombings. Nor did it significantly reform its intelligence or security services. It did, however, increase tenfold its intelligence staff devoted to investigating transnational jihadist networks and, like other countries, tightened coordination for counter-terrorist purposes of any relevant government departments.

The Indian context too illustrates how global and domestic politics interweave to shape demand for, and the implementation of, counter-terrorist legislation and measures. Jude Howell argues in this chapter that right-wing Hindu nationalist forces, building upon a background of communal tensions, adroitly constructed an image of Muslims and Islam as associated with terrorism and as disloyal to India, thereby justifying the introduction of repressive counter-terrorist measures. The terrorist attacks in Mumbai in late November 2008 served to catapult India onto the stage of international victimhood of global jihadist terrorism. The actions and discourses of the jihadists wove together domestic grievances concerning Muslims in India with international grievances around the Israel/Palestine conflict and US policy in Iraq and the Middle East. Prior to this the United States had treated terrorism in India as a domestic issue, only becoming concerned when it impinged on relations with Pakistan, which, like India, was a nuclear state. After the 2008 attacks, which targeted (among others) Westerners and iconic symbols of the West, the United States took a renewed interest in terrorism in India, which it now construed as threatening its interests.

Control and Regulation of Civil Society

A key theme that runs through most of the chapters is increasing control and regulation of civil society that has occurred since the launch of the War on Terror. An important corollary of this is a simultaneous strategy aimed at co-opting parts of civil society into the political and military prosecution of the global War on Terror. This forms the third theme and is dealt with later. However, at this point we observe that control and co-option are two essential parts of an evolving strategy toward civil society in the War on Terror.

The tightening of controls over civil society and the justification for these relies upon creating a veil of suspicion around the activities of civil society. As discussed in depth elsewhere (Howell and Lind 2009), this suspicion did not arise solely in the aftermath of the 9/11 attacks and the subsequent launch of the War on Terror. Rather, throughout the 1990s a number of trends casting doubts over the probity, legitimacy, and accountability of civil society were already emerging.

Simultaneously, donor agencies were gaining experience with engaging with civil society, establishing civil society-strengthening programs to nurture their activities and performance, both in service-delivery and advocacy work. However, they were also beginning to seek more effective and efficient ways of doing this, so as to reduce the transactional costs of working with a multitude of relatively small organizations. The United Nations, too, was trying to find new ways of relating to civil society that required further filtering and tidying-up of a cacophonous mass of disparate groups and voices. The launch of the War on Terror proved to be a juncture where these different trends converged, with the added twist that it deepened the suspicion of civil society.

The most visible manifestation of this suspicion of civil society is seen in the selective targeting of parts of civil society for regulation and control. Such control efforts have included the extension or creation of terrorist lists of individuals and organizations. Once designated, the assets, bank accounts, and property of designees are frozen, their movements are restricted, and their offices are closed. Processes of appeal against designation are lacking, and designees have met with an impasse when trying to establish the grounds for their designation. Another key control device is the Financial Action Task Force Special Recommendation VIII, which urges governments to monitor the flow of international funds to charities and between charities and their partners. This has led countries across the world to introduce new, or adapt existing, money-laundering legislation to cover charities. Other control measures include the tightening up of accountability and transparency mechanisms in regulatory frameworks governing charities and NGOs; the introduction of partner vetting systems, Anti-Terrorist Certificates, and anti-terrorist clauses in agreements between funders and funded bodies; and the registration of mosques and imams.

In the United States, an extensive legal and regulatory crackdown on the nonprofit sector has been justified as a necessary response to security threats, as Kay Guinane and Suraj Sazawal explain in this volume. The Patriot Act strengthened executive powers to designate terrorist organizations and seize their assets. There has been little recourse for organizations to contest being added to the Specially Designated Global List of terrorists, and the courts have tended to side with the government, which has justified blocking assets as a necessary measure to prevent funds being channeled to terrorists. Other controls introduced under the Patriot Act prohibit the provision of material support to terrorist groups, which has had a chilling effect on the work of US civil society groups working in conflict areas. The US counter-terrorism framework also includes broad surveillance powers that were used by the former Bush administration to infiltrate groups opposed to it policies. Guinane and Sazawal also explain how counter-terrorism objectives have greatly affected bureaucratic practices within the United States Agency for International Development (USAID), which has piloted a vetting system that requires its grantees to check the names of individual personnel in their partner agencies against security databases. They explain that what is so significant about the United States, beyond the generalized and clearly disproportionate impacts of its counter-terrorism regime on Muslim groups, is that it has sought to promote the adoption of similar legal and regulatory measures through its bilateral ties and in multilateral institutions.

Alison Dunn's chapter on the United Kingdom in this book examines in detail the effects of general counter-terrorist legislation and regulations targeted at charities on the voluntary sector part of civil society. She underlines the disproportionate and inappropriate effects of this general and sector-specific legislation on charities in England and Wales, thereby endorsing a more general finding of the International Commission of Jurists in 2009 on counter-terrorist legislation and its impact on human rights. She also suggests that the anticipatory, risk-based governance approach adopted by the Charity Commission of England and Wales to "protect" public confidence in charities also entails costs for charities in particular and civil society in general. Specifically, she argues that this approach threatens the very nature of civil society as an arena of diversity, creativity, and innovation. However in the case of Spain the expression of suspicion of civil society has remained at the level of political, public, and media discourse. Spain has not instituted any specific counter-terrorist legislation aimed at civil society or tightened its regulatory grip over civil society. Though the government tried at a national level to regulate imams, especially in the unregulated mosques and prayer meeting-places, it has not established any national regulatory system governing all mosques and religious meeting-places across Spain.

In the case of Uzbekistan the contradictions of US policy eventually cast suspicion over secular, foreign-funded civil society. In particular, the US pursuit of the War on Terror led it to, on the one hand, seek an alliance with Uzbekistan (a highly authoritarian state), while on the other hand its promotion of democracy led it to criticize human rights in Uzbekistan. Initially President Karimov welcomed US support in addressing the terrorist threat posed by the Islamic Movement of Uzbekistan and allowed foreign-funded NGOs and international NGOs to flourish so as to act as a buffer against the influence of fundamentalist Islam. However, following the Rose Revolution in Georgia in 2003, President Karimov became suspicious of foreign-funded and pro-democracy NGOs, especially once the United States started to raise human rights issues. Though the focus of repressive measures in Kyrgyzstan has been on religious institutions, an increasingly politically active, secular civil society has also come under suspicion as a potential regime threat. While President Bakiev declared religious extremism to be the greatest threat to national security, he also manipulated the security rhetoric, which gained added legitimacy through the War on Terror discourse, to cast suspicion over pro-democratic, secular civil society organizations.

The intense scrutiny of civil society in the Occupied Palestinian Territories is an extreme instance of how security discourses have buttressed arguments to further restrict the activities of non-governmental actors. Jeremy Lind explains that Israel has long suspected Palestinian NGOs of acting as fronts for militant groups, and therefore of being part of the so-called architecture of terror that threatens Israel's peace and security. The War on Terror provided a new global political framing of the Israeli–Palestinian conflict, allowing the Israeli government to step up its controls on NGOs operating in Palestine as justifiable to prevent attacks inside Israel. In essence, Israel has constructed a wall of security around the Occupied Palestinian Territories, creating enormous difficulties for Palestinian society as a whole but also challenges specifically for NGOs in terms of accessing populations in need of assistance and monitoring human rights abuses. However, as elsewhere, it is Islamic organizations that have come under the greatest suspicion. At the behest of Israel and the United States, and also out of its own political expediency, the Palestinian

Authority in the West Bank has closed several Islamic social welfare organizations that are alleged to be connected to Hamas, which Israel, the United States, and other donors designate a terrorist organization.

The Strategic Co-option of Civil Society into the Political and Military Prosecution of the War on Terror Regime

The flip-side of the restrictive measures discussed above are initiatives aimed at co-opting desirable parts of civil society into security and counter-terrorist agendas. Such initiatives might include programs aimed at preventing the recruitment of youth to radical and extremist causes, especially where these promote terrorist acts; reaching out to moderate voices in suspect communities to build a government-civil society alliance against terrorism; policies and resources to support curriculum reform in madrassas and the training of imams in mosques; and projects to encourage civil society groups to think through their role in countering terrorism and enhancing national security. The effects of the War on Terror regime are much more sophisticated, therefore, than a simple crackdown on civil society. It is a nuanced tale of dualities that refracts against the purposive dualities of good and evil framed by the War Terror regime.

This dual-pronged approach toward civil society marks a watershed with the "golden era" of the 1990s, when donor agencies conceptualized civil society as a harmonious, liberal, pluralistic site of non-governmental public action that was compatible with—indeed essential to—liberal democracies and market economies. With the launch of the War on Terror, governments and donors took a more circumspect approach to civil society, which they now conceptualized on the one hand as suspect and potentially complicit in terrorism, and on the other hand as still useful and malleable for a variety of political and policy purposes. This fed into a dual-pronged strategy toward civil society that constructed a "good" civil society that was to be engaged with, tolerated, and promoted and a "bad" civil society that was to be contained, observed, and controlled. While seemingly contradictory, these dualities of co-option and control are strategically complementary.

This dual-pronged approach has led to the selective targeting of particular groups and individuals in civil society for purposes of control or co-option. In many of the chapters, the point is made repeatedly that Muslim populations and their organizations have been targeted discursively, politically, and through policy initiatives. Such targeting has been aimed at both curtailing the identified undesirable groups and influences while simultaneously co-opting more "moderate" voices. In India the United Progressive Alliance government led by the Congress Party has sought to influence madrassas in India, particularly in areas such as

Bangladesh and Nepal, with a view to co-opting moderate leaders and clamping down on so-called extremist religious figures. Annie Pettitt's chapter on Australia points to growing concern about the discriminatory effects of counter-terrorist legislation on Muslim/Arab communities.

In Spain, political and media discourses focused on Muslim populations in the aftermath of the Madrid 2004 bombings. The government sought to forge closer alliances with Muslim communities by reaching out to established Muslim organizations such as the Sunni *Unión de Comunidades Islámicas de España* (Union of Islamic Communities in Spain). However, as Colas argues, this only underlined the government's lack of knowledge of these communities, as the established organizations were not representative of the heterogeneous mix of Muslim populations in Spain. Jude Howell describes how right-wing Hindu nationalist forces have created a climate of suspicion toward Muslims and their organizations in India, accusing them of being linked to global jihadism and behind the spiral of violent attacks in Indian cities over the last three years.

In India successive governments have, to varying degrees, recognized the usefulness of a registered, voluntary sector delivering social services both for implementing social policy and for providing legitimacy. Co-option of these parts of civil society serves thus to maintain order and legitimacy and justifies selective action against parts of civil society construed as undesirable. The service-delivery-oriented voluntary sector that relies on government and external funding in India has, as in other contexts, been late in its response to the effects of counter-terrorist measures on poor and marginalized groups and of right-wing discourses on Muslim communities. It has left the defense of civil society spaces to human rights groups, social movements, and minorities' organizations.

This dual-pronged strategy is, however, never neat and contained in its effects. Although some groups have been deliberately selected for control or co-option, it is also the case that counter-terrorist legislation, measures, and practices have also inadvertently affected other groups, whether through abusive practices or through the extension of terrorist measures to non-terrorist situations. As noted by Alison Dunn in her chapter on the United Kingdom, the International Commission of Jurists found in 2009 that extraordinary counter-terrorist legislation and widening police and state powers have, in many contexts, become applied to non-terrorist situations such as legitimate environmental and civil protests. Annie Pettit, in her chapter on Australia, notes the extension of tactics emerging through the counter-terrorist regime into ordinary policing, as evidenced in the lists of people drawn up by the police to be excluded from the 2007 APEC meeting.

Similarly, Jude Howell describes in the chapter on India how counter-terrorist legislation and measures have affected not only members of prohibited groups such as the Students Islamic Movement of India or Al-Umar-Mujahideen, but also vulnerable groups and minorities such as tribes, poor farmers, and Dalits. Corrupt and weak judicial and policing systems have led to hundreds of innocent people languishing in jails in India under suspicion of terrorism. In general, however, civil society in India has not suffered severe repression as a result of counter-terrorist legislation.

Deploying of Aid and International Development Policy and its Relation to Civil Society for Security Objectives

Our final theme relates to the use of aid and international development policy for broader security objectives, particularly as this relates to civil society. Just as political leaders and the media have cast the spotlight on Muslim populations and Islamic groups as suspect in terrorism, so too have donors discovered Muslims and Islamic organizations as part of the landscape of civil society. To this end, donor agencies have to varying degrees initiated some practical efforts to engage with Muslim youth for the purposes of preventing radicalism and extremism.

The collapse of the Soviet Union and its satellite states in 1989 heralded the end of the Cold War, ushering in a new phase in development strategy. No longer governed by the ideological imperatives of the Cold War, donor agencies from the late 1980s began to emphasize the goals of poverty reduction and "good governance." The democratic movements of the 1980s across Eastern Europe, Africa, and Latin America that Samuel Huntington (1992) described as the Third Wave of Democracy revived the concept of civil society. This fed into a paradigmatic shift in the 1990s away from a dualistic, ideologically informed development paradigm of state versus market to a triadic paradigm centering on the state, markets, and civil society, which were now conceptualized as co-existing in a harmonious and mutually reinforcing way. Donors began to engage strategically with civil society actors, though in practice their efforts were focused mainly on NGOs. In doing so they conceptualized civil society actors with the dual roles of partners or subcontractors in the delivery of services and as agents for promoting liberal democracy.

This period from the end of the Cold War in the late 1980s stretching up to the 9/11 attacks was a so-called golden age for civil society groups advocating around governance, democracy, and human rights issues (Howell and Pearce 2001). At the same time, neoliberal reforms that were being promoted by international financial institutions entailed reducing the role of the state in key sectors of the economy and in providing social welfare. Instead, private sector actors and civil society groups were encouraged to deliver social services as an alternative to the state.

The 1990s also saw a new role for UN agencies and development actors in the so-called New Wars of Kosovo, Bosnia, and Sierra Leone. An important development here was the gradual convergence of military and development actors in these conflict zones, a process that Mark Duffield (2001) aptly described as the securitization of aid. The 9/11 attacks took these linkages between development and security to a new level, binding them closer together in complex ways. The promotion of good governance and human rights that was so central to the use of aid throughout the 1990s in furthering liberal governance continued to be an important theme in development practice. However, it was increasingly over-shadowed by the newly important emphasis on "security" in the context of the War on Terror. Even though, rhetorically, the United States under the former Bush administration remained committed to promoting democracy overseas through Bush's "Freedom Agenda," in practice it cultivated relations with regimes that pledged their political and military cooperation in fighting the War on Terror.

The War on Terror thus revived a politics of aid that is reminiscent of the Cold War era, whereby regimes that cooperate in pursuing US security objectives are rewarded with various types of economic, military, and political assistance. At the same time, the neoliberal ideal to shrink the state and seek the participation of non-governmental actors in providing services continues to have significant influence over development approaches in the post-9/11 context. Indeed, the professed need to strengthen security has been used to justify interventionism intending to rebuild states in a neoliberal mould. For example, the post-Taliban con-stitution in Afghanistan envisions a pared-down state that largely serves a managerial function in market regulation and service delivery by oversee-ing a range of private-sector and non-governmental actors who are tasked with delivering development and social welfare (Howell and Lind 2009).

Mutuma Ruteere and Mikewa Ogada explain in their chapter on counter-terrorism initiatives and human rights in Kenya how the focus of US foreign assistance to Kenya has shifted since 2001. Bilateral relations between the United States and Kenya were fraught throughout the 1990s, as the country underwent a halting political transition from one-party rule to multiparty democracy. A US ambassador to Kenya during this time was especially vocal in criticizing the former regime of President Moi and back-ing civil society leaders in their calls for democratic reforms. A politically minded civil society blossomed as foreign donors, led by the United States, sought to promote democracy by strengthening the hand of non-governmental groups. Since 2001, the United States has been reticent in criticizing high-profile corruption in the Kenyan government, as it has instead sought to nurture strong bilateral cooperation on counter-terrorism in the Horn of Africa. It has provided technical and financial backing as well as military training assistance in support of the Kenyan government's counter-terrorism initiatives. The United States also pressured Kenyan authorities to pass controversial anti-terror legislation that was strongly opposed by civil society. Kenyan human rights groups have struggled to respond to these shifting aid dynamics since 2001, as they find themselves opposing the prosecution of the War on Terror in the region.

Some regimes have deftly manipulated the politics of aid since 2001 to solidify their own power and political standing. Joshua Rubongoya shows how the Ugandan President Yoweri Museveni was able to curry favor with the United States by backing its War on Terror in eastern Africa even at a time when his regime was cracking down on opposition political leaders and the media. Even while trumped-up charges were brought against the opposition leader, Dr. Kizza Besigye, under provisions of the Anti-Terrorism Act, for which he was brought to trial in the General Martial Court (a military court), Uganda continued to receive considerable economic and military assistance from the United States. Uganda contributed military support personnel to Iraq and was one of only two African countries to pledge peace-keeping troops to Somalia after the US-backed invasion in late 2006 using Ethiopian proxy troops. Therefore, the War on Terror was an opportunity for Museveni to renew the bilateral relationship with the United States, which is also the largest donor to Uganda.

The War on Terror regime has also affected how donor agencies, governments, and humanitarian workers conceptualize those in need of humanitarian assistance. This point is cogently argued by Nisrine Mansour in her study of the Lebanese government's response to two humanitarian situations. She suggests that in conflict situations civilians become defined along a spectrum ranging from "collateral damage" to "terrorists," which in turn determines their deservedness of humanitarian assistance. In the case of the first conflict in July 2006, when the government preserved Hezbollah's legitimacy and condemned Israel's state terrorism, the government provided humanitarian assistance to those affected by the Israeli invasion of southern Lebanon. In the second case, where it attacked FAI in Nahr Al Bared camp, it defined all the population in the camp as militants and those fleeing the camp were treated as terrorist suspects. Where the displaced had fled to other Palestinian camps in Lebanon, the government refused to provide them with humanitarian assistance, leaving them reliant on aid provided by the United Nations High Commissioner for Refugees (UNHCR) and NGOs.

In the case of Afghanistan, the War on Terror has deepened the process of securitization of aid, affecting military strategies and humanitarian and development work. Stuart Gordon traces the emergence in the United

Kingdom of a more joined-up approach to conflict situations that has drawn on past experiences of coordinated action between militaries, development institutions, and foreign ministries in Bosnia and Kosovo. He then relates this to the emergence of the new concept of stabilization, which was consolidated in the 2008 Road Map for Helmand province, Afghanistan, where British troops have been deployed since 2006. Stabilization refers to a strategy that fuses the military's use of soft measures, such as development and foreign diplomacy, to translate military victory into stability with a containment strategy drawn from new humanitarianism. It involved military and civilian workers working with local communities and local governments, with the goals of increasing local government responsiveness to local demands and strengthening the government's legitimacy through the delivery of basic social services. In this way the military became more involved in the soft side of stabilization activity, while civilian workers engaged more closely with the military.

Jeremy Lind's chapter on Palestine demonstrates the politicization of aid and international development policy for national and global security and political objectives. He illustrates the instrumental and political bifurcation of civil society by donors into a secular part, which they seek to nurture and support, and an Islamic part, which they view as problematic because of the contested nature of the relationship between Hamas and Islamist social welfare organizations. This is picked up in Guinane and Sazawal's chapter on the United States. They note that USAID has formed ties with a newly formed charity, Americans for Charity in Palestine, to channel private donations to charitable works in the Occupied Territories, ostensibly to bypass local Islamic groups that have been lumped with Hamas, a listed terrorist organization. Although this suspicion of Islamist social welfare organizations and the cultivation of secular NGOs and human rights groups pre-dates the 9/11 attacks, this provides the basis for donor strategy after the launch of the War on Terror.

Lind notes three ways in which the War on Terror regime impinges upon donor strategy toward civil society. First, the introduction of checks on grantees such as the USAID's Anti-Terrorist Certificate and its piloting of the Partner Vetting System has hindered access of many Palestinian NGOs to foreign aid. Indeed, some international NGOs, unable to forge agreements with Palestinian groups because of these new controls, have had to return to direct implementation of projects themselves. This reflects a point made by Alison Dunn in her chapter on the United Kingdom that the increasing burden on charities, especially those working overseas, to ensure that their partners are not linked in any way to terrorist activities, could lead to risk aversion. Second, the War on Terror regime has heightened suspicion of civil society in general. The Israeli government attempted unsuccessfully to pass a new NGO Bill in 2002 that would limit foreign contributions to Israeli NGOs. Third, and especially following the coming to power of Hamas in Gaza, the mobility of foreign aid workers to Palestine has become further restricted. International aid workers and activists have been denied entry to the Occupied Territories, visas have not been extended, and staff have been deported.

This bifurcation of civil society into a desirable secular part and a suspect religious part is also evident in aid policy in Central Asia. Western aid in Uzbekistan and Kyrygzstan has centered on supporting pro-democracy groups and liberal NGOs, not only for the purpose of promoting democracy but also to act as a buffer against the growing influence of radical Islam. The Uzbek regime initially welcomed international aid and the growth of foreign-funded NGOs as a bulwark against Islamist groups, for this dovetailed not least with its own security objectives. However, as noted earlier, the tables soon turned against the United States as foreign-funded groups became perceived as threats to Karimov's regime.

In the case of Spain, as Colas describes, the effects of the War on Terror regime on aid policy have been more tenuous. He concedes that transnational jihadist terrorism has facilitated the framing of North African immigration to Spain as a southern threat and has impinged on aid and civil society. However, he argues that Spain's emphasis on codevelopment in its international development policy—that is, fostering economic prosperity in North Africa through trade and economic links so as to reduce migrant flows to Spain—has outweighed any pressure to securitize aid and international development for security purposes. Similarly, in India aid policy has not been significantly reoriented toward national and global security interests, nor has donors' engagement with civil society fundamentally changed. Nevertheless, post-9/11 security concerns have crept into donor engagement with civil society, as reflected in efforts to forge new links with Muslim communities and madrassas.

Through these four themes, the book thus provides a close examination of the effects of the War on Terror regime on civil society. In doing so it draws attention to the multiple and varied strains that the War on Terror regime has placed on civil society actors, organizations, and spaces. By investigating a range of political contexts across Europe, Africa, Asia, and the United States, the book illustrates how these themes, effects, and strains unfold in diverse and complex ways. Given that the War on Terror regime is now well-entrenched in policy, legislative and regulatory frameworks, institutions, and bureaucratic practices in many contexts, this book seeks to alert politicians, policymakers, development agencies, and civil society actors in a critical and analytic way to some of the consequences of the War on Terror regime for civil society. This can then provide a basis for various actors to reflect critically upon ways of unraveling further the damaging aspects of the War on Terror regime for civil society.

Notes

1. We enclose this phrase in quotation marks initially to indicate that as authors we distance ourselves politically from this concept. We then continue to use it throughout without quotation marks. The concept is a widely used phrase that has become embedded in public and political discourse.

2. These include works by Mark Sidel (2007, 2008), Alison Dunn (2008), Conor Gearty (2003, 2007), John Cosgrave (2004), Jude Howell (2006), Jude Howell and Jeremy Lind (2009), Jo Beall (2006), and Beth Elise Whitaker (2007a), among others.

3. See Macrae and Harmer (2003), Christian Aid (2004), Cosgrave (2004), Fowler (2005), Woods (2005), Moss et al (2005), and Howell and Lind (2009). There has also been a general burgeoning of literature on terrorism since 2001. Post-9/11 literature on terrorism will account for over 90 percent of all studies on terrorism if current trends continue, according to Professor Silke, University of East London (Shepherd 2007).

4. Howell and Lind (2009) is one of a few publications to explore in-depth the effects of this two-pronged approach for civil society. Within the field of humanitarian assistance research and conflict studies, the effects of "hearts and minds" work on humanitarian space and workers has been accorded considerable attention.

5. The term "civil society" has been challenged for being too vague, too amorphous, and empirically imprecise. However, such critiques could apply to many social science concepts. Clearly the normative meanings it can take on vary ideologically, historically, and contextually. The concept continues to have considerable resonance in contemporary political, public, and media discourses, and it is appropriated by a range of actors for different ideological and political purposes. Through global media and communications, international relations, and aid operations, the term now circulates globally. Given its contemporary strategic relevance it is important to understand, therefore, the diverse politics surrounding it. For a very useful exploration of how it has been interpreted according to different disciplinary frameworks, see White (1994).

2

UK Counter-terrorism Provision and Civil Society: Ensuring Responsibility, Ignoring Proportionality

Alison Dunn

A recent study carried out by the International Commission of Jurists has revealed the damaging effect of international counter-terrorism policies on the progress of global human rights (International Commission of Jurists 2009). The report highlights in particular the way in which counter-terrorism laws since 2001 have been enacted with excessive haste, leading to regulation that is often inappropriate and disproportionate. Not only has this meant that pre-existing laws have been overlooked, but also that there has been an unreflective widening of police and state powers to arenas not previously considered within counter-terrorism's reach. In addition, the report found that many countries' emergency powers have been normalized; that is, that counter-terrorism measures enacted on a temporary basis to overcome extraordinary circumstances have acquired permanency (International Commission of Jurists 2009, 29, 36). The Jurists' report concluded that the reality of attempting to offer robust security has in fact been an erosion of protection, and that overall there has been a regression in legal provisions and the application of the rule of law.

Although examining provisions on a global stage, the Commission of Jurists' findings are certainly indicative of the position in the United Kingdom. In the last decade state and police powers have expanded exponentially and at speed. What were once temporary powers to deal with the extraordinary circumstances caused by a specific threat in Northern Ireland have now become part of the ordinary and permanent legal landscape.[1] That landscape is increasingly international and ideological in outlook, but where once international obligations could keep states in check, now such obligations can augment a disproportionate response to the threat of terrorism—or, where they do not, have sometimes been ignored. Requirements derived under United Nations Security Council Resolutions, European Union directives, and the intergovernmental Financial Action Task Force have placed obligations on states to have regulations that allow for more extensive surveillance and scrutiny of the use of assets.[2] At the same time the United Kingdom's counter-terrorism legislation has frequently derogated from the United Kingdom's obligations under the European Convention of Human Rights, and non-derogating measures have been found to be in contravention of the Convention. Controversial powers exist to impose control orders and detain without trial and deport persons suspected of terrorist acts, along with the increased use of secrecy and special advocates in trials that go beyond the controversial Diplock courts in Northern Ireland. All have contributed to putting in reverse the Labour government's election platform of expressly incorporating human rights norms into the exercise of executive, legislative, and judicial powers and into the everyday decisionmaking of public authorities.

The proliferation of state and police counter-terrorism powers and the erosion of human rights protection for individuals are not the only consequences of the United Kingdom's counter-terrorism program. The costs of laws and policies fashioned in haste, the failure to take into account existing legal measures, the expansion of powers without proper discussion or reflection, the normalization of emergency measures, and the resultant burden thereby created have also fallen heavily upon civil society. A direct regulatory focus upon this sector emerged following evidence that some of the 7/7 London bombers had charity connections. As a result, obligations have been imposed and policies developed for the sector in order to sweep away the "veil of legitimacy" that civil society organizations afford others for fundraising, channeling assets, or to foster radicalization (HM Treasury and Home Office 2007, para 3.83).

The language used to justify the imposition of these extra burdens upon civil society focuses upon protectionism. Increased regulation enables the public to be assured of the trust that they place in civil society organizations, as well as enabling individual organizations and the sector as a whole to be safeguarded from abuse (HM Treasury and Home Office 2007, para 3.83). This chapter will examine the ways in which the United Kingdom's counter-terrorism regulations and policies have ensured responsibility within the legal framework. In so doing it will argue that outside the rhetoric of protectionism, the United Kingdom's regulatory and policy approach toward civil society, particularly in creating a risk-based governance framework, has ignored the principle of proportionality. This chapter will argue that this shortcoming not only undermines the regulatory and policy agenda, but also has the potential to do significant damage to civil society organizations specifically, and the spirit of philanthropy more broadly.

United Kingdom's Counter-terrorism Strategies

Following the bomb attacks in London in July 2005, the government quickly released a 12-point action plan to combat terrorism, followed in 2006 by a more specific counter-terrorism scheme, termed "CONTEST" (Home Office 2006, Home Office 2009),[3] and a National Security Strategy in 2008 (Cabinet Office 2008). The CONTEST strategy has four strands: it seeks to ensure that acts of terrorism and the environment in which terrorism can be inculcated are prevented; that those who perpetrate such acts are pursued by the gathering of intelligence and by disrupting activity; that national services, the United Kingdom's interests, and the public are protected; and that the country is prepared for any act of terrorism and its consequences by a process of risk analysis and capacity building (Home Office 2006, paras 5–9, 32). Under the somewhat illusory banner of the "battle of ideas" (Home Office 2006, para 53), CONTEST represents an attempt to engage with the ideological as well as physical threat of terrorism.

To deliver on CONTEST and the National Security Strategy, the government has endeavored, with varying degrees of success, to adopt a multi-agency approach with the police, local authorities, and civil society to build community cohesion, alleviate community tensions, and generally enhance social conditions and environment so that the seed of radicalization cannot grow (Home Office 2006, para 6, 106; Cabinet Office 2008, 4.9, 2.5, 4.112). In an effort to marginalize religious extremism, this drive for community cohesion has been primarily focused on Muslim communities and has extended beyond addressing the conditions of social welfare per se to broader capacity building within the community, in particular by increasing participation of the whole community in local decisionmaking and by developing leadership (Home Office 2005; Department for Communities and Local Government 2007; Commission on Integration and Cohesion 2007).

Alongside this community agenda there has also been an extensive, controversial, and unprecedented legislative program that aims to deliver on the "pursue" and "protect" strands of CONTEST. To that end, legislation has provided a raft of criminal offences and related police powers to deal with those who commit or threaten acts of violence in an attempt to influence the government or intimidate the public in an ideological, religious, racial, or political cause.[4] Acts of terrorism can take place in or outside the United Kingdom, and include serious violence against a person, serious damage to property, endangering another person's life, creating a serious health or safety risk, or an action designed to seriously interfere with or disrupt electronic systems. If any of these actions involve the use of firearms or explosives, they will be counted as terrorism even where they are not designed to influence the government or intimidate the public. Under the legislation organizations "concerned in terrorism" can be proscribed, as can those that glorify terrorism.[5]

The reach of the legislation also extends to those who, although not themselves committing an act of terrorism, may nevertheless be associated with such an act, however peripherally. This approach seeks to be all-encompassing by drawing within the regulation's scope those individuals and organizations that may come into contact with terrorists or potentially be subject to their exploitation. The focus of this broader regulation is to create obligations of accountability and vigilance. It seeks to guard against vulnerability by requiring a strengthening of the internal governance processes of organizations. In addition, it creates specific obligations to disclose to relevant authorities information of suspicions of terrorist activity or information that could apprehend or convict a person involved in terrorism, as well as offenses against tipping off.[6] Civil society organizations fall within the ambit of this general regulation. Specific sector regulation applies more narrowly to the charity sector and takes a particular focus upon governance norms. In this regard the Home Office has emphasized the responsibility that falls upon the sector to commit to defeating terrorist exploitation of its organizations (Home Office and HM Treasury 2007, 4). The overall regulatory approach toward the sector can be summarized as both seeking to ensure responsibility is in place at an individual organizational level and at a supervisory level through oversight mechanisms. Each will be considered in turn.

Ensuring Organizational Responsibility

At the organizational level the United Kingdom's counter-terrorism measures seek to impose requirements of responsibility in at least two ways: through activity-based regulation and through governance norms. Primarily obligations are placed upon organizations to ensure that their activities and the activities of their officers, members, employees, and volunteers are not connected to terrorism. This responsibility on organizations is onerous. It goes beyond mere impartiality or disinterest to a requirement to actively ensure that the preparation, commission, or support of terrorist criminality is neither a direct nor indirect consequence of the organization's or its officers' activities. Neither must such activity be connected to the organization by association, such as through persons linked to it or by activities carried out on its premises by other parties. It is a criminal offence, for example, under the United Kingdom's Terrorism Acts of 2000 and 2006 to invite support for a proscribed organization or to be a member of one, to fundraise for the purposes of terrorism or otherwise facilitate the use of money or property for terrorism, to encourage an act of terrorism, direct an organization for terrorist purposes, disseminate terrorist information, or to wear an article of clothing that indicates support for terrorism. It is also a criminal offence to fail to disclose suspicions or information learned during the course of a "trade, profession, business or employment" that another may have committed one of these offences.[7] Money Laundering Regulations also require robust record keeping and clear financial audit trails.[8] It is thus incumbent on organizations to ensure that they have full and complete knowledge of all their officers, employees, and volunteers, that they are aware of who is using their premises and for what purpose, and that they can trace the legitimate provenance and end use of their funds and the use of any other assets belonging to the organization.

Although civil society organizations are not singled out by these regulatory obligations, which fall under the general counter-terrorism laws, nevertheless they may be more likely to bear the brunt of them. The complex application of organizational responsibility under the legislation becomes apparent when one considers the nature of civil society bodies; their fluid organizational structures; their reach to different parts of the community both home and abroad; the practical circumstances in which they have to operate, for example in delivering aid overseas and the use of informal value transfer systems; and the sheer plurality and diversity of persons connected to such organizations. Given the breadth of some of the counter-terrorism provisions and the extensive penalties for their breach (which can include custodial sentencing, suspension of officers, asset freezing and seizure, listing as a terrorist organization, and negative impacts on an organization's reputation),[9] the direct commission or commission by association of these offenses under the counter-terrorism legislation is a serious and very real concern.

Three examples illustrate the point. Under the Terrorism Act 2006 it is an offense to encourage an act of terrorism, but what civil society organization has not issued a fervent entreaty to its members or to the wider public to take action against the government on a contentious issue? Such activities are part and parcel of any awareness-raising or lobbying campaign. Yet if such an entreaty encourages another, directly or *indirectly*, to prepare or carry out an act of terrorism, the offence of glorifying terrorism will have been committed.[10]

This is not so far-fetched when one considers that the statement can be issued not only with intent to glorify terrorism, but also recklessly, and that the offence will have been committed merely if an act of terrorism has been encouraged. There is no need for the act to have been carried out. The breadth of the definition of terrorism makes the application of this provision more likely given that, at its foundation, terrorism is no more than an attempt with violence or threat of action to "influence government or to intimidate the public . . . for the purpose of advancing a political, religious, racial or ideological cause."[11] It is conceivable that a nonviolent call to lobby by a civil society organization seeking only to raise awareness of an issue that concerns it could indirectly encourage another to commit a violent act in the name of that cause. The commission of violent acts seeking to influence the government or intimidate the public, though rare, has certainly occurred in the past, for example in the name of fathers' rights, abortion rights, or animal rights—to mention just a few. The point is that the reach of this provision is potentially very wide and falls disproportionately upon those organizations that encourage others to be concerned about causes and contentious issues.

The provision can have a chilling effect too, discouraging legitimate organizations who may be fearful of misinterpretation from what would otherwise be legitimate activities of speech. The effect of counter-terrorism regulation, especially upon speech, is a widespread issue of significant concern to civil society.[12] Broad police powers to stop and search, the increased use of public order powers, and restrictions on locations of demonstrations have all been similarly employed in the context of civil society protests, chilling even legitimate action.[13] As Carter has pointed out in the Canadian context, often fear of the extent of the law can be as restrictive as the law itself (Carter 2006, 11).

A second example highlights the problems caused where there are layers of organizations with whom civil society organizations can be connected. A significant number of civil society organizations operate overseas, delivering humanitarian aid or operating other programs. Many of these organizations can only carry out their work in the field through the assistance of partner agencies. This may be because of practical considerations in the country of operation, such as a lack of knowledge or expertise, or because ruling regimes, local laws, or conditions require it. Where such partner agencies are utilized, civil society organizations will need to conduct extensive research and evaluation in order to ascertain the appropriateness of a potential agency, applying a "know your partner" principle. In order to stay within the regulation, an organization will need to ensure not only that the partner agency is not a proscribed or designated organization and that it provides appropriate end use of funds, but also that neither the agency nor its officers have any terrorist links.[14] Closer to home the multi-agency process of grant-making can cause regulatory burdens too; that is where civil society organizations make grants to individuals or bodies, who then distribute the grant to other organizations and so forth. It is unclear under the general legislation how many layers removed one goes in retaining a connection to the financing of terrorism, but questions have certainly been raised in relation to funding of the 7/7 bombers in this regard.[15]

Third, many civil society organizations are also members of coalitions, often as a means of sharing best practice, for campaigning, to raise awareness of an issue, or to raise the profile of the organization itself. Along with the benefits that coalitions afford to civil society organizations, they also present terrorism risks. To comply with the counter-terrorism regime, an organization joining a coalition would need to ascertain not only the coalition's aims and objectives, but also the status and associations of each of the coalition members and their officers in terms of support for terrorism or their designation under the legislation. In addition, to avoid fundraising for or facilitating the use of money or property for terrorist purposes, civil society organizations would need to determine the coalition's income streams, particularly where coalition projects are undertaken with funding outside the coalition members (Charity Commission 2009, para 8). As with partner agencies, the need for such a risk assessment here is extensive, intrusive, and burdensome.

Many of these activity-focused responsibilities require a governance-based response, and the United Kingdom's counter-terrorism measures seek also to impose specific governance obligations upon organizations. These are designed to ensure that risk-based control mechanisms are in place to build a defense to the exploitation of an organization by or for criminals who prepare or perpetrate terrorist acts (HM Treasury and Home Office 2007, para 3.82).[16] In this context specific scrutiny has been placed upon charities as the most "vulnerable" part of the civil society sector.[17] Despite a lack of concrete evidence, charities, along with money service businesses and international financial movements, have been identified as one of the key sources of terrorist financing in the United Kingdom (HM Treasury and Home Office 2007, para 3.82). Indeed, they are likely to come under greater focus as other avenues for money laundering and channeling funds are closed off (Home Office and HM Treasury 2007, 4). In particular, a charity's systems and processes for protecting the integrity of its assets in relation to ascertaining and ensuring legitimacy of both the provenance and end use of funds are a primary feature of these charity sector-specific governance mechanisms. General trust and charity law already place charity trustees under strict requirements to comply with a duty of care, to act in the best interests of charity beneficiaries, and to apply funds for charitable purposes only.[18] The latter requirement places obligations on trustees to ensure the receipt of legitimate monies and the proper end use of funds distributed directly by the charity or by its partner agencies. Complying with these requirements is onerous, time consuming, and expensive, particularly for organizations working overseas that will most frequently need to resort to the use of partner agencies to deliver aid or carry out a charity's purposes.

The recent inquiry into the operations of the charity Palestinian Relief and Development Fund (Interpal) by its regulator, the Charity Commission for England and Wales, highlights the extent and depth of the internal governance mechanisms required of charities (Charity Commission 2009). In this inquiry the Charity Commission focused as much upon the anticipatory nature of governance mechanisms in relation to determining potential risk of connections to terrorist activity as upon review mechanisms. The inquiry emphasized that, although charities should not altogether avoid risk, it is the responsibility of charity trustees to actively identify, evaluate, and manage any risk they face to ensure accountability. Given the nature and diversity of risk and the fact that it is liable to fluctuate according to often volatile political and socioeconomic conditions, charities should ensure that they have established robust and effective risk-assessment governance processes that are ongoing, proportionate, and flexible. It is important to recognize that for many charities working in different locations and on numerous projects, these governance processes will often be multiple and continual and in need of constant reevaluation.

The Commission's inquiry into Interpal followed allegations made in a BBC documentary program that the charity had links to terrorism through its partner agencies in the Occupied Palestinian Territories. It was alleged, inter alia, that these agencies promoted terrorist ideologies and, when distributing Interpal's aid, chose beneficiaries whose families had taken part in suicide bombings. Interpal had been earlier investigated by the Charity Commission in 1996 concerning allegations of links to Hamas, and also in 2003 following the designation by the US authorities of Interpal as a "specially designated global terrorist." The first investigation found no evidence of a link to terrorism or terrorist groups, and the second investigation was closed after the US authorities failed to provide evidence of the reasons for designating Interpal as a terrorist group (Charity Commission 2009, para 38).

It is notable that the US authorities failed to respond a second time during the course of the Charity Commission's most recent inquiry into Interpal. The findings of this third inquiry were that Interpal had robust financial audit trails with regard to the use of its funds by partner agencies.

This was evidenced in part by acknowledgment letters received from the beneficiaries. The Commission also found that there was no proof that Interpal's partners were promoting terrorist ideologies, or that beneficiaries were chosen just because they were children of suicide bombers. Nevertheless, the Charity Commission concluded that there were a number of significant governance and procedural failings in the way Interpal discharged its management burdens and that these required rectification.

The Commission emphasized that engaging with partner agencies who deliver aid on behalf of a charity does not shift responsibility from the charity to the partner, but rather increases the responsibility requirements placed upon the charity and its trustees (Charity Commission 2009, para 198). The risks for organizations here are multiple and complex, encompassing operational, financial, reputational, and external risks (Charity Commission 2009, para 196), to which could also be added risks of a legal and environmental nature. The primary duty of charity trustees operating through intermediary organizations is to be fully satisfied that any potential partner is an appropriate organization with whom the charity can work. This is not merely a question of fit but one of legal propriety. The Charity Commission emphasized that charity trustees should settle criteria for choosing a partner in advance and then seek out the knowledge and experience of those who may have worked with potential partner organizations in the past. In this context there is obviously a difficulty where a charity has moved into a new working environment or is seeking to partner an agency new to the field.

Trustees should also ensure that neither the agency nor its officers are designated or listed as proscribed organizations and that, where possible, the partner is registered and compliant with the local regulatory regime. If the partnership goes ahead, the charity should put in place a specific funding agreement with the organization that sets out methods of working and sanctions for lack of compliance. In addition, the charity should produce guidelines to partners on how beneficiaries are to be selected. Both compliance with the funding agreement and selection of beneficiaries by the partner agency should be actively monitored by the charity trustees, as well as the charity seeking independent verification of the work of the partner. Sanctions and contingency plans should be applied where necessary.

The bureaucracy-heavy governance mechanisms highlighted by the Charity Commission focus on ensuring that a charity has control of the partnership. This is essentially measured through facts—that is, knowledge of the partner and how funds are used, beneficiaries chosen, and operations managed. This enables the charity to continually reassess the risks it faces, particularly important in areas of conflict where the environment is volatile or where terrorists are known to operate. In relation to Interpal, evidence before the Charity Commission revealed that, although funding agreements were in place with partner agencies and the agencies were regulated under the local legal regime, and although Interpal had conducted site visits, questioned the agencies, and sought to verify their work, Interpal's investigation was little more than a "paper exercise" (Charity Commission 2009, para 133b). The Charity Commission found that Interpal's verification process had not been independent, Interpal did not appear to understand the local regulatory regime, and its trustees were apt to rely simply on the word of their partner agencies. The Charity Commission emphasized that it was incumbent on trustees to actively evaluate the information it received from or on its partners—for example, by checking the validity of the claims made by partner agencies, having planned in advance how this would be achieved.

Satisfying this standard is not merely a case of charities doing their best with the resources they have available, as Interpal had argued. Although proportionality was highlighted by the Commission, it was proportionality of investigation to the risk faced by the organization, which would be considerable in a conflict zone or where terrorist activities are known to take place. Ability to comply consistently and comprehensively with the extent and very high standards of these governance requirements raises significant concerns for charities, especially in terms of their financial capabilities, human resources, expertise, and the speed with which they need to act. It may well be that some organizations simply do not have the capacity for this level of anticipatory and ongoing evaluative governance. There would be no discretion here to negotiate a lesser standard.

The Charity Commission emphasized that a "know your partner" principle is relevant also in coalition working, where stringent governance mechanisms on knowledge, suitability, formalizing relationships, and contingency and exit strategies equally apply (Charity Commission 2009, para 199). In Interpal's case the coalition of which it was a member, the Union for Good, was found to have members who were either designated organizations or designated individuals. This meant that the charity engaged through membership of the coalition with entities designated as terrorists and potentially took part in projects funded by them. This would be unacceptable under general terrorism and charity law. As well as requiring Interpal to disassociate itself from the Union for Good forthwith, the Charity Commission also made it clear that there was a conflict of interest in regard to one of Interpal's trustees, who was also on the board of the coalition.

The importance of the duties and responsibilities of trustees was a consistent theme in this inquiry. Trustees are central in an organization's governance structure and are required to make "finely balanced" judgments on risk assessment (Charity Commission 2009, para 2). They need also to consider their own potential for conflict of interest and be wary of making statements or taking actions in a personal capacity that are irreconcilable with their office or their obligations under the counter-terrorism provisions, or that may be misinterpreted or harm the charity. Trusteeship is an onerous office and likely to become more so through the application of counter-terrorism governance norms.

The Charity Commission's findings and recommendations from its inquiry into Interpal highlight the onerous organizational responsibilities that charities face. Though focused upon a charitable organization, the Commission's approach to assessing risk should also apply more broadly to other civil society organizations. Although wider civil society is not subject to the same statutory duties as charities, nonetheless they will be subject to general counter-terrorism regulations and their own internal constitutional obligations. Good governance norms for partnership and coalition working would fall within expected practice for an organization's officers.

Ensuring Supervisory Responsibility

In addition to organizational responsibility, the United Kingdom's counter-terrorism regulation and policies also emphasize that responsibility lies within the overarching supervisory framework to oversee and monitor organizations, as well as to assist organizations to develop their own internal governance processes. For overall civil society the supervisory framework is piecemeal, with a particular emphasis placed upon charities. Separate charity regulators are in place across the different UK jurisdictions,[19] and although operating under different legislative regimes, these regulators have similar extensive powers to monitor and supervise charities within their jurisdictions. They also have similar statutory objectives that include enhancing accountability within charities, ensuring compliance with legal obligations, and promoting public confidence.[20] The latter is a significant requirement and a key motivator for protecting the reputation and good standing of charities against terrorist exploitation. The development of a counter-terrorism strategy for these different regulators is not yet complete, leaving a lack of coherence and consistency in provision. Given the infancy of the Scottish and Northern Irish regulators, the focus thus far has been on developing the supervisory approach of the Charity Commission for England and Wales, with a push for it to be a much more proactive regulator in this field working in partnership with the sector (Home Office and HM Treasury 2007, para 3.14).

The counter-terrorism approach to regulatory supervision can be characterized as an uneasy mix of standardization of behavioral norms and intervention. The policy seeks to prevent organizations acting as or becoming conduits for terrorist financing or other terrorist activities and, more broadly, to promote trust and confidence of donors in the civil society sector and the wider public by providing mechanisms for accountability. Tension exists between a drive for risk-based regulation, favored by the Home Office (Home Office and HM Treasury 2007), and an insistence within the sector for an evidence-based system (Quigley and Pratten 2007). From the sector's perspective, the use and abuse of its organizations by terrorist groups is rare, and so the regulation should reflect this level of risk. But, although the scarcity of discovered cases is acknowledged by the Home Office, there is an assumption that discoverability may not be a real indicator of the extent of exploitation of charities. For the Home Office, the latency of the risk remains a significant issue justifying a risk-based system (Home Office and HM Treasury 2007, 4.2). The Home Office's policy then pursues an anticipatory approach to diligence and assurance by organizations, focusing upon risk as to future conduct rather than evidence of existing conduct.

As the regulator taking forward the Home Office's policy, the Charity Commission has sought to develop a middle way, operating a zero-tolerance approach to terrorism, but emphasizing risk-based governance norms for organizations and evidence-based exercise of its own investigatory powers. The Commission has extensive powers to open inquiries into charities, to freeze accounts, and to suspend or remove trustees.[21] It exercised all of these, for example, in relation to the removal of the cleric Sheikh Abu Hamza al-Masri from the North London Central Mosque in Finsbury Park in 2003. That the mosque was eventually reopened with a new governing structure under advice from the Commission reflects the twin roles of the Commission as both enforcer and aide. The Charity Commission also can—and apparently has—used controversial powers under the Regulation of Investigatory Powers Act 2000 to undertake covert surveillance to investigate individuals and organizations to access and gather information.[22] The exercise of these powers should be used sparingly, because they and the Commission's investigatory powers sit uneasily alongside the Commission's role as guidance provider.

Despite the wide interventionist powers that it has, the Commission's expressed policy is to use its investigatory role and enforcement mechanisms only as a last resort. It gives preference to increasing its own oversight mechanisms and, within that, to building awareness and cooperation with charities (Charity Commission 2008, 3). To that end, a focus has been placed by the Charity Commission upon the importance of developing internal governance mechanisms within charities and promoting the development of a "risk assessment toolkit" to identify organizational weaknesses that could be exploited for terrorist purposes (Charity Commission 2008, 11–12).[23]

The Charity Commission's findings in the Interpal inquiry, noted above, were the first real test of its evidence-based approach under its supervisory regime. Lack of proof was central to the Commission's decisionmaking on the serious charges of Interpal's alleged links to partner agencies promoting terrorist ideology and distributing aid to the children of suicide bombers. That clear and unequivocal, rather than circumstantial, evidence was required by the Commission to link terrorist material to the partner agency and thereby to the charity was significant. Once the decision as to evidence was taken by the Commission, it reverted to a focus on internal governance mechanisms that, although stringent, nevertheless was reasonable in response to the risk faced by the particular organization. Such an approach by the regulator maintains a level of flexibility to address charities' organizational vulnerability to use and abuse by terrorists. It also maintains a measure of trust between the parties.

These factors should not be underestimated. The Charity Commission essentially buttresses charities from an initial investigation by the police or other state authorities. This provides an opportunity for a sensitive and knowledgeable investigation of the sort not seen in other jurisdictions such as the United States. The regulator has a clear understanding of the environment in which its organizations operate, complete with the constraints and opportunities. For the organization's part it has the opportunity to know the allegation against it, put its case forward, and answer the regulator's questions without the threat of an adversarial system or immediate listing without the opportunity to respond.

The advantage of the Charity Commission's role as a buttress is only a limited one, for the majority of civil society organizations stand outside of its regulatory powers. Although there are clear advantages to a lack of regulatory formalities for these broader civil society organizations, in a counter-terrorism context it presents a double difficulty. Although the Home Office's risk-based governance framework is expressed to be for charities, it is not inconceivable that the broad-based governance norms will be similarly applied to all civil society organizations, especially in relation to a "know your partner" or coalition or beneficiary principle. Furthermore, this then leaves much of the United Kingdom's civil society sector bound by high-level, risk-based governance norms but exposed to a less sensitive and less knowledgeable counter-terrorism investigatory framework.

No immediate salve is at hand for this regulatory gap. Proposals have been made for a specific counter-terrorism code of conduct from the European Commission to apply to all civil society organizations across all member states (European Commission 2005). This would have required an extension of regulatory powers such as those exercised by the Charity Commission to unregulated parts of civil society. Following consultation, however, the code was forcefully rejected by civil society organizations across the Union as a disproportionate, unworkable, and inappropriate instrument. Although some progress is being made on the code with a consultative contact group, it is some way from implementation.

Ignoring Proportionality

In their analysis of counter-terrorism regulation across the globe, the International Commission of Jurists noted in particular the difficulties caused by the application of inappropriate and disproportionate laws and policies (International Commission of Jurists 2009). Issues of proportionality and appropriateness are also raised in relation to the United Kingdom's counter-terrorism focus upon civil society and responsibility. For activity-focused obligations under the general counter-terrorism regulation, there are obvious concerns about the "net-widening" and ultimate "normalization" of offences that were once extraordinary powers (Waddington 2005). The listing of organizations and individuals as proscribed entities, the boundaries of the glorification of terrorism offences, the use of stop and search police powers to disrupt legitimate protests, and restrictions on the locations of demonstrations are all unnecessary and heavy-handed interferences with fundamental democratic rights of speech, assembly, and association.

But perhaps the most exigent developments for civil society under the United Kingdom's counter-terrorism laws are not the general provisions that most obviously restrict fundamental freedoms or chill participation in democratic activities, significant though they are. Perhaps organizations should be most concerned about those developments that are actually sector-specific, which have the potential to impact upon and frustrate day-to-day activities. In particular the very rapid development of the Home Office's sector-specific, counter-terrorism policies imposing organizational governance norms have potential to affect all organizations in the sector and cause regulation creep.

Good governance obligations placed upon civil society organizations have, to this point, been relatively piecemeal by comparison with the public and private sectors. The Home Office's approach, taken forward by the Charity Commission and applied in the findings of the Interpal inquiry, however, reflects a now-developing trend. Although the need for principles of good governance are generally accepted, particularly for organizations such as charities, which receive public money or generous taxation privileges, the setting up of governance standards and the choices made about their content, nature, and extent have created cause for concern.

This is particularly the case in relation to externally imposed standards. Although externally imposed standards permit a level of communality and harmonization with other fields and across terrorism targets, they can nonetheless represent a blunt legal instrument in terms of proportionality to risk. A desire for proportionality of approach applies equally, if not more, to the translation of counter-terrorism measures into standards of good governance toward civil society. The internationalization of the terrorist threat has brought with it a desire within the international community to have a coordinated, coherent, and consistent counter-terrorism response across states. This external pressure has effectively sidelined a sector-led development of governance practices drawn from the expertise of sector organizations (Quigley and Pratten 2007). It has led instead to the creation of imposed, risk-based governance policies specifically for charities that have very little real understanding of how, or the circumstances in which, such organizations operate. The imposition of governance benchmarks, set up in standardized form, not only increases compliance costs but often inhibits the activities of organizations. Indeed a plea from the sector (Quigley and Pratten 2007) for bespoke rather than external standards, as well as the need for partnership between regulators and the sector representatives in setting up counter-terrorism measures, was made in advance of the Home Office proposals but ignored.

A primary problem of the Home Office's risk-based approach to organizational responsibility is that it assumes an obligation without always inquiring into the propriety of imposing such an obligation. Some civil society organizations such as charities have specific statutory duties, for example, to carry out the charity's purpose, to safeguard the integrity and reputation of the organization, and to protect its assets. Placing governance obligations on trustees in these circumstances, particularly where the charity or its assets could be compromised by terrorist exploitation seems not only reasonable but essential. But are the governance mechanisms so applied necessarily a proportionate response in terms of creating obligations to, say, effectively monitor each and every officer, member, employee, and volunteer, or to require investigation of the use of a grant award to an organizations several hands removed? In addition to assuming a responsibility, the risk-based approach also assumes the existence of a level of risk that may neither be appropriate nor properly reflect reality. The Home Office's starting assumption, for example, is that the lack of reporting of significant activities of terrorism activity within civil society in recent years is a failing, indicative of poor sector awareness rather than possibly suggestive of the low risk of the sector.[24] The risk-based approach then, leaves little room for organizations to exercise their discretion, judgment, experience, or knowledge of the field.

The risk-based approach is also anticipatory, and this presumes that future unknown actions and circumstances can be translated into risk-based burdens. The Charity Commission, in its Interpal inquiry, recognized expressly that some civil society organizations operate in conflict, post-conflict, and disaster zones where political, social, and environmental conditions can be volatile and regimes unstable. Here risk to organizations can change very rapidly and be unpredictable. Similarly, risk-based governance mechanisms do not always take into account the restrictions of local conditions and local cultural practices, such as word bonds to cover agreements between organizations or the operation or use of informal value transfer systems such as hawala to transfer funds. Risk-based approaches further require high-level compliance mechanisms, which in turn depend upon knowledge, resources, time, and expertise, all four of which in civil society organizations can be in short supply. Even where resources are not in issue there is the difficulty of capacity, and of the ability to assess future conduct or future circumstances on which there is presently scant information or evidence (Brandon 2004, 997).

Finally, two consequences of risk-based governance systems are apparent. First a risk-based approach to expected conduct has the potential to effectively change the burden of proof for transgression, placing the onus on organizations to demonstrate their compliance with governance norms. A second consequence is that risk-based governance practices condition activities. In so doing they can lead to standardization of governance norms where good practice shades first into expected practice and then into quasi-legal principle. In this progress toward regulating behaviors, nuance and proportion can be lost. This is significant in a sector that thrives on diversity, creativity, and innovation. There is a real danger that standardizing conduct will stifle or chill sector activity.

In this context it is also worth mentioning that the focus upon responsibility and exposure to risk has broader effects too, primarily in creating risk aversion as actors seek to limit their potential liability. Risk aversion is prevalent not just in civil society organizations (which, for example, may move out of volatile environments), but also in a whole range of organizations that interact with civil society. For example, in recent years essential services such as banking, legal services, and accounting have been withdrawn from civil society organizations as a direct consequence of the potential liability that would flow to the service provider under counter-terrorism and money-laundering regulations. Initially such services have been withdrawn from organizations that have been listed as proscribed or designated terrorist organizations, or subject to official regulator investigation, such as Interpal.[25] But an emerging trend is the removal of service facilities from organizations that have no apparent link to terrorism or the commission of terrorist offences or that have not been the subject of a regulator inquiry.[26] There is no obligation on the part of the service provider to explain their actions, but failure to do so in these circumstances can easily lead to an inference of profiling. A wider point too emerges: not only does risk aversion impact upon civil society directly through the withdrawal of ancillary services, but it also removes an essential check and balance on organizations. If actors withdraw from the arena to limit their exposure to risk of liability, then they also remove themselves from a position of being able to detect and report criminal activity. It will be ironic if the disproportionate nature of the burden serves in part to defeat one of the main purposes of the responsibility.

Conclusion

Counter-terrorism regulation, as it applies to civil society in the United Kingdom, exhibits all the hallmarks of the broader failings of global counter-terrorism regulation recently highlighted by the International Commission of Jurists. There has been unreflective widening of legal provisions, normalization of emergency powers, the imposition of disproportionate burdens, and high regulatory barriers. Provisions have been imposed without understanding the sector or taking into account the nature of its organizations or the circumstances in which it operates. A significant chill factor is evident, and so too is risk aversion. All this has been achieved against the backdrop of protectionism. That is, that by ensuring organizational responsibility and supervisory oversight, organizations, individuals and the public will be protected from terrorist exploitation. But that protectionism, with all its advantages to public confidence, comes at a cost.

The vast majority of civil society organizations may not be directly affected by the United Kingdom's counter terrorism laws. This may be for a variety of reasons, perhaps because they do not work in certain fields or countries, or because they rarely undertake campaigning work or work within coalitions. Nevertheless, all civil society organizations should be alert to and concerned with the pace and extent of the legal developments in this field. First, anticipatory, risk-based governance norms apply without discretion. They have the effect of normalizing behavior and they are a short step away from standardization. Second, standardization is rather antithetical to the sector's ethos. Civil society occupies a unique space sometimes between the market and the state, and sometimes of the market or the state. As a sector it is broad, amorphous, and unique. It variously offers innovative, creative, and often rapid responses to need as well as maintaining traditionalism and conventional civic values. It has multiple bottom lines and multiple motivations for action. Civil society defies definition; it does not conform to customary ideas of organizational theory or rational choice. It is a sector little understood by regulators. In this light the imposition of external, risk-based governance norms represents a threat, however small, to the development of organizations and the spirit of the sector.

This is certainly not to say that there is no need for regulation in this field, because there obviously is. But regulation that allows for discretion and nuance, and that is sensitive to and understanding of the constraints and circumstances in which civil society organizations operate, would seem to be a better starting point.

Notes

1. The Terrorism Act 2000 marked the United Kingdom's first permanent counter-terrorism legislation.

2. See, for example, FATF, *Best Practices paper on Special Recommendation VIII* www.fatf-gafi.org/dataoecd/50/63/34424128.pdf, Third European Union Anti-Money Laundering Directive and the EU Counter Terrorist Financing Strategy, the Convention against Financing Terrorism, and UN Security Council Resolutions 1267, 1333 and 1373 (2001).

3. Annex 1 contains the initial action plan.

4. Definition of terrorism is provided in section 1 Terrorism Act 2000, as amended.

5. See Section 3, Schedule 2 Terrorism Act 2000, sections 21–22 Terrorism Act 2006.

6. See sections 19, 39B, and 39 Terrorism Act 2000.

7. See Section 19 Terrorism Act 2000.

8. See Money Laundering Regulations 2007, SI 2007/2157

9. See Section 1–4 and Schedule 1 Anti-Terrorism, Crime and Security Act 2001, Proceeds of Crime Act 2002 (as amended by the Serious Crime Act 2007), Terrorism (United Nations Measures) Order 2006, Al-Qaida and Taliban (United Nations Measures) Order 2006.

10. See Section 1 Terrorism Act 2006.

11. See Section 1 Terrorism Act 2000, as amended.

12. See Human Rights Watch 2007; Liberty 2004; Das-Gupta 2005.

13. Section 44 Terrorism Act 2000, Public Order Act 1986, Part 4 Serious Organised Crime and Police Act 2005.

14. Charity Commission, *Inquiry Report: Palestinians Relief and Development Fund (Interpal)* (London: Charity Commission, February 2009) para 55.

15. A BBC Newsnight Broadcast August 19, 2008, revealed that Children in Need had given a grant to the Leeds Community School which gave a grant to Iqra Community Centre which had been frequented by two of the 7/7 bombers.

16. The focus is provided by Financial Action Task Force, *Special Recommendations on Terrorist Financing* (2004), FATF Best Practices paper on Special Recommendation VIII, www.fatf-gafi.org/dataoecd/50/63/34424128.pdf

17. Gordon Brown, "Meeting the terrorist challenge," Chatham House, October 10, 2006. www.guardian.co.uk/politics/2006/oct/10/immigrationpolicy.speeches

18. See section 1 Trustee Act 2000, section 66 Charities and Trustee Investment (Scotland) Act 2005, section 1(1) of the Trustee Act (Northern Ireland) 2001.

19. These include Charity Commission for England and Wales, Office of the Scottish Charity Regulator, Charity Commission for Northern Ireland.

20. See provisions in the Charities Act 1993 as amended by section 7 Charities Act 2006, Charities and Trustee Investment (Scotland) Act 2005, Charities Act (Northern Ireland) 2008.

21. See section 8 Charities Act 1993.

22. These powers can be used where necessary on the grounds of national security, public safety, or public health, to detect or prevent a crime, in the interest of the economy, or to collect tax. See sections 26(7), 26(8)(a)–(e) and section 29(3). Documents obtained under the Freedom of Information Act reveal that the Charity Commission exercised its powers under this Act three times in 2007 (Evans and Lewis 2009).

23. A draft of this toolkit is scheduled for publication in 2009.

24. This point is acknowledged by the Home Office, *Review of Safeguards* paras 1.11, 3.1–3.8.

25. National Westminster Bank first closed Interpal's bank accounts in 2005 following a court ruling in the United States allowing the families of victims of a suicide bomb to sue those connected to the perpetrators: See *Weiss v. National Westminster Bank plc* 453 F. Supp. 2d 609 (E.D.N.Y. 2006). In January 2009 Lloyds Bank de facto withdrew banking services from Interpal by refusing to continue to act as a

clearinghouse for Islamic Bank of Britain through which it was clearing Interpal's cheques. Although a reason was not initially provided, the bank eventually announced that it could be subject to the United States' economic sanction laws (Mair 2009).

26. For example, Barclays Bank withdrew banking services from Ummah Welfare Trust (UWT), an Islamic charity operating in Pakistan, Palestine, Afghanistan, and other countries (Mair and Mason 2009).

3

"POLITICS AS USUAL": CIVIL SOCIETY AND DEVELOPMENT IN SPAIN AFTER 9/11

Alejandro Colás

Of all the Western states targeted by transnational jihadist terrorism over the past decade, Spain's response has arguably been unique. As opposed to the United Kingdom and the United States, there has been no substantial institutional reform, fresh legislation, or drastic policy initiatives in reaction to jihadist terrorism in that country. Instead, this chapter argues, Spain's institutional and societal response has been characterized by a reaffirmation of "politics as usual." The Madrid bombings of March 11, 2004, (known in Spain as the 11-M attacks) certainly placed questions of terrorism, civil society, and aid at the center of Spanish foreign policy. Over half of those sentenced for the 11-M atrocity were North African nationals, many of them stemming from Spain's former colonial zone in northern Morocco, and all were part of Spain's significant new Muslim populations, who have overwhelmingly come to the Iberian Peninsula in search of employment and socioeconomic betterment. Maghrebi residents in Spain—and the estimated half a million Moroccans in particular—have operated as a reserve army of labor, fuelling the country's economic growth since the early 1990s, and have, through their remittances, in turn played a critical role in the economic development of their countries of origin. Reflecting these intense, yet structurally asymmetric bilateral relations, Morocco is Spain's fifth largest recipient of official overseas aid and the country's main commercial partner among African, Caribbean, and Pacific states.

In this context, the 11-M attacks created a fertile terrain for the "securitization" of international aid and civil society in Spain. In line with Mark Duffield's influential account (2001), Spain's relations with its southern Mediterranean partners present all the necessary conditions for the establishment of a security-development nexus after 11-M. "Today," Duffield reminds us, "security concerns are no longer encompassed solely by the danger of interstate war. The threat of the excluded South foment-ing international instability through conflict, criminal activity and terro-rism is now part of that new security framework" (Duffield 2001, 2).

The rest of this chapter argues that jihadist terrorism has indeed facili-tated the framing of North African immigration to Spain in particular as a potential threat from the "excluded South," thereby also impinging on the country's aid policies and civil society. But equally, as I hope to demon-strate below, this framing has been both contested and implemented in distinctive ways in Spain, offering telling contrasts to other Western expe-riences. With this qualified support for the idea that the War on Terror has encouraged a convergence of aid and security, thereby also impacting upon civil society activity, the chapter explores the effects of this conver-gence—first, upon Spain's external relations; then, with regard to the Spanish state's relations with its Muslim citizens and residents; and finally, in relation to Madrid's policy and institutional response to jihadist terro-rism on its own soil.

Spain's Foreign Policy after September 11, 2001

The 9/11 attacks in New York had two immediate effects on Spanish politics, both with significant international dimensions. The first was to latch the country's domestic campaign against Basque terrorism onto the bandwagon of the global War on Terror. The Spanish premier at the time, José María Aznar of the center-right Popular Party (PP), was quick to align Madrid's foreign policy squarely behind that of Washington, exemplified most graphically in the Azores summit of March 2003 where Aznar flanked Bush and Blair in declaring their resolve to undertake regime change in Iraq, ostensibly as part of the global War on Terror (BBC 2003). The second reac-tion involved the securitization of North African migration across the Straits of Gibraltar. A week after the 9/11 attacks, the then Spanish Foreign Minister Josep Piqué proclaimed his administration's viewpoint that "Strengthening the fight against illegal immigration is necessary in order to combat international terrorism." He related this to journalists on Septem-ber 18, 2001, adding that it was "very likely" that people traffickers also handled the cross-border movement of terrorists (El País, 2001).

This statement neatly encapsulates much of the Spanish anxiety over migration as an agent of the security-development nexus in the aftermath of the 9/11 attacks and subsequently 11-M. The securitization of popu-lation movements in the western Mediterranean, however, long predates the 9/11 conjuncture. Since Spain's rapid ascendancy as a destination for

North African immigration in the 1990s, Madrid's diplomacy toward the Maghreb has been preoccupied with the control (and indeed the reduction) of migration flows from that region.

Initially, North African migration—whether legal or illegal—was associated among both state and civil society actors with questions of social integration and intercultural coexistence.[1] More alarmist and outright xenophobic sectors of Spanish society saw an "existential" threat to the country's presumed national identity, prosperity, and social stability emanating from mass Muslim immigration. For those more concerned with the welfare of African migrants themselves, it was the perilous— often fatal—crossing of the Gibraltar Strait or the Atlantic route to the Canaries, followed by the super-exploitation and denigration of many such workers once on Spanish territory, that warranted talk of security— in this context, of a more human kind. For a decade or so following Spain's accession to the Schengen Convention in 1991, successive governments—in the main of a staunch right-wring orientation—passed legislation aimed at regulating and reducing extra-European migration to Spain, generally in the context of alleged fears of foreigners "swamping" the country (Zapata-Barrero and de Witte 2007).

Madrid found different degrees of cooperation in this endeavor in Rabat, Tunis, and Algiers, but the policing of the Iberian Peninsula's coastlines was by the turn of the new century increasingly Europeanized through the newly hatched Justice and Home Affairs pillar (Huysmans 2000). It was furthermore deeply embedded in Europe's multilateral initiatives vis-à-vis the southern Mediterranean, such as the Euro-Mediterranean Partnership (EMP) launched at the 1995 Barcelona Conference and its successor European Neighbourhood Policy. As George Joffé has astutely observed, both these initiatives form "[i]n essence, a European security policy designed to render emigration from North Africa and the Middle East unnecessary by dynamizing their economic development and thus creating the necessary employment" (Joffé 2008, 154).

The buzzword accompanying this synthesis of security and development was "co-development," understood as a formula that replaced conventional, one-way international aid with the aspiration of an integrated Mediterranean free market that would foster prosperity and stability across all shores of the *Mare Nostrum*. Unsurprisingly, such a freedom did not extend to the international movement of people, although lip-service was paid in the relevant policy documents to the potential of harnessing remittances and voluntary migrant repatriation to economic growth in the southern Mediterranean countries of origin.

In line with this new development agenda, Spain's international cooperation agencies have, over the last decade, recast North African migration as an integral component of their proclaimed development strategy. The launch in 2000 of the four-year "Plan GRECO" (Global Regulation and Co-ordination Programme for Migration Policy—*Programa Global de Regulación y Coordinación de la Extranjería y la Inmigración en España*) aimed at facilitating the transfer of immigrant skills and capital back to their countries of origin, together with the association of migration to regional stability in Spain's 2001 Master Plan for International Coopera-tion, represent two notable instances of the ways in which migration flows have been reconceptualized as the basis of co-development. Closer scrutiny of how these aspirations have been translated into policy, how-ever, yields very little evidence of any significant impact on the ground. As Joan Lacomba and Alejandra Boni have recently suggested in an in-depth study of Hispano–Moroccan aid policy, "a detailed analysis concerning the exact nature of Spanish development aid in Morocco demonstrated that official Spanish cooperation policies in the area dedicate low priority to migration issues" (Lacomba and Boni 2008, 125).

It is with this backdrop—one where migration flows have already served as the conduit for the security-development nexus—that we can begin to understand the peculiarities of Spain's foreign policy response to the 11-M attacks. Once those accused of perpetrating the attacks were identified as Maghrebi nationals, the transnational flows across the Strait of Gibraltar were bound to become a focus of counter-terrorist efforts. Article 5 of the North Atlantic Treaty had already been invoked after 9/11 to launch NATO's *Operation Active Endeavour*, which was aimed at "patrolling the Mediterranean, monitoring shipping and providing escorts to non-military vessels through the Straits of Gibraltar to help detect, deter and protect against terrorist activity."[2] Bilateral cooperation in areas of policing, law-enforcement, and intelligence intensified across the Mediterranean littoral in the aftermath of the 11-M bombings, and on the multilateral plain, the tenth anniversary of the Barcelona Declaration in 2005 saw the signing of a Euro-Mediterranean Code of Conduct on Countering Terrorism. Despite failing to agree on a common definition of international terrorism, the signatories to the document seemed to have placed this issue at the forefront of the EMP, marking in the view of one expert observer, "a significant advance in the creation of a common political framework that acts as a normative and conceptual reference point" (Reinares 2005, 5).

With regard to the securitization of North African immigration, there is little evidence to date that the Spanish state has either expanded or intensified the existing monitoring of migration flows for security purposes as a direct result of the 11-M attacks. This is chiefly because, as we have thus far seen, there already exists an extensive regulatory infrastructure with managed population movements across the Mediterranean, and this is linked more to political-economic and human security concerns rather than to specifically terrorist threats. The operation of detention centers for illegal immigrants in the North African enclaves of Ceuta and Melilla, and other Spanish ports of entry, is associated with the political economy of migration rather than counter-terrorism strategies, whereas the closer policing of the peninsula's southern borders has not substantially affected the volume of migration flows—even if over the past five years it has resulted in an estimated 10,000 deaths among those trying to clandestinely reach Spanish territory (SOS Racismo 2008). To be sure, as scholars and human rights advocates have amply documented, the policing of Europe's Mediterranean borders has deepened and hardened over the past decade, often through the deployment of military forces (Lutterbeck 2006). Yet this intensification of Mediterranean border-control predates the 11-M (and indeed the 9/11) attacks, therefore complicating any direct causal relation between migration control and counter-terrorism.

From this perspective, the Spanish experience reinforces the kind of findings recently presented by Fiona B. Adamson in her survey on international migration and national security: "It is how states respond to global migration flows through policy formation and implementation that will determine the extent to which national security is enhanced or diminished by international migration" (Adamson 2006, 198). In other words, connections between transnational population flows and national security are never static or natural, but contingent and manufactured. Ultimately, the mutual economic gains to be derived from a Moroccan presence in Spain, coupled with the official commitment to co-development (however unsatisfactory its actual results), have, at the policy level at least, trumped any facile and straightforward association of migration with Islamist terrorism. North Africans will continue to work and live in Spain and return to their homelands at regular intervals. Such traffic may now be under closer scrutiny, but it has not been curtailed, let alone stopped.

The State, Civil Society and Spain's Muslim Populations

For most of the 1980s and 1990s, Spain remained largely unaffected by the revival of Islamism in the Maghreb—even when this took a violent turn in Algeria after 1992. By the start of the new century, however, Spanish authorities had detected and partially dismantled a network of jihadist terrorists in the peninsula coordinated by the Syrian-born Imad Eddin Barakat Yarkas, aka *Abu Dahdah*, and a related group of terrorists linked to the Algerian Armed Islamic Group (*Groupe Islamique Armée*,

GIA) (Jordán 2005; Jordán and Horsburgh 2006). A number of those identified by the Spanish and Maghrebi security services as escaped members of these networks reappeared as suspects in the Casablanca bombings of May 2003 and subsequently in 11-M itself. More recently, security forces have established connections between those involved in 11-M and the string of bombings that launched the North African branch of al Qaeda in the Spring of 2007 (Steinberg and Werenfels 2007). It is therefore reasonable to infer that jihadist terrorism in the western Mediterranean has become transnationalized, with states and societies on all shores involved and affected in fairly equal measure by the phenomenon.

In the absence of robust transnational or multilateral institutions to deal with cross-border jihadist terrorism, it is, logically enough, organs of the state that have been at the forefront of counter-terrorist initiatives at home. Civil society institutions, and Muslim associations in particular, have been interpolated as the preferred interlocutors in this endeavor. To this extent, what the 11-M events have spurred on is a (re)examination at the institutional, academic, and policy levels of the sociopolitical position of Muslims in contemporary Spain. In June 2004, the semi-official think-tank *Real Instituto Elcano* conducted a survey where 34.1 percent of respondents considered a "greater control of [Muslim] immigrants and mosques" as a priority in the fight against international terrorism (cited in Moreras 2005). Such securitization of Spain's Muslim populations and their places of worship, I will show below, has shaped much of public discussion and policy response to 11-M. But once again, the concrete instances of a structural transformation in Spanish State–Muslim relations as a direct result of 11-M are few and far between.

In the aftermath of 11-M, one arena where this paradox played itself out was in relation to the regulation and monitoring of Spain's mosques. The Iberian Peninsula has, of course, a long and distinguished association with Islamic civilization. Yet prior to the mass immigration of North Africans addressed earlier, the Muslim population of the country was composed of a few thousand Spanish converts, as well as students and professionals from the greater Middle East. The latter created the Muslim Association of Spain in 1971 (the first of its kind on the Spanish mainland), and in 1991 became the predominantly Sunni Arab organization, the *Unión de Comunidades Islámicas de España* (Union of Islamic Communities in Spain, UCIDE). The mainly Sufi converts, for their part, established the Islamic Community of Spain in Córdoba in 1976, becoming the *Federación Española de Entidades Religiosas Islámicas* (Spanish Federation of Islamic Religious Entities, FEERI) in 1989 (Arigita 2006; Taulés 2004). Both these organizations have sought to act as institutional representatives of Spain's Muslims, and the state affirmed this aspiration—albeit demanding their agglomeration into a single representative organization—by signing an Agreement of Cooperation in 1992 with the amalgamated Islamic Commission of Spain.

It was to these institutions that state authorities turned in the wake of 11-M in an attempt to address the issue of "Islamic extremism" in Spain. The problem, however, is that these organizations are largely unrepresentative of the Muslim populations of Spain in at least two senses. In the first place, they have limited membership among the bulk of Spain's Muslims, namely Maghrebi immigrants. For a variety of diverse sociological, cultural, and political reasons (including illiteracy/poor education, closer affinity with fellow-nationals rather than fellow-Muslims, and, in many instances, holding secular worldviews and lifestyles) most North African residents in Spain do not turn to UCIDE or FEERI for communal or political leadership. Indeed it is a secular immigrant workers association, the Asociación de Trabajadores Inmigrantes Marroquíes en España (ATIME) that has played this function over the past decade vis-à-vis the Spanish public. Paradoxically, although both the state and the Muslim faith organizations wish to formalize the relationship between Spain and its Muslim populations—identifying the latter as a minority religion rather than as an ethnic community—the bulk of Spain's Muslims seem more content with an informal expression of their faith and a more versatile definition of their identity as any combination of the following: Muslims, North Africans, Arabs, Berbers, or simply new Spanish citizens.[3]

This form of practicing Islam in Spain is expressed in the proliferation of informal, unregulated mosques or prayer rooms (*oratorios*) across the peninsula—the second major obstacle in the way of a purely institutional response to the normalization of relations between the Spanish state and its Muslim populations. Muslims wishing to carry out their religious obligations or seek out spiritual support in Spain have over 400 small prayer rooms to choose from, but only seven large, properly endowed mosques unevenly concentrated in Madrid, Barcelona, Valencia, and Andalusia (Moreras 2005, 134). The former are largely managed and administered by communities of believers without official links to governments and generally following Maghrebi Maliki rites.[4] The large mosques, on the contrary, have in the main been built and funded by states of the Arab Mashriq and the Gulf (particularly Saudi Arabia), and therefore tend to employ Hanbali rites and promote a Wahabi conception of Islam. The national, political, and doctrinal differences manifest in such variety of Muslim places of worship indicate the difficulty of representing Islam or Muslims in Spain as a single, homogenous religious, let alone a unified sociological entity.

Yet this is arguably what the Spanish state and some of its supporters among the Spanish Muslim populations did in the face of 11-M. The anxiety over the infiltration of unregulated mosques by Islamist extremists led to a call from the Spanish Minister of Justice for a regulation of Friday prayers through the creation of a state-controlled list of vetted imams. This proposal was soon rejected, but it has resurfaced in the form of several national and regional agreements and initiatives between the state and the officially recognized Muslim religious associations, aimed at regulating the appointment of imams, the issuing of fatwas, or the delivery of Muslim religious education in schools. The large, recognized Muslim associations have an economic and doctrinal interest in pursuing such initiatives, eloquently conveyed by the President of the Islamic Centre in Valencia, Amparo Sánchez, when she reiterated the call for the Spanish government to consider ways of monitoring the election of imams and supporting them economically so that properly qualified scholars could exercise this role (El País 2008). To take one illustration, only about half of imams currently undertaking this function in Catalonia do so on the basis of a fixed, officially remunerated contract—the rest are either itinerant or ad hoc imams selected from the community of believers itself on the basis of their high moral standing and pious reputation. Of these, according to official statistics, just 60 percent were able to demonstrate a qualification in religious studies (Moreras 2007).

Lack of further data makes it difficult to extrapolate from this Catalan experience onto the national, Spanish plane. Certainly the official, state-sponsored mosques in Madrid, Barcelona, Valencia, Fuengirola, and Granada employ clerics and scholars trained at world-renowned centers of Islamic scholarship, including Al-Azhar. But it is likely that the hundreds of smaller, community oratorios employ the itinerant or ad hoc imams just mentioned. Indeed, Jordi Moreras in this context invokes the suggestive figure of a "community imam" who "develops . . . tasks of a social character and communal mediation" (Moreras 2005, 139) as well as prescribed ritual functions, by way of conveying the prevalence of the informal, mobile, and often elusive forms of Muslim religious organization and practice in contemporary Spain.

It is these very qualities of Spanish Muslim oratorios—irregularity, mobility, and elusiveness—that have drawn the attention of State and Muslim authorities in the context of the War on Terror. The perception that unregulated mosques in Spain, as elsewhere in Europe, are serving as recruiting grounds for violent jihadists has validated this securitization of Muslim immigrants and their places of worship, even though in Spain the evidence of this kind of connection tends to be anecdotal (Jamal Ahmidan, one of the 11-M plotters, is for instance said to have occasionally preached at a Madrid oratorio).

Accordingly, both state authorities and relevant elements of Spanish civil society are keen to structure and formalize the role of Muslim associations and their mosques. At work here is the attempt at crafting legitimate mediators between the state and Spain's Muslims, in a manner comparable to the state's relations to Spain's other minority faiths. At one level, such a strategy is commendably even-handed and consistent with the democratic Constitution's commitment to religious tolerance and nondiscrimination. Yet implicit in such initiatives is a sense that it is Spain's Muslim population in particular that requires monitoring and integration, and that, once again, this is because of the potential links between jihadist terrorism and this particular demographic. To that extent the Spanish state has, after 11-M, seemingly sleep-walked into securitizing its relationship with Spain's Muslims by assuming that the character of whole populations can be reduced to their religious affiliation.

Institutional Reform and Jihadist Terrorism

As we have seen thus far, the Spanish state's response to the 11-M attacks has been fairly predictable in its combination of international counterterrorism cooperation with its European and southern Mediterranean neighbors, as well as domestic engagements with Spain's Muslim populations. In both these areas there has been a flurry of activity in the context of the global War on Terror, and this has certainly entailed the securitization of civil society. The concrete policy outcomes emanating from this activity have, however, been mixed at best. Where fresh policy initiatives in the wake of 11-M *have* been implemented, the particularity of the Spanish experience appears once more in that it has generally been channeled through existing political and juridical processes and institutions: securitization of civil society in Spain has been slightly deepened, but not significantly widened.

The third and final arena where this singular reaction is in evidence relates to the virtual absence of institutional or legislative reform in the face of jihadist terrorism. As against the two other Western states where global jihadist terrorism has struck, Spain has not witnessed the institutional reform of its intelligence services, the splitting of its Home Office, or the creation of new Departments of Homeland Security. Nor has it been the subject of draconian counterterrorist legislation such as the USA PATRIOT Act, the United Kingdom's 2000 and 2006 Terrorism Acts, or its subsequent experimentations with indefinite detention, extraordinary rendition, or outright torture (Haubrich 2003). Two existing legal-political institutions have instead been the focus of Spain's response to jihadist terrorism.

The first of these has been the courts (Human Rights Watch 2005a). The twenty-seven defendants associated with the 11-M attacks tried at the

Audiencia Nacional (Spain's highest penal court) faced various charges ranging from "terrorist assassination" to "acting in service of or collaborating with armed groups." They were subject to sentencing under the existing Penal Code (*Código Penal*).[5] The second institution is Parliament. As in the United States, the 11-M attacks were the subject of congressional scrutiny, although each parliamentary group delivered its own report. What is striking leafing through the recommendations of the three largest groups (Socialist Party, Popular Party (PP), and United Left-Green) is their insistence on using existing legislation and institutions to combat terrorism in the future. Only the PP recommended substantive changes to existing penal and administrative statutes in order to facilitate the monitoring and eventual expulsion of foreign terrorist suspects—even though current legislation allows for both of these options.

Instead what we have witnessed five years on from 11-M is an attempt at deepening the reach of existing judiciary/law enforcement agencies and tightening up coordination among relevant counter-terrorist departments of the state. There has certainly been a predictable shift in existing resources from national to international counter-terrorism, with a tenfold increase in the number of intelligence agents from the National Intelligence Centre dedicated to monitoring jihadist networks in Spain and beyond. There have also been, as we have seen, a range of state-sponsored initiatives at engaging with Muslim sectors of Spanish—and indeed North African—civil society with the well-meaning intention of fostering a "moderate" Islam in Spain and preventing extremism through recognition and integration. But all of this has happened chiefly through existing sociopolitical channels. If this account of Madrid's response to the 11-M carries any weight, two inter-related questions remain: why does the Spanish experience differ from that of other Western states subject to jihadist violence? And what, if anything, does such a response tell us about the connections between civil society, development, and security in the age of the "long war"?

In relation to the first of these questions, several lines of argument can be pursued. One is simply to emphasize that terrorism is not new to Spain, and that the country therefore requires no corresponding institutional overhaul or fresh legislation. Thirty years of experience with Basque and other extremist political violence has equipped Spain's democratic institutions with plenty of instruments to address the "new" jihadist terrorism. On this reading, the absence of radical judicial-institutional reform is a sign that the relevant organs of the state and law-enforcement are fit-for-purpose in combating terrorism.

There is much to recommend this view, not least the fact just mentioned that those accused of association with the 11-M bombings were processed through existing anti-terrorist legislation. For all intents and purposes, the 11-M hearings were conducted—and largely reported—as a domestic criminal case, with the international and transnational dimensions of the attacks presented—once again, in contrast to both the United Kingdom and the United States—as one of several, and not always the more prominent, components to the investigation. As Fred Halliday (2007) noted of Chief Judge Javier Gómez Bermúdez's final verdict, the criminological approach to 11-M underplays the political motivations behind jihadist terrorism: "The case was treated as a criminal one, thus framing it in terms of the conventions of crime (perpetrators and 'masterminds'—what in Spanish legal terminology are called the 'intellectual authors'). The demand of the victims and survivors to know who 'conceived of' or 'inspired' the cell's actions was in a similar vein. But the by-now-familiar decentralised, often self-starting, nature of Islamist groups across the world means that they cannot be understood in terms of a model of 'orthodox' criminal organisation" (Halliday 2007).

This muted approach to the international politics of the 11-M attacks has the virtue of both rejecting the collective stigmatization of Spain's Muslim populations and discouraging the kind of militarized responses that followed in the wake of 9/11. Yet it is also open to the charge of narrowing the explanatory terms of reference to an extent that minimizes or sidelines the international and transnational sources and consequences of the bombings, as well as failing to register the distinctive characteristics of what some experts have labeled a "fourth wave" of terrorism (Rapoport 2001).

While the courts criminalized terrorism, the Spanish Parliament—and, by extension, the Spanish "street" and media—became venues for the politicization of 11-M. This realization of the famed constitutional separation of powers can also be presented as a reason behind the absence of radical legal-administrative reform in the aftermath of 11-M. Put simply, the political response to the attacks remained political: it was neither judicialized, communalized, nor, as we have seen, significantly securitized. Instead, 11-M became the focus of a profound polarization between the political left and right in Spain. On this reckoning, the Spanish response to 11-M was to oust the PP from power and withdraw Spanish troops from Iraq. The 11-M attacks are explained in this way as a direct consequence of Aznar's slavish support for George W. Bush's foreign policy—especially the invasion of Iraq. The 11-M attacks were seen by many in the opposition primarily as a problem of external affairs. Consequently, the reorientation of Spanish foreign policy under the new Socialist administration was deemed to be a sufficient reaction to undermine any need for domestic institutional reforms or fresh policy initiatives.

Such an account of Spanish exceptionalism in the face of global jihadist terrorism has some cogency. There is, for instance, no question that the 11-M atrocity had a significant impact on the electoral defeat of the ruling party 72 hours after that event. But it is harder to establish that the impact resulted directly from the threat of al Qaeda terrorism as such, or indeed from Aznar's support for the Anglo-American invasion of Iraq. The available evidence suggests that the swing against the PP was a result of the disinformation by the incumbent government rather than any systematic rejection of its foreign policy, or the fear of further Islamist violence (Colás 2004). Indeed, since 11-M jihadist terrorism has ranked third, after Basque terrorism and the state of the economy, as the chief political concern of Spanish public opinion. A purely "externalist" reading of the Spanish reaction to 11-M also overlooks the strong continuities in Madrid's foreign policy toward the greater Middle East—Spanish troops may have withdrawn from Iraq, but they remain deployed in southern Lebanon and Afghanistan. All of this would suggest that, if the 2004 change of government was chiefly the result of Aznar's foreign policy, the new administration has not absorbed that particular message.

A third rationalization for the continuation of "politics as usual" after 11-M returns to the domestic level, contending that the absence of a significant second, third, or even fourth generation of Muslims in Spain has precluded the development of ethnic-religious "communities" that in other contexts, most notably the United Kingdom, have facilitated the sense of exclusion and grievance that, for some, help to explain the motivation behind the London 7 July bombers. This in turn would explain the absence of a communalization of counter-terrorism in Spain, and the accompanying dearth of strategic policies aimed at de-radicalizing domestic Muslim populations, like those witnessed in the United Kingdom (*Guardian*, 2008). Here the claim is that North African immigrants in particular form too small a percentage and too dispersed a population in Spain to constitute a "home-grown" expression of political Islam.

Accepting for a moment the otherwise suspect notion that it is exclusion or grievance that delivers suicide bombers, the peculiar demographic composition of Spain's Muslim population compared to that of most of its Western counterparts cannot in itself account for Spanish exceptionalism with regard to counter-terrorist policies. The problem with such ethno-communal approaches to the subject is that they tend to essentialize Islamist violence as the product of a readily available cultural or religious sense of identity and belonging. Once that identity or community is aggrieved, so the argument runs, political violence is bound to follow, taking on a religiously inspired rhetoric. Yet in the Spanish case, as elsewhere, the profile of those charged with the 11-M attacks does not correspond to a picture of pious individuals rooted in a religious community and alienated from wider society, but rather to men who were integrated at all levels of Spanish society—be it as professionals, students, or petty criminals—and whose affiliation to terrorism came not by way of communal radicalization but through careful recruitment via a dedicated transnational political network of Islamists.

Conclusion

We are left, then, with a final and perhaps rather glib and complacent conclusion, namely that Spain's response through a continuation of "politics as usual" after 11-M simply reflects the political maturity of the country's institutions and electorate, and its capacity to distinguish between a global jihad against the West on the one hand, and a host of complex political issues arising out of North African immigration, Euro-Mediterranean relations, or Spain's Muslim populations on the other. The Madrid bombings, I have argued, placed the limelight on a number of socioeconomic and political interconnections across the western Mediterranean that did elicit calls for changes in Spain's foreign policy, its domestic policies toward Muslims, and the country's institutional arrangements with regard to international terrorism.

The events of 11-M underlined the ways in which the complex social processes accompanying unequal development across different jurisdictions within a specific region—for instance, the population flow from the Maghreb into Spain's European territory—can become reduced to a national, or indeed European, security issue if they are associated with transnational terrorism. In other words, the Spanish response to 11-M and its aftermath can be read at one level as an expression of the securitization of development and civil society under the War on Terror. Yet equally, as I hope to have demonstrated above, such securitization is never entirely complete or successful. The observation that Christina Boswell has recently made in relation to the securitization of migration control in Europe after 9/11 also holds for civil society and development in Spain after 11-M: "[T]he two levels of political discourse (politics) and organizational practice (administration) operate according to distinct dynamics. Politics is concerned with mobilizing support through framing and advocating programmatic responses to issues of societal concern . . . The administration is less intensively engaged in reading signals from its environment about public legitimacy and its interests and goals are to a larger extent defined by internal organizational dynamics" (Boswell 2007, 606). Similarly, in the Spanish case, much of the political discourse surrounding 11-M emanated from, or was concerned with, the transnational dimensions of civil society, and the country's North African populations in particular.

Yet the "internal organizational dynamics" of the administration, coupled with the criminalization of the terrorist attacks themselves, has delivered minimal political change. The main reasons for this, I have ventured, are that, on this occasion at least, the institutional make-up of Spanish politics has proved robust enough to withstand shocks like those of 11-M, while connections between Spain's deep interdependence with its North African neighbors and terrorist threat from the "excluded South" have proved untenable empirically and theoretically. The socioeconomic and diplomatic challenges stemming from the sharp inequalities across the northern and southern shores of the western Mediterranean long predate the events of 11-M, and they are regrettably likely to long outlive the consequences of that fateful morning. In that respect at least, Spain can claim to have delivered an exceptional response, compared to most of its Western counterparts.

Notes

1. A good account can be found in Izquierdo 1996.
2. http://www.nato.int/issues/active_endeavour/index.html
3. Once again, however, schematically up to 50 percent of those Muslims surveyed in July 2007 identified themselves as practicing their faith irregularly or occasionally (34 percent) or not at all (16 percent) (Demoscopia 2007).
4. Sunni Muslims recognise four major orthodox traditions of Islamic legal exegesis: Hanafi, Shafi'i, Maliki and Hanbali. The latter two are generally deemed to be more conservative, and predominate in North and West Africa, and Saudi Arabia, respectively. Although all four schools recognize each others' legitimacy, and do not vary substantively, the Hanbali rite is arguably the most narrowly scriptural of the four.
5. For a useful documental dossier on the 11-M by the daily *El Mundo* available at http://www.elmundo.es/documentos/2004/03/espana/atentados11m/documentos.html. Downloaded June 6, 2008.

4

COUNTER-TERRORISM MEASURES AND THE NGO SECTION IN THE UNITED STATES: A HOSTILE ENVIRONMENT

Kay Guinane and Suraj K. Sazawal

Current counter-terrorism laws and enforcement policies in the United States began as an emergency response to the attacks on September 11, 2001, and remain largely unchanged eight years after the attacks. This legal and policy regime has created a hostile environment for US civil society and NGOs specifically. This chapter argues that it does not account for the realities of civil society operations, particularly international aid and development programming or charitable organizational structures.

The consequences of the United States' misguided treatment of charities in the name of national security are severe, in part because it diminishes civil society's ability to assist those in need. But the real tragedy in this story is the lost opportunity. Charities, foundations, and development organizations can contribute to the reduction of violent extremism through their charitable and advocacy work, a way of thinking that has become mainstream in international development work, as well. Whether their work is focused on reducing poverty, providing education and opportunity, or advocating against injustice, the net result could be the same: to shrink the space available for terrorism to flourish. But nearly eight years since the 9/11 attacks, US charities are still treated as a threat to security. Although the change in administration in Washington gave hope that the US government would adopt more measured responses to the threat of terrorism, the "War on Terror" has already become deeply embedded in laws, policies, and the bureaucratic practices of government agencies, as this chapter explains. Further, the US government has promoted the War on Terror regime internationally through diplomacy, aid, and new forms of civil-military cooperation. As the avowed leader of the global fight to defeat terrorism, the United States has an important role to play in terms of formulating counter-terrorism responses that respect human rights and encourage political deliberation.

Part 1 of this chapter reviews the laws and policies underlying the US counter-terrorism regime and analyzes their many flaws. Part 2 describes the negative and disproportionate influence US policy has outside the United States and suggests it conflicts with international law, including the Geneva Conventions. Part 3 focuses on impacts on US civil society, inclu-ding government infringement into civic space and the operational capacity of US NGOs. Part 4 describes the political context, rooted in the politics of fear, and suggests that a shift toward assessment—and hopefully reform—is taking place.

The US Counter-terrorism Regime

The Patriot Act of 2001 strengthened two laws that make it difficult for NGOs to engage in a range of legitimate activities, from grant-making to development and human rights advocacy. These laws include the International Emergency Economic Powers Act (IEEPA),[1] which gives the executive branch unchecked power to designate any group as a terrorist organization and bar all contact with them, and the Antiterrorism and Effective Death Penalty Act (AEDPA),[2] which prohibits providing material support to designated organizations.[3] IEEPA's designation and asset-blocking authority was originally passed to authorize embargoes and sanctions against nation-states, and then expanded to "national emergencies" created by the threat of terrorist organizations.[4] The use of IEEPA as a primary strategy in coun-tering terrorism has been counterproductive in the context of nonprofit organizations. It does not incorporate a mechanism to ensure that frozen charitable funds are ever spent for charitable purposes, so that what was meant as a temporary measure is in effect a permanent seizure.

Former US President George W. Bush invoked IEEPA on September 23, 2001, to issue Executive Order (EO) 13224, which authorizes the secre-tary of treasury and the secretary of state to designate terrorists on the Specially Designated Global Terrorist (SDGT) list.[5] EO 13224 expanded designation authority to include those "associated with" terrorists, with-out defining the term. Since that time the SDGT list has grown to include about 500 names. Under IEEPA the Department of the Treasury can block (freeze) assets if it finds there is a "reasonable basis to suspect or believe" an organization supports or is associated with terrorism. Rules of evidence do not apply, meaning that news reports, foreign intelligence, hearsay, and other forms of untested and potentially unreliable evidence can be used to block an organization's assets. A charity or its attorneys do not have the right to see secret evidence used to designate it. AEDPA authorizes the secretary of state to designate "foreign terrorist organizations"[6] and makes it a crime for any person or organization to knowingly provide, attempt to provide, or conspire to provide "material support or resources"[7] to a designated entity. AEDPA assumes all support furthers a designated organization's terrorist operations, regardless of its actual character.[8] Medical and religious materials are exempted from the definition, but humanitarian aid such as food, water, tents, and blankets are not (Cole 2004). The secretary of state and attorney general have authority to approve exceptions for "training," "personnel," and "expert advice or assistance" if it is found that the aid will not be used to carry out terrorist activities.[9] During the Bush administration these powers were not invoked to the extent necessary to remove barriers to aid.[10]

IEEPA sanctions programs are administered by the Treasury's Office of Foreign Assets Control (OFAC), an agency with money laundering expertise that has no expertise with respect to the NGO sector. IEEPA sanctions make no differentiation among and between charities, individuals, nation-states, banks, or other nonstate entities. As a result, when a charity or foundation is designated for providing material support to a prohibited entity, all of its US property and financial assets may be "blocked" (frozen) without notice.[11] When an organization's assets are frozen pending an investigation, there is no deadline on when the investigation must end. KindHearts for Charitable Humanitarian Development was shut down in February 2006 under this provision and its funds remain frozen even though it has not been designated (Blake and Yonke 2008). The 9/11 Commission Report published in August 2004 noted that this provision "raises particular concern in that it can shut down a US entity indefinitely without the more fully developed administrative record necessary for a permanent IEEPA designation" (Roth et al. 2004). Further, NGOs have no meaningful appeal rights if the Treasury Department designates them as supporters of terrorism, or if they are shut down "pending an investigation." They cannot present evidence on their own behalf to an independent reviewer, have no right to counsel, and cannot see much of the evidence against them. The courts are limited to reviewing the Treasury Department's procedures and will not accept evidence presented by the accused NGO (OMB Watch and Grantmakers Without Borders 2008a).

In November 2002, the Treasury Department released *Anti-Terrorist Financing Guidelines: Voluntary Best Practices for U.S. Based Charities.*[12] These guidelines were developed without public comment or input from the NGO sector. They address governance, disclosure, transparency, and financial practices, with an emphasis on groups that distribute funds to foreign organizations. Strict adherence to the guidelines provides no legal protection against designation and asset seizure. They have been widely criticized for mixing good governance with law enforcement, and the US nonprofit sector has called for their withdrawal.[13] The Treasury Guidelines Working Group, a network of nonprofits and foundations, developed the *Principles of International Charity* as a proposed alternative.

The US legal framework also includes broad surveillance powers passed after 9/11. Under the Bush administration these were used to track and infiltrate groups that publicly and vocally dissented from its policies and actions, such as the war in Iraq. Use of anti-terrorism laws and resources for this purpose has been justified under the Patriot Act's "domestic terrorism" provision, broadly defined as "activities that appear to be intended to intimidate or coerce a civilian population; to influence the policy of a government by intimidation or coercion; or to affect the conduct of a government by mass destruction, assassination, or kidnapping."[14] The law also lowered the threshold for the FBI to collect personal information about people inside the United States if it is "for an authorized investigation . . . to protect against international terrorism or clandestine intelligence activities." The government can seize an organization's records without showing probable cause of any criminal activity and without suspicion that the subject of an investigation is a foreign power or agent of foreign power.[15] Furthermore, controversial amendments to the Foreign Intelligence Surveillance Act (FISA) in July 2008 allow warrantless surveillance of foreign targets who may be communicating with people in the United States.[16]

Flawed Assumptions about the Role of Charities

The Bush administration consistently justified the emphasis on NGOs in its anti-terrorist financing efforts by claiming the sector is a "significant source of terrorist financing."[17] The Treasury Department guidelines claim that its internal investigations "revealed terrorist abuse of charitable organizations, both in the United States and worldwide, often through the diversion of donations intended for humanitarian purposes but funneled instead to terrorists, their support networks, and their operations."[18] These broad-brush accusations have never been supported by evidence. Instead OFAC cites "open source media reports" and refers to general information on its website.[19] An Annex[20] to the updated guidelines released in 2006 claims that charities and individuals associated with them account for 15 percent of total SDGTs. However, this claim is flawed, as using OFAC's information shows that US NGOs only account for 1.4 percent of total SDGTs.[21] Using the percent of designations as the measure exaggerates the threat posed by the abuse of nonprofits. When dollars are used as the measure, designated charities and foundations, both US and foreign, account for only 5.3 percent of total blocked assets.[22]

The view of the US Treasury Department is not shared by experts. The Terrorist Financing Staff Monograph to the 9/11 Commission claims that its own background investigations "revealed no substantial source of domestic financial support" for the 9/11 attacks (Roth et al. 2004, 3, 9). US money-laundering experts have questioned the cost effectiveness of the Bush administration's emphasis on the "financial war on terror" and the associated reliance on IEEPA's designation and asset-blocking provisions. Warde argues that, "Reforming the Islamic charities system was long overdue, yet post-September 11 policies proved mostly counterproductive; they weakened mainstream, 'controllable' charities, while building up informal, unchecked, and potentially dangerous charitable and donor networks" (2007, 130).

Mission Creep: From Anti-terrorist Financing to "Exploitation and Abuse"

The initial focus of counter-terrorism measures in the United States was on stopping financial support to terrorist groups. The Treasury Guidelines reflected this approach. In the Annex[23] to the September 2006 version of its Guidelines, the Treasury Department went a step further to include the need to prevent undefined terrorist "abuse of charities." The Annex says that the risk of terrorist abuse "cannot be measured from the important but relatively narrow perspective of terrorist diversion of charitable funds" but also includes the "exploitation of charitable services and activities to radicalize vulnerable populations and cultivate support for terrorist organizations and networks." There is no statutory basis for this expanded interpretation.

Despite its flaws, the early focus on preventing financial transactions with designated groups provided NGOs with some element of certainty about what groups and individuals they could partner with. Many NGOs have purchased software that helps them check their grantees and project partners against the SDGT list. But the criminal prosecution of the Holy Land Foundation (the largest Muslim charity in the United States before 9/11)[24] and its leaders in 2007 and 2008 undermined that certainty. The prosecution admitted that Holy Land spent $12.4 million for charitable activities, but argued that by working with nondesignated zakat committees in the West Bank and Gaza Strip, Holy Land was indirectly benefiting Hamas, a designated organization. Prosecutors argued that the defendants "should have known" the zakat committees were "otherwise associated" with Hamas (Krikorian 2007). The case ended in a mistrial in October 2007 (Eaton 2007) but in 2008 the leaders and Holy Land were convicted. The case is being appealed.

The government's theory in this case has serious implications for other non-governmental organizations. The legal theory used by the Treasury Department puts forward the idea that NGOs working overseas cannot rely exclusively on cross-checking the names of individuals and organizations with the government lists of designated terrorist organizations. This is because NGOs risk running afoul of counter-terrorism legislation if they provide support to organizations and individuals that do not appear on the official lists. Thus, NGOs must do their own due diligence checks on their overseas partner organizations to determine whether they might be subject to a classified investigation by US authorities or if their staff and leadership have political sympathies that may lead to accusations that they are "otherwise associated with" a terrorist organization. To make matters worse it appears that the Treasury Department is unable to keep the SDGT list up to date. During the Holy Land trial, an OFAC official testified that designation is not necessary to determine whether or not a group supports terrorism and that keeping up with front groups "is a task beyond the wise use of resources" and that Treasury targets umbrella groups instead.

The United States Counter-terrorism Regime on the International Stage

The United States has used its power and influence with international bodies such as the United Nations and the Financial Action Task Force (FATF) to promote its flawed counter-terrorism regime for NGOs and pressure other countries to adopt a similar approach. The outcomes of this are problematic. For example, Cortright points out that, "Counterterrorism legislation and measures against 'extremism' have been used to crack down on NGOs and political activists who criticize government policies. *The USA PATRIOT Act* sets the pattern for many states in widening the authority of police, intelligence, and security forces to investigate and detain suspects, with little regard for judicial oversight or the protection of individual rights" (Cortright 2008, emphasis added).

The United Nations counter-terrorism strategy has been heavily influenced by US policy. UNSCR 1373,[25] approved by the United Nations Security Council on October 30, 2001, strengthened FATF's authority to address terrorist financing. FATF, created in 1989 at the G7 Summit in

Paris to deal with money laundering and international financial crime, now finds itself in the realm of recommending regulation of philanthropy and charitable programming. It published recommendations for its members to combat terrorist financing, including Special Recommendation VIII: Nonprofit Organisations.[26] The language in the FATF Special Recommendations mirrors the US Treasury Department language by encouraging countries to "undertake domestic reviews of their NPO sector." In October 2002 FATF published a best practices guide that mirrors the Treasury's Guidelines.[27] Millar (2009) notes that the "UN Security Council's Counter-Terrorism Committee assesses 'the extent to which states have the necessary laws and regulations in place to ensure that charities and other nonprofits are not being used to finance or otherwise support terrorism.' This emphasis on the nonprofit sector derived from policy recommendations of the Financial Action Task Force, which were issued without corroborating evidence and without regard to the impact of such measures on CSOs (civil society organizations)."

The United States has also pressured European countries to adopt a Code of Conduct based on the Treasury Department Guidelines. In 2005 the European Commission's Directorate-General for Freedom, Security and Justice published a draft code of conduct for NGOs that was heavily criticized by European NGOs (Ethical Corporation 2005). The United Nations also created its own list of terrorists and terrorist organizations, and US-designated NGOs are automatically added to it. Other countries are expected to recognize these designations, even if they have not designated the NGO themselves. The problem is exacerbated by the fact that, like the United States, the United Nations lacks adequate processes for those placed on its list to appeal or challenge.[28]

Designations made by the United States in listing groups as supporting terrorism have led to problems in other countries. This is clearly illustrated in the case of the Palestinian Relief and Development Fund (Interpal), as explained in Alison Dunn's chapter. In November 2008, the British banking giant Lloyds TSB discontinued financial services to Interpal due to the United States' 2003 designation of the charity, even though it is not designated in the United Kingdom and has been cleared on three separate occasions of supporting terrorism following investigations by the UK charity regulator (Waller 2008). Interpal was eventually able to restore banking services through alternative methods. In a separate case, on December 16, 2008, Barclays Bank sent a letter[29] to the Ummah Welfare Trust (UWT), based in Bolton, England, announcing closure of its account. Barclays did not issue a statement explaining the action but many believe the primary reason is that UWT has relations with a number of groups designated by the US Treasury Department, including Interpal. A Barclay's spokesman said its decision was not "taken lightly," and the UK Charity Commission confirmed there was no current investigation into the group.

US Policy Conflicts with Red Cross Standards, Geneva Conventions

US law and previous Bush administration policy treats all provision of resources to terrorist organizations as commission of a terrorist act, regardless of its nature. This leads to bizarre results and contradicts international law. For example, Ahilan Arulanantham describes the long-standing policy of neutrality in humanitarian aid that President Ronald Reagan invoked in 1983, when he sent food aid to communist Ethiopia during the Cold War. Arulanantham explains that "[a]s with civil war and disaster situations around the globe . . . providing humanitarian aid to the most needy people in Sri Lanka almost inevitably requires working in areas controlled by, and dealing directly with, a designated terrorist group" (Arulanantham 2008, 3). In one of the most counterproductive applications of US law, the Department of Justice has fought the Humanitarian Law Project's efforts to provide the Liberation Tigers of Tamil Eelam (LTTE) and the Kurdistan Workers' Party (PKK) in Turkey with human rights and conflict resolution training in court, despite the fact that the program could contribute to a peaceful resolution of long-standing conflicts.[30]

These examples illustrate how compliance with US material support laws is in direct conflict with long-established standards for aid. The 1994 International Red Cross Code of Conduct[31] states in part that: the humanitarian imperative comes first; aid is given regardless of the race, creed or nationality of the recipients and without adverse distinction of any kind. Aid priorities are calculated on the basis of need alone; aid will not be used to further a particular political or religious standpoint; and that humanitarian aid shall endeavor not to be used as an instrument of government foreign policy.

IEEPA gives the president broad authority to prohibit humanitarian aid when he or she determines it would "seriously impair his ability to deal with any national emergency" or would engender US armed forces.[32] EO 13224 does not have any criteria for determining when aid would meet this threshold. As a result, there is a question of whether this aspect of IEEPA violates international law. White (2005) analyzes IEEPA in light of the 1949 Geneva Conventions. For signatory nations such as the United States, she points out that the Conventions "establish an impartiality standard in that they grant to humanitarian organizations the right of access to non-combatants during armed conflict."[33] IEEPA's failure to distinguish between impartial and discriminatory aid, or front groups that channel money to terrorism, "creates an environment in which the President can eviscerate these protections for non-combatants, placing the United States in violation of international law."

White (2006, 2i) further notes, "Both the Conventions and IEEPA protect against the risk of terrorist funding, but IEEPA goes beyond what is necessary and limits legitimate and necessary aid ... Unlike prohibitions created by use of the override authority, however, the Conventions do not inhibit activities of impartial organizations providing aid in satisfaction of the protective obligations that arise during an armed conflict." White recommends the International Committee of the Red Cross (ICRC) standards for defining impartiality as "no discrimination as to nationality, race, religious beliefs, class or political opinions"[34] as a measure of impartiality. Thus, the material support provisions in US anti-terrorism legislation since 9/11 mark a significant shift away from the tradition of delivering humanitarian aid according to principles of neutrality, impartiality, and independence.

Counter-terrorism, Aid, and NGOs

Due diligence requirements contained in post-9/11 anti-terrorism legislation have affected grant-making practices in agencies involved in international development. For example, USAID has required its grantees to sign "Anti-Terrorism Certificates," and since 2007 grantees have been required to vet the organizations that they are partnering with, to prevent funds from going to terrorists or terrorist organizations.[35] A proposed Partner Vetting System (PVS) would require USAID grant applicants to submit detailed personal information on "key individuals" to be shared with US intelligence agencies.

PVS generated immediate criticism from aid and advocacy groups. Despite numerous comments and calls from nonprofits for its withdrawal, the substance of the final rule issued on January 2, 2009,[36] remained largely unchanged. The Obama administration has delayed the rule, and it is expected that the new USAID administrator will make a decision on whether to drop, revise, or retain it. The personal data required from "key individuals" on the proposed Partner Information Form[37] includes name and government-issued photo identification number, place and date of birth, citizenship, gender, occupation, current employer, job title, home address, email address, and rank or title in organization. The rule seeks information "on each individual to receive training, equipment, or other direct benefits." This could mean beneficiaries are subject to information collection. According to USAID, the "Information provided to USAID by applicants will be transmitted to USAID employees who will check that information against one or more databases maintained by the intelligence community."[38] The American Civil Liberties Union (ACLU) argued that the databases "raise serious due process concerns . . . in light of the fact that the lists are error-filled and unreliable, with many false positives, and there is no effective means for challenging the fact that one is on the list" (American Civil Liberties Union 2007). The ACLU has detailed numerous instances where people have been put into terrorism-related databases because of activities supporting human rights, the environment, peace, and other causes (Rein and White 2009).

The final rule attempts to address due process concerns by providing that "any denial of funding by USAID as a result of PVS screening will be accompanied by a reason for that denial and an opportunity for the organization to appeal administratively." Because USAID will not confirm or deny whether an individual has passed or failed screening in terrorist databases, it will be difficult for applicants to pursue appeals.[39] USAID has not demonstrated a need for PVS. The Office of Inspector General issued a report[40] on December 10, 2007, in response to concerns that USAID provided funds to universities and students in Gaza that were allegedly linked to or controlled by Hamas. It found that, although procedural violations occurred, none of these grants assisted a designated terrorist organization. The students and universities were vetted more than once.[41]

In certain aid contexts, concerns that development and relief funds could be channeled to terrorist organizations have influenced the establishment of new organizations and structures to deliver aid. In August 2008[42] USAID and a newly created charity, Americans for Charity in Palestine, announced a new public–private partnership created to channel private charitable donations to groups in the West Bank and Gaza Strip through USAID. USAID issued a press release[43] when the parties signed a Memorandum of Understanding (MOU) stating that the project "seeks to offer a secure and efficient means of transferring charitable donations from individuals and entities in the U.S. to *USAID-managed programs* for the Palestinians" (emphasis added). Although many of the details including the contents of the MOU are not yet known, preliminary information raises significant concerns and questions for private philanthropy and the independence of the NGO sector.

Since the announcement, the US government has heavily promoted the agreement as a way to direct humanitarian aid to Palestine without violating US counter-terrorism laws. Patrick O'Brien of the Treasury raised concerns when he told a group of Muslim charities in August 2008 that, "It is our hope that this type of collaboration will take root and *serve as a model for other areas* of concern as well as encompass other funding streams including that of the international community" (emphasis added).[44] O'Brien assumes that independent aid distribution mechanisms operated through civil society are not as safe or effective as those provided by the government, when in fact the opposite may be true. There is also a question of whether USAID will turn the funds over to agencies controlled by political parties or factions favored by US foreign policy. This would politicize private philanthropy in violation of long-standing principles of neutrality and independence of civil society.

The cooperation of US NGOs has also been sought in counter-insurgency operations by the US military in contexts such as Iraq, Afghanistan, and the Horn of Africa. Since former US Secretary of State Colin Powell described NGOs as "force multipliers"[45] that help achieve the government's political and military goals in the war in Afghanistan in 2001, the problem of the military's increasing role in aid programs has generated criticism. At the same time, US charities and foundations are under pressure to ally themselves with the foreign policy and political goals of the US government, as epitomized by the pressure that has been placed on US NGOs to work within Provincial Reconstruction Teams (PRTs) in Iraq and Afghanistan, which combine civilian and military personnel and resources.[46] However, military objectives are prioritized, as can be seen in the alliances PRTs have built with warlords and corrupt local officials in order to strengthen stability (Perito 2005). Hence, there are risks for NGOs seen to be cooperating with the military.

This has added to the negative impression of US NGOs abroad, where many believe "that the politicization of aid before and during the [Iraq] war, and the resulting absence of clear distinctions between the US government and aid organizations, including those distinctively focused on independent humanitarian action, has created the perception that all assistance is part of the US agenda" (de Torrente 2004). A 2005 Department of Defense (DOD) directive calls on the military to build alliances with nonprofits for "stability operations" that are defined as "maintaining order in States and regions." As a result, "US NGOs thus today find themselves being approached in various countries by the US military with proposals for joint development and stability activities. Some NGOs and faith-based NGOs complain that the appearance of joint operations or visits by US military personnel imperil the NGO's reputation for neutrality and independence in the eyes of local communities" (McMahon 2007). This trend of increasing civil–military cooperation is alleged to have led to rising numbers of attacks on aid workers. For example, Patronus Analytical, a group measuring the security risks of places receiving humanitarian aid, finds that 90 percent of deaths of relief workers are nonaccidental, and the second leading cause of deaths for aid workers in politically turbulent areas is classified as "political/conflict" (Patronus Analytical 2007).

In December 2008 DOD officials met with humanitarian groups to outline a new plan, the Civilian-Military Cooperation Policy, which increases coordination with USAID programs "in all aspects of foreign assistance activities where both organizations are operating, and where civilian-military cooperation will advance USG foreign policy" (Moncreiff 2008). NGOs reacted strongly to the policy. InterAction, an umbrella organization for US NGOs, argues that aid funds will be allocated "to fund development projects favored by the military." It is also feared that the military will have greater influence on policymaking and funding of humanitarian aid programs. Elizabeth Ferris from the Brookings Institution [AU(SS)](OMB Watch 2008) claims that such a close relationship between the military and humanitarian groups will open the door for attacks on charitable groups by insurgents. She explains, "Once insurgent groups perceive that a humanitarian organization is acting to pursue military or political objectives that organization loses the protection it had by virtue of respect for humanitarian principles."

The Civilian-Military Cooperation Policy is now being reassessed, with the Foreign Affairs Committee in the House of Representatives considering renewal of the Foreign Assistance Act. On March 18, 2009, the committee held its third hearing[47] in an ongoing investigation into the proper role of the military in the government's foreign assistance efforts. The witnesses' testimony agreed that increased emphasis on security and use of the military for aid purposes has created problems, especially for US nonprofits that receive foreign assistance grants. The head of the US NGO Mercy Corps argued, "A chronic under-investment in civilian capacities has led to an over-reliance on military solutions and military tools." A partnership between two think tanks[48] convened stakeholders, including NGOs, in February 2009 to develop recommendations for an "imbalance in American statecraft, principally resulting from too heavy a reliance on the military" (Barton and Unger 2009). Noting the Obama administration's related policy review and statements by both Secretary of Defense Robert Gates and Secretary of State Hillary Clinton supporting an increased role for development in foreign policy, participants recommended expanding civilian agency capacity, including USAID, and leveraging international and non-governmental resources rather than trying "to go it alone." Nevertheless, if NGOs are to strive toward principles of neutrality and independence in their humanitarian work, then they will need to approach such a political embrace of development policy and civilian capacity with critical reflection and caution. Otherwise, they risk again being manipulated by larger military and political agendas.

Operational Impacts on Domestic NGOs

The degree of negative impact on charities, development, civil liberties, educational, religious, and grant-making organizations varies, but Muslim charities and their donors have been most heavily impacted. The pressure created by draconian sanctions, powers, and vague definitions has led many nonprofits to rely on checking terrorist watch-lists, signing anti-terrorism certification statements, and other administrative measures that cost time and money but do little to protect against diversion of resources to terrorism. Grant-makers say many of these measures are harmful to the grantor–grantee relationship (Fuller and Baron 2003).

Because the counter-terrorism regime is based on an IEEPA (an embargo statute), there is no process for funds of designated charitable organizations to be released or transferred for charitable purposes. Treasury regulations give OFAC full authority to allow transfer of these funds[49] to other charities upon request of a designated charity. However, the agency has declined all such requests as a matter of policy, saying such transfers are not in the national interest. Concerns that the funds be spent appropriately could be easily addressed. For example, each specific license application must include detailed information on all parties involved with the proposed transfer.[50] OFAC can place conditions on any license it grants, including reporting requirements;[51] it can amend or cancel the license at any time; and it can "exclude any person, property, or transaction from the operation of any license."[52] Requests denied by OFAC include the following cases. In 2002 Benevolence International Foundation asked OFAC to release nearly all its funds to a children's hospital in Tajikistan and the Charity Women's Hospital in Dagestan. The application included safeguards to ensure the money arrived at the proper destination.[53] In a separate case, after being shut down "pending an investigation" in 2006, KindHearts asked OFAC to release its funds to the United Nations, USAID, or any other humanitarian program.[54] Finally, in another case, IARA-USA offered to change their governance structure, financial accounting, and even personnel to "ensure that all of its funds reach its intended humanitarian designation."[55]

Because there is no appeal from OFAC's refusal to transfer funds, the money remains in limbo. In November 2006, a group of nonprofits asked the Treasury to release frozen funds "to trustworthy aid agencies that can ensure the funds are used for their intended charitable purposes."[56] The signatories requested a meeting with Treasury officials to discuss the proposal in more detail. Although two meetings have taken place, there has been no progress toward releasing the funds.

The overall regulatory regime has made aid operations more difficult. This is illustrated by the barriers to delivering aid in Lebanon because

Hezbollah, which has been designated as a terrorist organization by the Treasury, is part of the local government and aid delivery network, as Nisrine Mansour explains in this book. A report in the *Chicago Tribune* noted that "Every U.S. aid agency is facing the exact same problem," according to a spokesman for a US aid agency operating in Lebanon, who asked not to be named because the subject is "super, super, super sensitive." "We're waiting on word from the Treasury on that. We're waiting on some sort of guidance."[57] A Treasury spokeswoman, Molly Millerwise, said charities operating in the United States are barred from knowingly financing or "working with" Hezbollah. The question is what might constitute "working with," given that many Lebanese officials are affiliated with the group.[58]

A double standard in the Treasury Department's enforcement policies has evolved. Charities are shut down and their assets frozen indefinitely, while for-profit corporations are fined and allowed to continue to operate. The most egregious example of leniency for a for-profit corporation is the March 2008 plea agreement between the Department of Justice and Chiquita Brands International, which was fined $25 million for making payments to organizations designated as terrorists by the US. Between 1997 and 2004 Chiquita paid $1.7 million to the United Self-Defense Forces of Colombia and additional payments to the Revolutionary Armed Forces of Colombia, knowing the payments were illegal.

A Shift in the Policy Environment?

The ongoing "emergency" created by the 9/11 attacks has been characterized by the politics and rhetoric of fear. In this context national security concerns trump all other concerns. This has been seen in the courts, in Congress, and in the Treasury Department.

The Courts Change Direction

Legal challenges to the first wave of designations of US charities took several years, and in each case the courts deferred to the Treasury because of national security concerns. For example, in December 2002 the Court of Appeals for the Seventh Circuit found that the government's interest in stopping terrorism and preventing funds from being transferred out the country justified the use of secret evidence and lack of pre-seizure notice or hearing for the Global Relief Foundation.[59] Similarly, when the Islamic American Relief Agency-USA (IARA-USA) lost its challenge to the Treasury's designation and asset-blocking power in 2007, the Court of Appeals for the District of Columbia ruled that "[w]e may not substitute our judgment for OFAC's," even though the court said "the unclassified record evidence is not overwhelming, but we reiterate that our review—in an area at the intersection of national security, foreign policy, and administrative law—is extremely deferential."[60]

It now appears the political and psychological climate may be shifting. In late 2008 and early 2009, three courts ruled in favor of NGOs on the crucial issues of the overly broad definition of prohibited material support and due process rights for NGOs accused of supporting terrorism. These results open up the public discussion regarding when humanitarian aid should be barred and what process should be available to NGOs to challenge a Treasury designation. The following cases illustrate these changes.

In November 2008 a federal court ruled that the Treasury's designation and shutdown of Al Haramain Islamic Foundation in 2004 violated basic due process rights. The court also ruled that the definition of "material support" of terrorists is unconstitutionally vague.[61] In October 2008 the District Court for the Northern District of Ohio Western Division barred the Treasury from designating KindHearts for Charitable Humanitarian Development as a Specially Designated Global Terrorist "without first affording KindHearts with constitutionally adequate process," including notice and a meaningful opportunity to contest the basis for such a designation.[62] The Treasury shut down the group "pending investigation" in February 2006, but the investigation has never been concluded, and the group's assets, including about $1 million USD, remain frozen (American Civil Liberties Union 2008). In January 2009 the Court of Appeals for the Ninth Circuit upheld[63] a lower court ruling declaring the material support statute unconstitutionally vague. The Center for Constitutional Rights called on Congress to revise the definition of "material support" to exempt medical supplies and services, and to provide provisions for basic necessities such as food, water, and shelter to civilian refugees (Center for Constitutional Rights 2009).

Congressional Oversight

During the Bush administration, Congress generally failed to provide adequate oversight of how counter-terrorism policy impacts US organizations, their programs, and the people served. The few hearings that were held generally only heard from government witnesses, giving an incomplete and inaccurate picture. For example, in his May 2007 Senate testimony, Chip Poncy of the Treasury claimed the revised Treasury Guidelines "are based on extensive consultation between Treasury and the charitable and Muslim communities." He failed to disclose that, although there was consultation on the guidelines, a group of more than 40 US charitable sector organizations, including the Council on Foundations, called for their withdrawal.

A Senate Finance Committee hearing in April 2008 repeated this pattern. The committee declined a request by OMB Watch, a Washington advocacy group, that it hear from nonprofit witnesses, so that the only witness was Undersecretary for Terrorism and Financial Intelligence Stuart Levey. At the hearing Levey said, "We want humanitarian assistance to reach those who are truly in need through channels safe from terrorist exploitation," but did not disclose the Treasury's refusal to release frozen charitable funds to reputable nonprofits.

However, the picture has changed since January 2009. Oversight hearings in the 111th Congress have addressed a wide variety of topics impacting NGOs, including militarization of aid, the role of law enforcement in investigating advocacy groups, and government surveillance powers. Witnesses representing NGO interests have been invited to testify. There are indications that hearings focusing on the problems faced by the NGO sector will be scheduled in 2009. If this occurs, it will be the first oversight since 9/11.

A Goal for US NGOs: The State Department Guiding Principles for NGOs

One of the few positive developments for nonprofits in the past seven years is publication of the State Department-published *Guiding Principles on Non-Governmental Organizations* in December 2006. The preamble cites the United Nations Universal Declaration of Human Rights and other international standards that support "the right of freedom of expression, peaceful assembly and association." The ten standards recognize the essential role NGOs play in "ensuring accountable, democratic government" (US State Department 2006). The publication of these principles should provide a framework for the reform of US CTM laws and policies. In this way the trade-offs between counter-terrorism and reducing the spaces for civil society actors could be minimized.

Conclusion

Although there is reason to hope that the fundamental flaws in the United States' approach to counter-terrorism and charities may be subjected to re-examination and reform, there are significant barriers that must be overcome. Myths about charities as a "significant source of terrorist financing" must be dispelled. That will widen the scope of the discourse to include the role civil society and charities play in preventing and countering violent extremism. This will require re-examination of the regulatory scheme based in economic embargo laws that leave no room for human rights considerations. In this regard, the Department of Treasury's myopic view of the problem as one of terrorist financing and their invention of the myth of widespread terrorist "exploitation and abuse" of charities must be subjected to outside evaluation by the new administration and Congress.

The fundamental conflict between overly broad US laws barring "material support" of terrorism with the ban on discrimination in aid embodied in the International Red Cross Code of Conduct and Geneva conventions must be addressed immediately. This conflict puts US NGOs working in conflict zones or any area where terrorist groups are present in the untenable position of choosing to comply with human rights principles and risking criminal penalties, or withholding aid in order to avoid draconian sanctions for their organizations and their workers. The solution must move in the direction of compliance with the humanitarian imperative, and not toward greater government intrusion into the private philanthropic sector. The Department of Treasury's promotion of "alternative delivery mechanisms" involving funneling private donations through USAID goes in the wrong direction.

Government intrusion into civil society has also extended to surveillance and information-gathering that appears to be based on ideological orientation and the exercise of the rights of free speech and assembly. As long as government continues to perceive civil society as a threat rather than a fundamental counter-balance to extremism, this problem will continue to plague US NGOs. In addition to respecting human rights, a reformed counter-terrorism regulatory regime for US NGOs will end the diversion of resources away from mission-focused activities caused by attempts to avoid being shut down by the Department of Treasury. Although Muslim organizations have suffered the most from the misguided counter-terrorism regime, the entire sector is affected by greater regulatory scrutiny and the circulation of discourses that link charitable groups with terrorist networks. The damage extends further than the borders of the United States, as the flaws in the US regime have been incorporated into international contexts through the circulation of discourses casting suspicion over charities and NGOs, as well as general and specific legislation and regulations targeting the nonprofit sector.

Civil society in the United States, including charities, grant-makers, and human rights and civil liberties groups, must join forces to propose alternatives to the current counter-terrorism regime. It will not happen simply because of favorable court decisions, or even from changed attitudes in new officeholders. The sector is up to the challenge, and hopefully the new Obama administration and Congress will be, too.

Notes

1. 50 United States Code 1701.

2. Antiterrorism and Effective Death Penalty Act of 1996, Public Law 104–132, 110 Stat. 1214, 104th Cong., (24 April 1996). AEDPA was enacted in 1996 and later amended by the USA PATRIOT Act in 2001 and 2004, see http://www.abanet.org/natsecurity/patriotdebates/material-support.

3. These designations have resulted in $20.7 million USD in blocked assets. See US Department of Treasury, Office of Foreign Assets Control. Terrorist Assets Report Calendar Year 2007 Sixteenth Annual Report to Congress on Assets in the United States of Terrorist Countries and International Terrorism Program Designees (October 2008), 2.

4. International Emergency Economic Powers Act, US Code 50, sec. 1701–1707.

5. Executive Order 13224, 23 September 2001, http://www.treasury.gov/offices/enforcement/ofac/programs/terror/terror.pdf (5 May 2009).

6. US State Department, Office of Counterterrorism, "Foreign Terrorist Organizations," fact sheet, 11 October 2005, http://merln.ndu.edu/archivepdf/terrorism/state/37191.pdf (5 May 2009).

7. Providing Material Support to Terrorists, US Code, vol. 18, sec. 2339A(b)(1).

8. Anti-Terrorism and Effective Death Penalty Act of 1996, Public Law 13, 104th Cong., (3 June 1996). See material support provision at 18 U.S.C. § 2339A(b)(1).

9. Material Support of Terrorists and Foreign Terrorist Organizations, US Code, vol. 18, sec. 2339B(j).

10. Material Support of Terrorists and Foreign Terrorist Organizations, US Code, vol. 18, sec. 2339B(j).

11. Executive Order 13224, 23 September 2001, http://www.treasury.gov/offices/enforcement/ofac/programs/terror/terror.pdf (5 May 2009).

12. U.S. Department of the Treasury Anti-terrorist Financing Guidelines: Voluntary Best Practices for U.S.-based Charities. (This document is a revised version of the original *Anti-Terrorist Financing Guidelines: Voluntary Best Practices for U.S.-Based Charities* released by the U.S. Department of the Treasury in November 2002. The revised version incorporates comments received in response to the issuance of the draft revised Guidelines released for public comment in December 2005.)

13. Council on Foundations, "Working Group's Letter to Treasury about Treasury Anti-Terrorist Financing Guidelines," 18 December 2006, http://www.cof.org/files/Documents/International_Programs/TreasuryLetter.pdf (5 May 2009).

14. Uniting and Strengthening America by Providing Appropriate Tools Required to Intercept and Obstruct Terrorism Act of 2001 (USA PATRIOT Act), Public Law 107-56, sec. 802(a), 107th Cong., (26 October 2001).

15. USA PATRIOT ACT. Sec. 215 amends the business records of FISA to allow FISA court orders for FBI to access "tangible things (including books, records, papers, documents, and other items)."

16. The FISA Amendments Act of 2008, Public Law 110-261, 110th Cong., (10 July 2008).

17. US Department of the Treasury, "Screening Tax-Exempt Organizations Filing Information Provides Minimal Assurance That Potential Terrorist-Related Activities Are Identified," 21 May 2007, http://www.treas.gov/tigta/auditreports/2007reports/200710082fr.pdf (5 May 2009).

18. US Department of the Treasury, "U.S. Department of the Treasury Anti-Terrorist Financing Guidelines: Voluntary Best Practices for U.S. Based Charities," December 2005, 2-3. See footnote 13 for link to latest version; see http://www.ombwatch.org/article/articleview/3210/1/408 for a comparison of the 2002 and 2005 versions.

19. US Department of the Treasury, "Protecting Charitable Organizations," 9 March 2007, http://www.treas.gov/offices/enforcement/key-issues/protecting/index.shtml, Anti-terrorist Financing Guidelines, Annex at p. 14–16.

20. US Department of the Treasury, "U.S. Department of the Treasury Anti-Terrorist Financing Guidelines: Voluntary Best Practices for U.S. Based Charities," 2006 version, Annex 14–16, http://www.treas.gov/press/releases/reports/0929%20finalrevised.pdfhttp://www.treas.gov/press/releases/reports/0929%20finalrevised.pdf.

21. This figure is based on the authors' own calculations.

22. US Department of the Treasury, Office of Foreign Assets Control, "Terrorist Asset Report: Calendar Year 2006 Fourteenth Annual Report on Assets in the United States of Terrorist Countries and International Terrorism Program Designees," http://www.treas.gov/offices/enforcement/ofac/reports/tar2006.pdf.

23. US Department of the Treasury, "U.S. Department of the Treasury Anti-Terrorist Financing Guidelines: Voluntary Best Practices for U.S. Based Charities," 2006 version, Annex 14–16.

24. US Department of Justice, "Prepared Remarks of Attorney General John Ashcroft—Holy Land Foundation Indictment," press release, 24 July 2004, http://www.usdoj.gov/archive/ag/speeches/2004/72704ag.htm.

25. Press Release SC/7158, "Security Council Unanimously Adopts Wide-Ranging Anti-Terrorism Resolution; Calls for Suppressing Financing, Improving International Cooperation Resolution 1373" (2001).

26. FATF GAFI 9 "Special Recommendations on Terrorist Financing Interpretative Note Recommendation VIII: Non-Profit Organisations," October 2001.

27. FATF "Combating the Abuse of Non-Profit Organisations: International Best Practices," October 11, 2002.

28. United Nations Security Council 1267 List.

29. Barclay's, "Notice to Close Accounts/Terminate Banking Services," letter, 16 December 2008, http://www.uwt.org/Press/Press-Release/Barclays _letter.pdf (6 May 2009).

30. *Humanitarian Law Project, et al. v. Mukasey, et al.* No. 05-56753, United States Ct. of Appeals for the 9th Circuit, Dec. 10, 2007.

31. The International Federation of Red Cross and Red Crescent Societies, Code of Conduct, 1994, http://www.ifrc.org/publicat/conduct/code .asp (5 May 2009).

32. International Emergency Economic Powers Act, US Code, vol. 50, sec. 1702(b).

33. Geneva Conventions, Common Article 3, http://www.nytimes.com/ ref/us/AP-Guantanamo-Geneva-Conventions.html (5 May 2009).

34. Resolutions of the Geneva International Conference of 1863, Article 9, International Red Cross Handbook, 12th ed., ICRC-League, Geneva, 1983, p. 548.

35. Agency for International Development, "Privacy Act of 1974; System of Records," Federal Register 72, no. 136 (July 2007): 39042.

36. Agency for International Development, "Privacy Act of 1974, Implementation of Exemptions," Federal Register 74, no. 1 (January 2009): 9.

37. Agency for International Development, Partner Information Form, www.usaid.gov/wbg/misc/2007-27-Attachments.doc.

38. Agency for International Development, "Privacy Act of 1974; System of Records," Federal Register 72, no. 136 (July 2007): 39046.

39. See Lind's chapter on Palestine.

40. Agency for International Development, Audit of USAID/West Bank and Gaza's Assistance to Al-Quds University, the Islamic University in Gaza, and American Near East Refugee Aid, 10 December 2007, http://nefafoundation.org/miscellaneous/FeaturedDocs/USAIDOIG_IUGA udit.pdf.

41. Agency for International Development, "Privacy Act of 1974, Implementation of Exemptions," Federal Register 74, no. 1 (January 2009): 9.

42. American Charities for Palestine, American Charities for Palestine signs Historic Partnership Agreement with USAID, 31 July 2008, http://www.acpus.org/news/2008/11/20/8.

43. Agency for International Development, USAID Partners with Charity to Expand Assistance for Palestinians, press release, 1 August 2008, http://www.usaid.gov/press/releases/2008/pr080801_1.html.

44. US Department of Treasury, Opening Remarks of Assistant Secretary for Terrorist Financing Patrick O'Brien at Treasury's Charity Roundtable, press release, 15 August 2008, http://www.treas.gov/press/releases/hp1117.htm.

45. US Department of State, "Remarks by Secretary of State Colin L. Powell to the National Foreign Policy Conference for Leaders of Non-governmental Organizations," 26 October 2001, http://www.globalsecurity.org/military/library/news/2001/10/mil-011026-usia01.htm.

46. See Gordon's chapter on Afghanistan in this volume. US House of Representatives Committee on Armed Services, "Agency Stovepipes vs. Strategic Agility: Lessons We Need to Learn From Provincial Reconstruction Teams in Iraq and Afghanistan," April 2008.

47. United State House of Representatives Committee on Foreign Affairs, *Striking the Appropriate Balance: The Defense Department's Expanding Role in Foreign Assistance,* 111th Cong., 18 March 2009.

48. The Brookings Institution and Center for Strategic and International Studies

49. See 31 Code of Federal Regulations 501 and 597

50. 31 Code of Federal Regulations 501.801(b)(3).

51. 31 Code of Federal Regulations 501.801(b)(5).

52. 31 Code of Federal Regulations 501.597.502.

53. These funds amounted to between $700,000 and $800,000. The Office for Assets Control did not grant the BIF a license to dispense these funds, despite the appeal made by the BIF (National Commission on Terrorist Attacks upon the US, 2004, p. 14).

54. Letter from Office of Foreign Assets Control to KindHearts attorney Jihad Smaili, March 23, 2006.

55. Shereef Akeel, Letter from Attorney to OFAC, 7 February 2005.

56. See Letter to Henry Paulson, Secretary of the US Department of Treasury. Available at http://www.ombwatch.org/npadv/Paulson_letter.pdf.

57. Deborah Horan, "Charity strives to keep 'clean.'" *Chicago Tribune,* 29 Aug. 2006. Available at http://www.irw.org/news/inthenews/20060829.

58. September 2006: Treasury Guidelines Slowing down Humanitarian Aid to Lebanon, http://www.ombwatch.org/node/6394.

59. *Global Relief Foundation, Inc., v. Paul H. O'Neill,* 315 F.3d 748, United States Court of Appeals, Seventh Circuit, 2002.

60. *Islamic American Relief Agency (IARA-USA) v. Gonzales,* No. 05-5447, United States Court of Appeals for the District of Columbia Circuit, 13 February 2007, http://pacer.cadc.uscourts.gov/docs/common/opinions/200702/05-5447a.pdf.

61. *Al Haramain Islamic Foundation Inc., et al. v. US Department of the Treasury, et al.,* civil case no. 07-1155-KI, US District Court, District of Oregon, 6 November 2008, http://www.bernabeipllc.com/pdfs/Opinion.pdf.

62. *KindHearts for Charitable Humanitarian Development, Inc., v. Henry M. Paulson,* United States District Court for the Northern District of Ohio, Western Division. http://www.aclu.org/pdfs/safefree/kindhearts_memo.pdf.

63. *Humanitarian Law Project .v Michael Mukasey,* Civil Action No. CV-98-01971-ABC and CV-03-06107-ABC United States Court of Appeals for the Ninth Circuit. http://www.ca9.uscourts.gov/datastore/opinions/2009/01/05/0556753.pdf.

5

COUNTER-TERRORISM POLICING IN AUSTRALIA: IMPACTS ON CIVIL SOCIETY

Annie Pettitt

Since the 9/11 attacks in the United States, police and other law enforcement officials in many countries, including Australia, have been afforded increasingly expansive powers, including the use of preventative detention, control orders, and coercive questioning.[1] These exceptional police powers raise serious concerns regarding the impact on some sectors of society as well as on non-governmental actors. They also raise questions regarding the extent to which governments and law enforcement agencies are achieving an appropriate balance between strengthening security and protecting and respecting the human rights of all people, including "suspect communities."[2] In the name of protecting the community and combating terrorism, many counter-terrorism laws provide police and intelligence personnel with significantly increased powers, which enable them to act in ways that may infringe on the human rights of some members of society. Although counter-terrorism legislation may provide for the potential infringement of human rights, police and intelligence officers and their respective agencies are afforded significant operational discretion with regard to the manner in which they employ those powers. The challenge for democratic governments is how to ensure that exceptional counter-terrorism measures are applied in a manner proportionate to the actual threat and consistent with fundamental human rights principles.

This chapter proposes that the expansion of powers afforded to police and intelligence officials has had a disproportionately negative impact on the rights of minority and "suspect" communities. Further, it is argued that the exercise of counter-terrorism powers by police and intelligence officers has resulted from, and perpetuated, fear and prejudice within Australian society, leading ultimately to reduced social cohesion. This chapter is in four parts. The first part examines the impact of the legal definition of "terrorism." This is followed by an examination of the effects of the counter-terrorism regime on Muslim and Arab communities in Australia. The third part considers the proscription of "terrorist organizations" and examines the impact of offenses relating to association with proscribed organizations and their members. Finally, the slippage of exceptional counter-terrorism police powers into normal everyday policing, a concern often raised by human rights defenders, is examined through several examples of the Australian policing of community activists.

Defining "Terrorism" through Counter-terrorism: Australia's Counter-terrorism Regime

Acts of terrorism pose a unique threat in terms of mass casualties and serious impact to core infrastructure. Consequently, counter-terrorism legislation has sought to provide police and security agencies with tools for its prevention. This focus on prevention has resulted in a significant shift in the criminal law in terms of anticipating risk through the criminalization of conduct that may be linked to the preparation and coordination of terrorist acts. Attempts to prevent terrorism through legislative means, however, may in the longer term pose increased challenges to community cohesion (Pickering et al. 2007). This section details the development of counter-terrorism legislation in Australia since 2001 and examines several cases to highlight how it has affected the human rights of some social groups as well as civil society.

In the years since 2001 the breadth and content of the counter-terrorism legislative framework has represented an unprecedented shift in Australia's legal landscape (Pickering et al. 2007, 38). Prior to 2001, the only jurisdiction in Australia in which a "terrorist" act was an offense was the Northern Territory. Consistent with the development of counter-terrorism resolutions internationally, specific acts of terrorism, such as bombing, kidnapping, and hijacking, together with conspiracy to undertake these acts, had previously fallen within the general provisions of Australian criminal law. Between 2001 and 2008, however, there were no less than 49 separate pieces of counter-terrorism legislation enacted in Australia.[3] Thus, Australia has instituted a complex labyrinth of counter-terrorism legislation, the extent of which exceeds that of other comparable countries such as the United Kingdom, Canada, and New Zealand.[4]

In June 2002, with amendments that removed some of the more objectionable features, the Australian government secured the passage of a major package of counter-terrorism laws through the Senate.[5] The most significant of these, particularly with respect to policing, was the Security Legislation Amendment (Terrorism) Act 2002 (Cth), which amended the Criminal Code Act 1995 (Cth) with the addition of Part 5.3—Terrorism. The Act included a modified definition of "terrorist act" and "terrorist organization" from the initially proposed definition, which encompassed some forms of relatively nonviolent behavior.

As originally proposed, the definition of a terrorist act was extremely broad and extended into several areas, which may have adversely affected a large proportion of civil society. However, following significant public concern and two parliamentary inquiries, several important amendments were made to the definition of a terrorist act before the legislation was passed (Senate Legal and Constitutional Legislation Committee (SLCLC) 2002; Senate Legal and Constitutional References Committee (SLCRC) 2002). The original definition excluded "(c) *lawful* advocacy, protest or dissent; or (d) industrial action" (emphasis added) (SLCLC 2002, 10). Following public concern regarding the broad reach of the definition to potentially include a range of protest and civil disobedience actions, together with the recommendations of the parliamentary inquiries, the word *lawful* was removed (SLCLC 2002, 82). In addition, a requirement that action is not intended to cause harm was added to the exemption. Although the wide scope of the definition of a terrorist act is still a concern for many human rights observers (Scheinin 2006), the effectiveness of parliamentary scrutiny and open public debate in causing amendments to the original wording of the Act highlights the importance of open democratic processes and an engaged civil society.

The domestic definitions of what constitutes "terrorism" and "terrorist" activity in many countries share several common elements with one another and with the international Draft Comprehensive Convention on Terrorism (2002). This provides that an international terrorist offense is committed when death, serious bodily injury, or serious damage to property or infrastructure are caused, when the purpose of the conduct is to intimidate a population or compel a government or international organization to do or abstain from doing any act.[6] Surprisingly, when originally introduced the Australian definition did not contain a comparable element relating to intimidation or coercion. However, following the recommendation of the Senate Legal and Constitutional Legislation Committee (2002, 39) these elements were added. Accordingly, consistent with this aspect of the Draft Comprehensive Convention on Terrorism, in Australia an act or threat to act is now classified as a "terrorist act" if it has the intention of "coercing, or influencing by intimidation" the public or any government.[7] Such acts or threats not only include serious harm or death,[8] but also "serious damage" to property,[9] "serious risk" to public health or safety,[10] and "interference" with information, telecommunications, financial systems, essential services, and transport systems.[11]

In a significant departure from the international definition of terrorism, however, the Australian definition also stipulates that an action or threat of action is a "terrorist act" if it advances a "political, religious or ideological cause."[12] The accompaniment of a motivating ideology is, however, not unique to Australia; it can be found in the domestic legislation of many countries adopting general definitions of terrorism.[13] For example, the respective definitions of a "terrorist act" in Canada and the United Kingdom contain an element of coercion and intimidation of the public or government committed "for political, religious or ideological purpose, objective or cause"[14] and "for the purpose of advancing a political, religious or ideological cause."[15] The significance of the definition of terrorist offenses in all three cases is that they depart significantly from existing criminal law. For instance, in addition to having the intention to cause serious harm or death, the individual or group must have the intention to coerce or influence the public or government, *and* be motivated by a political, religious, or ideological cause. Thus, the crime becomes not the act itself, or even the intention, but rather the motivation.

Counter-terrorism legislation in Australia, which hinges on the definition of terrorism, is broad-ranging and includes new offenses for planning, threatening, and engaging in terrorist activity, as well as for inciting terrorism; it also prohibits membership in, training, and financing a terrorist organization and individuals or groups involved in terrorism. An independent review of Australian security legislation noted that a range of fundamental human rights—including the right to liberty and security of persons; the right to be free from arbitrary arrest; the presumption of innocence; the right to a fair trial; the right to freedom of opinion, expression, and assembly; and the right to seek asylum—have been directly or indirectly affected by this first raft of counter-terrorism legislation (Security Legislation Review Committee (SLRC) 2006, 42).

In 2005, prior to the completion of this independent review of the existing legal regime, a second wave of counter-terrorism legislation was introduced in Australia. The Australian government introduced the Anti-Terrorism Bill (No 2) 2005 on November 3, 2005. Receiving royal assent just six weeks later on December 14, 2005, the legislation included provisions for control orders and preventative detention, which are largely based on the United Kingdom's Prevention of Terrorism Act 2005.[16] The Anti-Terrorism Act (No 2) 2005 (Cth) empowers the Australian Federal Police (AFP) to request an interim control order if there is reasonable suspicion that an individual "would substantially assist in preventing a terrorist act" or "that the person has provided training to, or received training from, a listed terrorist organisation."[17] Although the Federal Court must review the request, issuing a control order does not require that the person be charged, tried, or found guilty of any offense. For these reasons it has been argued that the imposition of control orders fundamentally contravenes basic criminal justice values (Zedner 2008, 19). Control orders in Australia can be issued for up to 12 months for adults and 3 months for children between 16 and 18 years of age. Among other things, control orders provide for the use of tracking devices, restrictions on association, access to specified services and movement, and house arrest.

A key case testing the use of control orders involved Jack Thomas, who was acquitted of terrorism-related charges that were based on evidence obtained through the use of torture during his detention in Pakistan.[18] In August 2006 he was made the subject of an interim control order immediately upon his repatriation to Australia (Scheinin 2006). The grounds for the order were that Thomas had trained with Al-Qaida in 2001 and, hence, could assist Al-Qaida and other extremists in planning and carrying out future terrorist acts. The interim control order imposed a curfew from midnight to 5:00 a.m., required that Thomas report to police three times a week, and prohibited him leaving Australia. In October 2008, Thomas was retried before a 12-member Victorian Supreme Court jury. He was found not guilty of receiving funds from Al-Qaida but was found guilty of possessing a falsified passport.[19] Thus, he has been acquitted of all terrorism-related charges.

The Anti-Terrorism Act (No 2) 2005 (Cth) also empowers police to preventatively detain a suspect without charge or trial for up to 14 days if it is believed on reasonable grounds that they will engage in a terrorist act in the next 14 days. In addition, a suspect may be detained under a preventative detention order in the event that a terrorist act has occurred in the last 28 days and it is deemed necessary for the preservation of related evidence.[20] As a consequence of potential unconstitutionality, the Act requires cooperation between federal and state police services; it enables the AFP to detain someone suspected of involvement in a terrorist act for 48 hours, followed by a further 12 days' detention by state police services.[21]

The first person to be held under the provision for preventative detention was Dr. Mohamed Haneef, a 27-year-old Indian physician who first came to Australia in September 2006. Haneef was detained on July 2, 2007, for his suspected involvement in terrorism-related activities relating to the attack on Glasgow International Airport in 2007. After being detained for 12 days without charge, Haneef was charged under the Criminal Code Act 1995 (Cth) for giving his mobile telephone SIM card to his second cousin, Dr. Sabeel Ahmed, when he left the United Kingdom in July 2006. Ahmed's brother, Kafeel Ahmed, was one of the operatives involved in the attack on the Glasgow airport. On July 16, 2007, the Magistrates Court of Queensland granted Haneef bail after the commonwealth director of public prosecutions failed to convince the magistrate that his detention should continue. However, in a matter of hours after the ruling, the minister for immigration, Kevin Andrews, cancelled Haneef's visa on "character grounds" under the Migration Act 1958 (Cth) because he "reasonably suspected" that Haneef had an "association" with people involved in terrorism.

As a result, despite being granted bail, Haneef was moved directly into immigration detention. Eleven days later on July 27, 2007, all charges against Haneef were dropped after the commonwealth director of public prosecutions stated there was no reasonable prospect of securing a conviction. The minister's decision to revoke Haneef's visa, however, was not changed, and he was deported to India. While in India, Haneef appealed to have his visa reinstated. The Federal Court of Australia quashed Minister Andrews's decision on August 20, 2007, ruling that the term "association" should not include mere social, family, or professional relationships.[22] This decision was then reaffirmed on appeal.[23]

The cases of Thomas and Haneef highlight the serious breaches of human rights that can occur when governments and intelligence and police agencies are granted unprecedented executive powers. The use of evidence gathered overseas by means of force and torture, together with the restrictions placed on Thomas's liberty and freedom of movement following his acquittal, raise serious questions regarding the justifiability of incursions into the human rights of potentially innocent people. Ultimately, Haneef was held for nearly one month in detention, two weeks of which were without charge or the ability to apply for bail. Haneef's treatment by the AFP and the Australian government under former Prime Minister John Howard seriously undermines a number of fundamental aspects of the right to fair trial, including the presumption of innocence, access to judicial review of detention orders, and many elements of procedural fairness.

As these cases show, many Australian counter-terrorism measures continue to undermine the fundamental rule of law and important human rights and contain only limited checks on the exercise of executive power. These cases also reveal the serious impact that police powers can have on individuals caught up in the expansive reach of a counter-terrorism regime that is grounded in broad definitions and extensive executive powers. Although the exercise of powers under recent counter-terrorism law has directly impacted the human rights of only a small number of people, this is nonetheless serious, as these powers can be used against any person regardless of their nationality and cultural and religious background. The violation of human rights, even when only a few individuals are directly affected, has a broader impact on the society that permits such violations to occur. One need only think of Nazi Germany and the insidious and sustained impact of the Holocaust on German society. The existence of counter-terrorism laws that fail to establish an appropriate balance with respect for fundamental human rights has already impacted Australian civil society more broadly, resulting in an increase in fear and prejudice within Australian society and, ultimately, a reduction in social cohesion.

Who's Protecting Whom? Impact of the Counter-terrorism Regime on Muslim and Arab Communities

The suggestion that human rights and security can be "balanced" implies that they exist in inverse proportion to each other—a kind of "zero-sum" continuum in which more security equates to less human rights and more human rights equates to less security. The zero-sum metaphor of balance is based on a set of existing presumptions about the nature of "terrorism" and "counter-terrorism," and about who is a "terrorist" and who is a "victim." It is these underlying presumptions about what constitutes both terrorism and counter-terrorism that often provide the justification for extraordinary powers in exceptional times. The circuitous argument is such that the individual is effectively declared a terrorist before they have been tried or even charged, thus permitting the abrogation of their rights. This zero-sum type of balance lends itself to the a priori presupposition that an act is by definition "terrorist," or that someone is a "terrorist," and as a result they are treated as such by law enforcement and intelligence officials. They are effectively stripped of their humanity, and it becomes no longer conceivable to think of them as "human." They are "other" and are no longer worthy of human rights. McCulloch (2002) argued that this zero-sum equation is based on a view in which the world is divided into worthy, "human" insiders and outsiders unworthy of human rights. Thus, she concludes that the security that is sought to be paid for in human rights is one founded on insecurity and the suffering of the outsider "other."

Who exactly is the outsider, or the "other," is historically contingent and politically constructed. Indeed, images of "the terrorist" are relative and have changed over time. Herman (1993, 47) observed that "In earlier years, [the terrorist] used to look like someone from Eastern Europe who was Jewish in appearance; more recently, since the late 1970s, [the terrorist] has a darker complexion, suggesting an Arab." This practice of racial stereotyping exists not merely in the public imagination fuelled by tabloid media, but is institutionalized in policing policies and practices. This is exemplified by the five ethnic descriptors that continue to be used by the New South Wales Police Force (Middle Eastern/Mediterranean appearance, Pacific Islander appearance, Indian/Pakistani appearance, Black/African appearance, and South American appearance) in addition to the nationally agreed descriptors, which are limited to Caucasian, Asian, Aboriginal, and Other (Poynting et al. 2001, 67).

Since 2001 the Australian government's approach to the new threat of global terrorism has been principally focused on Islamic extremism, as revealed in the following:

> Australia's security environment has changed. We are now directly threatened by a new kind of terrorism. It is transnational and it is perpetrated in the name of a Muslim extremist cause . . . This new threat challenges us in ways which demand new and innovative forms of response. (Australian Government 2004, vii)

However, the Australian government has sought to insist that counter-terrorism laws and policies developed in response to the perceived threat of terrorism do not target Muslims. For example, following simultaneous police raids on Muslim homes in Melbourne and Sydney, Prime Minister John Howard stated: "This is not an anti-Muslim action."[24] Further, he argued, "There is nothing in our laws, nor will there be anything in our laws, that targets an individual group—be it Islamic or otherwise" (Howard 2005 a and b). Similarly, Philip Ruddock, Attorney-General, argued: "In formulating our new anti-terrorism laws, we were not targeting any particular religion or nationality. We are targeting terrorists—whatever their faith and whatever their race" (Ruddock 2006, 51). There appears to be a contradiction between the assertion on the one hand that the new counter-terrorism laws do not target Arab and Muslim communities and the continued use of racial and religious profiling as an "unintended" effect of countering terrorism. As such, it has been argued that Australian counter-terrorism laws simultaneously disavow and generate racial profiling; and as a consequence they further criminalize "suspect" subjects—in this case Australian Arab and/or Muslim communities (Pugliese 2006).

Since the introduction and subsequent review of counter-terrorism legislation in Australia, numerous academics and social and political commentators have raised concerns regarding its impact on the human rights of some sections of society and on civil society.[25] Indeed, the United

Nations Committee on the Elimination of Racial Discrimination (CERD) has also raised concerns that the enforcement of counter-terrorism laws may be having an indirect discriminatory effect on Muslims and Arabs in Australia (CERD 2005). On numerous occasions members of the Australian Muslim community, together with other community and human rights organizations, have raised their concerns of experiencing fear and alienation and of being targeted by police and the Australian Security Intelligence Organisation (ASIO) using their expanded counter-terrorism powers (HREOC 2004; Chong et al. 2005; PJCIS 2006, 23–37; SLRC 2006, 140–46). Of particular concern has been those powers that authorize ASIO to detain and question nonsuspects who are not thought to be involved in terrorist activity, but who might provide information relating to a terrorism offense that has occurred or may occur.[26] Under the Australian Security Intelligence Organisation Amendment (Terrorism) Act 2003 (Cth) detainees are obliged to answer questions, in effect removing the long-standing democratic right to remain silent and to refuse to answer questions on the ground that it may be self-incriminating to do so. McCulloch (2002) has argued that detention and questioning of non-suspects is not "based on reasonable suspicion of wrongdoing but instead suspicion of knowledge or state of mind."

Against the backdrop of the 9/11 attacks in the United States and the Bali bombings in October 2002, and following increased concerns regarding a rise in anti-Muslim and anti-Arab prejudice, in 2003 the Australian Human Rights and Equal Opportunity Commission initiated the Ismaε project (HREOC 2004). The aim of the project was to explore the extent and nature of discrimination and vilification being experienced by Muslim and Arab Australians since the 9/11 attacks. The majority of participants reported experiencing various forms of prejudice as a result of their race or religion and that these experiences had increased since 9/11 (HREOC 2004, 3). Although these experiences ranged from offensive remarks to physical violence, and included incidents involving strangers in public spaces, colleagues at work, and neighbors, participants particularly noted discrimination by police. Many noted that the most at risk were those readily identifiable as Muslim or Arab because of their dress, physical appearance, or name. The Ismaε report found that the biggest impact on Arab and Muslim communities had been "a substantial increase in fear, a growing sense of alienation from the wider community and an increasing distrust of authority" (HREOC 2004, 4). This fear and alienation was later realized in, and exacerbated by, racially fuelled street riots in Cronulla, Sydney in December 2005.

The Ismaε report notes that a substantial number of Muslims and Arabs felt that they were targeted by police and that young Arab men in particular were often treated unfairly. As one participant commented: "Of course Muslim and Arabs are targeted . . . Guys get abused, they get called 'terrorists' and 'Bin-Ladens' by the police" (HREOC 2004, 67). In addition, some felt that Muslims in Australia are unfairly targeted in counter-terrorism investigations conducted by ASIO and the AFP. For example, one participant reported:

> There is a fear in the community that one day you will wake up and your husband will be taken away under the new ASIO laws. The way the government treated people who underwent the raids was shocking. (HREOC 2004, 67)

It is not possible to verify an increase in stop and searches on Muslims and Arabs in Australia, because unlike in the United Kingdom police are not required to record the ethnicity of each person they stop and search.[27] There is therefore a lack of comparative data in this area. Nonetheless, anecdotally Muslim organizations continue to express serious concerns regarding the disproportionate impact on their communities. Discussing counter-terrorism laws introduced in 2005, which grant police increased powers to stop, question, and search people, Agnes Chong, cofounder and then co-convener of the Australian Muslim Civil Rights Advocacy Network (AMCRAN), argued:

> from the Muslim community perspective, greater street policing powers also increase the risk of discriminatory application, exposing visible communities—and the Muslim community is very visible—to arbitrary interference . . . Unrestricted coercive powers of this type have the potential to encourage racial profiling. There is a danger that decisions by front-line police as to who they will stop, search and question will be affected by commonly held prejudices and personal biases. (Chong 2006)

Furthermore, many anecdotal fears and concerns raised by Muslim and Arab communities relate to informal police questioning and practices as much as to formal stops and searches. Such claims are reinforced by the request made in 2005 by the Police Federation of Australia for the introduction of legislation to indemnify police officers against civil lawsuits for using racial profiling under new counter-terrorism laws. This request suggests that certain sections of society, especially Muslims and Arabs, are likely and expected to bear the brunt of counter-terrorism laws (Kearney 2005).

Criminalizing Relationships with Terrorist Organizations

Under Australian law there are two ways that a group can fall within the definition of a "terrorist organization." The first is if it is "directly or indirectly engaged in, preparing, planning, assisting in or fostering" a terrorist act regardless of whether or not one has actually occurred as a result of such actions. It may at first glance seem legitimate that a group engaged in planning and undertaking a terrorist act be designated a "terrorist organization." However, the first formal recognition of a group as a terrorist organization may not occur until charges have been laid, thereby exposing those who may be on the fringes of the group to unexpected and unwarranted liability. The second way that a group can fall within the definition of a "terrorist organization" is if it is banned or proscribed as a terrorist organization by the Australian Attorney-general. Although the latter is clearer, it raises serious concerns regarding the power of the executive government to ban organizations (SLRC 2006). Of particular concern with respect to the adverse impacts on human rights and civil society are offenses relating to a person's relationship with a terrorist organization, which were created by amendments made to Division 102 of the Criminal Code Act 1995 (Cth). Sections 102.2 to 102.8 make it an offense to

- Direct the activities of a terrorist organization (section 102.2)
- Be a member of a terrorist organization (section 102.3)
- Recruit a person to join or participate in the activities of a terrorist organization (section 102.4)
- Provide training to or receive training from a terrorist organization (section 102.5)
- Receive funds from or make funds available to a terrorist organization (section 102.6)
- Provide support or resources that would help a terrorist organization directly or indirectly engage in preparing, planning, assisting in or fostering the doing of a terrorist act (whether or not the terrorist act occurs) (section 102.7)
- On two or more occasions associate with a member of or a person who promotes or directs activities of a terrorist organization (section 102.8)

The Australian Human Rights Commission, together with numerous legal academics and community organizations, has consistently raised serious concerns regarding the scope of the association offenses relating to terrorist organizations.[28] When considering the introduction of the association offenses, the Senate Legal and Constitutional Legislation Committee

(SLCLC) raised concerns regarding legislative overreach and the potential capture of a wide range of legitimate activities under the rubric of "terrorism" offenses such as some social and religious festivals and gatherings, investigative journalism, and the provision of legal advice and representation (SLCLC 2004, 34). Moreover, the 2006 independent review of security legislation made several recommendations relating to the clarification and limitation of the association offenses, including the repeal of section 102.8. Indeed, noting that this offense transgresses the fundamental human right of freedom of association and interferes with ordinary family, religious, and legal communication, the SLRC (2006, 5) observed that this offense "is disproportionate to anything that could be achieved by way of protection of the community if the section were enforced."

Furthermore, consistent with recommendations of the SLRC and the Parliamentary Joint Committee on Intelligence and Security (PJCIS), the Australian Human Rights Commission has argued that the section 102.7 offense under which Haneef was charged is also excessively broad and should be amended to be defined with increased certainty (HREOC 2008, 7–8). Although the case against Haneef was later dropped, it demonstrated the potentially broad scope of the offense of "providing support and resources" to a terrorist organization.

Slippage of "Exceptional" Measures into Everyday Policing Impact on Civil Society

The impact of the counter-terrorism regime on civil society has also spread well beyond the bounds of what might strictly be called counter-terrorism policing. It has been proposed that the War on Terror and counter-terrorism strategies have been used as a pretext for expanding domestic surveillance and policing and for flexing the imperialist Western muscle (McCulloch 2004). Although this relationship may not be directly causal and conspiratorial, these elements are intricately entwined. Pickering et al. (2008) argue that the paramilitary model of counter-terrorism policing has resulted in an increasingly symbiotic relationship between law enforcement and terrorism. This relationship has given rise to concerns regarding the expansion of "exceptional" counter-terrorism powers into the general criminal justice system and everyday policing, a practice that criminologists have labeled "transubstantiation" (Stuntz 2002, 2157). Stuntz has observed that when police tactics designed to fight terrorists are approved, the same tactics are effectively being sanctioned for use against other sorts of criminals (2002).

To allow so-called exceptional circumstances to inform criminal justice policy propels us down a slippery slope in which the exception soon becomes the norm (Zedner 2008; Dyzenhaus 2001). The challenge for liberal democratic governments remains how to balance counter-terrorism measures with human rights in the first instance, and secondly how to ensure that any "exceptional" measures are temporary and proportionate to the actual threat. Concerns regarding the blurring between exceptional measures and everyday policing have been frequently raised by human rights defenders and activists in Australia.

This slippage has been witnessed in Australia in the area of immigration and security assessments, in which the reasons for an adverse security assessment have not been available to visa holders. For example, in June 2005, Scott Parkin, a US citizen and grassroots environmental and peace activist, entered Australia on a six-month tourist visa. However, ASIO later issued an adverse security assessment, which contained a recommendation that his visa be cancelled pursuant to section 116 of the Migration Act 1958 (Cth). His visa was cancelled on September 10, 2005, and a week later he was deported to the US (at his own expense) without being informed of the reasons for his adverse security assessment.[31] Parkin remains unable to travel to Australia and the fact of the adverse assessment seriously impedes his ability to travel outside the United States. Although a 2008 decision of the Federal Court of Australia relating to his visa assessment has opened the way for Parkin and others to apply for access to their adverse security assessment and other ASIO documents relating to their cases,[29] the director-general of ASIO has been resisting the release of documents relating to Parkin's assessment on the grounds of public interest immunity. To date Parkin and his lawyers have no better idea of the information on which the director-general acted.[30] The veil of secrecy surrounding ASIO security assessment information and criteria remains a matter for concern. Parkin's case illustrates the fine line between counter-terrorism intelligence and policing and the slippage into ordinary policing—particularly of "suspect" communities, including activist communities.

Similarly, a recent examination of the impact of the APEC Meeting (Police Powers) Act 2007 (NSW) (APEC Meeting Act) on protesters found that, prior to the Asia-Pacific Economic Cooperation (APEC) meeting held in Sydney in September 2007, many individuals intending to participate in protests reported police intimidation (Snell 2008, 21). The APEC Meeting Act granted police powers within the APEC security areas to establish roadblocks, checkpoints, and cordons;[31] to search people,[32] vehicles, and vessels;[33] to seize and detail prohibited items;[34] to give reasonable directions;[35] and to exclude or remove people from APEC security areas.[36] In addition, the publication in the *Daily Telegraph* of an "excluded persons list" comprising those persons the

New South Wales commissioner of police believed would pose a serious threat to the safety of person or property in the APEC security area, shows an intention to intimidate certain individuals. The power to create and disseminate such a list far exceeds any previous powers granted to police in Australia.

Conclusion

This chapter has explored some of the impacts of the Australian counter-terrorism regime on human rights and civil society. In particular, it has drawn out concerns regarding the broad reach of the definition of what constitutes a "terrorist act" and its impact on related offenses. Inextricably linked to the characterization of violent acts carried out by nonstate actors as "terrorist" is the erasure of state terrorism, both in the form of state-sanctioned violent activities and through coercive "counter-terrorism" mechanisms. In discussing which politically violent acts get labeled as terrorist and which do not, Hocking argued that "'terrorism' is better defined by reference to a response to it, rather than to any objective features within the act itself . . . the only definable aspect in the terrorism/counter-terrorism nexus is not terrorism, but counter-terrorism" (2004, 6).

In addition to control orders and preventative detention, the impact on civil society of the terrorism offense of association was examined. The association offenses, perhaps more than any other aspect of the expansive Australian counter-terrorism regime, pose the greatest risk to potentially innocent individuals who, once they are deemed terror suspects, become guilty until proven innocent, as the case of Dr. Mohamed Haneef shows. Moreover, these offenses, together with the seepage of counter-terrorism police powers into ordinary policing, continue to have an adverse impact on community cohesion. Although to date the use of provisions under new counter-terrorism law in Australia has directly impacted the human rights of only a small number of individuals, the impact on civil society— and particularly on Muslim and Arab communities—has been and continues to be serious. It is no coincidence that the Australian Human Rights Commission is currently undertaking an inquiry into the freedom of religion and belief. Indeed, one of the seven key areas being explored is the impact of the counter-terrorism legislative changes since 2001 on religious and ethnic communities. Although it may not immediately resolve concerns around the lack of respect and dignity afforded to stigmatized minorities, this inquiry illustrates both the importance of independent human rights institutions and the power of civil society to participate in democratic progress.

Legislation

Anti-Terrorism Act (No. 2) 2005 (Cth)
Anti-Terrorism Act 2001 (Canada)
APEC Meeting (Police Powers) Act 2007 (NSW)
Australian Security Intelligence Organisation Amendment (Terrorism) Act 2003 (Cth)
Border Security Legislation Amendment Act 2002 (Cth)
Crimes Act 1914 (Cth)
Criminal Code Act 1995 (Cth)
Criminal Code Amendment (Suppression of Terrorist Bombings) Act 2002 (Cth)
Major Events Security Act 2000 (ACT)
Olympic Events Security Act 1999 (ACT)
Security Legislation Amendment (Terrorism) Act 2002 (Cth)
Suppression of the Financing of Terrorism Act 2002 (Cth)
Telecommunications Interception Legislation Amendment Act 2002 (Cth)
Terrorism Act 2000 (UK)

Cases

Haneef v Minister for Immigration and Citizenship (2007) 161 FCR 40
Minister for Immigration and Citizenship v Haneef (2007) 163 FCR 414
O'Sullivan v Parkin [2008] FCAFC 134 (Unreported, Federal Court of Australia, Ryan, North and Jessup JJ, 18 July 2008).
R v Thomas (2006) 14 VR 475

Notes

1. I would like to thank Professor Jude Howell and Dr. Jeremy Lind for their generous and valuable editorial comments.

2. Patty Hillyard has explored the concept of "suspect communities" in his examination of the impact of the counter-terrorism regime in Britain (1993).

3. This information was valid as of September 8, 2008, and is based on information on the Australian Parliamentary Library's website http://www.aph.gov.au/library/intguide/law/terrorism.htm#terrstate at that time.

4. For a valuable overview of Australian counter-terrorism legislation, see Lynch and Williams (2006).

5. This first raft of counter-terrorism legislation included: Security Legislation Amendment (Terrorism) Act 2002 (Cth); Criminal Code Amendment (Suppression of Terrorist Bombings) Act 2002 (Cth); Suppression of the Financing of Terrorism Act 2002 (Cth); Border Security Legislation Amendment Act 2002 (Cth); and Telecommunications Interception Legislation Amendment Act 2002 (Cth).

6. See Article 2(1) of the Draft Comprehensive Convention on Terrorism, contained in the Report of the Ad Hoc Committee Established by General Assembly Resolution 51/210 of 17 December 1996, 57th sess, Supp no. 37 (2002) UN Doc A/57/37.

7. See *Criminal Code Act 1995* (Cth) s 100.1(2)(c).

8. See *Criminal Code Act 1995* (Cth) ss 100.1(1)(a) and (c).

9. See *Criminal Code Act 1995* (Cth) s 100.1(1)(b).

10. See *Criminal Code Act 1995* (Cth) s 100.1(2)(e).

11. See *Criminal Code Act 1995* (Cth) s 100.1(2)(f)).

12. See *Criminal Code Act 1995* (Cth) s 100.1(2)(b).

13. Ben Golder and George Williams (2004) distinguish this type of general (or deductive) model of defining terrorism from a specific (or inductive) model, which describes specific actions as terrorist in nature rather than providing a prescriptive definition—an approach that has historically been adopted internationally and domestically.

14. See *Anti-Terrorism Act 2001* (Canada) s 83.01(1).

15. See *Terrorism Act 2000* (UK) ss 1(1)(b)–(c).

16. When announcing the proposed measures, Prime Minister John Howard stated that the control order and preventative detention provisions were "similar to those available in the UK" (Howard 2005a).

17. See *Anti-Terrorism Act (No. 2) 2005* (Cth) sch 4, s 104.2(2).

18. See *R v Thomas* (2006) 14 VR 475.

19. See "Jack Thomas not guilty of taking al-Qaeda cash," *The Sydney Morning Herald* (Sydney), 23 October 2008, Online http://www.smh .com.au/news/national/thomas-cleared-of-taking-osamas-cash/2008/10/23/ 1224351422036.html at 3 February 2009.

20. See *Anti-Terrorism Act (No. 2) 2005* (Cth), sch 4, s 105.4.

21. For an interesting discussion regarding the constitutionality of preventative detention in Australia, see Renwick (2007).

22. See *Haneef v Minister for Immigration and Citizenship* (2007) 161 FCR 40.

23. See *Minister for Immigration and Citizenship v Haneef* (2007) 163 FCR 414.

24. See ABC News Online, "PM Denies Raids Anti-Muslim," 9 November 2005, http://www.abc.net.au/news/newsitems/200511/s1500786 .htm at 4 September 2008.

25. See, for example, submissions made to the Australian Senate Legal and Constitutional Affairs Committee regarding a range of inquiries into proposed counter-terrorism legislation; the 2006 independent Security Legislation Review Inquiry (The Sheller Report); and the Clarke Inquiry into the case of Dr. Mohamed Haneef.

26. See *Australian Security Intelligence Organisation Amendment (Terrorism) Act 2003* (Cth) s 34C(3).

27. Compare with statistical evidence gathered and examined in Quershi (2007).

28. See especially submissions made to the Senate Legal and Constitutional Legislation Committee Inquiry into the provisions of the *Anti-Terrorism Bill (No. 2) 2004* (Cth).

29. See *O'Sullivan v Parkin* [2008] FCAFC 134 (Unreported, Federal Court of Australia, Ryan, North and Jessup JJ, 18 July 2008).

30. Personal communication with Parkin's legal team.

31. See *APEC Meeting (Police Powers) Act 2007* (NSW) s 10.

32. See *APEC Meeting (Police Powers) Act 2007* (NSW) s 12.

33. See *APEC Meeting (Police Powers) Act 2007* (NSW) s 11.

34. See *APEC Meeting (Police Powers) Act 2007* (NSW) s 13.

35. See *APEC Meeting (Police Powers) Act 2007* (NSW) s 14.

36. See *APEC Meeting (Police Powers) Act 2007* (NSW) s 24–6.

6

FALSE CHOICE? THE WAR ON TERROR AND ITS IMPACT ON STATE POLICY TOWARD CIVIL SOCIETY IN UZBEKISTAN AND KYRGYZSTAN

Daniel Stevens and Kanykey Jailobaeva

When reflecting on the impact of the War on Terror on civil society, the full global consequences must be weighed up. Although relatively peripheral to academic and popular debate, the countries of Central Asia were central to the operations of the War on Terror, with both Uzbekistan and Kyrgyzstan having grappled with a Taliban-allied group and then hosted United States military bases in support of the operations in Afghanistan. This chapter offers an analysis of how the broader War on Terror affected these countries' policies[1] toward civil society, first briefly setting the context, then analyzing each country in turn before concluding on how the similarities and differences between these cases contribute to our understanding of the impact of the War on Terror on the fortunes of civil society internationally.

The 9/11 attacks occurred just a decade after Kyrgyzstan and Uzbekistan had become independent, and they were still in the process of adjusting from being Soviet republics to independent states in the world community. The post–Cold War order was not only facing new types of security threats, but the 1990s also featured a surge of interest in the value of civil society in guaranteeing liberal democracy, market reform, and cohesive societies.[2] As such, the idea of building civil society was a significant theme in these countries' interactions with the international community. In particular they were recipients of international aid programs supporting civil society development.

Exactly what civil society meant, what it looked like, and what its role was to be in Central Asia are politically contentious issues,[3] but, broadly speaking, Western donor organizations perceived a need for these former "totalitarian" societies to build/rebuild a plurality of social organizations in order to embed liberal democracy, advance economic development, and substitute for a retreating state in providing a social safety net. A number of organizations, most notably USAID and the Open Society Institute, developed programs for funding and training an emergent, modern NGO sector, as well as latterly engaging with more traditional community structures. Here we adopt a structural definition of civil society: those organizations that are neither formally part of the state or the market. It would include inter alia, NGOs, community organizations, and other cultural and religious groups.

Civil Society, Security, and Aid in Uzbekistan

In the case of Uzbekistan, the War on Terror had a significant impact on state policy toward civil society, which we could broadly categorize as passing through two main stages, each subdivided into two phases. The first stage could be termed as "tactical tolerance" and can be subdivided into an earlier phase of receiving limited external support (up until 2001) and then a second phase from 2002 to 2003, when external support rapidly expanded. The pivotal point was the Rose Revolution in Georgia of November 2003 (Ilkhamov 2005, 300). From 2004 a second stage of "controlled localization" began, in which the sector's independence was severely constrained and foreign funding cut off. The years 2004–2005 featured a retrenchment of civil society activity. However, from 2006 this second stage has entered a new second phase, in which both carefully selected foreign funding and increased state funding are available to support the NGO sector. The sector is seen as strategic in maintaining a social contract between state and society,[4] in which individuals trade their freedom to engage in independent organizing in return for the state taking responsibility for addressing issues of social concern. These shifts in policy largely relate to state regulation of NGOs, and to a lesser extent community (*mahalla*) institutions. The regulation of religious groups, a separate category of organization under Uzbekistan's legislation, was much more consistent throughout the whole post-independence period, with only minor fluctuations around a policy of very strict control. The question we turn to now is to what extent the War on Terror was a key factor in triggering these shifts in state policy toward the NGO sector.

The initial focus of the War on Terror in the theatre of Afghanistan had profound implications for Uzbekistan, whose government was initially an enthusiastic supporter of the action taken against the Taliban. For Uzbekistan had also been dealing with its own Afghanistan-based terrorist threat, that of the Islamic Movement of Uzbekistan (IMU). Prior to 1999

Uzbekistan had considered itself an oasis of stability in a region that had witnessed civil war and rapidly deteriorating living standards. However, in February of that year a series of car bombings in the capital Tashkent raised the specter of a serious terrorist threat. This threat was reinforced in the summers of 1999 and 2000 by incursions into the country's border areas by the IMU (International Crisis Group 2002, ii), which in September 2000 was designated by the US State Department as a terrorist group (US State Department 2007).

The IMU had found an ideological ally and safe harbor with the Taliban, which by then was in control of much of Afghanistan. The Taliban advance against the Northern Alliance in 2000, which at the time raised concerns that it might reach the border with Uzbekistan (Rashid 2000), only served to heighten concerns that the group would be able to project its threat even further into the country.

Fears that the socioeconomic disruptions faced by the population might fuel increased domestic support for the IMU and other radical Islamic groups—such as Hizb ut-Tahrir (the Islamic Liberation Party), with its aim of establishing an Islamic state governed by Sharia (Khamidov 2007)—meant that international humanitarian aid was broadly welcomed. Even though the concept of foreign-funded NGOs was viewed by the government with suspicion, if these NGOs could introduce additional resources to help the government manage socioeconomic problems, then they were broadly tolerated and even actively welcomed at the regional level (Stevens 2004, 165–80). With the NGO leaders being drawn from former party figures and the intelligentsia, they were seen as a potential secular ally in deterring the population from embracing fundamentalist religious ideologies (Stevens 2007, 50). Western development aid was also seen as a useful buffer against another perceived threat—that of the excessive influence of the former "colonial" power Russia (Pannier 2000).

This first stage of tactical toleration entered a new second phase of increased external support after the events of 9/11. For the United States-led attack on the Taliban bolstered support for the government of Uzbekistan, with a strategic partnership signed that elevated Uzbekistan to a position of key ally of the United States and promised a significant increase in aid to shore up the economy. President Karimov met with President Bush in the Oval office and was reputedly assured that on the issue of human rights, the United States was not going "to teach you" (Daly et al. 2006, 21). Exactly what signals were given to the Uzbekistan government about a reciprocal commitment to political reform is difficult to decode, but with subsequent contacts with President Karimov being largely mediated by defense secretary Donald Rumsfeld, one can surmise that the urgency of the situation and the perceived value of Uzbekistan's air base near the border with Afghanistan meant that the strategic partnership was primarily presented as a military one, cemented by a common notion that such terrorists needed to be dealt with swiftly and ruthlessly.[5]

In the short term, this led to an increase in civil society aid. In particular there was an expansion of USAID programs supporting local NGOs, administered by a growing number of US-based NGOs. Democracy support organizations that had previously been largely absent, such as the National Democratic Institute, International Republican Institute, and Freedom House, became increasingly active in the country. The operating environment was still challenging, and suspicions of these activities throughout the state system blunted the impact of the programming. However, the government's concerns were subordinated to the foreign policy goal of partnership with the United States and its assistance in addressing the terrorist threat. It was thus fitting that the international NGOs supporting civil society development were registered under, and reported to, the Ministry of Foreign Affairs (Open Society Institute 2004, 40).

However, by the end of 2003 a conflation of factors created a tipping point in state policy toward the NGO sector, marking the demise of the first stage of state-NGO relations. Operations in Afghanistan had significantly weakened the IMU—losing its base and also many of its fighters, including reputedly its leader (International Crisis Group 2007, 11) in fighting alongside the Taliban. In 2002 and 2003 there were no significant terror incidents in Uzbekistan. The threat of terror seemed to be receding, but was now replaced by a new emerging threat. In short the Uzbekistan ruling regime began to perceive the United States not as a guarantor but as a threat to its own survival. This may have been partly shaped by growing doubts about the motives of the United States in invading Iraq. Initially, Uzbekistan was one of the 48 members of the "coalition of the willing" (Daly et al. 2006, 84). Karimov contrasted the United States' decisive action with the inactivity of Europe (Radio Free Europe/Radio Liberty 2003), but eventually decided against contributing troops and became less vocal in support of the campaign.

But it was the "Rose Revolution" in Georgia in November 2003 that convinced the government that the United States, and more specifically its support for "civil society," was a significant threat. There is a debate as to what extent a "color revolution" was perceived as a real threat or as pretext for deepening the regime's control (Lewis 2008, 265), but either way it resulted in real change in state policy and a reassessment of the value of the strategic partnership with the United States, and therefore the tactical toleration of civil society that had existed up until then.

The period of controlled localization between 2004 and 2005 was marked by measures to cut off the foreign funding for NGOs in a number of ways (Ilkhamov 2005, 300–2). First, all international NGOs were required to re-register with the Ministry of Justice and, starting with the most political,[6] were pulled up on operational irregularities, with the resulting closure of nearly all of those engaged in grant-making to NGOs or working on democracy-related issues.[7] A second tactic was to restrict bank transfers of grants, with some grant-making organizations having nearly all their grant transfers returned to them.[8]

What was of particular interest is that, although there was a readily available and internationally voguish justification for such banking restrictions, there was little attempt to justify this using the pretext of combating terrorist financing. There have been measures on terrorist financing (Uzreport.com 2009) but the thrust of the crackdown on NGOs was not on Islamic groups, but on Western, pro-democracy groups. These, according to a 2005 presidential speech, were "founded with use of sponsors' funds" and operated outside their charter, pursuing "ordered aims" and, as such, "have no future in Uzbekistan." President Karimov argued that "democracy and various so called 'open society models' cannot be exported and imported" and that "I want to underline once more that we are against any revolutions and fundamentalism in any appearance when it comes to reforming and modernisation of the country" (Uzreport.com 2009). There were also state-supported insinuations that the United States was actually now aiding terrorist groups to destabilize the regime (Radio Free Europe/Radio Liberty 2005).

Now with foreign support and field-monitoring cut off, a sweeping-up operation ensued, closing those local NGOs that refused to fall in line with the new, controlled approach, represented by the newly created National Association of NGOs. An estimated 269 NGOs were closed down between August 2005 and February 2007.[9] Although difficult to determine exactly, it would seem that the government calculated that whatever social contribution these NGOs were making was outweighed by the collective threat they posed as potential bases for a "color" revolution. Now that the terrorist threat had receded, the value of the United States as an ally had diminished, and by 2005 the US air base in Khanabad was closed down. Who exactly was to blame is the subject of some debate (Daly et al. 2006, 87), but with the United States that year joining its voice to the call for an international enquiry into the multiple deaths that occurred during a complicated mix of terrorist activities and popular protest in the regional city of Andijan in May 2005, the partnership had dramatically broken down.

The seemingly erratic swings in Uzbekistan's foreign policy are a reflection of a bifocal US policy in the region—promoting democracy and fighting terror (Carothers 2003). The pursuit of the War on Terror chimed with the political discourse in Uzbekistan, but with the immediacy of the post-9/11 moment passing, voices were increasingly heard criticizing the United States' choice of ally and highlighting the human rights record of Uzbekistan. The government of Uzbekistan began to perceive "two faces" of the United States. On the one hand the United States (represented by the Defense Department) supported ruthless action against terrorist threats, but on the other hand (represented by the State Department) it seemed to be criticizing Uzbekistan for its own attempts to pursue the War on Terror—publicly criticizing its human rights record and calling for an international enquiry into the Andijan events,. This was perceived as hypocrisy and treacherous. During the Uzbekistan parliamentary session, when the closure of the United States air base was publicly discussed, the senator for the air base region proclaimed that a "man with two faces cannot be a friend of Uzbekistan" (Agonist 2005).

As of 2005 the regime promoted the theme that "Uzbekistan will not be dependent on anyone," also the name of a presidential book that spring, and this policy was applied to the civil society sector. The notion of "civil society" was not rejected; if anything, the concept became even more entrenched in the government's public discourse, reiterating a long-standing commitment to move from a "strong state" to a "strong society" (Jahon 2007). International links were significantly curtailed, and a process of localization of civil society began, mirroring the economic policy of import substitution and developing local suppliers for Uzbekistan's manufacturing sector. In the place of foreign funding, the government started developing structures not only to regulate NGOs, but also to provide them with funding. A series of measures were adopted to implement this, the most recent of which amended the law on NGOs and envisaged setting up a public foundation and a parliamentary commission on supporting NGOs (Uzreport.com 2008). So-called GONGOs (government organized NGOs) have become increasingly high profile in society.

Since 2007 there are signs of a softening of the hard line against foreign engagement with civil society, but now with the local NGOs negotiating from a position of strength. For example, Fund Forum, a politically well-connected foundation, offers political protection for international organizations who want to retain programming in the country in various social sectors (Uzbekistan Press Agency 2008). For just as the terrorist threat was perceived to have diminished between 2001 and 2002, so the threat of a color revolution was perceived to have diminished since 2005, as there have been no more large outbreaks of political opposition. In both cases a policy of suppression has been successful in the short term, but at the risk of provoking a realignment of opposition groups into a broad-based opposition in exile that would bring together more radical opposition groups and the previously more moderate NGO sector (Stevens 2007, 60).

Up until now opposition groups have been extremely fractious and ineffective in maintaining a constituency within the country, but the prospect of a slowdown in growth and economic hardship over the next few years could see repeats of localized popular protest on issues such as the freedoms of petty-traders, provision of gas, and allocation of land. Connections with these prosaic issues and the more abstract campaigning on political freedom by exiled groups[10] could spell longer-term trouble for the current regime. As such the regime needs to address the social concerns of the population. The promise of a state-controlled civil society is that it could both mobilize additional resources and civic engagement in a carefully controlled way, thereby averting any regime change.

Overall the War on Terror is best seen as having shaped the framing of the external threat, a theme that has been consistent throughout the period of this analysis. From colonial Russia to the IMU to subversive, Western-funded NGOs, the nation-building project in Uzbekistan is furthered by maintaining a sense of external threat that would unite and mobilize the population behind the regime.[11] But the dramatic shifts around 2003 can be attributed to the "two faces" of the War on Terror that the government of Uzbekistan perceived (Daly et al. 2006, 8). The marriage of "freedom and force" that lay at the heart of the conduct of the War on Terror—the expectation that the overwhelming use of force and abrogation of international legal norms could engender new political systems that would then exercise self-restraint in protecting freedom— was rejected as hypocrisy from the perspective of a country like Uzbekistan. The proponents of the War on Terror were seen as having an eagle eye for human rights violations perpetrated by the government in its own, albeit ham-fisted, War on Terror, but then turning a blind eye (and maybe even actively encouraging) the same behavior when it suited the broader War on Terror.

This in turn shaped perceptions of the freedom agenda as it manifested itself in the activities of international NGOs engaged in democracy promotion through civil society development. The ease with which the government was able to frame it within a "great game" discourse of external powers fighting for control over Central Asia was rooted in a popular perception that the 2003 events in Iraq and Georgia were two sides of the same coin—an extension of US influence. NGOs that accepted such support were as such hirelings, a fifth column threatening the independence of the country.

Civil Society, Security, and Aid in Kyrgyzstan

The case of Kyrgyzstan, Uzbekistan's southern neighbor, echoes some of these themes. For at the same time as fighting terrorism, the Kyrgyz government has used the War on Terror as cover for advancing its own purposes in suppressing both civil society in general—particularly its rights for assembly—and religious groups in particular.

As in Uzbekistan, civil society in Kyrgyzstan started to develop rapidly after independence with the assistance of foreign democratization aid; however, it did so at a much greater pace as a result of the relatively more liberal policy of the Kyrgyz government led by Askar Akaev. In the early 1990s, Kyrgyzstan was the most liberal and reform-orientated country in Central Asia (Gleason 1997), embracing the idea of civil society and democracy to a greater extent than its neighbors. This in part reflected its greater need for the financial and political support of the international community in tackling the particularly severe social and economic crisis that emerged after the collapse of the Soviet Union (Gleason 1997, 94–96). Therefore, a legislative environment conducive to the emergence and operation of civil society was established. For example, the law on NGOs adopted in 1996 was called by the International Centre for Non-For-Profit Law "one of the most progressive of its kind in the former Soviet Union" (ICNL 1996).

As a result there has been a proliferation of NGOs, whose number has grown from 611 in 1993 (Shishkaraeva et al. 2006, 63) to 11,035 in 2008 (Open Kyrgyzstan 2008). Kyrgyzstan has become the country with the highest NGO density in Central Asia (Garbutt and Heap 2002), whereas Uzbekistan, with a population over five times greater,[12] has never claimed to have more than 5,000 active NGOs. Likewise the lifting of the Soviet restrictions on religion has increased the number of religious organizations, with, as of 2008, 2,158 registered Islamic organizations. There are also a large number of Christian organizations (primarily Russian Orthodox and Protestant) and some Jewish and Buddhist organizations (Marat 2008).

In Kyrgyzstan, the radical Islamic group Hizb-ut-Tahrir has also managed to gain some support among the local population, particularly those most affected by the difficult socioeconomic conditions (IMS and PAJ 2008). For the time being, the movement has used nonviolent methods, such as the distribution of religious literature, to promote its goals (Khamidov 2007). The IMU and another group named Akramiya were mainly focused on Uzbekistan, but have an influence on Kyrgyzstan, especially in its southern parts where it shares a long border with Uzbekistan through the Ferghana valley (Khamidov 2007).

The 1999 and 2000 IMU incursions into Uzbekistan used the south of Kyrgyzstan as a transit route and began to emerge as a threat to Kyrgyzstan's own stability, such that the government sought international assistance from both Russia and the United States (IMS and PAJ 2008, 15). After 2000, there were four incidents caused by radical Islamists in the south of Kyrgyzstan. For example, in December 2002 IMU members carried out a terrorist act in one of the markets of Osh city (IMS and PAJ 2008, 15).

Consequently, fighting terrorism and national security became pressing issues for the Kyrgyz government, particularly taking into account the poor condition of its military power. Their chosen strategy was fighting radical Islamism by banning the activities of the radical movements and tightening control over religious organizations. Furthermore, the Kyrgyz government allowed the US government to establish an air base on its territory to fight the Taliban in Afghanistan after 9/11 (Global Security Org 2009). This clearly showed the commitment of the Kyrgyz government to fighting radical Islamism.

Although the anti-terrorist measures of the Kyrgyz government were primarily focused on religious organizations, there was also an impact on the secular parts of civil society, namely NGOs, following to some extent the pattern described in Uzbekistan of an increasing perception of NGOs—a former ally—as an emerging threat to the incumbent regime. The national security issue came to the forefront during the parliamentary elections in 2005 as an instrument for the government to repress the political activity of NGOs. This accelerated a trend that had started in the late 1990s, when Akaev changed his vision on the development of the country from a liberal to a more authoritarian one. He started centralizing power (Anderson 2000) by pushing amendments in the constitution to extend presidential authority (Singh 2003).

Before the parliamentary elections in 2005, there were some signs that Akaev still wanted to retain his influence over politics through having a political heir. As in Uzbekistan, he had watched with anxiety the Georgian and Ukrainian revolutions, which resulted in the replacement of their respective governments. Therefore, he started criticizing civil society groups for their intention to cause instability in the country when, according to him, it was under potential siege from Islamic radical groups such as Hizb-ut-Tahir, a faint echo of the charge in Uzbekistan that Western governments and Islamic terrorists were twin threats to national stability. As a result, attempts were made to restrict the rights of civil society groups to stage demonstrations (Beshimov 2004).

This suggests that the government of Akaev sought to use the issue of national security and the War on Terror as an instrument to restrain NGOs in order to keep the regime in power. Whereas in Uzbekistan the charge of foreign interference was more directly made, the restrictions in Kyrgyzstan were justified more in terms of the imperatives of the War on

Terror. Another key distinction is that the crackdown on civil society in Kyrgyzstan was not as harsh as in Uzbekistan. It did not include any of civil society curtailment methods of the Uzbek government, such as controlling funding of NGOs or the mass closure of NGOs and donor agencies working on civil society and democracy issues. In fact, it did not go further than an informational war, some restrictions on demonstrations, and the intimidation of a small number of watch-dog NGOs and human rights activists. For example, the Kyrgyz Committee on Human Rights was refused registration, and its leader had to flee to Europe (Freedom House 2006), and a few NGOs were subject to checks by the National Security Services (Jailobaeva 2008a). This comparatively soft approach arguably resulted in the removal of Akaev during the "Tulip revolution" in March 2005.

In addition, unlike in Uzbekistan, the profile of radical Islamism has continued to grow since 2005. There were six more incidents caused by radical Islamic groups in the south of Kyrgyzstan, and their nature became much more political. In 2007, the Bishkek Department of Interior Ministry Press Service reported that a number of people had been arrested for distributing Hizb-ut-Tahrir leaflets, which discouraged citizens from supporting the democratic institutions of Kyrgyzstan (IMS and PAJ 2008) in the upcoming elections. Furthermore, in 2008 the National Special Service identified 30 units of religious-extremist organizations, revealed 90 facts of religious extremism, and found 4,957 copies of religious extremism literature. Religious extremism has been declared by the government as the most serious threat to the national security of the country (24.kg News Agency 2008a).

In other words, the post-Tulip revolution government continues to see radical Islamism as an issue in Kyrgyzstan. However, it has used the War on Terror for two different purposes—just as the previous government did, but with tighter control and suppression. In 2009 President Bakiev signed a new law on religion. It introduced a number of new rules for religious groups including: 1) the number of people needed to officially register a religious organization increased from 10 people to 200 people; 2) the involvement of children in religious organizations and proselytizing was banned; and 3) the distribution of religious materials in public places, children's institutions, schools, and from house to house was prohibited (Radio Free Europe/ Radio Liberty 2009).

The government claims that the new law on religion is an anti-terrorism measure and will enable police to contain radical Islamism better. Further, it states that the new law is necessary to restrain evangelical Christianity, which is seen as "a second social scourge" (Eurasianet 2008). This clearly suggests that, under the War on Terror, the government suppressed not only radical Islamists, but also all religious groups, and, most importantly, it restrained people's right to freedom of religion. The new law has been criticized by human rights organizations for not meeting international human rights standards (Forum 18 2009). Furthermore, some experts on religion noted that the adoption of such a law did not ensure that the problem of terrorism would be solved. Conversely, it might intensify the religious activeness of people and even make religious organization clandestine, particularly those whose membership is below 200 people (Marat 2009).

Furthermore, the government is also restricting the rights of NGOs in order to limit their political engagement. The political transition taking place in Kyrgyzstan since 2005 has increasingly drawn NGOs into the political domain. Some NGO leaders joined political parties, and as a result NGOs have become associated with the political opposition. The government sees such a politicization of NGOs as a threat to its power, particularly taking into consideration its experience with the revolution. As the next presidential elections in 2010 draw closer, it seems that the government is starting to use the national security rhetoric to suppress the political activeness of NGOs for its own political purposes.

Demonstrations proved to be one of the most effective ways for civil society to express its voice in Kyrgyzstan. Therefore, the Kyrgyz government restrained this ability of civil society by amending the law on the freedom of assembly. The new law puts strict restrictions on public demonstrations for public safety. According to it, "Citizens cannot protest next to 'strategic facilities' including all government buildings. Further, they should also get permission from the government in advance to have a demonstration. There are also limitations on the times when protests can be held" (Radio Free Europe/Radio Liberty 2008). This is a considerable change because before people had only to notify authorities about their demonstration in advance (Russian and Eurasian Security 2008).

Furthermore, the government has attempted to more strictly control NGOs by checking their funding and activities. In 2006, the Ministry of Justice initiated investigations of those NGOs functioning in Kyrgyzstan that receive foreign funding. He stressed that the investigation should identify NGOs that might be a threat to the national security of Kyrgyzstan. The Minister also emphasized that the government should support those NGOs that work on the advancement of Kyrgyzstan's development (Human Rights Watch 2006). NGOs expressed deep concern in relation to this initiative. In response, the Minister said that his proposal was aimed at fighting "religious extremism" (Human Rights Watch 2006). However, this initiative still remained on hold at the time of writing this chapter.

In comparison with Uzbekistan, where the government is taking the initiative to shape and fund civil society, in Kyrgyzstan the government lacks a clear program. In fact, most collaboration between state institutions and the NGO sector, regardless of the area and scale of their activities, takes place within projects funded by donors. Because donors prefer to fund one-off and short-term projects, the government–NGO relationship tends to be temporary and unsustainable. The lack of a state program on NGOs has led to a desultory and sometimes discriminatory government–NGO relationship. The government and its institutions tend to work more with social service NGOs than with civil activist groups, because the latter are considered to be more active in advocacy and policy-making processes (Jailobaeva 2008b). Moreover, the Kyrgyz government did not make any effort to localize NGOs as the Uzbek government did. Although there is a new law on state contracting as of June 2008 in Kyrgyzstan, the prospect of NGOs being financed by the government is very slight (24.kg News Agency 2008b) because there is no funding in the state budget for this purpose. Kyrgyz NGOs are still largely funded by donor organizations (Jailobaeva 2008c).

Conclusion

In conclusion, the cases of Kyrgyzstan and Uzbekistan first bring into focus a number of themes that are common to countries where democratic institutions are relatively underdeveloped. Second, the differences between the two highlight the importance of local political context in mediating the relationship between the War on Terror and state–civil society relations. Third, they shed light on some of the dilemmas facing the international community as it seeks to hold in tension demands for increased security and at the same time greater liberty.

First, the common themes are that, in both Uzbekistan and Kyrgyzstan, state policy toward civil society organizations has become more restrictive, particularly since 2004 in Uzbekistan and 2005 in Kyrgyzstan. The fact that the timing in both cases does not neatly coincide with the most intensive period of anti-terrorist activity in the region (between 1999 and 2002) suggests that the US-led War on Terror was not the only factor in shaping policy toward civil society, and that its impact was mediated by other factors. However, the "warlike" pursuit of the terrorist threat has clearly shaped political dynamics in both countries—where national security is elevated to an almost supreme value, where non-government organizations come to be perceived as anti-government organizations, where collateral damage on those elements of civil society that are not directly contributing to the terrorist threat becomes politically acceptable, and where suspicions are raised about external funding of civil society.

The image of the West in general, and the United States in particular, has also been a clear casualty in the War on Terror. Signs in early 2009 that Kyrgyzstan was requesting the closure of the US air force base illustrate the extent to which US room for maneuver in the region is severely hampered by its reputation as a self-interested and unreliable ally. One of the factors pushing Kyrgyzstan to end this cooperation with the United States is the forthcoming presidential elections, and a calculation by the president that being seen to lean toward Russia and away from the United States will be politically popular. Although difficult to quantify given the absence, particularly in Uzbekistan, of robust opinion polling, the waves of anti-Americanism that have swept the world in the post-Iraq invasion era have clearly changed the contours of popular opinion in the region.

However, what is particularly instructive in comparing Uzbekistan and Kyrgyzstan is that despite their common regional location, Soviet heritage, Islamic terrorist threat, and role in the international War on Terror (both hosting United States bases to support the campaign in Afghanistan), this chapter has identified significant differences in which local political context mediated the impact of the War on Terror on state policy toward civil society. Kyrgyzstan emerged from the Soviet Union in a much weaker position than Uzbekistan—smaller, less resource-rich, and more ethnically diverse and geographically fragmented. All these factors made Kyrgyzstan more vulnerable to a committed band of terrorists able to exploit these vulnerabilities—its weaker military, mountainous areas, ethnic and political tensions between the north and south of the country, and the more serious economic situation.

This vulnerability led in turn to it being more dependent on external support, both in directly dealing with the terrorist threat (calling in US and Russian assistance where Uzbekistan prided itself on dealing with it alone) and also developing the country. Although the liberal policy partly has roots in the country's political culture, it was also driven by this need to align its development model with those of international development agencies and bilateral partners. This alignment has led to a relatively more tolerant and targeted approach to civil society regulation—focusing more exclusively on religious groups and also restricting civil society activity only in its most politically overt forms such as demonstrations at times of political flux. It has also meant Kyrgyzstan has refrained from shutting the door to international support for civil society groups.

With signals that Uzbekistan may also be relaxing its stance toward international organizations, there is an opportunity for international organizations to continue to shape the evolution of civil society in both countries. Successful interventions, however, will need to take into account these changes in state policy toward NGOs and address some of the underlying concerns. For the War on Terror more broadly has shaken the previous image of civil society as some inherently positive dynamic (Eade 2000, 10) and increased suspicions about its role and relationship with state actors. This is definitely true in the cases of Uzbekistan and Kyrgyzstan, where civil society has been put on the defensive—framed as a fifth column for foreign interests in Uzbekistan or, in a milder version, as a distraction to the government as it seeks to deal with an Islamic fundamentalist threat. Civil society now has to more clearly articulate its contribution to national development and stability, and international assistance programs now have to take this into account—focusing increasingly on building up the capacity of NGOs not just to run projects, but to strategically position themselves within the broader political context in ways that emphasize their domestic roots and contribution to nationally owned development plans.

Notes

1. By state policies we refer to an approximate tendency aggregated from a variety of legislative acts, resolutions and practices of different state actors, rather than a single coherent policy document.

2. In the 1990s "civil society" was described as "the Rome of today's internationalism; wherever we may begin, we will arrive at this debate sooner or later" (Van Rooy 1998, 1).

3. An introduction to the debate in this region can be found in Babajanian, Freizer and Stevens (2005).

4. The idea of a social contract draws from the idea of a social compact between state and individual in Uzbekistan as outlined by Kandiyoti (2007, 33).

5. The president was quoted as saying on state-run TV that "I call on everyone to unite and protect our country from enemies like this, to come forward against them as one fist" (Associated Press 2004). The president is also cited as claiming that terrorists "must be shot in the forehead! If necessary, I'll shoot them myself" (Bingol 2004).

6. The Soros foundation was the first to close, followed by accusations against the US National Democratic Institute of International Relations, International Republican Institute, and Freedom House (Press Service of the President of the Republic of Uzbekistan 2004).

7. The National Democratic Institute remained open, and to some extent Human Rights Watch (though its most recent appointment of Country Director has been refused accreditation). These are the exceptions that prove the rule—widely seen as tokens to demonstrate the

government's commitment to dialogue in reaction to the European Union's biannual reviews of sanctions on the country, originally imposed after the Andijan events in 2005.

8. Author's interviews with international donors, March 2005.

9. According to unpublished research by one international organization.

10. For example, a recent coalition known as the "Coalition Against Forced Child Labour in Uzbekistan" has called for both respecting human rights commitments and land reform to ensure broader ownership and control. Further information available at www.laborrights.org.

11. For an elaborate argument to this end see March (2003).

12. This is based on population figures provided in UNFPA (2008, 93).

7

CIVIL SOCIETY, THE "NEW HUMANITARIANISM," AND THE STABILIZATION DEBATE: JUDGING THE IMPACT OF THE AFGHAN WAR

Stuart Gordon

Following the end of the Cold War, development donors increasingly disengaged from what they labeled as "fragile states." However, with the onset of the global War on Terror, this trend gradually reversed. This led to considerable changes to the way in which some Western donors approached countries characterized by large-scale violence, poor governance, and the absence of the rule of law. As opposed to seeing these as marginal areas, these situations were portrayed as actual or potential sources of terrorism, organized crime, weapons proliferation, global pandemics, and violent conflict—in short, as potentially posing a significant and direct threat to international peace and security. By treating the essentially internal crises of failed states as existential threats to the international system, the international community has increasingly sought to manufacture stability through the benign logic of economic development and governance reform among and within democratic states. This has precipitated an increased willingness to engage with these contexts with the related aims of "stabilizing" them before instigating wider social transformations in the direction of a "liberal peace."

In order to achieve such ambitious objectives, most Western governments and international organizations have sought to align the full spectrum of policy responses, including diplomatic, development, humanitarian, and defense policies. These integrated (or comprehensive) responses have drawn attention to the need for improved internal mechanisms for horizontal coordination between different departments and agencies. Within governments this has precipitated the birth of new offices, processes, and initiatives charged with effecting these changes to the capacity for horizontal coordination within governments. At the strategic level these have included the Stabilisation Unit (originally the Post Conflict Reconstruction Unit) in the United Kingdom, the Canadian Government's Stabilization and Reconstruction Task Force, and the Office of the Coordinator for Reconstruction and Stabilization in the United States. At the operational level, initiatives such as the Provincial Reconstruction Team (PRT) have been charged with delivering integrated strategies. Furthermore, the concept of "stabilization" as a discrete set of activities separate from traditional development and conflict diplomacy has emerged as a powerful policy discourse.

In a practical sense this has led to a tremendous growth in interactions between the military and civilian elements within governments, while also changing the relationships between, on the one hand "civil society" within beneficiary communities, and, on the other, intervening militaries. These approaches are not without controversy, and the humanitarian community in particular has been vocal in its criticisms. The core criticism is that policy integration leads to a blurring of the boundaries between humanitarian and political activity, reducing humanitarian space and the capacity for agencies to access vulnerable communities. However, in the past donors have been criticized just as sharply for failing to link humanitarian responses to broader responses that include appropriate forms of diplomatic and military engagement.[1]

These integrative processes are not fundamentally new. Rather the politics implicit in the global War on Terror have deepened a process of securitizing aid that was already underway in the 1990s, impacting both on military strategies and the activities of humanitarian agencies, creating a complex convergence of security objectives and development processes. This chapter charts these changes in both the British military and the humanitarian community before exploring the impact on civil society in Helmand, Afghanistan, between 2006 and 2009.

The United Kingdom: Joining Up Security and Development?

Within the apparatus of the UK government, different departments have been subject to this "joining up" agenda in different ways and with different levels of enthusiasm. The Ministry of Defence (MOD) has developed a particular zeal, enshrining its growing appetite for joined up approaches in its "comprehensive approach" doctrine, described as:

> a conceptual framework which could be used to reinvigorate
> the existing, Cabinet Office-led, approach to coordinating the

objectives and activities of Government Departments in identifying, analysing, planning and executing national responses to
complex situations. Post-operational analysis of situations and
crises at home and abroad has demonstrated the value and
effectiveness of a joined-up and cross-discipline approach if
lasting and desirable outcomes are to be identified and
achieved. (MOD 2005, 1-)

This enthusiasm for comprehensive working lies in a number of interrelated factors: changes in the department's understanding of the complex
nature of conflict; experience of operations in the Balkans, and subsequently
the global War on Terror (or GWOT); and finally debates relating to the
transformation of the military itself (the "Effects Based Approach" or
EBA).[2] In terms of the former, the MOD has been heavily influenced in its
understanding of the complexity of conflict by the "human security" agenda
(UNDP 1994). This shaped both its understanding of conflict causality and
its appetite for harnessing the capacity of other actors to address root
causes. This approach was reinforced by its experiences in the Balkans from
1991, where it discovered crises involving a complex "interplay of civilian,
para-military and military groups and individuals, International Organisations (IOs) and the mass Media" (Ministry of Defence 2005, 1–1) The
MOD's Joint Doctrine Note, "the Comprehensive Approach," encapsulated
the MOD's rediscovery of the limits of the military instrument in transforming conflict and the significance of what has increasingly been termed
the "civilian effect" (Ministry of Defence 2005).

Largely reflecting the United Kingdom's experiences with the UN Protection Force (UNPROFOR) mission in Bosnia, the MOD's focus on comprehensive working was initially on transforming relationships with the
non-governmental and UN humanitarian systems at the tactical level.
However, NATO's response—first to the refugee crisis emanating from
Kosovo in 1998/1999, and subsequently to the stabilization of the region
as a whole—reinforced the growing sense that the scale of crises made
tactical-level coordination, defined largely in terms of shared understanding and some cooperation between like-minded individuals, insufficient. In
response to this, the level at which cooperation occurred was elevated to
the operational level—initially with the establishment of (limited) Department for International Development (DFID) and Foreign and Commonwealth Office (FCO) representation in the UK Defence Crisis Management
Organisation—in particular at the Permanent Joint Headquarters. However, subsequent experiences in Sierra Leone (2000) and during the inva-
sions of Afghanistan (November 2001) and Iraq (2003) highlighted the
continuing absence of machinery at the military strategic level for

planning across government. The principal remedy to this was the establishment of the cross-Whitehall Post Conflict Reconstruction Unit (PCRU) in 2004.

The MOD appeared to place considerable faith in the PCRU's capacity to deliver a comprehensive approach and continued to articulate its understanding of the need for cross-governmental working in its own doctrine publications—principally *The Military Contribution to Peace Support Operations* (MOD 2009) and subsequently in the *Comprehensive Approach* (CA) (MOD 2005)—but made little real progress in enhancing its own capabilities in this area. Rather, it even stimulated opposition in the other departments at what was seen as an overly evangelical approach to whipping them into line in support of the MOD.

Nevertheless, other pressures continued to reinforce enthusiasm for a more comprehensive approach, particularly what became known as the "transformation agenda." This approach, originating in the US Department of Defense, sought to leverage a broad range of largely technological changes (particularly stealth, sensor, information technology, and communication technologies) in order to transform military capabilities through what was termed an "effects-based approach" (EBA). The EBA was itself rooted in two fundamental notions: first, that of understanding the enemy as a complex, adaptive system of systems; and second, identifying and then concentrating action against the key nodes and links that comprised that system. Such an approach resonated strongly in the United Kingdom, offering both a means for addressing the complexity of the contemporary battlefield and for offsetting the deleterious impact of budgetary pressures on capabilities. However, it threatened to erode boundaries between the military and civilian domains by encouraging more holistic views of what sustained or undermined an enemy's will and capacity to fight.

Nevertheless, the agenda, as played out in the United Kingdom, was somewhat different from that in the United States. While adopting the ethos of the original US "transformational" agenda (albeit less well resourced), there were also a range of largely British elements. These included embedding the changes in the pursuit of an "ethical foreign policy," a stronger preference for "softer" effects (leveraging diplomatic, information and development actors), and a much greater willingness to countenance less hierarchical forms of cooperation between the defense and foreign ministries. Collectively, these strengthened the demand for civilian departments, principally the FCO and DFID, to support the MOD in both transforming conflict through rapidly applied development activity and the provision of a political vision that would make possible a sustainable peace and the consolidation of tactical military victories.

While growing in the MOD, the appetite for and capacity to engage in comprehensive working showed marked variations in other departments, particularly DFID and the FCO. In a very practical sense neither had career incentives for working in what the MOD termed "expeditionary environments." In the case of DFID the issues ran much deeper, reflecting a department configured around a "poverty reduction" rather than a traditional "national interest" agenda. DFID's focus on poverty reduction in support of the United Nations' millennium development goals was enshrined in legislation (the 2002 International Development Act) and militated against the type of cooperation presumed by many within the MOD. Development *best practice* also warned against seeking to use money as a "weapon system"—highlighting the potential to undermine peace and the beneficiary state, to create perverse incentives, and to reinforce the war economy (Anderson 1999 and 2000). Although the evidence largely supported the DFID position, the assumptions made by some within the MOD were voiced more powerfully; in the context of wars in which UK servicemen were losing their lives, DFID found it difficult to make their arguments stick.

DFID's capacity to articulate the risks of the MOD approach was further undermined by a sense among some military officers that the organization preferred to work around conflict rather than on it. In 2002 it had largely disengaged from planning for the invasion of Iraq, reflecting a widespread opposition to the conflict within DFID (and stemming from the attitudes of the then Secretary of State Claire Short), but also reflecting the culture of large parts of the department as a whole. DFID's creation and rapid expansion in 1997 had led to heavy recruitment from the NGO sector, a community that was unlikely to favor the type of robust interventionism evident in Iraq. Furthermore, the rapid expansion of DFID's budget since 1997 placed considerable pressure on the organization in terms of ensuring effective program management.

The rather elegant solution, and one that again reflected best practice among donor states, was to pour money through multilateral partners and national state structures, building beneficiary state capacity in more sustainable ways than the direct delivery of "public services" by donors. However, elements of the British Army labored under the assumption that development workers *did* projects, rather than funded or supported capacity-building strategies. Meanwhile DFID argued, and with considerable justification, that since 2004 they had invested in the PCRU to deliver the type of conflict stabilization work that middle-ranking officers within the MOD expected. This became a source of interdepartmental tension from 2006 with the deployment of troops to Helmand.

The FCO also struggled with operationalizing "joined up" approaches in theatres such as Iraq and Afghanistan. Configured throughout much of the Cold War around delivering what could be termed "strategic diplomacy," it found it difficult to find appropriately experienced staff, as well as structures and strategies that could deliver the type of local-level diplomatic engagement necessitated by the tribal politics of both conflicts.

The Convergence of Humanitarian and Military Strategies

The changes in the relationship between development and military actors *within* government have been paralleled by changes in the relationship between humanitarian actors and political processes. This trend was visible most clearly in the growth of multi-mandate organizations that blended the traditional discourse of humanitarianism with "developmental" and rights-based approaches to aid. Similarly, the growth in humanitarian "commercialism," brought about by the professionalization of the aid industry and its growing dependence on UN and state donor money, pushed the boundaries of traditional Dunantism.[3]

During the 1990s the humanitarian discourse was also heavily influenced by the reconceptualization and broadening of the concept of security. As analysis shifted from a focus on states and the ideological competition of the Cold War to a focus on population growth, poverty, and environmental decline, the potential role of "assistance" in security strategies grew, paving the way for the idea of aid as peacemaker. Throughout the early 1990s, relief assistance increased significantly, both in absolute terms and as a percentage of official development assistance.[4] This trend attracted increased scrutiny of the workings of relief agencies, particularly in conflict situations, and led to changes in the way in which NGOs related to beneficiary governments. In particular the declining significance of state sovereignty translated into "renewed powers to judge the quality of governance in recipient countries and, if necessary, withhold resources on political grounds" (Humanitarian Policy Group 2000, iii).

Macrae argues that by the middle of the 1990s two critiques had begun to dominate humanitarian policy circles. First, "relief assistance was failing to reduce the vulnerability of populations in the medium- to long-term. Emergencies were dragging on without an obvious end in sight; relief interventions were not sustainable, nor were they necessarily the most effective way of helping populations to maintain their dignity and re-establish their livelihoods" (Humanitarian Policy Group 2000, 2). Second, she argues that evidence had begun to mount that "as part of the diversification of the financing of contemporary conflicts, warring parties were turning to relief to sustain themselves. Relief, it was argued, was doing more harm than good" (Humanitarian Policy Group 2000, 3). The combination of these two critiques led, she argues to a tantalizing possibility: that if relief fuelled conflict, then, if more skillfully applied, it could also reduce it.

This approach was not universally popular. Analysts such as David Rieff challenged whether "an ideal based on both universal values and unbending neutrality can be politicized successfully" suggesting that the "price for such a transformation would seem to be very high—perhaps too high" (Rieff 2002, 35). Rieff implied that the situation was portrayed in terms of an extreme dilemma: that contemporary humanitarianism would need to compromise its Dunantist origins or be condemned to a humanitarian "moment," in which only the most limited symptoms of human suffering could be addressed. However, he stressed the danger that the expansion of humanitarian mandates beyond lifesaving support ran the risk of overstretching humanitarian mandates and responsibilities, as humanitarians increasingly identified violence against civilians as a humanitarian issue and placed pressure on the belligerents to open up humanitarian space and access. Where this failed, it was but a short elision into an approach designed to trigger political, military, or judicial processes for enforcing civilian protection.

Rieff (2002, 1–33) has been critical of this trend, arguing that humanitarianism has portrayed itself as "a saving idea that cannot save." Furthermore he described how frustration with the inability to change the political conditions that have produced humanitarian crises has led the humanitarian community to sacrifice their integrity and independence in order to get into the much bigger business of "armed protection of threatened civilians and neo-liberal state construction." He concluded that humanitarianism is ill-equipped to resolve the issues that it increasingly portrayed itself as capable of confronting.

The price of this bargain has, however, involved attaching contemporary humanitarianism to an interventionist or containment agenda of the Western powers, echoing, says Hugo Slim (2003), the process through which European missionary philanthropy became a component of nineteenth-century colonialism. For Rieff, contemporary humanitarianism has arrived at its own "Constantine moment"—passing from a movement based on private faith to becoming a state-based orthodoxy, leading to what he describes as "state humanitarianism" (Slim 2003b, 1). Having bought fully into the logic and pursuit of liberal peace, it is possible to argue that the securitization of development processes has become largely inevitable.

For liberal, Western states the convergence of this "new humanitarianism" with significant elements of security strategy makes sense both morally and strategically. In terms of the West's response to its war in

Afghanistan, it has resulted in a strategy rooted, at least in a declaratory sense, in these new instruments of liberal state-building. This has given birth to a new policy discourse, that of "stabilization." This represents a fusion of the "new humanitarianism" and the state-building agenda—or, more specifically, the military's pursuit of "soft security" instruments sufficient to transform its tactical success on the battlefield into more sustainable forms of stability (a precursor to peace), and a conflict management/containment strategy drawn from the "new humanitarianism." This fusion can be seen in the draft Stabilisation Unit Quick Impact Project Handbook's definition of stabilization's aims as being to:

> support places that are emerging from violent conflict towards a period of peaceful development, often through external military and civilian support to weak host governments. The support is focused on extending the legitimacy and capability of that government and providing immediately tangible benefits to the population—"quick wins"—that underpin their confidence in the state and the political process that it represents. Stabilisation activities explicitly aim to impact positively upon formal and informal political dynamics at all levels and to contribute to a non-violent political settlement or interim accommodation. (Stabilisation Unit 2009a, 11)

In terms of specific tasks, it suggests that stabilization supports the development of the state, through

- Facilitating a political settlement between parties competing for power
- Supporting the state to fulfil its core functions, such as territorial control and control of the state's finances
- Facilitating the legitimate government's ability to deliver what is expected by the population and what gives it its authority to represent them. (Stabilisation Unit, 2009a, 12)

The stabilization process focuses on what are described as the four Ps: the prevention or containment of conflict; the protection of people, key assets, and institutions; the promotion of political processes that lead to greater stability; and preparation for longer-term development (Stabilisation Unit 2009a, 13; 2009b, 12–14). It continues to argue that in a "counter insurgency and conflict environment the 4 Ps converge upon the idea of reaching a 'tipping point' on the path to a *self sustaining peace* where stabilisation actors support institutional and societal capacities to constrain conflict 'drivers' and extend the political, military and moral authority of the state."

Such a model conceives of Afghanistan's instability as largely a product of fundamental failures of governance and economic development, while the solution is described in terms of managing a transition toward a democratic system raised on the temporary foundations of internationally provided security, political, and economic assistance. Arguably the United Kingdom has been at the vanguard of developing this model in terms of its strategy in Afghanistan with a much greater focus on governance and provincial institutional capacity building than, for example, the United States in the east.

The development of this ambitious approach threatens to fundamentally reconfigure the relationships between the British military, assistance strategies, and beneficiary communities and can be described as an effort to engineer the emergence of proto-elements of civil society and facilitate their linkage with the state authorities. As such it is a far more sophisticated model than the traditional "hearts and minds" approaches that have characterized military efforts in this area to date.

The United Kingdom's Model of Liberal State Building

Arguably the strategy has passed through two principal stages. The first was a period (from 2006 until late 2007) of adjusting an initial and unrealistic "peacekeeping strategy" to the realities of Helmand. The second, beginning in early 2008, was one of consolidating activity around a new plan that more accurately reflected the stabilization priorities and was labeled as the "Helmand Road Map."

The first stage began with the United Kingdom's deployment of troops into southern Afghanistan in support of the extension of NATO's presence beyond the north. In October 2005 the Cabinet Office commissioned the Post Conflict Reconstruction Unit (PCRU) to lead interdepartmental planning for a strategic framework encompassing both civilian and military activity in Helmand. This resulted in the UK Joint Plan for Helmand, a masterful study in policy coherence that claimed consistency with the Afghanistan Compact, the Interim Afghan National Development Strategy, the Government of Afghanistan's National Drug Control Strategy, the UK Strategic Plan for Afghanistan, NATO's International Strategic Assistance Forces strategy, and the emerging Afghan Development Zone concept. It also provided a vehicle for binding and seeking coherence between the DFID, the FCO, the Afghan Drugs Interdepartmental Unit and MOD planning. It was also one of the first occasions in which three very different departments of state were able to establish an interdepartmental strategy—arguably providing a greater range of strategic options and a means for developing synergies.

The UK plan, echoing the Malayan "ink spot" strategy, focused on Lashkargar, Helmand's provincial capital. It envisaged British and Afghan troops providing a framework of security sufficient for development work to slowly transform the political, social, and economic fabric of the town and generate "effects" that would spill over beyond the town itself. The transformation was to be funded with some £6 million of UK money allocated to small-scale, quick-impact projects (QIPs) in 2006/2007 and the DFID providing an additional £30 million through a multi-year, rural livelihoods program. The DFID money was to be channeled through the Afghan Ministry of Reconstruction and Rural Development, while the QIPs were to be managed by the civilian and military staff of the British Provincial Reconstruction Team (PRT).

However, the initial plan contained serious weaknesses. Planning developed in a virtual information vacuum, with only limited access to Helmandi power-brokers. This was compounded by President Karzai's removal of the Helmandi Governor, Sher Mohammed Akhundzadha (SMA), an individual who would otherwise have been expected to have been a major interlocutor and source of information. The information vacuum was compounded by Whitehall's focus on Iraq and the resultant diversion of critical assets, reducing further the access to local actors and the information that was necessary to develop more detailed implementation planning. Furthermore, the plan did not provide a clear blueprint for a counter-insurgency campaign or an effective means of reconciling the Counter Insurgency[5] (or "COIN") strategy with the counter-narcotics approach. Nor did the plan adequately reflect the impact of the US-led Kajaki Dam project on military operations.

As with most of the international community, the United Kingdom's national planning also reflected many of the assumptions of the post-Bonn period, which envisaged a largely top-down, technocratic, and apolitical approach to state-building, neglecting the sub-national, state-building agenda. Furthermore, the post-Bonn process implied a form of cooperation between donors and Afghan leaders that presumed a shared understanding of and commitment to reversing state failure and managing reconstruction in the interests of all. Many Afghan elites, however, did not share either that diagnosis of failure or the state-building objectives, seeking instead to maximize the potential benefits accruing to them from the political, financial, and military resources that flowed from Kabul.

The initial UK plan was derailed almost from the outset. By mid-June 2006 the removal of SMA had created a power vacuum and, in northern Helmand, elements of the Taliban and narcotics barons harnessed what amounted to a popular uprising against the remnants of SMA's regime. Governor Daoud and President Karzai placed considerable pressure on the United Kingdom to re-establish control—making British commanders painfully aware of Karzai's view that he could lose the presidency if the northern districts of Helmand were to fall. Despite having little more than a battle group of infantry (less than 600 combat troops), the United Kingdom deployed small groups of troops into several of the isolated and beleaguered towns, beginning what became known as the "platoon house" strategy.

The deployment met unexpectedly fierce resistance from the Taliban, who employed conventional tactics to drive out the British. The British clung on grimly, withstanding siege and near-constant attack until, in October 2006, commanders negotiated a controversial arrangement with local tribal leaders. In exchange for guarantees that the Taliban would be prevented from retaking the town of Musa Qaleh, the British withdrew. Predictably, the Taliban retook the town in February 2007.

However, the British military presence in Musa Qaleh had been untenable almost from the outset. With insufficient troops to deter Taliban attacks, the weakness of the British military deployments encouraged both direct Taliban assaults and increased the British reliance on defensive airstrikes. Not only was the resulting collateral damage deeply unpopular with the civilian population of Musa Qaleh, but the Taliban portrayed the British presence as supporting an unpopular leader, SMA. The platoon house strategy had other deleterious side effects. The serious deterioration in security during the summer of 2006 contributed to an acrimonious debate in Whitehall over whether the United Kingdom was "on" or "off" plan. Assessments of the security situation grew increasingly pessimistic, and the focus on the fighting in the north of Helmand combined with the growth in the Taliban's use of asymmetric tactics to affect both DFID and the FCO's willingness to send staff to the region—both because of the inherent security threat and the sense that the environment was not conducive to development work. This slowed further the buildup of civilian capacity in the PRT and reduced the military's capacity to translate tactical military success into more enduring results.

While in theory the British approach was more comprehensive than that of the Americans, at least in terms of harnessing foreign, defense, and development ministries to a common plan, the first two years were characterized by considerable difficulties in making the model work. The UK Joint Helmand Plan's approach envisaged a top-down and largely apolitical approach that failed to adequately take into account Helmand's dangerous volatility, the nature of Afghan political society, and the paucity of implementing partners willing to operate in such an insecure environment and seriously underplayed the mechanisms and resources necessary to focus and integrate the relevant civilian lines of operation within a COIN plan. This resulted in nearly 18 months of strategic drift in which much of the United Kingdom's overall effort dissipated, and the assumptions underpinning the original UK plan increasingly broke down.

However, with the deployment of a replacement Brigade every six months, there was a slow increase in troop numbers (from one UK battle group in the summer of 2006 to five by the end of 2008), allowing them to hold ground more effectively in areas beyond Lashkargar while using more mobile elements to disrupt Taliban activities in the areas beyond. While troop levels grew, the need for a detailed, operational-level stabilization "road map" to bring the diplomatic and development strategies into line became increasingly apparent throughout 2007. As the military's capabilities grew, the weakness in civilian capacities became more noticeable, causing a degree of frustration, particularly as subsequent brigades invested increasingly in aligning themselves with the gradually expanding PRT. In particular, 52 Brigade's deployment at the end of 2007 coincided with the arrival of a team from the then PCRU (Post Conflict Resolution Unit, now Stabilisation Unit), who agreed jointly to produce the "Helmand Road Map." This bottom-up initiative coincided with a change of Prime Minister and a renewed emphasis by Whitehall on Afghanistan— creating space for a refresh of policy. It also coincided with the arrival of a charismatic and influential Ambassador, Sir Sherard Cowper Coles, who shepherded the plan through the pitfalls of Whitehall.

The Road Map set out a broad range of security, counter-narcotics, development, and governance objectives, reflecting existing UK, NATO, and Government of Afghanistan policy frameworks, resulting in a far more detailed plan than the original "UK Joint Plan for Helmand." However, the latter's legacy was clear, with the Road Map combining the former's top-down, state-building approach with significant efforts to stimulate local governance structures and enhancements to their capacity to draw down national programs and the work of line ministries. It envisaged stabilization and political advisers being deployed into the Forward Operating Bases. These would work with district authorities and local communities to build their trust in government and to sponsor the growth of community-based structures with which formal government could link. The underlying intent was to channel political dialogue, largely defined in terms of the voicing of community aspirations and grievances, through political channels maintained by the provincial authorities.

This meant focusing the UK "security" effort on supporting the disruption and containment of the military threat posed by the Taliban and creating a space for collaboration between the Afghan authorities and the key populations of Helmand. The dialogue was to be led by the Afghan Provincial Authorities and underwritten by their timely delivery of basic public services—principally security, health, education, and some rural infrastructure work—and a demand-led economic recovery. This would be augmented by the United Kingdom's support to key ministries in order to create a government that was increasingly responsive and able to deliver visibly against key expectations in the major population centers.

The implicit intention was one of cajoling populations into relationships with their district authorities—crystallizing diverse and ad hoc meetings between elders and governors/mayors into more habitual processes conducted through more enduring institutions such as the Community Development Councils or their "Afghan Social Outreach Programme" equivalent. There was recognition that such processes were not easily constructed. They are generally rooted in a population's belief that: local and national political structures are more capable and responsive than any realistic alternatives offered by the insurgency; district- and community-based institutions are viewed as sufficiently credible and robust that concerns can be raised *with* them; resources are able to pass down, *through* such institutions; some public services can be delivered *by* them; and disputes could realistically be played out *within*, rather than without, them. In effect the strategy required manufacturing an "appetite" for government, something that had become rather alien to the tribes of Helmand, as well as a more capable and responsive set of provincial and district authorities.

In addition to this change in strategy, the United Kingdom effected significant increases in both military resource levels and the organization of its effort. By the end of 2008 some five British battle groups were deployed, while the PRT and the Brigade headquarters had been combined into a "Civil–Military" Mission headquarters. This was led by an FCO civilian and resourced with more civilian staff than any other Afghan-based PRT. In addition to stabilization advisers being deployed "forward," the military established "Military Stabilisation Support Teams" (MSST) in the key districts, seeking to extend significantly the reach and capability of the "civil effect."

The reliance on civil servants and, increasingly, the military as direct providers of "stability" processes was a change in approach when compared with the intended instrumentalization of humanitarian organizations sought by the military during the 2003 invasion of Iraq. Such militarization reflected both the inability of humanitarian organizations to operate safely in Helmand and the security restrictions placed even on civil servants. However, the perceived significance of the activity compelled the MOD to adopt "stabilization" as a core activity for the Army, reflected both in a substantial increase in the manpower dedicated to this activity in Helmand and also the permanence of the Military Stabilisation Support Team (MSST)[6] concept and the sense that this required an enduring capability and manpower resources.

In addition to these changes, the military also sought to increase the permanence and cohesion of its command arrangements, increasing the tour lengths of several key appointments from six to nine months. In parallel, the United States deployed elements of a Marine Expeditionary Unit, increasing both NATO's deployed manpower and the funding available for rapid development projects.

Controversies—The Transformation Agenda

The principal difficulty with the approach encapsulated in British strategy is that it is predicated on a particular vision of what the state "does." This leads to particular understandings of the process of state failure and a predisposition toward particular mechanisms for, and approaches to, the problem of state-building. Sarah Lister echoes this theme, arguing that different perspectives on the process of state building are bounded by an underlying theoretical tradition that encompasses perspectives from Locke to Weber. The Lockean perspective conceives of the state as a mechanism for fulfilling a social contract. Hence, she argues, state failure is perceived to be a product of the incapacity to deliver essential goods and services. The Weberian approach conceptualizes the state as having a legitimate monopoly of the use of force. Thus state failure implies the inability of a state to produce and maintain such a monopoly.

These conceptualizations have implications for our "understanding of the state and its functions" (Lister 2007, 2). Although she freely admits that there is a significant degree of consensus on what states provide (she suggests the provision of security, representation, and welfare (Lister 2007, 2)) the danger is that the focus on what states "do" encourages the reduction of state-building strategies into an almost technocratic, depoliticized, and impersonal process of formal capacity building—with the development of institutions and rules being designed to restore the state's capacity to deliver core functions in pursuit of its own legitimacy (Chesterman et al. 2005, 41). Consequently, it encourages a perception of the state in terms that are largely rationalistic, rule-based, and institutionally framed rather than as institutions and processes that are themselves the legacies of and contemporary vehicles for highly politicized interactions (Corbridge et al. 2005, 5).

Lister provides a concise explanation of the process by which the Afghan state "failed" and the dangers that this creates for state-building strategies in such a context. Echoing the seminal work of Rubin Barnett, she argues that, prior to the Soviet invasion, centralized institutions of the state coexisted uneasily with a "fragmented and decentralised traditional society" characterized by a process through which tribal and religious leaders created what she describes as micro-societies "that related to central and other powers on the basis of negotiation and patronage" (Lister 2007, 3) Following the Soviet invasion and the ensuing years of armed conflict, this uneasy coexistence broke down as power shifted from traditional institutions to new ones defined by control of military and financial resources "generated by participation in the conflict and the war economy" (Lister 2007, 3).

This process of fragmentation and decentralization was accompanied by a parallel process through which commanders created alliances based on geographically distinct areas, mobilizing ethnic, tribal, and lineage allegiances to support or resist the central authorities and creating alternative, hierarchically arranged systems of patronage and power.[7] The development of central state authorities that followed the US-led invasion in 2001 realized significant tensions between these powerful "remnant" or "conflict" institutions and processes and those entailed by state-building. Lister provides evidence of a damaging merging of warlord and criminal processes with the rebuilding of the new Afghan state in a form of politics that is felt in the relationships between civil society and the institutions and policies of the state, government ministries, governors, and provincial development structures. The negative consequences of this fusion may be felt in terms of the emergence of other conflict forms and the growth of disillusionment within civil society that undermines the legitimacy of the state-building process and even broader forms of "consent."

The British military has been drawn into this process of state-building at the local level and has tended to focus on limited forms of project-based institutional capacity building. This is rooted in a view of the process as largely apolitical or, at the most, as a kind of "low-level local politics" that can be frustrating but somehow separated from the state-building process itself. The result has been the development of military approaches to state-building that have tended to focus on building the institutional capacity of Governor's or Provincial Development Committees, often without necessarily understanding the impact on local-level political dynamics. The corrupt and incompetent nature of the emerging Afghan state in particular has made such conceptualizations particularly dangerous, leading to difficulties at the local level with reconciling powerful, local-level patronage interests with the development of legitimate institutions and policies.

In order to plot a course that avoids these potential consequences, state building, especially at the local level, cannot be reduced to a technocratic process of capacity building separate from the low politics of the local tribal structures, criminal elements, warlords, or even the petty bureaucratic politics between the governor and national line ministries. Rather, state and institution building at the local level needs to be recognized as the arena in which individuals and groups negotiate power and transform these into policies and structures that shape the overall state-building process itself.

In part the military can be forgiven for their approach. They have been victims of the international community's general "Lockean fixation" with the state as a provider of a social contract rather than as a vehicle through which community politics (in every sense) is played out. They have also been drawn into the vacuum left by the neglect of this level of state-building by the international community with its almost exclusive focus on the national level of Afghanistan's government between 2002 and 2005. But there are also significant issues related to post-Cold War defense transformation. The British military's expeditionary strategy has largely focused on how power is exercised and delivered rather than how it is felt within civil society. This has contributed to errors of judgment such as the "projectization" of state building and the use of warlords in the struggle against the Taliban. Furthermore, the reliance on "networked" warfare and light, deployable forces has provided a military rationale for reduced troop numbers that legitimizes political discomfort with deploying forces beyond a "light footprint." The direct consequence has been that troop levels in both Afghanistan and Iraq have been insufficient to establish the degree of control that was seen in either post-Dayton Bosnia or Kosovo (Quinilivan 1995, 59–69). Arguably the result has been that the moderate voices have been unable to take advantage of a "redrafting of the rules" by which power is mediated in the post-conflict setting—largely because the rules have not been altered fundamentally. Chesterman eloquently explains this point:

> States cannot be made to work from the outside. International assistance may be necessary but it is never sufficient to establish institutions that are legitimate and sustainable . . . international action should be seen first and foremost as facilitating local processes, providing resources and creating the space for local actors to start a conversation that will define and consolidate their polity by mediating their vision of a good life into responsive, robust and resilient institutions. (Chesterman et al. 2005, ii)

Conclusion

The stabilization approach is in many ways an extension of efforts to set international interventions within a more coherent political framework, while also being a direct product of frustration with the short-term nature of essentially humanitarian interventions to complex emergencies and conflict environments. However, the stabilization discourse overlaps with a number of similar approaches including the UNDP-led "Early Recovery Agenda" and significant elements of the "community driven reconstruction" (CDR) approach pioneered by the World Bank, USAID, and the International Rescue Committee (IRC). Such overlaps offer both opportunities and challenges for the governance and delivery of stabilization—and for its relationship with humanitarian action and counter-insurgency strategies.

However, the linkages between the various models of "early recovery," stabilization, and humanitarian action threaten to blur further the boundaries between the humanitarian and stabilization discourses. There are also significant challenges in terms of the ambitious nature of the stabilization discourse itself. The approach in Helmand has been one of using projects to stimulate broader political engagements between the Helmandis and their provincial leadership. However, weak gubernatorial leadership between 2006 and 2008, shortages of UK civilian staff, and the rapid six-month rotation of both military and civilian elements has created a situation in which stabilization planners lacked a sufficiently detailed knowledge of Helmand's political and tribal dynamics to support the legitimization of the Helmandi authorities, at least for the first two years of the British involvement. In such a context the challenge has been for stabilization programs to retain their connection to a political settlement between a government and their citizenship. Perhaps the greatest threat arising from this is that the overwhelming imperative for outsiders to support the legitimization of a government, and the profound difficulties inherent in doing this, will lead to even greater pressures to misuse humanitarian assistance.

Notes

1. See, for example, *The International Response to Conflict and Genocide: Lessons from the Rwanda Experience,* Steering Committee of the Joint Evaluation of Emergency Assistance to Rwanda, March 1996, available on the reliefweb website.

2. The EBA is defined as "The way of thinking and specific processes that, together, enable the integration and effectiveness of the military

contribution within a Comprehensive Approach." Joint Doctrine Note 1/05 *The Effects Based Approach* (MOD internal document).

3. "Dunantism" (named after the Swiss philanthropist and cofounder of the Red Cross movement Henri Dunant) refers to the principles enshrined in the Red Cross code of conduct and referring to a limited vision of impartial, independent, and neutral humanitarian assistance that is largely based on responding to emergency needs.

4. Nicholas Leader and Peter Colenso argue that in "1999–2001, donors on the DAC allocated about $5.5bn a year to humanitarian aid, around 10% of ODA. If others sources are included, such as money from western publics to NGOs and aid to post-conflict peace activities, the figure doubles to 10bn. Global humanitarian aid has grown, both in overall terms and as a share of aid." See Leader and Colenso (2005, 39).

5. The term "counter-insurgency" refers to the armed suppression of a rebellion coupled with tactics that seek to break the link between the insurgents and the population that they claim to represent—often described as "hearts and minds."

6. Prior to the 2007 assault on the town of Musa Qaleh, the UK military established a "Military Stabilisation Support Team" comprising CIMIC and engineers staff to deliver a stabilization plan largely formulated by the civilian stabilization advisers. The perceived success of this model led to smaller teams, subordinated to Stabilisation Advisers, being established in each of the major Districts in which UK troops were deployed in Helmand.

7. This argument owes much to the seminal work of Barnett Rubin (2002) and others (Saikal 2006, Maley 2006)

8

COUNTER-TERRORISM POLICY POST-9/11 AND THE SELECTIVE IMPACT ON CIVIL SOCIETY: THE CASE OF INDIA

Jude Howell

In late November 2008, gunmen entered Mumbai by boat to launch a spectacular terrorist attack on symbolically significant sites in India. They went on to hold hostages for several days in the internationally renowned Taj Hotel, which is frequented by international visitors and India's prosperous elites. Parallel to this, hostages were taken at the Nariman House Jewish Centre in Mumbai; customers in a coffee shop near the Taj Hotel were randomly fired upon; and a hospital and local market were also attacked. The choice of these locations and the language used by the terrorists to justify their actions—such as discrimination against Muslims in India, anti-Jewish statements and the conflict in Kashmir—pointed to the increasing circulation of global jihadist discourses across the globe and its interweaving with local grievances and tensions. These were not the first terrorist attacks in India. However, they were significant in that they launched India onto the international stage as a victim of global jihadi terrorism, along with Madrid, New York, London, Nairobi, and Dar es Salaam, thereby drawing India deeper into the politics of the War on Terror.

This chapter examines the effects of the War on Terror regime on counter-terrorism and civil society in India. It begins by analyzing the politics of counter-terrorist legislation in India, particularly since the launch of the global War on Terror regime in 2001. It highlights the role of right-wing Hindu nationalist forces in constructing Muslims and Islam as associated with terrorism and promoting the introduction of repressive counter-terrorist measures. In the second section it explores the effects of this political manipulation of the War on Terror discourse on civil society. The chapter argues that, although civil society in general has not been subject to widespread repression as a result of various counter-terrorist measures, parts of civil society have been selectively affected. In particular Muslims, marginalized groups, and oppositional movements have become discursively associated with terrorism and subjected to the blunt edge of counter-terrorist practices. The final section assesses the responses of different civil society actors to the selective effects of counter-terrorist practices.[1]

Politics of Counter-terrorism Post-9/11

The Mumbai bombings of late November 2008 catapulted India onto the international stage of victimhood from global jihadist terrorist networks. Terrorism in India was no longer framed as a purely domestic issue that Western governments could conveniently overlook. With the taking of Western hostages at the Taj Hotel and the killing of a Jewish priest at the Jewish community centre, the US and UK governments became acutely aware that terrorism in India also threatened their national security interests. Moreover, with a group calling itself the Indian Mujahideen claiming responsibility for some of the attacks in Jaipur, Ahmedabad, New Delhi, and other cities in 2007 and 2008, the Indian government became increasingly concerned about homegrown Islamic extremists linking domestic grievances to global jihadist agendas. UK and US government officials rushed to India in the aftermath of the Mumbai attacks, offering advice and expertise on counter-terrorist policy and practice. As former US Secretary of State Condoleezza Rice commented in New Delhi on December 3, 2008, "Everybody needs help . . . The very nature of this terrorist threat is that it crosses borders . . . India and the United States have been cooperating . . . but we're going to do it in a more intensive and urgent manner."[2]

However, terrorism and counter-terrorist measures in India are not new. India's first anti-terror law, the Terrorist and Disruptive Activities (Prevention) Act (TADA), was passed in 1985 upon the assassination of former Prime Minister Indira Gandhi by her Sikh bodyguard and was used to crack down on Sikh militancy in the Punjab (Singh 2004, 149). Previously the Indian government used special military powers granted under the 1958 Armed Forces (Special) Powers Act to curb the secessionist struggles in Kashmir and the Northeast. TADA was renewed again in 1987 and thereafter every two years. The provisions of the law were effectively diluted over time through court rulings. Following reports that TADA was being used selectively against particular social groups, such as workers in Gujarat, farmers' movements, and Muslims during outbreaks of communal violence, the law was allowed to lapse in 1995. There was then a legal hiatus between 1995 and 2000 when no specific anti-terrorist law was in place.

The US and UK governments viewed alleged acts of terrorism in India as matters for domestic concern. They were not viewed as impinging significantly upon the security of the West, except when they threatened to destabilize relations between India and Pakistan, both nuclear-armed states. Moreover, since Independence in 1947 the Indian government has viewed the three main threats to be the conflict in Kashmir, secessionist movements in the Northeast of India, and the Maoist-inspired Naxalite movement. The latter started in 1967 and has increasingly enveloped vast swathes of the country. Indeed, in November 2008, only days before the bombings in Mumbai, the Prime Minister Manmohan Singh stated in a conference of Directors and Inspectors General of Police that left-wing extremism posed "perhaps the most serious internal security threat" to India.[3]

With the election of a Bharatiya Janata Party (BJP)-led government in 1999, political pressure increased for the introduction of a new anti-terror law, despite concerns among some legislative assembly members that such laws more often than not targeted minority and vulnerable groups. Indeed, in his comprehensive analysis of recent counter-terrorist legislation in India, Ujaawala Singh notes how the Law Commission's 173rd Report omitted to mention threats from Hindu fundamentalists such as the Shiv Sena in its analysis of threats within the country (Singh 2004, 150). The 9/11 attacks and the media attention that accompanied this created a climate of concern around jihadist terrorism that right-wing Hindu nationalists were quick to exploit.

The subsequent attack on the Kashmir Assembly in November 2001 and the bombing of India's parliament a month later further fuelled the debate on terrorism. The BJP artfully manipulated these events to argue for stricter counter-terrorist measures. In this way they pushed through the Prevention of Terrorism Ordinance (POTO), which many interpreted as a crackdown on Islamic militants, although the official rationale made no such specific reference (Singh 2004, 150).[4] Subsequent debates in parliament on the need for a bill on terrorism were peppered with references to a global fight against terrorism and the presumed role of Pakistan in hosting and supporting militant groups that threaten India's security. Following the adjournment of Parliament after the December attacks, a second ordinance on the prevention of terrorism was promulgated. Parliamentary and presidential approval for a bill on terrorism was then given in March 2002, when the Prevention of Terrorism Act (POTA) became law.

Part of the BJP strategy for pushing through the POTA was to construct Muslims in India as linked to global jihadist terrorism. Since the launch of the War on Terror, the BJP has built upon a background of communal unrest stretching back to the riots in Ahmedabad in the late 1960s to fuel suspicion of Muslims, to attribute violent incidents to Muslim groups, and to link Muslims to global jihadism. By communalizing the police force and other government institutions, especially in Mumbai and Gujarat, the BJP and related right-wing Hindu forces have been able to perpetuate this discourse and give it literally greater force through the coercive apparatus of the state.

The BJP and the Rashtriya Swayamsevak Sangh (RSS)[5] have played a key role in constructing and promoting an image of Muslims as would-be terrorists. They have deliberately fostered an image of Muslims in India as disloyal to India, owing allegiance primarily to Pakistan and complicit in allegedly Pakistani-inspired terrorist attacks in India. In the wake of the 9/11 attacks and the influence of a War on Terror discourse that links Islam with terrorism, they have extended this image to include the idea that Muslims in India are linked in to global jihadi networks, thus elevating the "problem" of Indian Muslims to a global level. This is reflected in the language used in the aftermath of the 9/11 attacks and that was deployed after the deaths of 58 train passengers in Godhra, Gujarat in 2002. These poisonous claims have gained traction and legitimized historical prejudices and fear of Muslims, especially among the burgeoning Hindu middle classes. As an employee at the Dalit Foundation commented: "Dalits are a social movement and this is viewed differently to say the Muslims, who can easily be branded as agents of Pakistan or North East India."[6]

Three days after the attack on the Twin Towers in September 2001, the Chief Minister of Gujarat, Narendra Modi, participated in a debate on Star News TV, an Indian news channel, on the provocative topic "Is Islam the Cutting Edge of Terrorism?" In the debate he stated that, "All Muslims are not terrorists but all terrorists are Muslims," a refrain that had appeared in the US and Europe and had now found its way via the global media to India.[7] Modi's statement sought to project the link between terrorism and Muslims beyond India and beyond the India/Pakistan axis into a global context.

The effects of right-wing Hindu nationalists' exploitation of a global discourse linking Muslims to terrorism is vividly demonstrated in the way the BJP manipulated the events of Godhra in February 2002 to unleash formidable attacks upon Muslims in Gujarat. Right-wing Hindu nationalist leaders adeptly shifted the responsibility for the deaths of 58 passengers travelling on the Sabarmati Express in February 2002 to Muslims. The train was carrying a large group of Hindu pilgrims who were returning to Gujarat after having visited the site of the demolished Babri Masjid to demand the construction of a Hindu temple in its place. The BJP-ruled Gujarat government arrested suspects under POTA. The BJP declared this not only to be a terrorist incident, but also one that was linked to

Muslims. The attribution of the Godhra tragedy to "Islamic terrorism" fuelled violence across Gujarat, leading to the deaths of 2,000 Muslims and the displacement of 200,000 Muslims (Varadarajan 2002, 9).

When the United Progressive Alliance government, led by the Congress Party, came to power in September 2004, it made good on a campaign pledge to repeal POTA. However, this did not apply retrospectively, and those detained under the Act continue to be incarcerated, and their cases remained open. Moreover, several of the provisions in POTA exist in other legislation, such as the Armed Forces (Special Powers) Act, the Disturbed Areas Acts applying in the Northeast and Jammu and Kashmir, the Maharashtra Control of Organised Crime Act (MCOCA),[8] and the Unlawful Activities Prevention Act (UAPA 1967, 2004). In 2004, several key amendments were made to UAPA incorporating provisions from POTA. Other loopholes in the law have meant that in practice the state has relinquished very few powers. These amendments thus had the effect of making permanent extraordinary anti-terror provisions in law (People's Union for Democratic Rights 2005a, 8).

In December 2008 in the aftermath of the Mumbai attacks, the lower house of the Indian parliament passed the Unlawful Activities (Prevention) Amendments Bill. It increased the period of detention of suspects from 90 to 180 days. The bill evoked debate around safeguarding constitutional rights, the targeting of Muslims, and the need for new legislation with a multitude of security laws already in place. Though the BJP has been outspoken in calling for harsher counter-terrorist legislation in the wake of the Mumbai bombings, the attempt by Gujarat Chief Minister Modi immediately after the attacks on the Taj Hotel to capitalize politically on events backfired, winning him condemnation in the national media. Nevertheless, there was a strong political imperative to be seen to be taking action, and the bill passed easily. Despite Modi's media blunder, BJP national leaders, such as L.K. Advani, continued their criticisms of the Congress Party for repealing POTA (Lakshmi, 2008). The government emphasized the importance of reforming also the police, criminal law, and the justice system. The communalization of police forces in some states and police handling of the Delhi bomb blasts in September 2008 raised legitimate concerns over whether greater powers could be entrusted to police and judicial forces that had in the past targeted Muslims.[9]

The Effects on Civil Society

Union and state governments have viewed civil society organizations with ambivalence. On the one hand, political leaders and government officials have harbored suspicion of civil society, the most extreme example of this being the crackdown on oppositional groups in the Emergency of 1975–1977. On the other hand, union and state governments have simultaneously adopted an instrumental approach to service-delivery NGOs, encouraging their activities as a cost-efficient way of delivering social policy. The Congress Party adopted this dual-pronged strategy of control and encouragement during most of its periods of rule. In general, though, civil society has not been subject to widespread repression as a result of the global War on Terror regime, or indeed other security objectives.

However, counter-terrorist legislation in India, and the more recent political manipulation of the War on Terror by right-wing Hindu nationalist forces, has affected selective parts of civil society in different parts of the country. In particular Muslims, marginalized groups, and oppositional movements have become discursively associated with terrorism and subjected to the blunt edge of counter-terrorist practices. As the Sachar Committee Report (Sachar et al. 2006, 11), the first specific investigation of the status of Muslims in India,[10] stated: "One aspect of this understanding [the general sense of unease among Muslims] relates to patriotism. They carry a double burden of being labelled as 'anti-national' and as being 'appeased' at the same time . . . Muslims need to prove on a daily basis that they are not 'anti-national' and 'terrorists' . . . In general, Muslims complained that they are constantly looked upon with a great degree of suspicion not only by certain sections of society but also by public institutions and governance structures."

Furthermore, aspects of the War on Terror regime have intersected with state–civil society relations and, in particular, government suspicion of foreign donors and NGOs. This is reflected in the reworking of the Foreign Contributions Act, which is the regulatory framework surrounding NGOs and the contractual arrangements of foreign donors. As an interviewee commented, "The government is worried the [foreign] money could be used for other purposes such as terrorism, anti-nationalist causes. We have asked for proof for such suspicions but we haven't received any. The government says there is a lot of pressure from the UK and USA."[11]

As in other countries, counter-terrorist legislation in India has involved prohibiting groups and movements. As of 2007, 32 organizations have been listed under the Schedule of Terrorist Organisations. Most of these are linked to secessionist causes such as the Khalistan Zindabad Force, the Jammu and Kashmir Islamic Front, or the Manipur People's Liberation Front, to ideological causes such as the Communist Party of India (Marxist-Leninist), or to religious fundamentalism such as the Students Islamic Movement of India (SIMI), Al Qaeda, or Al-Umar-Mujahideen. Agreement to ban a particular organization has also factored in the efforts of the Indian government to build alliances with regard to regimes in neighboring states. At the behest of the Nepalese government, New Delhi banned Akhil Bharatiya Nepali Ekta Samaj (ABNES), a Nepali migrants' welfare organization with no apparent background of involvement in terrorism in India.

This case highlights the partial and political use of the POTO/POTA (Singh 2007, 146–147). However, it is noteworthy that extremist Hindu nationalist groups were not banned under POTA. In response to the ban on SIMI through the POTO in October 2001, the then Madhya Pradesh chief minister, Digvijay Singh, and the Samajawadi Party leader, Mulayam Singh Yadav, in Uttar Pradesh, demanded similar bans for Hindu fundamentalist groups such as Bajrang Dal, Shiv Sena, and the Vishwa Hindu Parishad (VHP) (Singh 2007, 145).

As discussed in the previous section, right-wing Hindu nationalist forces have played a central role in shaping a perception of Indian Muslims as disloyal to India and loyal to Pakistan and as increasingly associated with global jihadi terrorism. This has cast suspicion upon Muslim communities, their leaders, and their organizations, promoting a view that Islam and terrorism are intrinsically related. These suspicions have been greatest in Northeast India along the Bangladesh and Nepal borders, where the union government has investigated several mosques and madrassas (Alam 2004). In Gujarat the communalization of state institutions, including the police, along with years of rule under right-wing Hindu nationalists, have intensified suspicion of Muslims. Indeed it is noteworthy that all those arrested under POTA following the Godhra train fire were Muslims.

Political leaders have also exploited the political opportunity opened up by the War on Terror to relabel oppositional groups and movements as terrorist organizations. Whereas politicians and the media previously referred to secessionist and political movements in the Northeast and groups in areas affected by the Naxalite insurgency as extremist, violent, or radical, since 2001 they have increasingly described these as terrorist organizations. In this way states have been able to justify repressive action against these groups and sought to delegitimize their causes, thereby undermining any popular appeal they might have had.

Due to weak governance systems in the police and judicial system, counter-terrorist legislation in India, such as TADA and POTA, has at times been applied discriminately against certain minorities and political opponents. In Gujarat, Rajasthan, and Jammu and Kashmir, the majority of those arrested under TADA were Muslims, whereas in Jharkhand and Andhra Pradesh tribals and peasants associated with Marxist-Leninist groups were targeted (Singh 2007, 52–53). A fact-finding mission by lawyers and human rights activists in 2003 found there were over 3,200 cases lodged under POTA. Of these, most accused were illiterate, poor, landless, and/or Dalit and adivasis.[12]

A member of the Sachar Committee explained in an interview how this demonization of Muslims had led to feelings of insecurity, stating, "We have had public hearings. The major issues are . . . the problem of security is a key one—in Andhra Pradesh, Jammu and Kashmir, Maharashtra, Gujarat and Uttar Pradesh. In Uttar Pradesh there is apprehension about travelling outside, about whether it will be secure for Muslims to go outside, how people will identify and treat you as a Muslim."[13] In one instance a 16-year-old woman was arrested under POTA in Jharkhand for organizing women in her village around gender issues (Gonsalves 2004, 2). In 2003, over 287 people were detained in Gujarat alone under POTA. Most of these were Muslims who were arrested in the aftermath of the Godhra tragedy. Just under a third of these were charged with conspiracy to commit a terrorist act rather than any specific crime (Mander 2004). Thus counter-terrorist legislation was being used selectively and politically against particular communities, which had become suspect because militant groups had formed around their grievances.

The vague definition of terrorist activities under POTA had enabled states such as Tamil Nadu, Gujarat, and Uttar Pradesh to apply the legislation widely to a range of activities and people, who were then labeled as terrorists or antinational (People's Union for Democratic Rights 2005a, 1). In both Tamil Nadu and Uttar Pradesh the incumbent governments invoked POTA against leading political critics and opponents.[14] In Tamil Nadu the Chief Minister Jayalalitha ordered the arrest of a political adversary, the MDMK[15] leader, Vaiko, for making a speech in support of Tamil nationalism in Sri Lanka and the banned Liberation Tigers of Tamil Eelam (LTTE).[16] In Uttar Pradesh, the state government and police were alleged to have misused security legislation and criminal codes to quell resistance to mining operations after coming under pressure by the World Bank and mining companies.[17] Furthermore, in December 2005 the BJP-dominated Chhattisgarh state assembly passed its own Special Public Safety Act, which widened the net of civil society groups vulnerable to accusation of being "unlawful" or engaging in "terrorist" activities beyond the ban on Naxal groups that already existed under the UAPA 2004 (Singh 2007, 310).

Compared to the recurrent circulation of a political and public discourse linking Muslims to terrorism, only scant attention has been accorded to the perpetration of violence and terrorist acts by right-wing groups. As a well-known scholar based in Gujarat commented, "What Hindu organizations do is not called terrorism, but if it is Muslims, then it is terrorism."[18] According to some reports, right-wing Hindu groups linked to the Bajrang Dal and RSS were implicated in attacks on mosques in Parbhani in 2006, in Purna and Jalna in 2003, and in the bombings in Malegaon, Maharashtra in 2006 and 2008 (Swami and Katakam 2006; Shapoo 2008). Chief Hemand Karkare, head of the Anti-Terrorist Squad in Maharashtra, had reportedly uncovered evidence implicating Hindu nationalist groups in the Malegaon attacks. Following his death in the Mumbai terrorist attacks in November 2008, the Indian media reported that his death was the work of the RSS, VHP, and Bajrang Dal in revenge for his unearthing of right-wing Hindu terrorist activities.[19]

Although specific actors in Indian civil society have been targeted under anti-terror provisions in law, generally counter-terrorism responses have had a minimal impact on relations between the union state and the charitable and welfare-oriented part of civil society, referred to variously as the "voluntary sector," "social action groups," "people's organizations," or "NGOs." This sector has grown substantially since the mid-1970s. By 2000 there were estimated to be over 1.2 million NGOs in India, only half of which were registered (Bal 2006, 17).[20] Of these an estimated 85 percent are "one-man NGOs," raising doubts about the transparency and accountability of NGOs in general.[21] According to the umbrella organization Voluntary Action Network India, the majority of registered organizations are religious in nature.[22]

As mentioned earlier civil servants, political parties, and central and state governments have approached civil society with both caution as well as encouragement. Whereas the BJP-led National Democratic Alliance government was suspicious of foreign-funded organizations, the Congress-led coalition government that took over in 2004 has fostered a more favorable environment for the voluntary sector. In this spirit the National Planning Commission, the agency responsible for coordinating government relations with voluntary organizations, drafted a new policy framework to govern registered organizations.[23] Broader global concerns around the transparency and accountability of NGOs as well as specific global discourses around links between charities and terrorism have provided a backdrop to these initiatives. For example, a European diplomat we interviewed commented:

> Our position is that the FCRA/FCMC [Foreign Contributions (Regulation) Act/ Foreign Contribution (Management and Control) Bill] is a good thing because civil society has to be accountable. There are more than one million NGOs and many are pocketing funds. Funding is going through right-wing Hindutva groups and then being used to persecute minorities. UK money went to earthquake relief and schools

but funds were used to persecute religious minorities . . . We
have a lot to do with NGOs because of our programme and
project funds. We are disappointed with NGOs here. It is too
territorial and self-interested. It is charismatic individuals and
all about money.[24]

The Indian government has introduced new anti-money laundering
legislation that includes new due diligence requirements relevant to NGOs.

The government's draft proposal in 2005/2006 for a new Foreign
Contribution (Management and Control) Bill reflected, inter alia, anxiety
about the abuse of charities by terrorist groups as well as long-standing
suspicions about external funding of oppositional groups. One interviewee
from the donor community suggested that the Indian government has used
the threat of terrorism to restrict foreign contributions to NGOs.[25]
Through skillful negotiation representatives of the voluntary sector were
able to persuade the government to remove the word "control" from the
proposed bill.

Debates around this bill reflect differences in perspective within
government toward the voluntary sector. While the National Planning
Commission under Congress governments has sought a more conciliatory
and instrumental approach to NGOs, government officials within the
Ministry of Home Affairs (MOHA), which is responsible for security and
for the FCRA Act and amendments to it, continue to analyze the world
through the lens of the Cold War. They view foreign-funded NGOs with
suspicion, either as pawns of external governments seeking to lever influence over internal politics or as terrorist front groups.[26] An interviewee in
an umbrella NGO commented, "They [MOHA] will say that NGOs are
getting foreign money and they will accuse NGOs of supporting terrorism."[27] Similarly a diplomat commented on government suspicion of
NGOs: "There is still a Cold War mentality here and a suspicion that
NGOs are the enemy within. Foreign funding is under suspicion . . . Cold
War horses here are very concerned about NGOs being used as conduits
for foreign influence and that some are terrorist fronts . . . The Cold War
mentality is seen in the Ministry of Home Affairs."[28] Negotiation between
the government and NGOs over the proposed Foreign Contributions
(Management and Control) Bill thus invoked concerns from the security-
related institutions about the purposes of foreign-funded NGOs. The
global War on Terror regime was no doubt one of several contextual
factors shadowing these negotiations.

Compared to contexts such as Afghanistan, Palestine, or Kenya, the
War on Terror regime has not led to significant changes in how donor
agencies have engaged with civil society in India. Nonetheless, to a limited

extent, post-9/11 security concerns have seeped into donor engagement with civil society in India. This is apparent, for instance, in efforts to cultivate new engagement with Muslim communities and madrassas, as USAID has done.[29] It is also apparent in how DFID officials have used the discourses of the War on Terror to promote agendas of social inclusion. As a DFID official commented, "We need to use the space that security creates regarding its links with social exclusion and conflict . . . We have been successful in pushing social exclusion because of the security issue. Here in India we should push for more evidence and analysis of social exclusion and deprivation . . . So security can be a useful stick and it can work both ways. You can use it opportunistically."[30] Also indicative of the growing interest in Muslim communities is the UK government's courting of Muslim groups in India. For example, representatives from Jamiat Ulama-I-Hind in New Delhi were invited to participate in a dialogue with municipal heads in the United Kingdom and Whitehall officials on the issue of community cohesion.[31]

Apart from these advances toward Muslim communities in India, the effects of the War on Terror regime have also filtered into contractual arrangements between donors and local civil society organizations. According to an interviewee from an international NGO, it came under pressure from DFID to introduce partnership agreements with organizations it worked with locally. These agreements required the partners to state that they were not involved in any terrorist activities.[32] They also received a document and training from headquarters on money-laundering so as to ensure that grants were not misused. Similarly, international foundations such as Ford have introduced new anti-terror clauses into their standard grant agreement letters. As elsewhere, the inclusion of these new clauses has raised eyebrows among Indian civil society groups, some of whom have voiced their opposition. Only one Indian NGO has refused to sign a Ford Foundation grant letter of agreement because of the anti-terrorism clause (Sidel 2008, 18), though it later withdrew this refusal after reassurances from Ford.[33] Apart from this new clause, Ford has not otherwise fundamentally reoriented its engagement with civil society in India for security objectives.

Responses of Civil Society

Observers of Indian civil society often describe it as diverse, active, and vibrant, reflecting India's pluralistic and relatively mature democracy. We might then expect civil society actors to challenge counter-terrorist measures that impinge on their work and to defend the spaces of civil society. Such an assumption has to be balanced, however, against the fact that civil society in India is deeply divided, contested, and fragmented, reflecting the sharp and complex divisions along communal, class, caste, and regional lines. One interviewee commented: "There is a vibrant civil society but it is riven by political factionalism."[34]

Since the early 1980s civil society was becoming the theatre of communalist politics, and in particular the rise of various Hindu nationalist groups such as the RSS. They have deliberately sought to further complicate caste and religious politics by mobilizing tribals and Dalits as a tactic to undermine the work of Christian missionaries in tribal areas (Sabrang Communications Private Limited 2002, 70–73). As discussed earlier these groups have fomented hatred of Muslims and drawn on funding and support from nonresident Indians in the United Kingdom and United States to promote Hindu nationalist ideology (Sabrang Communications Private Limited 2002, 70–73). However, greater global interconnectedness has also opened up possibilities for subaltern groups to organize. New Dalit groups such as the Dalit Foundation in Delhi, Dashara in Bihar, and Apna theatre group have drawn attention to the lack of Dalits in leadership positions in voluntary-sector organizations in India.[35]

Apart from these social divisions, the nature of regional state–civil society relations varies considerably, affecting not only the scope in general for social action, policy influence, and negotiation, but also responses to counter-terrorist initiatives at both the union and state levels. In Northeast India and Kashmir, for example, union state repression of secessionist groups and movements has in turn constrained the spaces for collective action. Compared to other parts of the country, NGO activity in the Northeast and Kashmir is relatively limited. As the head of a peace-building group explained to us: "A lot of people feel scared to work in Kashmir. The politics are so complex that you tend to keep away . . . The secular democratic space in Kashmir is almost zero."[36] Similarly, with reference to the Northeast, the head of a foundation in New Delhi commented, "The insurgents do not welcome NGOs. They might welcome civil society but they have their own idea of how this should be. In the North East NGOs have neither the confidence of the state nor of the militants."[37] The constraints on central government intervening through the armed forces or police in state affairs facilitated the anti-Muslim riots of 2002 in Gujarat. Moreover, judicial wrangling over the respective authority of the Supreme Court and local courts (in the case of POTA in Tamil Nadu, for example) highlight the fragmented and contested nature of union-state relations, which in turn make civil society advocacy and the sources of redress to which civil society can appeal much harder to navigate.

There are also significant tensions between people's movements and the more formally organized NGOs that have proliferated from the mid-1970s onward. For example by the early 1980s the Indian left was castigating externally funded NGOs as "agents of imperialism," so that civic groups seeking popular legitimacy distanced themselves from the label of NGO (Jenkins 2007a, 64–65). Though the movement-NGO dichotomy continues to prevail rhetorically, in practice, since the mid-1990s, increasing linkages across civil society such as occurred at the World Social Forum in Mumbai in 2004 have blurred boundaries between NGOs and movements (Jenkins 2007b, 20–26; Chandhoke 2003).

Given, then, the highly diverse, differentiated, and fractious landscape of civil society in India, it is instructive to explore how different civil society actors have responded to counter-terrorism measures, practices, and discourses. In India, as in other political contexts such as Kenya, the United Kingdom, and the United States (Howell and Lind 2009), human rights organizations, lawyers, and individual activists have led opposition to counter-terrorism practices and advocated for the rights of terror suspects. Human rights lawyers who sought to defend terror suspects have been labeled by politicians and the media as sympathizing with terrorists. For example, a Supreme Court lawyer who has defended people accused under POTA of terrorism was contacted by the media after the bombings in Delhi in October 2005 and accused of being responsible for terrorism. She explained, "The papers rang me and said I was responsible for the bombings because I opposed legislation like POTA, and this encourages terrorists."[38] Similarly, a human rights activist who participated in the Independent Citizens' Initiative on Chattisgarh, an area increasingly occupied by Naxalites, complained that the government suspected them of supporting the Naxalites.[39]

The People's Union for Democratic Rights (PUDR) and the Human Rights Law Network have documented the arrest and interrogation of suspects under anti-terror provisions in law, highlighting the tendency for poor and marginalized groups to be detained without trial for long periods despite a lack of evidence (PUDR 2005a and b). In one case, Syed Abdul Rahman Geelani, a lecturer from the University of Delhi and an activist on Kashmir, was arrested for planning the attack on the Indian parliament in December 2001. He was repeatedly tortured during his imprisonment before being released after several years. His co-accused is still detained, and Geelani requires constant protection.[40]

Formally registered, service-delivery-type voluntary organizations have generally been silent on the state's counter-terrorism responses, including on issues of public debate such as the targeting of Muslims and the government's security cooperation with the United States. Two features of the Indian voluntary sector help to explain their failure to speak out. First, some NGOs are masked, profit-making ventures by individuals and do not aspire to work on issues of social justice. Second, many mainstream, service-delivery-type organizations depend on donors or the Indian government for funding to provide welfare. As Sheth and Sethi (1991) explain, they have become "instrumental appendages" of the state. Intense competition for funds means that many groups are reluctant to stake a position on political issues and have lost sight of the larger political picture.

The political blindness of many Indian civil society groups is apparent in other areas. For example, developmental and welfare NGOs have not taken up the social exclusion of Dalits. Instead, these issues have been addressed mainly by human rights groups, as well as more recently established Dalit rights organizations.[41] The depoliticized nature of mainstream civil society in India is also evident in their lack of engagement and work in conflict areas such as Kashmir and the Northeast. Despite the mission statements and rhetorical claims of many voluntary sector agencies, it is as though poverty and development in these "difficult" parts of India are somehow irrelevant. As one interviewee in an international NGO commented, "There is a culture of silence around these issues [the Naxals and Jammu/Kashmir]. The media reports on attacks but no one debates this. There is an insurgency in Jammu/Kashmir and this is seen as a Jammu/Kashmir issue and nothing to do with general society or developmental NGOs."[42] One of the few organizations to work in conflict areas such as Jammu/Kashmir is the Aman Trust, which funds local groups to provide trauma counseling and health care for orphans.[43]

The depoliticization of parts of Indian civil society has had clear implications for the protection and promotion of the human rights of disadvantaged groups, and particularly when they become subject to counter-terrorist initiatives and abusive police action. This was poignantly revealed in the weak response of voluntary sector agencies to the conflagration of violence in Gujarat in 2002, particularly compared to their responses to the devastating earthquake in Kucch (also in Gujarat) in 2001. The head of a human rights group in Ahmedabad, the state capital, argued, "It is interesting to compare the poor response (of civil society) to the violence and the earthquake response, which was exemplary. There was violence on a huge scale and massive displacement. You see the number of groups that were providing relief in response to the violence dwindling to 10 or 12. It was such a contrast with the earthquake response. During the earthquake there were civil society organizations fighting one another to deliver aid."[44]

Similarly, the former head of an international NGO lamented the voluntary sector's inertia, not only on the part of the Gandhian organizations but also cooperatives and self-help associations. In his words, "There were silences by civil society on the violence in Gujarat."[45] The Gujarat state government, which itself was implicated in orchestrating the anti-Muslim attacks, provided little relief or rehabilitation for Muslim victims. Moreover, very few civil society organizations offered assistance leaving the bulk of the response to Muslim religious trusts and organizations— such as the Islamiya Relief Committee (Luce, 2007, 161–62), the Indian Muslims Relief Charities,[46] the Jamiat Ulema-i-Hind, and Jamiat Islami— and to Muslim-dominated panchayats.[47] A well-known human rights activist stated, "There were no international NGOs there (responding to the violence) . . . It was not only the government that abdicated its responsibility (to protect). Civil society did so, as well."[48]

There were some smaller initiatives led by non-Muslim organizations as well as by human rights and social justice organizations. For example, two months after the violence, the Society for the Promotion of Rational Thinking, along with Action Aid, Citizen's Initiative, Janpath, and the Gujarat Sarvajanik Relief Committee, organized the Sah Nirman rally in Ahmedabad. Over 3,000 victims of the violence walked for five kilometers as a moving, multimedia installation paying tribute to the victims of the riots (*Hindustan Times,* 13 September 2002, reprinted in Varadarajan 2002, 352–355). The Citizen's Initiative brought together a number of local, national, and international groups under an umbrella to distribute food and grains in relief camps that were mainly serviced by Muslim organizations.[49] The Jesuit-run St. Xavier's Social Services Centre, the inter-faith Gujarat Sarvajanik, secular groups such as Samerth, Janvikas, ANHAD, Sanchetna, and individual secular activists were particularly active in providing relief. Since then, organizations such as ANHAD and Action Aid have been active in peacebuilding work, organizing conventions for Dalits and Muslims and camps for young people to counter right-wing ideology.[50]

At the national level journalists, social and political activists, NGOs, lawyers, human rights groups, and students widely condemned the state-led pogrom in Gujarat. As Nussbaum (2007, 31) explains, many individuals horrified at the events of 2002 flocked into Gujarat to organize relief work and to document the deaths, attacks, and rapes and disseminate their findings on the internet. One of the most detailed records was provided by the Concerned Citizens' Tribunal, which was organized by Teesta Setalvad from Maharashtra state. Setalvad also played a key role in the legal NGO "Communalism Combat" and was pivotal in seeking justice for the victims in the Best Bakery Case, in which over 20 Muslims were killed during the attacks in March 2002. However, BJP politicians allegedly pressured the key witness to renounce her statement, and Chief

Minister of Gujarat, Narendra Modi, called for public scrutiny of NGOs (Nussbaum 2007, 40).

Several factors account for the failure of voluntary sector agencies, development-oriented NGOs, and trades unions in Gujarat to speak out against the anti-Muslim violence. First is the dependency of many civil society organizations in the state on government contracts. This would also explain the extraordinary growth of the voluntary sector in Gujarat in recent decades, which otherwise would attest to the strength of civil society. A human rights official commented, "Civil society is growing on state largesse to provide services, not because of a record of protest and providing alternatives."[51] The head of an organization that worked in the relief camps added to this view, "Many mainstream NGOs did not want to be part of it (the relief response) because they are running huge government schemes . . . You can count on your fingers the number of people who looked at the issue, openly petitioned and submitted court cases. Only maybe 30 out of thousands of NGOs in Gujarat spoke out. Some refused to respond."[52] A second and related factor was that, as is true of mainstream civil society groups elsewhere in India, voluntary sector and service-delivery type organizations in Gujarat were blind to processes of marginalization and exclusion affecting Muslims. They focused on poverty alleviation and delivering welfare to the poor without appreciating the exclusionary processes and power relations that were producing peoples' social exclusion.

A third factor was the increasing fragmentation and polarization of civil society in Gujarat since the 1980s. The loss of jobs in the textile industry following its mechanization was particularly damaging, because the trade unions for textile workers previously brought together Hindu and Muslim workers. Moreover, textile factory owners were alleged to have fomented Hindu nationalist sentiment to drive a wedge between the workers and break the collective resolve of the workers. The loss of jobs and diminishing power of the unions saw the rise of Hindu nationalists who filled the void. What was also especially painful for the small human rights organizations that did respond to the violence was the silence of the Gandhian groups, who were alleged to have been "saffronized"—in other words, to have come under the influence of Hindu nationalists. Thus, they were less inclined to show support for Muslims and still less so in a context in which Muslims had been linked with terrorism.

Finally, another factor was Chief Minister Modi's intimidation of civil society. He campaigned for chief minister on a populist platform that was anti-Pakistan and against human rights groups. Specifically, his campaign tactics sought to discredit the National Human Rights Commission (NHRC) and civil society. In his campaign literature and advertisements in local newspapers, he posed the questions, "Who is the NHRC for?" and "Who is civil society for?," implying that these were forces pandering to the interests of Muslims. A prominent social justice activist in Gujarat explained, "He spoke about civil society in the language of 'five stars.' The hidden meanings of his rhetoric were that civil society is foreign-funded, that they travel widely and stay in posh hotels. He called them 'pseudo-secular.' Few NGOs challenged him, as many of them depend on the state's largesse."[53] Therefore, the reticence of mainstream NGOs and voluntary welfare-delivery organizations to respond in the aftermath of the violence reflected the nature of these organizations as "instrumental appendages" of the state, as Sheth and Sethi (1991) had observed.

Apart from this general discrediting of NGOs, there are also accounts of intimidation of corporations and NGOs that considered providing relief support. For example, a housing finance corporation in Gujarat was reportedly warned by the BJP that if they gave any support to relief work, their bank branches would be stoned and burned.[54] Similarly, when the National Minorities Commission awarded a Jesuit priest a human rights award, an ally of Chief Minister Modi apparently tried to discredit him by complaining that he was funded by Muslim organizations and only worked with Muslims.[55] Set against this background, it is not surprising that local civil society, and the voluntary sector in particular, has not responded to the effects of abusive police practices, biased judicial processes, and the selective use of counter-terrorist legislation against marginalized groups.

The November 2008 Mumbai attacks stimulated intense public debate on terrorism and how the government should respond and frame its policies with respect to domestic legislation, police reforms, and relations with Pakistan. Human rights groups cautioned against passing any hastily crafted laws and warned against increasing the powers or resources of the police and intelligence agencies when they had failed to win the public trust and proved themselves to be so incompetent in preventing and responding to the attacks. It was also notable that many ad hoc groups emerged to protest policing and administrative incompetence and voice outrage at their politicians. Vigils and protests were held throughout India. Muslims held their own demonstrations against the attacks, with protesters waving placards calling for war on Pakistan. The heads of prominent Muslim organizations, including the Vice-Chancellor of Jamia Millia Islamia, the All-India Babri Masjid Reconstruction Committee, and the Shahi Imam of Jama Masjid in Delhi, condemned the attacks as "un-Islamic" (Dash 2008; Raha 2008). Jamiat Ulama-I-Hind, along with secular groups, organized a peace march in 12 cities that had been sites of terrorist violence in 2008 (Raha 2008). However, when Jamia Millia Islamia, a government-funded public university, established a fund to provide legal assistance to two of its students who were arrested in the September 2008 Batla House police raid in Delhi, BJP politicians accused the university of using public funds to support terrorism, thus once more trying to link Indian Muslims with global jihad.[56] Some Muslim commentators have lamented the way that some Muslim leaders have felt compelled to publicly denounce the Mumbai attacks, as they perceive such public denunciations to reinforce the idea of Muslims as a separate and suspect population.[57]

Conclusion

This chapter examined the intersection of the War on Terror regime with domestic politics and its effects on counter-terrorism and civil society in India. Against a background of rising communalism, right-wing Hindu nationalist forces have adroitly constructed an image of Muslims and Islam as a suspect, disloyal minority community associated with terrorism and Pakistan. Following the launch of President Bush's War on Terror and the subsequent attacks—first on the Kashmir assembly and then on Parliament in Delhi—BJP leaders wove the language of the War on Terror that linked Islam with terrorism into its own domestic cloth of anti-Muslim rhetoric. In this way they linked Muslims and Islam in India with broader, global jihadi discourses and networks.

The terrorist attacks in Mumbai in late November 2008 catapulted India onto the stage of international victimhood by fundamentalist Islamic groups. This reopened a debate about the tightening of counter-terrorist measures and an overhaul of the police and criminal justice system. Though BJP leaders tried to capitalize on events to call for a resurrection of specific counter-terrorist legislation, the Congress-led UPA government has so far resisted any hasty attempt to reinstate the POTA. Nevertheless, many aspects of the POTA that had been repealed by the UPA were in any case already incorporated into other legislation and measures.

Counter-terrorist legislation, measures, and practices in India have in general not led to a major crackdown on the spaces and activities of civil society in India. However, their effects have been partial and selective, targeting in particular minority communities and vulnerable groups. Muslims, Dalits, tribals, and poor farmers have been particularly affected. Despite India having a diverse and vibrant civil society, responses to restrictive legislation and practices have been complex and differentiated. Resistance to counter-terrorism measures and their effects on minorities and vulnerable groups has come primarily from human rights groups. Though groups across India denounced the violence against Muslims in Gujarat in 2002 and assisted with relief and documentation of the attacks, only a handful of civil society organizations in Gujarat publicly challenged the attacks or assisted later with relief work.

Furthermore, mainstream civil society in general has been remarkably detached and silent about the effects of restrictive legislation on civil society spaces and groups in areas of conflict in India, such as the Northeast and Jammu/Kashmir. The silence of mainstream civil society in the face of restrictive and abusive security legislation and judicial practices, and the impact on minority groups, including Muslims, relates not only to the fractious and divided nature of civil society in India but also to the growing dependence of mainstream, voluntary-sector organizations on government grants. This, as in other contexts, has led to a disarming depoliticization of parts of civil society.

Notes

1. This chapter draws on field research in India carried out between 2006 and 2008. In all, over 58 interviews were conducted in India with key informants in bilateral and multilateral aid agencies, human rights networks, developmental NGOs, and voluntary sector groups, as well as with relevant civil government officials, journalists, Muslim leaders, members of the Sachar Committee report, and academics. I also jointly organized a roundtable on this theme with the Voluntary Action Network of India (VANI) in December 2006, involving government policymakers, NGOs, foundations, academics, and community leaders. I am grateful to the Economic Social Research Council Non-Governmental Public Action program for funding this research. I am also grateful to Nadia Burza for initial research assistance and to Chris Pallas for later documentary research assistance.

2. US Department of State. "Remarks with Indian Minister of External Affairs Pranab Mukherjee." New Delhi. December 3, 2008. Available at: www.state.gov/secretary/rm//2008/12/112622. Accessed on March 25, 2009.

3. www.satp.org/satporgtp/countries/india/document/papers/ pmspeechnnov08.htm. Accessed on March 25, 2009.

4. As Singh (2004, 150) points out, it is noteworthy how the POTO/POTA, unlike the TADA, does not refer to "threatening harmony between communities" as an act of terror, suggesting that the POTO/POTA legislation is cast within a Hindu nationalist framework that effectively links Muslims to terrorism.

5. As Varadarajan (2002, 3) explains, the RSS serves as an umbrella organization linking the BJP to more violent, right-wing Hindu elements such as the VHP and Bajrang Dal.

6. Author's interview with Dalit Foundation. Delhi. December 6, 2006.

7. Varadarajan (2002, 7) and author's interview. Siddharth Varadarajan. Delhi. December 4, 2006.

8. The MCOCA has been applied in Maharashtra since 1999 and Delhi since 2002. The Gujarat assembly passed a similar bill in June 2004, which also contained provisions similar to in POTA. So if POTA was repealed, the Gujarat government could, through this law, continue to detain people in the state arrested under POTA (Singh, 2007, 288; 293–5). MCOCA was used in the parliamentary debate on the Prevention of Terrorism Bill in 2002 as a model for the new law, primarily on the basis of its high conviction rate.

9. The police responded swiftly to the blasts, engaging in a dramatic shootout with suspected terrorists in a Muslim neighborhood of Delhi. Two suspects were killed, both students from Jamia Millia Islamia University (Author's interview. Media co-ordinator, Jamia Millia Islamia. Delhi. December 8, 2008). However, the official account given by police was discredited by the press and rights groups and revealed fundamental mistrust of the police forces ("Indians question police response to recent bombings." *The New York Times,* October 3, 2008).

10. The Gopal Singh Committee report of 1983 related to minorities, Muslims, Scheduled Castes, and Scheduled Tribes and other so-called weaker sections of society.

11. Author's interview, VANI, Delhi. May 29, 2006.

12. The term "adivasi" refers to "indigenous people" or "original inhabitants" of India. Of the 5,653 distinct communities in India, 635 are considered to be "tribes" or "adivasis" (Bijoy 2003).

13. Author's interview, Sachar Committee member, January 6, 2006.

14. In Uttar Pradesh the Chief Minister Mayawati invoked POTA against Raja Bhaiyya, an independent Member of the Legislative Assembly and Minister in the BJP-BSP coalition government and his eighty-year-old father, a move that was widely seen as an act of political revenge. Similarly, in Tamil Nadu the Jayalalitha government arrested the MDMK leader Vaiko under POTA (for further details see PUDR 2005b, 7).

15. This is the Marumalarchi Dravida Munnetra Kazhagam Party, which was supportive of the LTTE in Sri Lanka, an organization banned in 1991 under the 1967 UAPA.

16. For further details see PUDR (2005b, 7) and Singh (2007, 222–231).

17. Author's interview with senior human rights activist. New Delhi. December 12, 2005.

18. Author's interview. Achyut Yaagnik. Ahmedabad. December 9, 2006.

19. Times of India. December 7, 2008. Page 2.

20. Author's interview. VANI. New Delhi. May 29, 2006.

21. According to the Income Tax Act, voluntary organisations raise over US$60 billion domestically, with a further US$6 billion coming from government and international agencies. It is noteworthy that the bulk of this funding is channelled to fee-charging hospitals and schools and to religious organizations.

22. Author's interview. VANI. New Delhi. November 28, 2006.

23. There are at least 285 ministries and departments at all levels engaging with NGOs. (Author's interview. VANI. New Delhi. May 29, 2006.)

24. Author's interview. British High Commission. New Delhi. December 6, 2006.

25. Author's interview. DFID official. New Delhi. November 30, 2006.

26. Author's interview. DFID official. New Delhi. November 30, 2006.

27. Author's interview. VANI. New Delhi. May 29, 2006.

28. Author's interview. British High Commission. New Delhi. December 6, 2006.

29. For example USAID's Madrasa Quality Education Program running from 2004 to 2008 in Andhra Pradesh aims, inter alia, to incorporate the state government-approved curricula, raise teaching standards, and conduct employment training.

30. Author's interview. DFID. New Delhi. November 30, 2006.

31. Author's interview. Jamiat Ulama-I-Hind. New Delhi. December 13, 2006.

32. Author's interview. International NGO. New Delhi. November 28, 2006.

33. Author's interview. Ford Foundation. New Delhi. December 2008.

34. Author's interview. Aman Trust. New Delhi. December 4, 2006.

35. Author's interview. Dalit Foundation. New Delhi. December 6, 2006.

36. Author's interview. ANHAD. New Delhi. November 29, 2006.

37. Author's interview. National Foundation Institute. New Delhi. December 5, 2006.

38. Author's interview. Supreme Court lawyer. New Delhi. December 13, 2005.

39. Author's interview. Commonwealth Human Rights Initiative. New Delhi. November 28, 2006. Interestingly, the Naxalites also sent a letter to the Independent Citizens' Initiative, complaining that they had accused the Naxalites of violence too.

40. Author's interview. May 27, 2006.

41. It should be noted that Christian Aid has taken a lead in championing the causes of Dalits and adivasis, though in doing so it has to deal with the suspicion that, as a Christian organization, its primary purpose is religious conversion (Author's interviews. DFID. New Delhi. November 2006. Christian Aid. New Delhi. November 28, 2006).

42. Author's interview. CARE UK. New Delhi. May 25, 2006.

43. Author's interview. Aman Trust. New Delhi. December 4, 2006. It also works in Gujarat and on caste violence in Bihar.

44. Author's interview. Janvikas. Ahmedabad. December 8, 2006. For an excellent, textured analysis of the violence in Gujarat and discrimination in earthquake relief, see Simpson (2006, 2008).

45. Author's interview. Centre for Equity Studies. New Delhi. November 30, 2006.

46. Author's interview. ANHAD. Ahmedabad. December 7, 2006.

47. For a detailed account of the failure of Gujarat state to provide adequate relief for those displaced in the riots see Varadarajan (2002, 307–330), which includes a substantial extract from the PUDR "State, Society and Communalism in Gujarat," New Delhi, May 2002. The term "panchayat" refers to village assemblies, which form the basic unit of administration in the Indian governing system.

48. Author's interview. Centre for Equity Studies. New Delhi. November 30, 2006.

49. Author's interview. Samerth. Ahmedabad. December 7, 2006.

50. Author's interviews. Action Aid. Ahmedabad. December 9, 2006. ANHAD. New Delhi. November 2006.

51. Author's interview. Janvikas. Ahmedabad. December 8, 2006.

52. Author's interview. Samerth. Ahmedabad. December 7, 2006.

53. Author's interview. Managing Trustee. Janvikas. Ahmedabad. December 8, 2006.

54. Author's interview. Local NGO. Ahmedabad. December 8, 2006.

55. Author's interview. Jesuit priest. Ahmedabad. December 11, 2006.

56. Author's interview. Jamia Millia Islamia. New Delhi. December 7, 2008.

57. Author's interview. Jamia Millia Islamia. New Delhi. December 7, 2008.

9

CIVIL SOCIETY IN SRI LANKA DURING AND AFTER THE 5TH PEACE PROCESS: CHANGING SPACES FOR ADVOCATING POLITICAL TRANSFORMATIONS AND DELIVERING SOCIAL WELFARE POST-9/11

Kristian Stokke

The post–Cold War period has seen the emergence of a dichotomizing discourse on civil society. Whereas the 1990s were characterized by a strong emphasis on the positive political and developmental contributions of civil society to peacebuilding in intrastate conflicts, the period since the 9/11 attacks in the United States has brought a critical focus on the transnational advocacy work and resource mobilization of civil society associations linked to "terrorist" insurgency movements. Thus a discursive distinction has emerged between "good civil society," associated with the transnational agenda of liberal peacebuilding, and "bad civil society," associated with intrastate and international terrorism. This dichotomization creates a basis for contrasting strategies by state and international actors; instrumental use of "good" civil society for liberal peacebuilding and regulation and repression of "bad" civil society as part of counter-terrorist measures.

These contrasting strategies are well illustrated by the changing policies toward civil society in Sri Lanka's protracted intrastate conflict and the appropriation of global discourses on defeating terrorism by the Sri Lankan government since 2005 to introduce new controls on the spaces for political deliberation and human rights advocacy. Civil society organizations (CSOs), focusing on political advocacy work, and non-governmental organizations (NGOs), involved in humanitarian rehabilitation and development, were instrumentally used in the internationalized attempt at crafting liberal peace during the government of Prime Minister Ranil Wickramasinghe

(2001–2004). These civil society roles in liberal peacebuilding were, however, politicized by the Sinhalese ethnonationalist opposition during the peace process, and civil society associations have been targets for state repression under the government of President Mahinda Rajapakse since 2005. While the former period was marked by a relatively inclusive definition of "good" civil society, when even some Tamil welfare and development organizations associated with the Liberation Tigers of Tamil Eelam (LTTE) received international aid, the latter period has brought authoritarian repression of both Tamil and Sinhalese NGOs and CSOs. Thus, the global War on Terror has added another layer of complexity to the long-running conflict and made it increasingly difficult for advocacy groups to seek an effective political engagement in the conflict while also encumbering the delivery of aid to conflict-affected areas.

This chapter examines the multifaceted and changing politics of civil society during and after Sri Lanka's 5th peace process. Given that the current repression of liberal civil society stems from its assigned functions in the peace process, the chosen point of departure is the role of civil society in peacebuilding (Edwards 2004). The literature on civil society is marked by a distinction between civil society associations engaged in political advocacy and NGOs involved in service delivery. This bifurcation is reflected in Sri Lanka's civil society and the utilization of CSOs to advocate liberal peace and NGOs to deliver humanitarian rehabilitation and neoliberal development during the 5th peace process. This instrumental use of associational life undermined the autonomy of liberal civil society and paved the way for oppositional politicization during the peace process and state repression after the resumption of warfare. The current authoritarian control of civil society is especially hard felt for Tamil welfare organizations that are accused of channeling funds from the Tamil diaspora to the LTTE. However, international humanitarian organizations, as well as Sinhalese and multiethnic CSOs involved in advocacy of liberal rights, democracy, and peace, have also experienced a curtailment in political space. Thus, the global War on Terror has intersected with the conflict in Sri Lanka in such a way as to cast greater suspicion over parts of civil society involved in peacebuilding and promoting democratic rights, while at the same time justifying the Rajapakse government's commitment to defeating the LTTE militarily.

Civil Society in Peacebuilding

The concept of peacebuilding has emerged in the last two decades in the context of the post–Cold War, neoliberal world order. This period has been marked by a certain kind of armed conflict—intrastate and in the global

South, rather than interstate wars at the centre of the world order—with associated geopolitical representations and interventions. In the context of escalating globalization, such "new wars" have been construed as global security threats in Northern geopolitical discourse, thereby providing a rationale for international armed interventions or nonviolent promotion of liberal peace (Duffield 2001; Kaldor 1999; Miall et al. 2005). The latter mode of intervention—nonviolent and cosmopolitan peace promotion—seems to contain two defining characteristics. First, given recent experiences with elite-negotiated transitions to liberal democracy and structural adjustments to neoliberal globalization, it is assumed that liberal peace can be crafted through internationally facilitated elite negotiations (Paris 2004). Second, based on the understanding that underdevelopment constitutes a fertile ground for armed insurgency, it can be observed that international peace promotion includes a strong emphasis on replacing vicious cycles of underdevelopment and armed conflict with virtuous cycles of neoliberal development and liberal peace (Collier et al. 2003). Therefore, conflict resolution through elite negotiations is supported by instrumental and conditional use of humanitarian and development aid (Anderson 1999; Goodhand 2006).

In this situation, with internationalization of conflict resolution and securitization of development aid, a new emphasis on peacebuilding has emerged (Miall et al. 2005). Peacebuilding gained international recognition through the UN Secretary General Boutros-Ghali's *Agenda for Peace* in 1992 (Boutros-Ghali 1992), emphasizing developmental efforts supporting peace. Such peacebuilding was initially conceptualized in a narrow manner as post-conflict reconstruction to consolidate peace and prevent the recurrence of violence after cessation of hostilities, but the term has since been broadened to mean comprehensive conflict transformation before, during, and after a violent conflict. Toward this end, the agenda for peacebuilding was supplemented by the UN *Agenda for Democratization* in 1996 (Boutros-Ghali 1996) and the understanding of democratization as an integral part of peacebuilding was furthered in the *Framework for Cooperation in Peacebuilding* in 2001 (Annan 2001). This means that since its inception in the early 1990s, peacebuilding has come to mean a long-term and comprehensive conflict transformation process aimed at preventing the outbreak, recurrence, or continuation of armed conflicts (Paffenholz and Spurk 2006).

Associated with this shift from a narrow to a broad approach, there has, however, been a tendency for peacebuilding to become vague and all-inclusive, without clear priorities and strategic connections. This has led to calls for a more disaggregate specification of the dimensions of peace-building and a stronger emphasis on the strategic connectivity between the different components of peacebuilding (Smith 2004). Contemporary analyses and practices display a certain convergence around four overarching dimensions of peacebuilding, namely to "enhance public security, generate economic recovery, facilitate social healing, and promote democratic institutions" (Jeong 2005, 12–13). Along the same lines, Smith (2004) points to four broad areas of peacebuilding: (1) to provide security (for example, disarmament, demobilization, and reintegration of combatants; mine clearing; and security sector reforms); (2) to establish the socioeconomic foundations of long-term peace (for example, reconstruction and investments in economic infrastructure, public health, and education; repatriation of displaced people; and reconstruction of livelihoods); (3) to establish the political framework of long-term peace (for example, institutional reforms toward democratization and good governance; development of political parties and civil society associations; legal reforms and strengthened rule of law; and implementation and monitoring of human rights standards); and (4) to generate reconciliation and justice (for example, truth and reconciliation through commissions or other forms of inquiries, and bridge-building activities in the form of dialog between antagonistic groups and through media, education, and cultural events).

Smith argues that this toolkit for peacebuilding may serve as a starting point for strategic policy formulation as well as disaggregate analyses of the roles of civil society actors in peacebuilding. This agenda has been further pursued by recent World Bank studies that identify key functions for civil society in conflict situations (Paffenholz and Spurk 2006, World Bank 2006). Within the field of security, civil society may perform key roles in protecting citizens' lives, freedom, and property as well as monitoring activities of state and nonstate actors in regard to conflicts. Civil society organizations may also contribute toward reconciliation by socializing citizens into norms of tolerance, mutual trust, and peaceful conflict resolution and promote social cohesion by constructing bridging social capital across societal cleavages. In the development field, NGOs and self-help groups are expected to engage in service provisioning. Finally, civil society organizations may also contribute toward political transformations through public communication of interests and intermediation between interest groups and the state.

Apart from the security-oriented functions that are specific to conflict situations, the others correspond to the roles that are emphasized in the general discourse on civil society, namely (1) to generate social capital and inclusion in society; (2) to provide political representation for popular interests and demands; and, (3) to support development through self-help and service provisioning (Edwards 2004). In the Sri Lankan case, where the conflict revolves around questions of self-determination, human rights, and livelihoods for the Tamil minority and the peace process has emphasized humanitarian rehabilitation and development, the use of civil society for peacebuilding has also had a prime focus on development and political transformation rather than security and reconciliation. These are also the civil society roles that will be highlighted in the following discussion.

Civil Society

Civil society has received increased attention in academic literature and international policy making for development and democratization. Coming out of the crises and neoliberal critique of statist ideologies and models—be it Eastern state socialism, Western welfareism or Southern developmentalism—civil society has become an instrument for shrinking the role of the state through a combination of self-help in society and non-governmental service delivery. Civil society is constructed as a "third sector" of voluntary associations that perform developmental roles based on comparative advantages in participatory and cost-effective poverty alleviation. This was the main focus within neoliberal development discourse in the 1980s, in the context of structural adjustment to global economic liberalism. The role for civil society was, however, widened in the 1990s with growing concerns about the quality rather than quantity of state regulation and the emerging focus on good governance. The role of civil society thus came to include a political function of exerting organized pressure on the state and promoting the good governance agenda of improved public sector efficiency, democratic accountability, human rights, and rule of law (Smith 2007). Whereas the developmental role constructs civil society as comprising NGOs, this political watchdog role draws attention to CSOs involved in political advocacy and popular representation. From the latter perspective, civil society is a sphere of associational life that fosters socialization, norms of civility, and tolerance, but focuses first and foremost on the formation and communication of public interests (Edwards 2004). Civil society associations are assumed to produce and empower active citizens, each of whom would not individually have the capacity to exert influence on public officials and transform political institutions or society in a democratic direction.

This means that the interest in the development role of civil society has been supplemented with a renewed interest in the democratic function of civil society. With democratic transitions and the emergence of new social movements in recent years, there has been increased attention to the role of civil society in representing people vis-à-vis the state and government (Carothers 2004; Grugel 2002; Törnquist et al. 2009). Whereas some observers place high hopes on civil society as an alternative to political parties, others raise critical questions about how and to what extent CSOs provide political representation for people and their interests. Belloni (2008, 186), for example, argues that "this ideal vision of civil society must be weighed against the reality of a fragmented, factionalized, and occasionally xenophobic version of civil society" with limited ability to promote social inclusion and political representation. This calls for cautious analyses of the actual role of civil society associations as a mediating link between people and the governing of public affairs (Törnquist 2009).

In general terms, political representation through civil society organizations is preconditioned by the relations between CSOs and the state (that is, the character of the political space and the CSOs' capacity to utilize political opportunities) and between CSOs and the groups they seek to represent (that is, the authorization and accountability of CSOs as people's representatives). Research on democratic transitions and movement politics has demonstrated that the political spaces for CSOs (in terms of formal institutions and political practices) are highly varied even in consolidated democratic regimes (Bastian and Luckham 2003), and that civil society organizations are often under-resourced and fragmented, with limited capacity to unify diverse identities, interests, and strategies and provide effective political representation (Habib et al. 2006; Priyono et al. 2007). It has also been observed that, although civil society organizations claim to be legitimate representatives of popular interests, they often lack a clear and institutionalized mechanism by which people join as members and authorize the leaders (Houtzager and Lavalle 2009).

The implication of this is that it is necessary to examine the political dynamics of state–civil society relations in order to comprehend the manner and extent to which civil society contributes to peacebuilding. Moreover, civil society in the global South is not a straightforward matter of national state-society relations, but is also shaped by international state and civil society actors. Such multi-scale, state–civil society relations frame associational life along a continuum from ideal-typical, service-delivery NGOs to advocacy-focused CSOs. State–civil society relations may also vary from coexistence and collaboration to contention and conflict, as exemplified by Sri Lanka during and after the 5th peace process.

Postcolonial Civil Society in Sri Lanka

The dual face of civil society in theory is reflected in a bifurcation of actually existing civil society in Sri Lanka. There is, on the one hand, a long tradition of political advocacy by civil society organizations that emerged with colonial transformations from the mid-nineteenth century and changed character in the post-colonial context of liberal democracy, authoritarianism, and ethnic conflict. There is also, on the other hand, an almost equally long tradition of voluntary work for social welfare that emerged with Christian missionary activities and Buddhist and Hindu revivalism in the late nineteenth century (Orjuela 2004). More recently, a large number of NGOs have emerged and been involved in delivery of humanitarian relief and social welfare in the context of protracted warfare and neoliberal state retrenchment.

This dual character of civil society—with roles that separate CSOs from NGOs but may often be combined within one and the same organization—is also found in a two-pronged use of civil society for peace-building during Sri Lanka's 5th peace process. Whereas Colombo-based research and advocacy CSOs were supported as contributors to the public discourse on liberal peace, domestic and international NGOs were engaged in delivery of humanitarian rehabilitation and social welfare in war- and tsunami-affected areas. As the peace process became increasingly politicized, CSOs and NGOs came under heavy criticism for their support for the liberal peace agenda, their close links to the international facilitators and donors, and their weak popular basis. In order to comprehend and assess this character, instrumental use, and politicization of civil society it is necessary to historicize the development and transformation of associational life in Sri Lanka.

Civil Society Organizations and Left Politics

Although there is a rich literature on Sri Lanka's political history (Uyangoda 2009), relatively little has been written on the historical making and transformation of civil society. One notable exception is a short but analytical essay written by Uyangoda (2001) that examines the links between civil society activism and Left party politics. His main argument is that the Left parties, especially the Lanka Sama Samaja Party (LSSP) and the Communist Party (CP) that emerged in the 1930s and played a key role in promoting democracy and social welfare, were preconditioned by the existence of a vibrant associational life. Colonial capitalist transformations yielded new class cleavages and mobilization, and Christian missionary activities produced Buddhist and Hindu grievances and revivalism, but colonialism also meant the institutionalization of a public sphere (Orjuela 2004).

This combination of new grievances and a public sphere where they could be articulated gave rise to a broad array of associations that constructed and represented caste and class interest or Buddhist and

Hindu religious identities. Uyangoda thus observes that "the second half of the nineteenth century saw the birth of something that had not previously existed in Sri Lankan society—a mode and space for organization and activity outside the structures defined by the state and the Church, or political and religious authorities. This marked the inauguration of modern associational politics" (2001, 203). These new forms of interest and identity mobilization in the late colonial period served as a basis for radical class politics and conservative ethnonationalist mobilization through political parties in the transition period from colonial rule to independence (1931–1948) and after Independence in 1948 (Stokke 1998).

Uyangoda (2001) emphasizes the key role of colonial civil society in furthering social emancipation through liberal constitutionalism and democracy. This agenda was in stark opposition to the conservative politics of the elite within the Ceylon National Congress. The Left political parties provided a coherent mobilization framework for radical associational politics, combining a strong emphasis on liberal democratic ideals of equality, justice, and rights with an ideological commitment to revolutionary change and socialism. This meant that radical civil society activism was, to some extent, brought into the ambits of the state, especially as the Left parties underwent a strategic reorientation from contesting the state to participating in government and reforming the state. In the former phase the Left parties dismissed bourgeois democracy but nevertheless pushed the state toward democratic and welfare reforms. From the late 1960s the Left parties turned to coalition politics and entered government positions with the Sri Lanka Freedom Party (SLFP), thereafter viewing the state as the supreme agency of social transformation.

Uyangoda describes this as a desertion of relatively autonomous civil society politics and observes that this co-optation of CSOs became detrimental when the state-led development model of the Left was discredited and replaced by economic liberalization in 1977. In the absence of a credible Leftist political model and the loss of radical intellectual leadership in civil society politics, there "emerged in Sinhalese and Tamil societies a tendency towards ethno-nationalist hegemony of counter-state politics" (Uyangoda 2001, 210). The antecedents of this ethno-nationalist hegemony can be found in the aforementioned religious revivalism in the late colonial period, combining advocacy work against missionary activities with religious social voluntarism. In the post-colonial period this formed a basis for elitist incorporation of people into electoral politics through ethnic identity mobilization, first spearheaded by the Sri Lanka Freedom Party but later also utilized by Left parties and the conservative United

National Party (UNP). This created strong—and at times contentious—links between the state and Buddhist associations in civil society, with Buddhist monks playing complex roles as both spiritual leaders and political activists (Frydenlund 2005; Tambiah 1992).

While co-optation of civil society and the demise of Left politics undermined radical associationalism in the 1970s, new civil society formations emerged with economic liberalization, ethnonationalism, authoritarianism, and armed conflict in the 1980s (Orjuela 2004). These new CSOs focused on political issues that were generally ignored by the old Left such as human rights, media freedom, women's rights, and peace. Inspiration was sought in the values embedded in the Declaration of Human Rights and the International Covenant on Civil and Political Rights, thus continuing the pre-existing focus on human rights and democracy among radical CSOs (Committee for Rational Development 1984).

Being generally Colombo-based and operating as professional research institutes and advocacy think-tanks,[1] these new CSOs contributed to the political-intellectual debates but were constrained by the authoritarian control and political violence in the 1980s and early 1990s. With the coming into power of the SLFP-led government of President Chandrika Bandaranaike Kumaratunga on a peace and democracy mandate in 1994, these human rights- and democracy-oriented CSOs and their activists of university lecturers, journalists, and human rights lawyers gained prominence as professional think-tanks and political intellectuals. This influence was particularly visible in the government work and public debate on devolution of power as a solution to the ethnic conflict (Bastian 1996). When this mode of conflict resolution failed and the government turned to a "war-for peace" agenda in the late 1990s, the state-civil society relations were strained, but the CSOs gained new prominence with the internationalized elite negotiations for liberal peace that was initiated in late 2001 (Rupesinghe 2006). At that point, however, their support for Westernized promotion of liberal peace combined with their narrow social basis as professional and Colombo-based think-tanks made many CSOs easy targets for criticism from Sinhalese ethnonationalist forces.

NGOs and Neoliberal Development

In addition to these politically oriented civil society organizations, Wickramasinghe (2001) points to the emergence since the late 1970s of a large number of domestic and international NGOs involved in humanitarian relief and development in the context of economic liberalization and armed conflict. NGOs have existed in Sri Lanka from the

early British colonial period as local counterparts to Christian missionary activities and since the late nineteenth century in the form of voluntary welfare work linked to Buddhist, Hindu, and Muslim revivalist
movements (Orjuela 2004). By the time of independence in 1948 there
was a large number of NGOs involved in social welfare and poverty
alleviation, but these were soon overshadowed by the growth of the
welfare state. With neoliberal state retrenchment and reduced welfare
programs in the 1970s, there were growing needs for social assistance
from non-state sources. Nevertheless, it was only with the shift to
"neoliberalism with a human face" in international development cooperation and the turn to populist poverty alleviation politics in Sri Lanka
from the late 1980s that the NGO sector gained its current strength and
prominence.

Starting in the mid-1950s, Sri Lanka was for two decades characterized
by a "democratic socialism" that was built around state-led economic
development and comprehensive welfare programs. The driving force
behind this was the strong influence of Left parties and, later, the political
elite's practice of granting material and symbolic concessions to the intermediate classes. As this model failed to generate dynamic economic
growth, a deep structural crisis emerged and was followed by a macro-
economic policy shift to economic liberalization. This crisis also produced
a sweeping electoral victory for the UNP in 1977, providing a basis for
authoritarian centralization of state power, postponement of democratic
elections, exclusion of Tamil minority representatives, and intensified control of political dissent (Venugopal 2008; Stokke 1997).

As much as this turn to majoritarian authoritarianism diminished the
political leverage of Tamil minority representatives, it contributed to the
radicalization of Tamil nationalism from federalism to separatism and
from parliamentary negotiations to armed struggle (Stokke and Ryntveit
2000). Likewise, as the shift to economic liberalization violated the social
contract between the ruling elite and the Sinhalese intermediate classes, it
also produced a militant and radical Sinhalese youth movement (Janatha
Vimukthi Peramuna, JVP) that brought the state close to collapse in the
late 1980s (Gunaratne 1990). In this context of a devastating two-front
civil war against militant Tamil separatism and against revolutionary
Sinhalese ethnonationalism, the government of President Premadasa
embarked on a strategy combining harsh military repression of the JVP
uprising, Indian intervention to disarm the Liberation Tigers of Tamil
Eelam (LTTE), and populist material and symbolic concessions to regain
political legitimacy among the intermediate Sinhalese classes. A key
feature in the latter was poverty alleviation based on self-help and non-
governmental service delivery (Stokke 1995).

In this context of neoliberalism with a human face, the Sri Lankan state has redefined its relations to domestic and international NGOs in broad agreement with aid discourses on governance, participation, and partnership (Orjuela 2004). Wickramasinghe observes that this has created a large NGO sector with three principal subsections:

- An international NGO sector serving the humanitarian needs of the country stemming from the ethnic conflict.
- A few large and well-distributed national NGOs involved in poverty alleviation projects in conjunction with the state or complementary to the state.
- Myriad small NGOs sometimes called CBOs (community-based organization) involved in grassroots, rural development. (Wickramasinghe 2001, 76)

This rise to prominence of a professional NGO sector has produced complex relations between service-delivery oriented associations, aid donors, state institutions, and political actors. State-NGO relations in Sri Lanka have gone through various contrasting stages. The government was relatively indifferent to NGOs throughout the period with a strong welfare state in the 1950s and 1960s, and it remained ambivalent even as the NGO sector grew amid state retrenchment in the 1980s. The late 1980s and early 1990s brought more complex and contentious relations. Although there were new openings for partnership, there were also personalized confrontations between President Premadasa and prominent NGO personalities. The main point of contention, beside personal animosities, was the accusation that large foreign funds were flowing into the NGO sector without the knowledge or concurrence of the government (Orjuela 2004).

Following the change of government in 1994, state–NGO relations were much less conflictual, but the criticism regarding lack of transparency and accountability vis-à-vis people and government in Sri Lanka remains the same and was intensified in the 5th peace process. Although open conflicts between the state and NGOs have been rare, state-NGO relations tend to be superficial and tenuous rather than characterized by mutuality and partnership. Thus Wickramasinghe observes that "cooperation between NGOs and government agencies is limited and mainly takes place at the local level on poverty alleviation projects" (2001, 101). There are, however, links through the patrimonial network mode of politics that has come to characterize Sri Lanka since the demise of the comprehensive welfare state. Whereas NGOs are often seen as instrumental for achieving and maintaining positions of political power, NGOs depend on beneficial relations to political patrons and international donors. This creates asymmetrical power relations between donors/patrons and recipients/clients while orientating accountability relations toward the donors/patrons rather than to the popular constituencies of NGOs. These characteristics made the NGO sector conducive for instrumental use in support of peacebuilding in the 5th peace process and hence also a target for criticism by actors opposed to Westernized, liberal peace.

Civil Society in the 5th Peace Process

Based on post-colonial politicization of ethnic identities and the failure to accommodate Tamil demands for minority rights and self-determination, the period since 1983 has been marked by protracted armed conflict between the Government of Sri Lanka (GOSL) and the Liberation Tigers of Tamil Eelam (LTTE). Tamil nationalism emerged as a nonviolent and democratic movement for federalism, but was later radicalized into militant separatism (Manogaran and Pfaffenberger 1994; Stokke and Ryntveit 2000; Wilson 2000). This armed conflict has been interspersed by five attempts at political conflict resolution; the Thimpu Talks in 1985; the 1987 Indo-Lanka Accord; the 1990 LTTE-Premadasa talks; the LTTE-Kumaratunga talks in 1994–1995; and the 5th peace process between the LTTE and the government of Prime Minister Ranil Wickramasinghe in 2002–2003 (Balasingham 2004; Gooneratne 2007; Rupesinghe 2006). The last peace process was characterized by a military-territorial balance of power between the protagonists, international promotion of elitist conflict resolution, and instrumental use of aid and civil society for peacebuilding.

Internationalized Crafting of Liberal Peace and Neoliberal Development

Sri Lanka's 5th peace process began shortly after the elections in December 2001 and included six rounds of peace negotiations between the GOSL and the LTTE in 2002–2003 (Raman et al. 2006, Uyangoda and Perera 2003). This process produced a Ceasefire Agreement from February 2002 to January 2008 and was characterized by an extensive international involvement in agreement with the merging of security and development in post–Cold War geopolitics (Duffield 2001). A broad range of governmental, intergovernmental and non-governmental actors performed roles as facilitators, monitors, and donors, operating within political spaces defined by international geopolitics and the power constellations and strategies of actors in Sri Lanka. The Government of Norway facilitated negotiations between LTTE and GOSL and organized Nordic ceasefire monitors within the Sri Lanka Monitoring Mission

(SLMM). Comprehensive peacebuilding efforts were funded by the cochairs to the donor conferences (Japan, the European Union, United States, and Norway) and also supported by international financial institutions such as the World Bank and the Asian Development Bank. Finally, a broad range of international NGOs and United Nations organizations were involved in humanitarian and development programs, especially after the 2004 Indian Ocean Tsunami disaster. Thus, the question of peace became thoroughly internationalized through the development aid relationship and by placing peacebuilding at the center of conflict resolution (Bastian 2007; Goodhand and Klem 2005).

In order to comprehend the character and politicization of peacebuilding, it is necessary to examine the political preconditions and dynamics of conflict resolution. Although the 5th peace process was internationalized, it was first and foremost shaped by domestic power politics, especially the balance of power between the GOSL and the LTTE and the constellations and strategies within Sinhalese majority politics. The war reached a "mutually hurting stalemate" in the late 1990s, following a series of military victories for the LTTE that brought extensive areas under their control and segmented a de facto dual state structure (Shanmugaratnam and Stokke 2008; Stokke 2006; Uyangoda 2005). This balance of power brought the protagonists into negotiations and kept them from resuming warfare, despite the breakdown of the negotiations, until the balance was altered through military preparations and changing positions among the international actors in favor of the GOSL.

The peace process was also structured by Sinhalese majority politics, as the government was based on a weak coalition with limited powers to promote institutional and constitutional changes (Uyangoda 2005; Uyangoda and Perera 2003). Sinhalese politics is characterized by fragmentation and intense rivalry within the political elite. In addition, the voters are mobilized according to ethnic identities, with entrenched political practices of ethnic outbidding and instrumental opposition to minority rights and devolution of power (de Votta 2004). This created a situation where the government had limited prospects for political conflict resolution through constitutional reforms and had to search for strategies of conflict management and resolution within limits set by the existing constitutional and institutional arrangements.

These constellations produced a peace process with distinct characteristics. It was, on the one hand, designed as "track one" negotiations between the warring parties without any parallel process for other stakeholders (Uyangoda and Perera 2003). This narrow definition of stakeholders reflected the military realities but was also a strategic decision to prevent the negotiations from being derailed by opportunistic tactics of potential "spoilers." However, this meant that the Sinhalese political opposition of Sri Lanka Freedom Party (SLFP), Janatha Vimukthi Peramuna (JVP), and Jathika Hela Urumaya (JHU), the Muslim minority, non-LTTE Tamil groups, and the broad diversity of both liberal and ethnonationalist civil society organizations were all excluded from the peace negotiations. The content of the negotiations was also narrowly defined to questions about the Ceasefire Agreement and joint mechanisms for interim development administration, postponing questions of devolution of power, human rights, and substantive democratization (Rainford and Satkunanathan 2008; Shanmugaratnam and Stokke 2008). Thus the core political questions that were behind the making and perpetuation of the conflict remained largely unaddressed.

On the other hand, the peace process was also characterized by an unusual sequencing of peacebuilding and conflict resolution as humanitarian rehabilitation was used as a trust-building and depoliticizing precursor for conflict resolution (Bastian 2007; Shanmugaratnam and Stokke 2008; Sriskandarajah 2003). The negotiating teams from the GOSL and the LTTE agreed to address immediate humanitarian relief and rehabilitation needs in the war-torn areas and to establish a joint interim mechanism to plan and implement development projects in the Northeast. This choice of design was a pragmatic adjustment to the political realities and obstacles to conflict resolution, but also a reflection of the existence of severe crises of development. While the GOSL faced a growing budget crisis with soaring military expenses and rising costs of living that posed a serious threat to survival of the government, the LTTE faced a humanitarian crisis and an increasingly war-weary Tamil population who had suffered under massive destructions of livelihoods (Bastian 2007; Kelegama 2006; Rupesinghe 2006). This situation made both protagonists enter the peace process with a desire to address humanitarian rehabilitation and development challenges.

These particular characteristics of the peace process granted CSOs and NGOs distinct roles in regard to peacebuilding (Liyanage 2006; Uyangoda 2003). Colombo-based think-tanks within the radical CSO tradition were supported in their role as public-political intellectuals advocating positive peace through comprehensive political transformations. Domestic and international NGOs were engaged in delivery of humanitarian rehabilitation and public services, especially as the protagonists failed to implement a joint mechanism for disbursement of aid.

CSOs Advocating Liberal Peace

Orjuela (2004) draws attention to the broad diversity of peace organizations in Sri Lanka and observes that these became popular clients for international aid from the mid-1990s. Her study lends support to the conclusion that the peace movement remained ethnically divided and organizationally fragmented with relatively limited ability to utilize the political space to effectively promote peace or to foster integration and reconciliation in civil society.

One highly visible component within this broad mass movement is a group of Colombo-based think-tanks involved in research and public advocacy. These institutions for intellectual activism combined a leftist focus on social justice and a liberal focus on human rights and democracy. Over time most of them have come to give prime attention to human rights and democracy in the context of severe rights violations and protracted armed conflict, thereby downplaying their former political economic critique of capitalist development. With the internationalized attempt at conflict resolution, peace studies and advocacy became a key orientation of many of these think-tanks, often in the form of consultancy work for international donors but sometimes also as more autonomous basic research. Some prominent examples of such think-tanks include the Centre for Policy Alternatives (CPA),[2] the Foundation for Coexistence (FCE),[3] the International Centre for Ethnic Studies (ICES),[4] the National Peace Council (NPC),[5] and the Social Scientists' Association (SSA).[6] On the Tamil side, a similar role was performed by the Centre for Just Peace and Democracy (CJPD)[7] based in Switzerland.

The main contribution of these think-tanks is the introduction of contemporary academic debates on conflict transformation into the public-political debate in Sri Lanka (Centre for Just Peace and Democracy 2006, Rupesinghe 2006, Uyangoda 2005). A key role in this was played by the Colombo office of the German Berghof Foundation for Conflict Studies.[8] The basic argument was that lasting peace beyond mere cessation of hostilities ("negative peace") is contingent on substantive political transformations (Ferdinands et al. 2004). As much as the Sri Lankan conflict is produced within the political field, lasting peace is contingent on comprehensive transformations of political institutions and practices.

Reflecting the de facto dual-state structure at the time, the academic and political debates on conflict transformation had two principal foci: the needs and means for political transformation of the LTTE and the GOSL. The Sri Lankan state, on the one hand, can be described as a consolidated electoral democracy that is characterized by majoritarianism within a unitary and centralized state. During the 5th peace process there were numerous studies and public interventions on the need for transforming political institutions and practices in the direction of substantive devolution of power (beyond minimalist administrative decentralization) and substantive human rights and democracy (beyond formal rights and elections). These challenges are inseparable but the public debate and the peace negotiations focused more on the geographic arrangements of state power than on substantive, rights-based democratization (Raman, Moorthy and Chittaranjan 2006).

LTTE, on the other hand, can be described as a militaristic movement with few formal mechanisms for democratic representation. The early stage of the 5th peace process was marked by academic and political debates about whether transformation of LTTE—especially in the form of disarmament and renouncement of separatism—should be a precondition for peace negotiations or whether transformation to political movement could be achieved through peace negotiations and practical collaboration in humanitarian rehabilitation. In this debate, the Colombo-based CSOs displayed a willingness to consider LTTE as a stakeholder with potential for political transformation that was in striking contrast to the singular focus on LTTE as a "terrorist organization" among Sinhalese ethnonationalist actors. In practice, no demands for political transformations were imposed on LTTE as a prerequisite for negotiations. Instead, the peace process followed a pragmatic development-to-peace approach that to some extent widened the space for LTTE. The LTTE made certain strategic adjustments to this new political context and especially pursued a strategy of state-building in areas under their control as a precursor to future power-sharing arrangements (Stokke 2006).

It can be observed that there were some points of convergence between the peace agenda of the GOSL, the cochairs, and the Colombo think-tanks, although the latter championed much more comprehensive political transformations than the "negative peace" that was envisioned by the government. Although this convergence was somewhat superficial, it nevertheless meant that the CSOs were seen as part of the process and that their role was politicized by the Sinhalese ethnonationalist mobilization against the peace process. As the peace negotiations stalled, Sinhalese political elite actors that had been excluded from the process and key electoral constituencies in the intermediate classes who had experienced social exclusion from the government's neoliberal development model joined forces against the government and their agenda for liberal peace and neoliberal development. The government and the international actors were criticized not only for undermining the sovereignty and integrity of the unitary state, but also for failing to deliver in the field of livelihoods and social welfare. The CSOs were construed as complicit in this externally imposed and elitist liberal peace agenda, and they were criticized for being far removed from and unaccountable to the Sinhalese popular masses. Thus the legitimacy of

CSOs was contested, as they were portrayed as being closely associated with the state and international donors.

NGOs Delivering Neoliberal Development

A defining feature of the peace process was the unusual sequencing of peacebuilding and conflict resolution, starting with humanitarian rehabilitation before addressing core political issues. The GOSL and LTTE reached an early agreement to address immediate humanitarian and rehabilitation needs—in sharp contrast to the previous 4th peace process (1994–1995), when the focus was on conflict resolution through constitutional reforms. This primacy of development politicized the question of interim development administration in the Northeast (Rainford and Satkunanathan 2008). In the absence of a joint mechanism, international NGOs and their local partner organizations were granted a key role in the delivery of aid, as this was the only remaining conflict-sensitive option.

The question of interim development administration became highly contentious, as it impinged on the question of future power-sharing arrangements—that is, whether Sri Lanka should be a unitary state, a federal state, or two separate states (Shanmugaratnam and Stokke 2008). For the LTTE it was an absolute necessity that the interim administration should have substantive powers and a guaranteed position for the LTTE in order to ensure both immediate rehabilitation and future self-determination in the Northeast. The government agreed to establish an interim joint mechanism in the form of the Subcommittee on Immediate Humanitarian and Rehabilitation Needs in the North and East (SIHRN). However, they faced a strong opposition to this from the SLFP and JVP, who viewed interim administration as a threat to the sovereign unitary state. Given this strong Sinhalese opposition and the weak position of the government in Parliament, they tried to find an interim arrangement within the limits of the unitary constitution. This was insufficient to accommodate the LTTE, while their counterproposal for an Interim Self-Governing Authority (ISGA) was seen by the Sinhalese opposition as a precursor to secession. In the end, the peace negotiations stalled over this question of power sharing in interim development administration.

These experiences were repeated after the 2004 tsunami disaster. Overwhelming humanitarian needs and promising signs of mutual goodwill immediately after the disaster were soon replaced by politicization of aid and its administration. Recognizing the political obstacles to efficient and fair distribution of emergency aid, the international donors urged that a joint mechanism should be established between the GOSL and the LTTE.

But this mechanism was again subjected to divisive politicization, and when the Post-Tsunami Operational Management Structure (P-TOMS) agreement was finally signed, it was put on hold by a Supreme Court ruling that found key elements to be against the constitution of the unitary state. Thus, the opportunity created by the tsunami for implementing a special mechanism with potential for revitalization of the peace process was missed.

In the absence of any functioning joint mechanism, the actual delivery of rehabilitation and development was increasingly handled by NGOs, especially after the 2004 tsunami disaster. This meant that rehabilitation and development were delinked from the Sri Lankan state and from the administrative institutions in LTTE-controlled areas.

There was a strong growth in the number and activities of international agencies after the signing of the Ceasefire Agreement in 2002 and an especially tremendous growth after the 2004 tsunami disaster. The assessment of the tsunami disaster response documents a strong proliferation of international NGOs, but also widespread problems of weak links between disaster relief and long-term development, lack of synergy between international capacities and local capacities, and weak accountability of international NGOs to local communities (Telford et al. 2006). There is also the problem of weak links from rehabilitation to institutional reforms for devolution of power and substantive democratic representation. All of this meant that, despite the development-to-peace design of the process, the actual delivery of rehabilitation and development had weak strategic links to political conflict transformation, both in government- and LTTE-controlled areas. This was due to the failure to institutionalize LTTE/GOSL joint mechanisms for development administration and the subsequent bypassing of these political authorities when the actual delivery was handled by international NGOs and their local counterparts. Moreover, NGOs, like the CSOs, came under severe criticism for being elitist outsiders with accountability relations to international donors rather than being embedded in local society and contributing to the development of state capacity in social welfare and development.

Civil Society and the Resumption of War

The regime change in 2005 from the UNP-led government of Prime Minister Ranil Wickramasinghe to the SLFP-led government of President Mahinda Rajapakse marked the change from a liberal peace agenda to an offensive "war against terrorism." This resumption of warfare between a militaristic, ethnonationalist, and increasingly authoritarian government and a militaristic and ethnonationalist insurgency movement dramatically changed the context for civil society organizations, both the development-oriented NGOs and the political-advocacy CSOs. The most severe repression has been experienced by Tamil welfare NGOs associated with the LTTE.

During the 5th peace process, both sides continued to work on the balance of power through military, political, and discursive means. The government used media and diplomatic relations actively to frame the LTTE as a "terrorist" organization in order to curtail their ability to draw on international relations and resource mobilization, but also to acquire international legitimacy for the coming "war against terror" (Nadarajah and Sriskandarajah 2005). Hence, there was an overlap between the discourse of the war against terrorism propagated by the Sri Lankan government and the US-led global War on Terror. It is precisely because the discourse of the global War on Terror was circulating and was being used to legitimize the introduction of counter-terrorism structures in the United States and elsewhere that the Sri Lankan government could so fruitfully appropriate the language of the war against terrorism to delegitimize the LTTE and impose restrictions on the delivery of aid by Tamil-aligned civil society groups. The Rajapakse government intensified this diplomatic-discursive campaign while also building new alliances with Asian states (such as Pakistan, China, and Iran) that strengthened their military capacity and provided diplomatic leverage vis-à-vis the cochairs and India.

The LTTE combined military preparations and a strategy of institutionalizing de facto self-determination as a precursor to power sharing arrangements in a peace agreement. The main focus in the LTTE's statebuilding strategy was external and internal security, but there was also an additional focus on social welfare and development (Stokke 2006). This was to some extent facilitated by the inflow of aid, some of which was channeled through NGOs that either had an association with the LTTE or had to accept partnership or coordination with the LTTE-controlled organizations. Thus the LTTE collaborated with external actors to address humanitarian and development needs, including first and foremost the Tamil diaspora, but also foreign donors and even Sri Lankan state institutions. The most prominent example of diaspora-funded Tamil NGOs is the Tamils Rehabilitation Organisation (TRO). Their mode of operation has been to rely on resource mobilization within the diaspora, but after the tsunami disaster TRO also worked in partnership with international donors and the NGOs to channel aid to affected areas and people.

With the change of government and the resumption of warfare, TRO came under critical scrutiny and harsh regulation in Sri Lanka and abroad (especially in Canada, Australia, the United Kingdom, and the United States), including freezing and confiscation of funds. The justification for this was the claim that the TRO was a front organization for the LTTE that collects and transfers funds from the diaspora. Politico-administrative pressure on the TRO typifies the greater scrutiny of Tamil civil society associations generally in the context of the global War on Terror. For example, in a separate case, the UK charity regulator, the Charity Commission, investigated alleged links between the Tamil Students Union and the LTTE. The Commission found that one of its trustees was on a designated list of terrorists. However, rather than banning the charity, as it had done with the TRO, the Commission used its powers to suspend the trustee and authorized the charity to continue its work (Howell and Lind 2009).

The Rajapakse government has also utilized authoritarian repression against actors they fear could derail the agenda of crushing the LTTE by military means. This is manifested in vigilant confrontations against international state, UN, and NGO representatives that have criticized the government for human rights violations and war crimes or called for humanitarian pause, ceasefire, and political negotiations. Within Sri Lanka, there has been an increase in political violence against suspected LTTE sympathizers, but also against the democratic oppositions and media workers. Harassment and assassinations of journalists and media, including the much-publicized assassinations of Sivaram Dharmeratnam in 2005 and Lasantha Wickrematunge in January 2009, have had a stifling effect on critical journalism.

Many of the aforementioned CSOs focusing on political advocacy in the field of human rights, democracy, and peace have also experienced various forms of authoritarian repression. A greater willingness to control and repress the activities of foreign civil society organizations, for example by way of visa restrictions and government inquiries into foreign funding, have curtailed the international networking of many Sri Lankan CSOs. This has been especially visible with the reorganizations of the International Centre for Ethnic Studies in Colombo and the closing of the Colombo office of the Berghof Foundation in 2008. In addition there is the use of threats and warnings that give CSO activists a sense of operating within an omnipresent surveillance regime with a constant potential for negative sanctions. This makes many activists and CSOs impose self-discipline in order to avoid unwanted attention and possible repression.

All of this means that the transition from the 5th peace process to the ongoing war has dramatically altered the situation for CSOs. Whereas the need for humanitarian relief and human rights advocacy has increased, the political space for NGOs and CSOs has been reduced in the face of an increasingly authoritarian regime and an atmosphere of patriotism and war euphoria. These changes have had a clear disciplining effect on many organizations, as can be seen in the reduced and less conflict-oriented NGO program activities and the less active and visible public advocacy by CSOs than earlier. This means that the oppositional politicization of CSOs and NGOs during the peace process has formed a basis for more authoritarian state repression during the war and a resultant self-disciplining within both NGOs and CSOs.

Conclusion

Recent years have seen a renewed interest in the political and developmental roles of civil society. However, this interest has been revised in the wake of the 9/11 attacks, which led to the formulation of new security frameworks. These integrate aspects of development and civil society into counter-terrorism, but also curtail the political spaces for "bad civil society" to organize. The War on Terror has provided an opening for governments around the world, for their own domestic political reasons, to introduce various controls on dissident voices—ostensibly to limit the presumed threat of terrorism. In countries in conflict such as Sri Lanka, the global discourse of defeating terrorist networks has been appropriated to recast deeply entrenched civil wars and insurgencies as "new" threats justifying militaristic responses and a more uncompromising stance in political negotiations.

The Sri Lankan experience points to the complex and contextual politics of civil society, the diversity of associations and roles, and the changing state-society relations. The 5th peace process was characterized by a twofold utilization of civil society to advocate liberal peace and deliver humanitarian rehabilitation and neoliberal development. Both roles politicized civil society while the intended peacebuilding outcomes failed to materialize. In fact the instrumental use of CSOs and NGOs in peacebuilding branded them as "bad" civil society in regard to the Rajapakse government, making many associations victims of various forms of state repression in the context of a proclaimed "war against terror." Thus, the shifting global political context after the 9/11 attacks has made it possible for the Sri Lankan government to redefine the threat of Tamil ethnonationalism in terms of "terrorism," thus justifying a hard strategy to crush the LTTE militarily while limiting the space for deliberation and negotiation on the core political issues underpinning the long-running conflict.

Notes

1. Some civil society organizations that exemplify this occupation of the public space are the Civil Rights Movement, Centre for Society and Religion, Citizen's Forum for Democracy, Committee for Rational Development, Social Scientists' Association, Workers' and Peasants Institute, Movement for Inter-Racial Justice and Equality, the Movement for Defense of Democratic Rights, Marga Institute, International Centre for Ethnic Studies, Institute of Policy Studies, and Centre for Policy Alternatives.

2. http://www.cpalanka.org

3. http://www.fce.lk

4. http://www.icescolombo.org

5. http://www.peace-srilanka.org

6. http://www.ssalanka.org

7. http://www.cjpdonline.org

8. http://www.berghof-foundation.lk/

10

THE CHANGING DYNAMICS OF CIVIL SOCIETY AND AID IN THE ISRAEL–PALESTINE CONFLICT POST-9/11

Jeremy Lind

Civil society has been a key battleground in the long-running conflict between Israel and the Palestinians. It is an important platform for articulating nationalist ideals and political objectives on both sides, as well as a way of mobilizing popular support and legitimacy. The uneven power relations that pervade the conflict extend through civil society and are displayed in the differential treatment of Jewish and Arab groups inside Israel as well as in the deeply embedded suspicion of Palestinian organizations that predates the latest phase of the conflict stretching back to the outbreak of the Al Aqsa intifada in September 2000. There is a long background to these suspicions, which Israel has used to justify its imposition of various administrative controls on Palestinian NGOs, prominent human rights activists, and Islamic groups.

Israel intensified its scrutiny of Palestinian civil society groups after the escalation of violence in September 2000 and again in the aftermath of the 9/11 attacks in the United States. In particular, the War on Terror has provided a new frame for understanding the conflict and occupation and the different actors involved. Israel has justified its intensified security crackdown of the Occupied Territories by linking its conflict with the Palestinians to the War on Terror. This has included new controls on the activities of Palestinian groups and international aid agencies, including restrictions on issuing visas and work permits as well as limits on the movements of aid workers, human rights observers, and peace activists. The role of aid has become problematic in this context as a tool that is used to shape the underlying conditions for negotiating a political settlement to the conflict. In recent years, donors have courted secular groups as a way of circumventing Palestinian political leadership and countering the rising stock of Islamic civil society. However, this greater foreign interest has not helped improve the image of secular Palestinian groups, which are viewed as elitist and self-serving. Rather, the post-9/11 political circumstances have created unique pressures for secular and human rights groups to demonstrate their legitimacy and credibility to Palestinian people by opposing the political objectives of the War on Terror that have come to shape the use of development aid.

This chapter examines the changing dynamics of aid and civil society in the Israel–Palestine conflict since the 9/11 attacks in the United States. It begins by sketching the political framing of civil society and the politics of aid. The chapter goes on to examine the ascendancy of Hamas and the spreading influence of Islamic social welfare organizations associated with Hamas. The chapter then examines the impacts of various Israeli security and administrative measures on the spaces and actors of civil society working in the Occupied Palestinian Territories.

Occupation, Conflict, and the Politics of Aid

The dynamics of the occupation and conflict that have been so significant in defining the space for civil society, in both Palestine and Israel, have dictated the delivery of aid in the region as well. Although consideration of the causes of the conflict and the nature of the violence is beyond the scope of this chapter,[1] this section examines how understandings of the conflict and its impacts have influenced the ambit of aid policy and practice.

Many Palestinian civil society organizations trace their roots to the efforts at mass mobilization in the 1970s by various leftist factions or to the national front strategy of the Palestinian Liberation Organisation (PLO) (Hammami 2000). The outbreak of the first intifada in 1987 reaffirmed the popular roots of these factional organizations. The efforts of these groups in responding to and advocating for people's needs had shaped positive perceptions of their ability to deliver. These perceptions conferred legitimacy upon these organizations, among both Palestinians and aid givers. Encouraged by donors to create formal structures and standardize their operating procedures to seek funding, many popular committee structures formed during the intifada had morphed into professionalized NGOs by 1991.

In the years following the Oslo Agreement in 1993, the chief role of aid was to help deliver a peace dividend to Palestinian people and thereby sustain support for the negotiating process, the levels of which were diminishing over time (Lasensky and Grace 2006). Donors sought to cooperate with the new Palestinian Authority (PA) in promoting economic development and for this reason directed greater levels of aid through its structures, which entailed reduced support for civil society. However, creeping concerns of mismanagement, corruption, and ineffectiveness caused donors to bypass the PA by redirecting support through NGOs, which were thought to be more proficient in delivering services. Foreign assistance to NGOs also derived from the thinking that they would act as a watchdog on the PA and thus promote democracy and good governance. By the late 1990s, donors led by USAID, the largest donor of Palestinian democracy and governance groups, began courting secular groups to work with as a way of thwarting the growing influence of Hamas (Roy 2000). As explained below, aid expectations are that (secular) NGOs act as "responsible" civil society or "counter-society" and uphold human rights vis-à-vis a state that is not fully sovereign and a PA that is not trusted (EMHRN 2004). Secular NGOs are also expected to serve as a counterweight to Islamist parts of civil society.

In the meantime, throughout the 1990s relations soured between secular NGOs and the PA as NGOs' expanding political influence—at least within international aid circles—came to be recognized. Relations between the PA and the Islamic social welfare groups associated with Hamas were comparably better, mainly because they were not viewed as a political threat, as explained in the following section. Indirectly, aid funding of secular organizations was adding to this antagonism and feelings that NGOs were in competition with the PA. Beginning in the 1990s, politicians in the PA made statements vilifying NGOs as "fat cats" that exploited donor funds for their own enrichment at the cost of an increasingly destitute population. Explaining these tensions, Hammami (2000) posits that PA officials felt threatened by scrutiny of their actions undertaken by human rights organizations. She notes that PA officials would differentiate between "bad" elements in the human rights community and "good" national organizations that provided services during the occupation, which would also relieve pressure on the PA to meet people's needs.

This drumbeat of criticism undermined popular perceptions of Palestinian NGOs, as explained later. Many Palestinians reportedly regard local human rights groups as being elitist and detached from society (Guest 2007). Historically, although foreign funding enabled NGOs to stake an independent stance, processes of professionalization encouraged by donors have imposed their own logic and constraints and distanced many organizations from the grassroots (Guest 2007). This in turn has contributed to negative public attitudes of Palestinian NGOs, as many lack downward accountability relations that might otherwise provide a measure of legitimacy to deflect criticism. Advocacy efforts by Palestinian NGOs, for example, are internationally focused rather than for any domestic audience, and the promotional literature of many organizations is in English (Guest 2007).

The outbreak of the Al Aqsa intifada in September 2000 induced a further reconfiguration in the role of aid. Israel combined military operations against militants with policing and security measures to cut off and isolate the Palestinian Territories, producing dire humanitarian consequences and inflating poverty levels (Amnesty International UK et al. 2008; House of Commons 2007; OCHA 2007a; UNCTAD 2006). The worsening situation for Palestinians raised the imperative to respond to spiraling needs as well as prevent the collapse of the PA through direct budget support, which came namely from the European Union and Arab states (Lasensky and Grace 2006). Annual donor funding to the Palestinians has doubled since 2000 as peace prospects have diminished (House of Commons 2007, 12). A greater proportion of aid was committed to meeting humanitarian needs. The ratio of development to emergency assistance flipped from 7:1 in 2000 to 1:5 in 2002 (DFID 2004). Aid was also used to cover salaries in the public sector, the size of which swelled after 2000 to absorb the ranks of the unemployed who were prevented from crossing into Israel for work.

The global framing of the Israel–Palestine conflict in the post-9/11 context has clearly impacted upon aid policy and practice as well. Fast (2006, 19) explains, "Aid agencies . . . have been forced to move from a developmental, post-Oslo approach that assumed and required a more political and active engagement with government-as-service provider to providing these basic services in the absence of governmental resources." The clearest manifestation of the War on Terror on aid policy was the suspension of aid to the PA following the January 2006 legislative elections, which saw Hamas come to power. As a condition for aid, the US and European donors insisted that the new Hamas-led government recognize the right of Israel to exist and renounce the use of violence. What followed was an intense struggle for power between Hamas and Fatah, the party of the Palestinian President Mahmoud Abbas. In June 2007, Hamas overwhelmed Fatah forces in Gaza in four days of intense fighting. In the aftermath of the putsch, Abbas broke off relations with Hamas and dissolved a unity government that had been formed three months earlier following a Saudi-negotiated power sharing agreement (Robinson 2007). Abbas dismissed the PA Prime Minister, Ismail Haniya, from Hamas and replaced him with Salam Fayyad, an independent who was trusted by Western countries. The Hamas putsch basically split the Occupied Territories into two separate political and administrative bodies: Gaza under a Hamas government and the West Bank under the PA government (Robinson 2007).

Following the split in 2007, the policy pursued by the United States and Israel was to assist the more moderate PA in the West Bank under Abbas as a strategy of undermining support for Hamas. The political objective to shape the negotiating environment clearly steers trends in aid, which are thus responsive to understandings of the different actors involved in the conflict as well as competing security claims they make. That aid is intended to promote the political objectives of certain donors is explicit in the DFID Country Assistance Plan for the Palestinian Territories: "We [DFID] will liaise with other parts of the UK government to ensure that the UK's development, humanitarian and political objectives support each other" (DFID 2004, 3).

Donor support for strengthening secular organizations has become newly prominent in a context of political impasse and worsening conflict, as well. The treatment of secular Palestinian civil society groups in aid as a moderating force to promote public buy-in to peace negotiations with Israel serves the political objectives of donors to minimize the influence of Hamas and Islamic civil society. However, donors' expectation that civil society do its bidding by advancing a moderate position in the conflict poses a political dilemma for groups that receive aid. Principally, it confirms the suspicion of many Palestinians in the Occupied Territories that NGOs are corrupt, self-serving, and exist primarily to advance external interests in the conflict in contrast to the expectation that they act as advocates for the security of Palestinians. Ordinary Palestinian people suspect that international support of Palestinian organizations is intended to defang militants and improve Israel's security (Guest 2003).

There is a dissonance between the anticipated role of civil society that drives donor support and the popular perceptions that international NGOs and Palestinian groups oppose both the occupation and the aggression and human rights abuses by the Israeli Defence Forces (IDF). Fast (2006) noted that the conflict, lack of political settlement, and human rights situation have prompted some international NGOs to adopt a solidarity stance with the Palestinian cause. But this also compromises their ability to operate by renewing Israeli suspicions that NGOs are politically aligned with Palestinians, which has occasioned intensified bureaucratic controls of NGOs, as seen below. The paradox of donor assistance is that it derives from certain views of the conflict and explicitly political motives to intervene, yet aid recipients are expected to demonstrate neutrality and moderation.

Thus, the development of Palestinian NGOs was set by the situation of long-running occupation and conflict but was subsequently steered by aid politics as many groups elected to professionalize and abandon grassroots organizing. Over time, accountability relations of NGOs have become skewed as organizations became oriented to donor priorities and requirements for bureaucratization. But there is another side of the story in the development of civil society in the Occupied Territories. The detachment of many secular Palestinian groups from grassroots organizing, and the erosion of their internal legitimacy, has seen the ascendancy of Islamic movements to fill the void. The fundamental dilemma for secular Palestinian organizations favored for donor funding is to balance popular expectations to stake a distinctly political position with donor insistence that they conform to an image of moderation and neutrality. Moves to fashion new grassroots structures to rival Islamist social welfare organizations, referred to below, presage further struggles in defining the role of secular Palestinian civil society groups.

The Social and Political Ascendancy of Hamas

The election success of Hamas in the Palestinian legislative elections in January 2006 was a political earthquake that reverberated throughout the Middle East and internationally. The victory shocked governments in the region, including Egypt and Jordan, whose regimes have sought to suppress Islamists (Usher 2006). It triggered a political crisis that assumed global dimensions in the context of the War on Terror. Israel, the United States, Canada, and the European Union consider Hamas to be a terrorist organization and hence not a credible partner in peace negotiations. However, the legislative election victory of Hamas was testament to its widespread support at the grassroots, which has granted it the legitimacy and credibility to rule. Belatedly, this was recognized by international actors in the conflict and has come to inform the strategy pursued by Israel and the United States of isolating the Hamas-led government in Gaza as a method of obstructing its ability to govern and thus undermine its legitimacy to rule.

Although enjoying broad grassroots support, Palestinian views of Hamas are decidedly mixed. In the January 2006 legislative elections, Hamas won 76 seats against Fatah's 43 in the 132-seat chamber (Robinson 2007). However, Fatah and the secular parties won the majority of the popular vote (55 percent), because 74 independent Fatah members stood against the movement's official list, whereas Hamas united behind one list (Usher, 2006). A poll conducted in the aftermath of the election by the Palestinian Center for Policy and Survey Research showed that 75 percent of Palestinians supported reconciliation with Israel based on a genuine two-state solution, including 60 percent of those who voted for Hamas (Usher, 2006). In general, the movement enjoys greater support in Gaza than it does in the West Bank.

In the view of many Palestinians, Hamas created a kind of shadow civil society long before its reputation for carrying out suicide bombings in Israel (Remnick 2006). Its roots date to the aftermath of the 1967 Six-Day

War, when the Muslim Brotherhood founded organizations to supervise religious schools as well as created neighborhood libraries and sports clubs (Abu-Amr 1994 in ICG 2003). A Gazan by the name of Sheikh Ahmed Yassin took a leading role in establishing a range of charities and social welfare organizations and took over professional associations and the Islamic University of Gaza, all of which were linked to authorities in mosques (Remnick 2006). In 1973 he set up the Islamic Center in Gaza to consolidate his charitable efforts and promote the influence of Islam through *da'wa*—social work and preaching.

Initially, Israel did not oppose such charity and even encouraged the formation of grassroots groups, which it thought could absorb the energies of Palestinian youth (ICG 2003). Focused on combating Yassir Arafat, Israel thought, correctly as it turned out, that the Islamists threatened the PLO and so did little to obstruct the spread of Islamic social welfare activity (Remnick 2006). As armed resistance to Israel led by the PLO intensified in the 1980s, Islamists began importing arms and organizing their own militias to keep up their influence over male youth. The Islamists joined the first Intifada that began in 1987, and Hamas, an Arabic acronym for the Islamic Resistance Movement, was born (Remnick 2006).

The political ascendancy of the Islamists began in the 1980s, when they prevailed in student elections in universities of the West Bank. By the late 1990s, Islamists won elections in chambers of commerce in the Occupied Territories and, more recently, municipal elections. By competing in the elections of representative public institutions and bodies and in professional guilds, Islamists were able to establish themselves in active politics throughout the 1990s (Shavit 2006). However, during this time Hamas studiously avoided pressing a political or military agenda to oppose the occupation (Roy, 2000). Roy explains that the role of an opposition and its ability to mobilize Palestinians politically was difficult at the time due to widespread popular alienation from politics and the lack of appeal of political Islam at the time. Instead, Hamas focused on providing social welfare to the poor, which also meant it was spared intense scrutiny by the PA and Israel (ICG 2003). By providing social welfare and assisting the poor, Hamas was also able to build up grassroots popularity and support while drawing a contrast between itself and the ineffectiveness and corruption that characterized the PA. Thus, it was able to tap into popular dissatisfaction with peace negotiations and the perception that they favored Israel's security over the needs of Palestinians.

Roy (2000), who documented the prevalence of Hamas in providing social services, estimated that 40 percent of all social institutions in the Occupied Territories were Islamic but that this figure was higher in certain sectors, such as education and the care of orphans. Roy identified several attributes of Islamic social welfare organizations in one of the most comprehensive studies of these groups to date. Roy noted that their staff and management is professional and highly trained; they focus on quality service provision; most operate independently of one another and of other non-Islamic organizations; they focus on meeting the needs of the poor and marginalized; and they are not selective in who can participate and benefit from their charitable works. ICG (2003) notes that Islamic social welfare organizations do not insist on allegiance to Hamas as a quid pro quo for receiving support. Social solidarity is enshrined as an important organizing principle in Hamas's charter, defined in articles 20 and 21 as "extending help to all the needy, both materially and morally, or assisting in the execution of certain actions. It is incumbent upon the members of the Hamas to look after the interests of the masses the way they would look after their own interests."[2]

Roy also noted that most Islamic social welfare organizations are official and legally registered with the appropriate Palestinian ministries. This clearly contrasts with a common perception in the West that Islamic civil society operates in the shadows and conducts its activities illegally. Instead, Islamic social welfare groups have been more diligent than secular organizations in Palestine at registering. Islamic organizations sought to comply with registration requirements, fearing they might otherwise come under greater pressure both internationally and by PA authorities (ICG 2003, 10). A report by the International Crisis Group explains that PA officials were not inclined to deny registering Islamic organizations because they took pressure off the PA to provide services. On the other hand, some human rights organizations in the Occupied Territories have refused to register in protest at the requirement to register with the PA Ministry of Interior (Hammami 2000). The background of mistrust and suspicion between the PA and secular civil society groups was also important in explaining the reticence of some organizations that wished to demonstrate their independence by staying apart from the registration regime (ICG 2003).

Israel's policy of undermining the PA was strengthening the Islamists indirectly. The importance of Islamic social welfare groups increased in relation to the combined impact of punitive Israeli sanctions against the Palestinian population as well as the disintegration of the PA (ICG 2003). By organizing in this context of chronic conflict and expanding social and economic needs, Islamic social welfare groups were able to build up their credibility by delivering aid. It is also significant that in their thinking and practice they linked their charitable activity to a system of shared values and principles that emphasized solidarity and justice.

The political fallout of the War on Terror has seen Islamic social welfare groups come under suspicion. As early as 1989, during the first intifada, Israel outlawed Hamas and considered mere membership to be a punishable offense (ICG 2003). The suspicion of Hamas has become more widespread since the declaration of the War on Terror and the designation of Hamas as a terrorist organization by the United States in 2001. The International Crisis Group (2003, 16) detailed three categories of suspicion concerning Islamic social welfare organizations. First, that they provide direct support to the Hamas military infrastructure through the illicit transfer of funds. Second, that they support Hamas through recruitment and incitement. Lastly, that they indirectly support Hamas through delivery of relief aid, which ultimately strengthens the ideology and practices of the movement. Hamas denies channeling funds to Islamic social welfare groups, which in turn emphasize their compliance with regulatory requirements and their financial probity and transparency. Still, Hamas plays an important role in guiding foreign contributions to Islamic organizations (ICG 2003).

Debates on Islamic social welfare organizations have turned on whether they are independent and autonomous from the political and military activities of Hamas or whether the different sides constitute an integrated whole. The Israeli government alleges that the Islamic social welfare infrastructure associated with Hamas provides financial incentive for individual involvement in terrorism and that the movement's mosques and imams incite hatred and violence against Israel.[3] It has also voiced concern that the social welfare activity by Islamic groups garners popular support for the movement's larger political objectives and attacks by militants. The Israeli government has sought to crack down on Islamic social welfare groups, arguing that there is no distinction between the militant and charitable sides of Hamas as a political movement. A 1998 statement attributed to the Hamas founder Sheikh Yassin claimed that the political and social branches of Hamas could not be distinguished from the military: "We cannot separate the wing from the body . . . If we do so, the body will not be able to fly. Hamas is one body" (Quoted in *Reuters* report, in Remnick, 2006).

Over the years, retaliatory action by the Israeli government and the PA against Islamic social welfare organizations have included shutting down organizations, seizing documents and assets of these groups, and arresting the heads of charitable associations.[4] The ascendancy of Hamas as a rival to the political supremacy of Fatah has ensured it has come under closer scrutiny by the PA. The Islamic Charitable Society in Hebron has repeatedly been closed at the behest of Israel. It includes schools, a medical clinic, and an orphanage and has received funding from Western NGOs, Arab groups, and private donors. In 2002, its former director, who was in Hamas, was arrested for helping to finance and plan an attack on the nearby Israeli settlement of Adora. In September 2005, Israeli troops took over the administrative building, confiscating documents, fax machines, printers, and computers and then sealing the doors. Khalil Herbawi, the director, commented, "The Israelis say that we take care of children whose parents martyred themselves ... But we take all the orphans, the ones whose parents are suicide bombers or who died of cancer or heart attacks. Of the thousand orphans here, only 20 or 21 are orphans because of suicide bombing. Another 20 or so are children of collaborators who were killed. So it evens out" (quoted in Remnick 2006). In April 2008, property belonging to the charity was seized under Israeli military orders.

The move follows a clampdown in recent years by the Palestinian President Mahmoud Abbas and Fatah loyalists in the PA on Islamic social welfare groups to curry favor with Israel and the United States while also targeting the Hamas political base. Since the Hamas takeover of Gaza in June 2007, Abbas has moved systematically against Islamic militants in the West Bank. His security forces have arrested hundreds of Hamas supporters, and he has issued tougher anti–money–laundering regulations to cut off Hamas funding from abroad (Laub 2007).

In December 2007, Abbas authorized the closing of 92 charities linked to Hamas that were formed by prominent local and religious leaders and under the supervision of the Ministry of Religious Affairs. In public statements to justify the closures, the Palestinian information minister claimed that the charities had morphed into financial enterprises that acted as a conduit of support for the activities and political objectives of Hamas. The former Palestinian Prime Minister Salam Fayyad announced the formation of 11 new charity committees to take the place of those that had been shut. The clearly intentioned objective to stunt the political rise of Hamas by targeting Islamic groups and installing new grassroots structures in their place misses the point of how Islamic organizations and, by association, Hamas were able to attain widespread, grassroots credibility and legitimacy. As the ICG (2003, 21) notes: "Hamas seeks to derive prestige and political profit from social welfare activism precisely by maintaining the professionalism and integrity of such institutions rather than politicizing them."

As an important means for political mobilization, civil society groups have been the target of a crackdown by different Palestinian political factions as well as Israel and by governments providing aid to the Palestinians. Hamas has also pressured NGOs they regard as proxies for peddling Fatah's political influence. After suffering defeat in the 2006 legislative elections, Fatah registered scores of new NGOs that were started by Fatah loyalists as a way of sustaining their political influence (Guest 2007). However, once it assumed power in Gaza, Hamas adopted

a firm stance in registering NGOs and sought to crack down on *dakakin*—
"shops," or bogus organizations vilified by politicians that have been so
damaging to the reputation of NGOs. For a time, Hamas blocked all
NGOs from registering, but its hand was forced by a court ruling in favor
of several NGOs that had challenged the government. Still, in 2006 the
Hamas government shut 20 NGOs and referred three organizations to the
attorney general for corruption investigations (Guest 2007).

A former Israeli military intelligence officer, quoted in *The Nation* on
the significance of the Hamas triumph in the 2006 legislative elections,
commented, "The decades of work that Hamas did in mosques and
schools and charity organizations transformed Palestinian civil society
from within. What suddenly erupted today has been simmering beneath
the surface for a generation" (Shavit 2006). Islamic social welfare groups
have been essential to sustain Hamas politically by delivering services and
responding to people's needs for health care and education. The wider
crackdown on Islamic organizations affiliated with Hamas has indicated
the new battle lines being drawn in the conflict, and the intent of Fatah to
loosen the dominance of Hamas in the field of grassroots organizing.

Civil Society in Dystopia

The grassroots force of Hamas, and its ability to amass political power
through social welfare and charitable activity, has altered political calculations in the conflict and renewed pressure on Islamic civil society. Hamas's
political ascendancy has coincided with suspicions that have arisen since the
9/11 attacks concerning the possible role of civil society in helping terrorists.
In particular, the War on Terror has provided a new frame for viewing the
Israeli occupation and conflict as well as the different actors involved,
including the Islamic social welfare groups that have come under renewed
scrutiny. Israel has sought to convey itself as a victim of Palestinian terrorism and to link its actions to the US-led War on Terror as a way of reshaping the negotiating context in its favor. This has had three main
repercussions for aid and civil society working in the Occupied Territories:
it has changed access to foreign aid; cast suspicion on Islamic civil society
with implications for their ability to fundraise and organize; and restricted
the mobility of aid workers and, hence, limited humanitarian access.

The linking of the conflict to the War on Terror has had a profound
impact on aid and civil society by shaping perceptions of the different
actors in the conflict. The distrust of Palestinian civil society ratcheted up
a notch following the 9/11 attacks. Israeli officials issued feverish pro-
nouncements linking the activities of Palestinian groups to terrorism. In
May 2003, the Israeli Foreign Minister alleged that Palestinian NGOs and

most human rights organizations in the OPTs provide shelter for Palestinian terrorists (EMHRN 2004). The declaration of the War on Terror was a pretext for a renewed Israeli crackdown, which human rights campaigners allege was meant to intimidate and prevent human rights workers from carrying out their work (EMHRN 2003).

In general, donors have introduced new monitoring and greater checks on their grantees in response to questions around the probity of NGOs that have arisen in recent years. These relate not only to suspicions of the links of NGOs to extremists, but also to evidence of severe mismanagement of donor funding by NGOs, as exemplified in a scandal in 2003 implicating the Palestinian Society for the Protection of Human Rights and the Environment (LAW), which at the time was one of the largest NGOs in the Occupied Territories. The scandal lent legitimacy to claims peddled by Israeli politicians that Palestinian NGOs were corrupt and untrustworthy and reinforced the tendency of donors to increase checks on their Palestinian grantees.

There are no documented cases of NGO donor funding being transferred to a terrorist organization in the Palestinian Territories,[5] and only a small number of NGOs are thought to have links with extremists (DFID 2004, 7). Still, these concerns clearly shape public attitudes of aid, which in turn influences moves to introduce new bureaucratic practices of control as well as enhanced oversight of civil society funding. In 2009 the British media reported claims by the Tax Payers' Alliance, which campaigns for lower taxes, that DFID aid to the PA was being used to fund school textbooks "promoting terrorism and encouraging young Palestinians to hate the West" (Gloger 2009).

Strict eligibility requirements for receiving US assistance, which were tightened in the 2005 Foreign Operations Bill, have also complicated the delivery of US aid to the Palestinians. The requirements prohibit grantees of US assistance from being involved in or otherwise supporting terrorist activities. Within the OPTs, US government funds may not be used to support any organization thought to be affiliated with Hamas, which is on the US list of officially designated terrorist organizations. USAID has piloted a Partner Vetting System in its West Bank and Gaza program. This requires grantees to check the personnel details of their partners overseas against an intelligence database.[6]

Since 2003, USAID has also required its grantees to sign "Anti-Terrorism Certificates" (ATCs) that compel them to undertake due diligence checks as a precaution against indirectly supporting terrorist activity. The ATC applies to all organizations with either a US base or a US partner, as well as organizations that receive US funding (Fast 2006). While USAID officials de-emphasize the importance of ATCs,[7] in practice many relief and development NGOs have experienced new difficulties in engaging with Palestinian organizations. The legal obligation of aid agencies to verify the background and possible links of their partners with designated terrorist organizations has caused many international NGOs to shift to direct implementation (Fast 2006). Many Palestinian NGOs have refused to sign the ATC. The Palestinian NGO Network (PNGO), an influential NGO lobby, called on its members to refuse any grants awarded by USAID as a protest against the ATC requirement, which it claims is intended "to create internal conflict among Palestinians" (NGO Monitor 2007). The alignment of many charitable actors with Hamas and the political stance of other groups that refuse to sign USAID ATCs have meant there is a dearth of implementing partners in the Occupied Territories.

In practice, these checks have made it more difficult for Palestinian NGOs and Islamic organizations to access funding, not least because many groups have worried about undue political interference by donors in their activities and dealings with partners on the ground. Many rightly worry that accepting donor funding under these conditions may damage their standing as being impartial and neutral, especially in a situation in which there is such widespread distrust of NGOs on all sides.

A second repercussion of framing the conflict as connected to the War on Terror has been to heighten suspicion of civil society and, in turn, intensify moves to crack down on suspect groups. Against the backdrop of the occupation and the lack of a fully sovereign authority in the Palestinian Territories, the Israeli government has long been wary of Palestinian civil society as a terrain for mobilizing popular support for the resistance and nationalist ambitions of different Palestinian political factions. The War on Terror has legitimized Israeli suspicions of Palestinian civil society and Islamic groups as well as provided justification to act on its claims that these actors are associated with terrorism. Israel has stepped up its controls on what it perceives as suspect elements of civil society, including Palestinian NGOs, human rights organizations, Islamic social services organizations, and international NGOs. There has been a crackdown on Islamic social welfare groups in the Occupied Territories in disregard of their professionalism and diligence to adhere to regulatory requirements. These groups have been shut down, their assets seized, and their staff have been detained on the basis that they provide support to Hamas. The objective of emasculating Hamas's political base is the primary consideration informing the security clampdown on these groups.

Palestinian civil society members and Islamic religious figures in Israel have also come under intensified political pressure. A respected Islamic scholar, and founder of the Islamic Movement in Israel, was arrested in May 2003 along with 14 Palestinians holding Israeli citizenship. Israeli authorities alleged that the Islamic Movement engaged in the unlawful transfer of money from illegal, foreign NGOs and companies to Hamas (EMHRN 2004). The offices of Palestinian NGOs in Israel have also been raided, most notably Adalah, which came under official investigation in August 2002 by the Israeli government regulator (EMHRN 2004).

International Islamic organizations providing relief in the Occupied Territories were also targeted. In May 2006, Israel labeled the Birmingham(United Kingdom)-based Islamic Relief a Hamas front after Israeli security services arrested Ayaz Ali, the organization's program manager for Gaza. Ali was held for three weeks and interrogated by Israel's Shin Bet security service for allegedly providing assistance to Hamas institutions and organizations, including the Al Wafa and Al Tzalah associations, which are illegal in Israel.[8] However, Islamic Relief claims that Israeli intelligence confused the proscribed group, Jamaiat Al-Wafa LiRayat Al-Musenin, with a well-known hospital in Gaza called Al-Wafa, which both the United States and United Kingdom have funded, and Al-Tzalah with a reputable firm of auditors used by Islamic Relief (McGreal 2006). The Israeli government alleged Islamic Relief's activities were carried out by Islamic social service groups whose activities are intended to further Hamas's ideology and that are controlled and staffed by Hamas operatives.

There is deep suspicion in Israel of human rights organizations and international NGOs, which are perceived as promoting the political aims of Palestinians. This suspicion extends to and includes international donor agencies, which are thought to reflect an allegedly anti-Israel bias in their funding and activity. In 2002, an NGO Bill was proposed in the Knesset that would have limited foreign contributions to Israeli NGOs. The Bill would have required NGOs to seek permission from the Registrar of Associations, which would have had increased powers to follow and supervise the work of NGOs (EMHRN 2004). The Bill was never passed, yet it served a political purpose by casting suspicion over NGOs, which are widely thought to promote the Palestinian position by using the language of human rights and international law. The following quote from a newspaper editorial in Israel on the involvement of Christian Aid, the Anglican Church, and other Palestinian organizations in a divestment campaign captures the thinking of Israeli officials: "Public campaigns reflecting stark anti-Israel themes are characteristic of much of Christian Aid's activities, as well as the agendas of other groups claiming to promote human rights and relieve suffering . . . In the cycle of demonization, radical church leaders channel 'charitable' funds to extremists . . . then cite their claims in justifying divestment campaigns and similar activities using the false flag of human rights" (Steinberg 2005). Pro-Israel websites and blogs such as "NGO Monitor" have sought to discredit

NGO claims of impartiality and neutrality. A typically disdainful entry on the "NGO Monitor" website claims, "NGO statements and press releases use the politicized rhetoric of human rights, such as "collective punishment" and "crimes against humanity," in selective and one-sided condemnations of Israel" (NGO Monitor 2008).

There is a clear political motivation to purporting allegations that NGOs are misused. For instance, the "NGO Monitor" website claims that DFID funding "goes towards politicised NGOs that campaign on external agendas as opposed to internal development, and use their status to demonize Israel" (NGO Monitor 2005). It cites the Humanitarian Practice Network at the Overseas Development Institute as an example of "a humanitarian remit being misused to make externally focussed attacks against Israel." Negative perceptions of NGO misuse and links with extremism have also influenced the use of aid to support security-minded measures. For example, under an objective to promote private sector development as a way of establishing an economic basis for conflict resolution, DFID has provided capacity support to the Palestinian Monetary Authority on the design and implementation of anti-money laundering/counter-terrorist financing legislation (DFID 2006).

Another impact of linking the conflict to the War on Terror has been that it has provided the Israeli government rationale to introduce a host of controls on the activities of non-governmental actors. These controls have consisted of physical barriers as well as bureaucratic practices that tighten the spaces for civil society to act, and in some cases prevent their access to populations in need. The pressures on Palestinian civil society, and international organizations and groups seeking to help the Palestinians, exemplify the constraints imposed on Palestinian society writ large. Restrictions on Palestinians' freedom of movement encompass physical barriers, including the separation wall between Israel and the West Bank, checkpoints, and road closures as well as a permit regime to control the movement of Palestinians and non-Palestinians alike between the Occupied Territories, Israel, and beyond.

The regime of security restrictions on the movements of Palestinians has been taken to its logical extreme in Gaza, which has been described as "a large, beachfront prison." Israel, which claims it is no longer an occupying power following its disengagement in 2005, maintains a de facto occupation. It has tight control of two of the three land borders and patrols the sea and airspace over Gaza. The only open checkpoint at Erez has been described as "a dystopia of barbed wire, metal cages and full-body searches" (Goldberg 2006).

Israel has denied entry to international aid workers and activists to the OPTs, refused visa extensions, and deported international volunteers and staff. In May 2003, Israel introduced a disclaimer that internationals wanting to enter Gaza had to sign stating that they had no association with International Solidarity Movement (which has supported international activists to protest and obstruct operations by the IDF inside the OPTs) or other organizations that seek to disrupt military activities. Host organizations were required to sign waivers proving that the international volunteer would not conduct any acts of terror (EMHRN 2004). Foreigners entering the Gaza strip must seek written authorization from the IDF as well as sign a "waiver" that absolves Israel of responsibility for any death or injury caused by Israeli soldiers (EMHRN 2003). Noncompliance may result in deportation and future denial of entry into Israel (EMHRN 2004).

It has also become more difficult for internationals to acquire work permits and visas. Expatriates working in Israel require a permit from the Ministry of Interior (Fast 2006). Many enter initially on a three-month tourist visa, but aid agencies have argued that extensions beyond this period have become increasingly difficult to obtain. Many organizations have found it more difficult to hire and retain international staff, especially those with passports from Muslim countries or countries that do not recognize Israel. Furthermore, Israeli NGO staff is barred from traveling to Palestinian-controlled parts of the West Bank and all of Gaza (Fast 2006).

As well as having the obvious impact of making it more difficult to reach beneficiaries, these bureaucratic restrictions on the entry of international aid workers and activists have been part of the de facto Israeli policy to isolate Palestinian civil society internationally. As well as activists from the International Solidarity Movement, other international staff that have been barred from entering the Occupied Territories include staff from the Ford Foundation, a Dutch–Belgian team of medical doctors, and the secretary general of the International Federation of Human Rights Leagues (EMHRN 2004).

Palestinian NGO workers are routinely denied permission to travel abroad to attend conferences, no matter the topic of the conference (Guest 2007). The general director of the nonpartisan human rights group Al-Haq, Shawan Jabarin, has routinely been banned from leaving the Occupied Territories. Human rights campaigners argue that these restrictions have nothing to do with safeguarding Israel's security but instead are meant to obstruct the work of Palestinian human rights workers (EMHRN 2008). When crossing the barrier from the West Bank into east Jerusalem and other Palestinian enclaves cut off by the barrier, all Palestinians, regardless of their affiliation with international agencies, are required to leave their vehicle and walk through a pedestrian lane where they go through a metal detector, have their property x-rayed, and, for some, are subjected to a full body search (OCHA 2007b).

As well as these checks on the entry and movement of NGO workers and activists into the Occupied Territories, aid workers and the offices of civil society organizations have been attacked by Israeli security personnel. Up to the end of 2007, eight journalists had been killed by Israeli occupation forces since the beginning of intifada in September 2000 (PCHR 2007). There were 85 documented incidents where journalists had been fired at by Israeli forces. Journalists had been beaten, detained, and denied access to areas where military operations were occurring; media equipment had been confiscated; and journalists' freedom of movement was restricted. Several peace activists have been killed. The case of Rachel Corrie, an American peace activist killed by an Israeli military bulldozer while protesting the destruction of Palestinian homes, received global media attention owing to its particular brutality. Israeli forces have also attacked peaceful demonstrations by Palestinians against Israeli settlement activities such as the closure and confiscation of Palestinian land (PCHR 2007). Israeli military attacks on UN ambulances and the arrest and detention of UN employees have been mentioned in the annual reports on safety and security for UN and humanitarian personnel (Fast 2006).

Conclusion

The terrain of civil society has been a central battle line in the conflict between Israel and the Palestinians. Civil society has been important to how both Palestinians and Israelis constitute and pursue their respective ideas of security. Non-governmental actors have been important for mobilizing support, advancing nationalist ambitions and notions of statehood, and otherwise promoting the political ideals of either side. At the same time, the conflict has irrevocably shaped the field for civil society action. This is observed in the constraints on organizing, as well as in how civil society defines its role and relations with the state and political movements. Considering the close coupling of civil society and politics in the conflict, it is unsurprising that civil society has been treated as a legitimate target in security crackdowns. However, the War on Terror has renewed scrutiny of civil society actors in the conflict, lending legitimacy to new controls on their activity and bringing out further complexities for how civil society defines itself and articulates its roles in a shifting global political context.

Civil society is important to the achievement of strategic aims of all sides in the conflict. Many of the pressures on civil society relate to outlooks of their role and contribution to forming and pursuing a notion of security that is advanced by different sides. For Israel, Orthodox groups and diaspora networks have provided pivotal support in protecting and promoting the Jewish identity of the state. Palestinian expectations are that civil society resist the occupation by documenting and speaking out against human rights abuses by the Israeli military as well as responding to the social and economic needs of the poor. International donors have looked to secular Palestinian civil society groups as a way of working around Islamic movements and to Palestinian political leaders to promote liberal peace ideals. These different outlooks also inform the different and contrasting treatments of various categories of civil society. They also point to the different perceptions at play. Palestinian civil society actors that have enjoyed international credibility—namely, secular and human rights organizations—lack grassroots credibility, whereas Islamic civil society that possesses widespread popular support is not viewed as legitimate by Israel or international powers.

Although the burden is on "bad" civil society to remove the suspicion that surrounds their activities, the problems of Palestinian civil society relate ultimately to the lack of a political settlement and the problems of using aid as a way out of the existing political impasse. Aid has become discredited as an instrument to extend support to groups that bid for the various bilateral political interests in the conflict, and thus it is ineffective as a tool for building in the popular legitimacy that is lacking in secular groups. The isolation of Islamic civil society has only drawn the lines in the conflict more starkly and may risk a boomerang effect by enabling Islamic groups to claim greater legitimacy by presenting themselves as victims of the unfair treatment of Palestinians in general. The importance of civil society in the conflict, and the threats to its internal and international standing, has never been greater.

Notes

1. For scholarly analysis on the roots of the Israel–Palestine conflict and its shifting dynamics over time, see Tessler (1994), Said (2001), Meital (2006) and Smith (2007b).

2. Hamas Charter. 1988. Article 21. Available online at http://avalon.law.yale.edu/20th_century/hamas.asp.

3. "Hamas's use of charitable societies to fund and support terror." Israel Ministry of Foreign Affairs. September 22, 2003. Available online at http://www.mfa.gov.il/MFA/MFAArchive/2000_2009/2003/9/Hamas-s%20use%20of%20charitable%20societies%20to%20fund%20and%20su.

4. "The Hamas—background." Israel Ministry of Foreign Affairs. August 24, 1997.

5. Author's interview. USAID official. Washington, D.C., April 24, 2008.

6. Author's interview. USAID official. Washington, D.C., April 24, 2008.

7. Author's interview. USAID official. Washington, D.C., April 24, 2008.

8. "British national arrested for assisting Hamas." Israeli Ministry of Foreign Affairs, press release. May 29, 2006. Available online at http://www.mfa.gov.il/MFA/Terrorism+Obstacle+to+Peace/Terrorism+and +Islamic+Fundamentalism/British+national+arrested+for+assisting+Hamas +29-May-2006.htm.

11

Only "Civilians" Count: The Influence of GWOT Discourses on Governments' Humanitarian Responses to "Terror"-Related Conflicts

Nisrine Mansour

In the past decade, "terrorism" has occupied the imagination of governments and populations alike. Civilians have become equally at the center of insurgents' violent attacks and states' military retaliation. In the repercussions of 9/11 unilateral and multilateral state responses became controversial, as they brought significant distress to populations caught in the line of fire of the so-called new humanitarian and counter-terrorist wars. What is "new" about these wars is not so much the identification of insurgent military activities as "terrorist," as this label was used in several previous battles in the last century; rather the novelty lies in the ways in which the global War on Terror (GWOT) regime reformulated the state's security priorities in relation to civil space (Howell and Lind 2008, 2009). In their military campaigns, states have increasingly compromised civilians' "immunity," a basic premise found in International Humanitarian Law (IHL).

Prior to this reformulation, governments justified their failure to protect populations within the IHL framework, pointing to constraints of low capacity or political complexity (Lischer 2007). Through the examples of Afghanistan and Iraq, the new GWOT regime shook the moral foundations for the protection of civilians and the provision of humanitarian support. The GWOT regime effectuated a double shift in governments' concern with the safety of populations and internal and cross-border displacement. At the moral level, governments absolved themselves from their obligation to protect these populations and provide them with humanitarian assistance.

At the operational level, they tightened their grip over the management and provision of humanitarian assistance, a role previously championed by multilateral agencies and NGOs (Lischer 2007). The new security grounds had a central premise: contesting the nature and the value of the "civilian" status of these populations. As civilians were variably identified as anything from "collateral damage" to outright "terrorists," the distinctions between the military and civilian categories in relation to the right to protection became unsettled. A gradual normalization of civilians' losses ensued (Owens 2003).

The dynamics and implications of these shifting boundaries are still largely unexplored. Analyses of the influence of GWOT on state–civilian relations under the GWOT regime have included useful insights on the security-imbued "humanitarian" discourses of superpowers engaging in counter-terrorism (Hajjar 2007; Ayub and Kouvo 2008; Finnemore 2004; Lang 2004). Similarly, valuable discussions have flagged the erosion of the IHL as a universal regime moral code in these operations (Hajjar 2008; Molier 2006). However, both perspectives reveal little about the practical implications of these issues at the national level of analysis of state–civilian relations. The lived experiences of populations under conflict situations have been pertinently elaborated through research on humanitarian relief and conflict-induced displacement (Chatty 2007; Feldman 2007; Montclos 2008; Agier 2002a). These accounts have been concerned with various types of conflict situations and are yet to engage with the specific influences of the GWOT regime. This chapter bridges these three perspectives to analyze the ways in which national governments translate and enact national security discourses into their humanitarian assistance to civilians within the GWOT era. It seeks to show that state–society dynamics are far from coherent, and governments' humanitarian policies toward various affected populations are rather imbued with conflicting security discourses and practices.

The chapter argues that, in the post-9/11 era, governmental humanitarian assistance has been reshaped according to security concerns around affected populations. Rather than fully incorporating or rejecting it, governments use this new GWOT security framework to various degrees, according to the specific political context, to reconfigure the "target" populations, both as civilians and as militant groups who operate within them. This influence is manifested at two levels. First, despite their international political alliances, governments frame the legitimacy of militant groups according to local and regional geopolitical factors that are enmeshed with, but not restricted to, the GWOT regime. They classify militants in relation to these influences into variable security categories ranging from armed resistance to illegitimate terrorism. Second, governments subsequently redraw the concept of "civilians" in relation to their definitions of militant groups in terms of their legitimacy. The conceptual distinctions between civilians and militants become elastic, affecting their entitlement to protection and humanitarian assistance. For this it is important to explore how the representations of the target populations are manifested in governmental security claims and how they are reflected in their humanitarian policies. As the intertwining between security and humanitarian discourses exercises constitutive and transformative power on affected populations, it is useful to conceptualize these humanitarian policies as a regime of governance with serious implications on populations.

To illustrate this argument, the governmental security and humanitarian discourses in two cases of "summer wars on terror" in Lebanon are contrasted. The first case is commonly known as the July 2006 War, a major military operation launched by Israel on Lebanon following Hezbollah's kidnapping of two Israeli soldiers in early July and that lasted until mid-August 2006. The second case is known as the Nahr Al Bared Clashes and was launched by the Lebanese army against Fateh Al Islam (*Islamic Sway*), a little-known Islamist group in the Nahr Al Bared Palestinian "camp,"[1] and lasted between June and September of 2007. Although the two wars are very different in scope, they are underpinned by a similar "anti-terrorist" logic involving militant groups with specific religious and ethnic attributes and resulting in the displacement of entire populations associated with them, namely Lebanese Shi'as and Nahr Al Bared Palestinian residents, respectively. These two cases are useful in illustrating how the influence of the GWOT regime on national humanitarian assistance is complex and varied, and how different wars incur different crises, issues, and responses.

In selecting these cases, I am aware that the position and role of the Lebanese government were very different, as it was at the receiving end of Israel's GWOT operation on Hezbollah. However, this difference does not affect the line of argument. It provides a contrasting backdrop showing the variability and complexity of the influence of local and global security discourses on civilians.

The chapter also does not aim to elaborate on the validity of the distinction between categories of civilians and militants. This discussion has been aptly and amply debated within humanitarian relief and conflict studies with some interesting conclusions regarding "civilian ambiguity." Such ambiguity occurs as populations are inevitably involved in wars through social, political, and economic ties with militants (Slim 2007). The chapter discusses the implications of adopting these categories as morality frameworks that organize state–civilian relations.

The argument elaborating the influence of the GWOT regime on humanitarian assistance is explored in three sections. The first section shows that the government formulates the legitimacy of the two conflicts according to local and global security concerns that impact the framing of militant groups. The subsequent section discusses the conditions for the construction of populations into varying degrees of "civility." The third section discusses the implications of these constructions for the government's humanitarian assistance policies. The chapter concludes with some research and policy remarks.

Justifying Wars and Framing Militants

This section explores the Lebanese government's formulation of security concerns in relation to the two militant groups involved in the two aforementioned conflicts. It looks at the ways in which the Lebanese government positions militant groups according to the GWOT terrorism framework.

"Terrorism" was recently singled out as a special form of hostility that exceeds the usual violence frameworks. Popular definitions like the one used by the UN Security Council describe terrorism as "criminal acts, including against civilians, committed with the intent to cause death or serious bodily injury, or taking hostages, with the purpose to provoke a state of terror in the general public . . . [and] intimidate a population" (cited in Roberts 2005, 102). This definition is underpinned by the two elements of "threat" and "fear" and places civilians at its center. In this sense, the GWOT logic is constructed in tandem across security and humanitarian discourses (Wheeler 2002). This understanding of terrorism, adopted by war theorists and governments alike, is inherently vague. It does not elaborate on what constitutes a "threat" (and what constitutes "civilian"), leaving a large margin of interpretation as to what terrorism actually means. With "threat" and "fear" adopted as two rationalities based on emotive perceptions of security, governments constructed dissident militant groups as "terrorists" on the basis of their ideological considerations of "evil" (Roberts 2005).

In the two cases, the government judged the legitimacy of the two militant groups based on hybrid security discourses adopted from the GWOT regime and the local political and historical context. The labeling of Hezbollah as a terrorist organization by the United States and Israel is a case in point.[2] Both powers regard Hezbollah as a staunch enemy and have placed it on their terrorist lists. The group's local legitimacy and popularity is as complex as it is substantial—and as it is controversial. The pro-Western government of Lebanon at the time of the two events found the paramilitary status and pro-Syrian and -Iranian links of Hezbollah problematic. The party, however, enjoyed legitimacy as a major political player and as a popular representative of the majority of Lebanese Shi'a population.[3]

The convoluted history of the Palestinians' presence in Lebanon bears the repercussions of the ongoing Israeli–Palestinian conflict and their mass deportation since 1948. Their historical armed resistance and the existence of 400,000 refugees in Lebanon trigger as much sympathy as controversy. After 1967 various Palestinian militant groups used Lebanon as a political and military platform. Lebanese political parties are fiercely divided over the legitimacy of their armament and the long-term solution for their displacement.[4] The continued displacement of Palestinians due to Israeli occupation, and the massacres they were subjected to during the civil war by right-wing Lebanese militias, granted them much political support.[5] Yet some political parties blame them for their role in the civil war. They are also considered a threat to Lebanon's precarious sectarian balance should they be granted Lebanese citizenship as a part of the final solution for the Israeli–Palestinian peace process. The Fateh Al Islam group became an example of this "threat" and came to symbolize the reinterpretation of refugee camps as "security islands" (Khalidi and Riskedahl 2007).

Despite this complexity, the government has had two different stands toward these militant groups. Hezbollah's legitimacy, although contested, was preserved. In contrast, Fateh Al Islam was drawn into the GWOT archetypal "terrorist" and "evil" profile. This distinction drew on a pool of complex local political constructions of social groups within Lebanese society, which categorized groups according to their perceived threat to national security and according to how they were embedded in the Lebanese context.

First, the groups' threat to national security was constructed in terms of intent to harm. Hezbollah was nationally perceived as a resistance movement whose arms were turned "outwards" toward the ultimate Israeli enemy (Norton 2007). In this sense, its military and political power was not perceived as a national threat. Moreover, the July 2006 war took place amid a series of chronic and episodic outbursts of internal violence characterizing the post-conflict Lebanon.[6] Launched between July 12 and August 14, 2006, this war was the first massive operation by Israel against Lebanon since the withdrawal of Israeli forces from the occupied Lebanese south in 2000.[7] In a clash over the kidnapping of two Israeli soldiers, Israel launched its "Second Lebanon War"[8] with the goal of "dismantling" the "terrorist" organization (Halevi 2006). For such a targeted mission, the conduct of military operations resulted in one of the most devastating tolls of human and material losses besides the civil war.

In this one-month war, the Israeli army carried out massive bombings of all villages in the southern part of Lebanon as well as in the southern suburbs of Beirut and systematically destroyed major national economic and physical infrastructure. As Israel's goal of eradicating Hezbollah was not realized, the group proclaimed a symbolic "divine victory" (*nasr ilahi*) despite the crushing costs on civilian populations (MacGinty 2007). The toll of Lebanese civilian deaths reached 1,191, out of whom 30 percent were children (Presidency of the Council of Ministers 2006a). Around one million inhabitants were displaced, constituting 25 percent of the total population. The total bill of direct damages was estimated to be US$4 billion, with 130,000 residential units destroyed in addition to thousands of businesses, 300 factories, and countless national infrastructure outlets.

The government's stand toward Hezbollah shifted considerably as the conflict progressed. In a reflection of the internal political tensions, it initially fiercely discredited its military actions and questioned its legitimacy by branding it as "a satellite arm of Teheran" (*Le Figaro* 2006). However, with the sweeping humanitarian crisis induced by the Israeli operations and the persistence of Hezbollah's defense, the government recognized Israel as a greater national threat. It joined Hezbollah in denouncing Israel's "state terrorism" and geared its discourse away from the group to focus on the humanitarian crisis (Siniora 2006).

In contrast, the government framed Fateh Al Islam as a threat to national security mainly due to very different local political conditions. The group's threat was concentrated in its intention to harm by targeting the state's national symbol, the Lebanese Army.[9] On May 19, 2007, Fateh Al Islam, a formerly unknown militant group, carried out a hold-up of a bank in Tripoli and killed 20 Lebanese Army soldiers. The group sought refuge in Nahr Al Bared, one of the 14 Palestinian "camps" that had accommodated a total of 400,000 Palestinian refugees since 1948.[10] The threat of the group was also articulated in terms of its irrationality. Its actions were deemed unjustifiable and the group was likened to "cancerous cells that could multiply" (Lebanese Ministry of Defence 2007a). The security forces identified the group as predominantly composed of Palestinian militants belonging to the same conservative strand of Salafi Islam as Bin Laden's Al Qaeda.

Once the terrorist link was established, the Lebanese defense minister and the chief of army took the lead in an operation specifically aimed at "eradicating" the group (Lebanese Ministry of Defence 2007a). This operation bore a striking resemblance to the "counter-terrorist" discursive practices deployed by Israel in the July 2006 war against Hezbollah. The army imposed a blockade and conducted systematic bombing of the Nahr Al Bared Camp. Twenty days into the operation, the defense minister declared "mission accomplished," reiterating the ill-fated counter-terrorism victory claims of President Bush in Iraq (Lebanese Ministry of Defence 2007b). This announcement was soon declared premature, as the

group showed no sign of surrender. The army intensified bombing operations of the camp in an attempt to track the hideaways of the group within
residential areas. On September 2, 2007, the army declared a victory,
stating that the militants were killed or captured and that their leader was
presumed killed in the war zone, although his body was never found.

The Nahr Al Bared clashes were of a much smaller scale than the July
2006 war, as it was mostly restricted to the outskirts of the second largest
city of Tripoli, where Nahr Al Bared is located. However, its repercussions
on the inhabitants were more devastating in relative terms. The human
losses of the clashes were estimated at 40 Palestinian civilians, 80 Fateh Al
Islam militants, and 169 military personnel. All 33,000 Nahr Al Bared
inhabitants were displaced. In addition, the indiscriminate shelling of the
Lebanese army destroyed 85 percent of residential units and most
economic outlets, resulting in a large-scale, conflict-induced displacement
crisis (UNRWA 2007).

Second, how these groups were embedded in the Lebanese context also
plays an important role in the framing of these militant groups in GWOT
discourses. This is manifested at two levels. The first level concerns the
extent to which they are perceived to be "indigenously" positioned within
the broader Lebanese sociopolitical context on the basis of political constructions of ethnicity; and the second level relates to the density, breadth,
and direction of their networks among the social groups within which
they operate.

As a militant group, Hezbollah gradually asserted its powerful position
on the Lebanese political scene by moving from 1992 onward from radical
militancy toward active social participation in service delivery and
involvement in representative politics (Harb and Leenders 2005). It gained
legitimate political status through instituting an ultra-national "Islamic
sphere" (*hala islamiyya*) based on a reorganization of a "resistance
society" and the establishment of a "holistic" social network (Harb and
Leenders 2005). Hezbollah's performance in the July 2006 war provided
a renewed platform for this power. It brought significant regional support
to the group, reinstating its defiant position facing Israel. It also gained
substantial popular support from the vast majority of the Shi'a population, which constitutes 40 percent of the Lebanese population. Hence, the
group was able to face the government's initial criticism by accusing them
of treason and alignment with "Israel, Lebanon's ultimate enemy"
(Islamic Resistance in Lebanon 2006).

The dynamics of the construction of Fateh Al Islam in relation to the
Lebanese sociopolitical context were very different. The government
primarily discredited Fateh Al Islam as an exogenous infliction by relying
on a central discursive premise: its constitutive relation to the Palestinians

as an "alien" social group present in Lebanon. Historically succeeding Lebanese governments considered Palestinian camps to be autonomous foreign territories, as they allowed Palestinian armed groups control over them through the Cairo agreement in 1969 (Khalidi and Riskedahl 2007). Although the Lebanese parliament revoked this agreement in 1987, it still observed it in practice. Fateh Al Islam was further dismissed because it had an insignificant historical-political mark on the official and popular Palestinian and Lebanese political scene. The group was recent and obscure, detached from any of the prominent Palestinian factions such as the Palestinian Liberation Organization (PLO), the Islamic Resistance Movement (Hamas), or the Popular Front for Palestinian Liberation. The government focused on profiling the leader of the group as a minor and unstable dissident offshoot from two Palestinian factions. It was an insignificant group that could be easily dismissed and targeted by the government (Lebanese Ministry of Defence 2007a).

Elasticity of Civilian–Military Boundaries

The new security discourses had an impact on the way governments categorized populations according to varying degrees of "civility" and, in this way, defined their right to protection. These categories were drawn in relation to the legitimacy of militant groups, reflecting the elasticity of the discursive boundaries separating civilians and militants.

The construction of social categories is a relational process that contributes in "kind-making," a process whereby a label attached to people alters their perceptions of themselves (Hacking 1986). This relation is specifically pertinent as we trace the ways in which the GWOT regime redefined the civilians in relation to militants. Prior to the rise of this discourse, the enemy was generally defined as "groups of people [who] might lie beyond the realm of normal moral obligation in times of war and political violence" (Slim 2003, 485). This definition implies that there is another group of civilians that governments are morally bound to protect (Wheeler 2002). This right to protection is based on two ethical principles. First, civilians are considered "inherently innocent," such as the case of the traditional vulnerable groups of children and women; and second, "noncombatants," comprising people who refrain from harming the other side (and specifically noncombatant men), are similarly considered innocent. The GWOT regime overthrew these definitions by questioning the extent of involvement of civilians in war-related activities.[11]

As a result, the protection of civilians is compromised on the basis of three types of justifications. First, civilians are considered "collateral damage." Their civilian status is recognized, but their safety is sacrificed in the face of the bigger threats brought by terrorists. Second, civilians are deemed "human shields." They are still entitled to protection, but the responsibility shifts from the state actors to the warring groups who choose to hide among them. The "innocence" premise for civilian protection is shaken here, as it implies that they could also be blamed for providing cover for the militants. Third, civilians are "legitimate targets," as they are considered active participants in terrorist activities. This approach embraces the "total enemy" view as it shifts civilians to the terrorist category and denies them any right to protection.

The two cases illustrate the changing link between the two categories. In the July 2006 war, the government only focused on civilians when it changed its stand on Hezbollah and rejected the "terrorist" label being pushed by Israel. It then constructed the population as civilians predominantly on the basis of their "innocence." In the first week of the war, the government paid little attention to the welfare of the southern populations and focused instead on the political and economic implications of the attacks. It primarily blamed the group for their "bad timing" of the military operation that fell at the start of the high tourist season in Lebanon (*Le Figaro* 2006). It took the government nine days of escalating death tolls, massive destruction, and exodus of populations before it finally denounced the attacks as an "aggression against the civilians and the vital institutions in the country" (Presidency of the Council of Ministers 2006b).[12] Within this discursive shift, the southern populations became the symbol of the Lebanese population and were placed at the center of multiple governmental humanitarian appeals. They were represented simultaneously as "innocent victims" and "valiant people of Lebanon" (Presidency of the Council of Ministers 2006c). At the same time, any reference to Hezbollah was dropped.

In the case of the Nahr Al Bared clashes, the government adopted the GWOT discourse to justify their actions. This approach meant that entire populations were included within the terrorist militant category. Periodic statements from the minister of defense and the chief of the army interweaved inhabitants within the activities and profiles of Fateh Al Islam.[13] The pool of militants was noted to be "drawn from many inhabitants of other Palestinian camps in Lebanon" (Njeim 2007). Inhabitants were also constructed as sharing similar essential values with militants, as reports focused on intimate social relations between them. Militants "settled in the Nahr Al Bared Camp and got married to female inhabitants and rented numerous flats there" (Njeim 2007). The inhabitants of Nahr Al Bared were also stripped of their "innocent civilians" status through an emphasis on their criminality. In order to boost their capital, militants reportedly recruited outlaws from the Nahr Al Bared inhabitants and benefited from the trafficking activities they held on the camp's sea-front (Njeim and Bal'aa 2007).

Finally, Palestinian populations were further militarized as the fleeing inhabitants were considered "terrorist suspects." Their exodus from the camp was under the tight grip of the Lebanese army. People were searched, and most men were taken into military custody for investigation on their possible links with the Fateh Al Islam (Human Rights Watch 2007). Investigation was accompanied by incidents of harassment, torture, and arrests, bringing fear to the populations. There was a systematic forced displacement, as the Lebanese Army did not allow any inhabitants back into Nahr Al Bared to check on their homes and family members left behind (Khalidi and Riskedahl 2007). The army banned all humanitarian assistance inside the camp apart from the evacuation of the wounded, despite civil society's appeals for access. The Lebanese Army considered any inhabitants left behind to be terrorists with no right to protection.

Civilians as Citizens

As affected populations were defined in relation to various militant categories, their status for protection and support was reflected in differentiated governmental responses. The differential treatment of both groups of internally displaced persons (IDPs) suggests a particular governmental approach that frames some civilians as "citizens" and others as "non-citizens."

The humanitarian priorities of the Lebanese government were framed accordingly. In both cases the humanitarian assistance patterns during the period of the conflict consistently favored Lebanese IDPs. One indication of this disparity can be traced through the IDPs' mobility within the "displacement space." In the July War of 2006 the displaced southern populations were granted free movement to any less hazardous northern areas, ranging from the capital Beirut to the mountains. They were hosted in public facilities, including schools and other governmental buildings. The government designated the High Relief Commission to coordinate the official humanitarian operation, complementing other efforts by various civil society and political actors, including proponents and opponents to Hezbollah.[14]

The displacement experience of the Nahr Al Bared population tells another story. Upon fleeing the camp, inhabitants suffered restricted mobility. The population sought refuge exclusively in other Palestinian "camps," mainly Beddawi—a few kilometers from Nahr Al Bared—whose population almost doubled to around 30,000 in the first two weeks of the conflict (UNRWA 2007). Governmental involvement in humanitarian relief to these populations was practically nonexistent, and was entirely left to the UNRWA and NGOs.[15] The government's response was typical of a "host government" that often has little interest in engaging with refugees (Kaiser 2006).

The neglect for Palestinian IDPs was also reflected in the government's documentation of the human losses. In the July 2006 war, the daily coverage of losses focused on civilians, including their names, ages, and hometowns, with no indication of the losses incurred by Hezbollah militants. In the case of the Nahr Al Bared clashes, the government's focus was the reverse. The Ministry of Defence issued a daily count of military losses among both the ranks of the Lebanese army and Fateh Al Islam. The Palestinian civilian losses were mostly not recorded. This focus on military losses stimulated local animosity toward Palestinian inhabitants. Because their plight was unrecognized and they were neither framed as "innocent" nor as "civilians," they were collectively held responsible for the killing of 169 Lebanese army soldiers, two-thirds of whom belonged to the nearby villages.

The Lebanese government reinforced the "civilian as citizen" nexus through its marginal interest in the welfare of Palestinian IDPs and its focus on the Lebanese inhabitants surrounding Nahr Al Bared. The Prime Minister gave "instructions to intensify support to these families . . . and found it necessary to attend to the crises that the Lebanese are enduring as a result of Fateh Al Islam's aggression" (Presidency of the Council of Ministers 2007a). The Palestinian IDPs were hardly mentioned. Their refugee status was confirmed as their needs were allocated and presumably met by UNRWA. A new category of refugees-IDPs was created and its population rendered invisible in the governmental discourse.

Populations placed under this new label incurred a double vulnerability. Governments in general use different labeling techniques to categorize populations into several subcategories (Zetter 2007).[16] The double displacement of the Palestinians—initially from their homelands as refugees, and subsequently from Nahr Al Bared—subjected them to the double labeling of "refugees-IDP" that enhances their "extraterritoriality" (Bauman 2002) and places them further "outside of society" (Brun 2003). As the government confounded "civilians" with "citizens," it excluded Palestinians from both the civilian category and the framework of immunity and protection granted to citizens.

Humanitarian Assistance as an Extension of Security Governance

This section draws the link between security-related constructions of civilians and post-conflict humanitarian assistance. It analyzes the ways in which humanitarian assistance is a type of "humanitarian management" (Agier 2002a), a technique facilitating the reproduction of a broader system of security governance.

The two cases indicate that governmental humanitarian assistance led to two types of reproduction of security governance. In the July 2006 war, where the Lebanese government did not cast Hezbollah within GWOT frames, the official response and reconstruction plan reproduced the political legitimacy of the militant group. In the Nahr Al Bared clashes where counter-terrorist discourses were adopted, the governmental reconstruction plan reproduced the exclusion of and control over Palestinians as "undesirable populations" (Agier 2002a). These processes of reproduction could be seen in first, the rearrangement of political authority in relation to populations, and second, in the establishment of spatial control over them.

The rearrangement of political authority was primarily channeled through major reconstruction plans following the massive destruction of residential infrastructure. In the case of the July 2006 war, tensions between the government and Hezbollah resurfaced following the cease-fire and the massive humanitarian crisis. Both raced to gain political ground through compensation to, and reallocation of, IDPs. Hezbollah took the lead through bypassing government funding and providing efficient short- and long-term planning and execution.

In terms of short-term assistance, Hezbollah's agency for reconstruction, Jihad Al Bina, entered the affected areas in the morning after the cease-fire, distributing an estimated total of US$190,000 in cash handouts to damaged residential and business units in the southern suburbs of Beirut and the southern part of Lebanon (MacGinty 2007). Further compensation followed, subsidizing temporary relocation such as rental, furniture, and subsistence costs. As regards long-term reconstruction, Hezbollah relied on sympathetic governments such as Iran and Qatar, which preferred to deliver substantial direct funding to affected communities (Presidency of the Council of Ministers 2006a). It also extended its efficient network of agencies to provide systematic social support for communities drawing from local and international private donations (MacGinty 2007). On the other hand, while the government secured substantial funding amounting to US$900 million, it could not draw political gains from it. The funds were primarily channeled through the "Council of the south," a governmental reconstruction agency dedicated to South Lebanon and practically run by the speaker of the parliament, a close ally of Hezbollah (Presidency of the Council of Ministers 2006a). The government's remaining reconstruction funds for the southern suburbs were restricted to disbursement of compensation bills as Hezbollah took over the reconstruction plan.

In the case of Nahr Al Bared, the government presided over the relief operations under a banner of physical reconstruction. Halfway through the clashes, the Prime Minister uncovered his efforts to initiate a reconstruction plan in cooperation with a major Lebanese construction firm (Presidency of the Council of Ministers 2007a). This untimely announcement was in stark contrast to the minimal interest given to the humanitarian needs of the IDPs. With the end of the clashes, the government reasserted its ownership over the operations by publicly launching a master plan that would turn Nahr Al Bared into a "model camp." The master plan reflected the previously discussed differential constructions of "civilians" among the displaced population. It was divided into two sections. The UNRWA was designated to reconstruct the Palestinian neighborhoods, known as the "old camp," while the Lebanese government exclusively catered for the minority of Lebanese inhabitants residing in Nahr Al Bared's "new camp" areas. The relief and reconstruction bill for both sections amounted to US$382.5 million, one-third of which went to the areas inhabited by Lebanese residents (Presidency of the Council of Ministers 2007b).

The initiative also generated a political "production of locality" (Appadurai 1996, 182 cited in Agier 2002b) governing relations between inhabitants and the Lebanese broader social space at internal and external levels. First, the government directly intervened to rearrange the internal politics of the camp. It instated the Palestinian Liberation Organisation (PLO), its major Palestinian ally, as the representative Palestinian political patron on the reconstruction board. The appointment of the PLO served to extend the government's control, overriding the other factions and ignoring its contested popularity among the inhabitants (Lamb 2007). Second, at the external level, the Lebanese government acknowledged the opposition of the Lebanese population surrounding Nahr Al Bared to any reconstruction initiative. As the camp was nearly wiped out after the conflict, the neighboring towns and municipalities sought to reclaim the lands onto which it had illegally expanded over the years. The government had to include protesting communities in the redevelopment plan in order for it to go ahead. The tension between the two communities was reflected in the prime minister's speech at the launch of the master plan (Presidency of the Council of Ministers 2008).

The governmental humanitarian response also perpetuated the inequalities that inhabitants were subjected to due to their status as "refugees." The master plan overlooked crucial issues around the livelihoods of the Nahr Al Bared inhabitants that were historically framed in political and security discourses. The Lebanese laws ban Palestinian inhabitants from practicing 73 liberal professions (Halabi 2004). As a result, inhabitants tend to overwhelmingly rely on the informal sector and be confined to low-skill or unskilled manual labor within the camp (UNRWA 2007). With the destruction of the camp, unemployment rates of the Nahr Al

Bared inhabitants rocketed to 90 percent (UNRWA 2007). The vast majority of the population had to rely on cash handouts from UNRWA and NGOs. This was another example of the ways in which humanitarian assistance entrenched long-lasting economic (and political) discrimination and vulnerability (Jacobsen 2002).

The humanitarian assistance installed a particular regime of governance as reconstruction plans were used as tools for negotiating spatial control over populations. In the southern suburbs, the damages to high-density, urban infrastructure were massive, including the headquarters of Hezbollah. The group insisted on managing the reconstruction and the execution process through Wa'ad, a Hezbollah-affiliated firm established specifically for that purpose. The group took control of the spatial rearrangement of the area despite the fact that reconstruction costs were mostly drawn from donations made to the government's budget.[17] In this way, the government's role became that of an auxiliary—a surveyor and an aid broker—while Hezbollah declared ownership over the space as well as the communities it was servicing.

The reconstruction plan of Nahr Al Bared sought to contain the inhabitants within the defined social space and establish the Lebanese government's authority over them. It sustained the idea of refugee camps as a "space for confinement" for "undesirable refugees" (Agier 2002a). Two modalities were together as part of a "technology of power" (Malkki 2002). Gentrification promised a revamping of the urban space with a focus on aesthetics and living environment (UNRWA 2008). The plan included many inviting features, from gated communities to giving attention to light, space, and green spaces. However, it still framed the area within the political category of a "camp" and thus as an exile that fell short of being an open city (Agier 2002a). A less publicized aspect was the rearrangement of policing managed by the Lebanese Army. The new design blocked the camp's access to the sea and installed instead a military base for the Lebanese army (Khalidi and Riskedahl 2007). The internal security of the camp was also handed over to the army, contrary to the earlier understanding between Lebanese and Palestinian authorities. The camp was redrawn from a "security island" to a meta-confinement space for Palestinian non-civilians who became further "suspended in transit" (Bauman 2002).

Conclusion

This chapter explored the ways in which the GWOT regime influences government–civilian relations in non-Western conflict situations. It argued that this influence is conditional upon the sociopolitical local context. When adopted, counter-terrorism discourses become part of governments' humanitarian-security frameworks that contest the "civilian" status of populations and their entitlements to humanitarian assistance. Most importantly, the variable process of adopting certain security discourses is translated into an elastic use of the categories of militants and civilians.

Governments adopted the GWOT regime framework when the legitimacy of militant groups was contested. The conditions for framing militants as "terrorists" depend on the extent to which they are constructed by the governments as a threat to national security, and the degree of their rootedness in the broader political context, such as the portrayal of Fateh Al Islam as an outsider criminal gang, similar to the Al Qaeda profiling.

The variable influence of the GWOT discourses directly impacts populations within which militant groups operate. Governments rearrange affected populations in relation to an elastic categorization of civilian and militant boundaries. When governments frame militants in "terrorist" categories, they also include the affected populations within them and compromise their civilian immunity, as in the case of the Palestinian inhabitants of Nahr Al Bared. In contrast, when the operations of the military groups are legitimized, they are included within the "civilian" category granted to affected populations. In these categorizations GWOT discourses have a partial influence. They are enmeshed with local historical and political nationalist constructions of social groups, reflected in the way the ideas of "civilians" and "citizens" are conflated. Contrary to some studies arguing that internally displaced persons tend to be more vulnerable than refugees (Lischer 2007), the chapter shows that that Palestinian refugees faced a double vulnerability stemming from the early constraints imposed by their initial status of "refugees" and their more recent status as "non-civilian" (read non-citizen) IDPs.

These constructions translated into governmental humanitarian assistance as a technique for reproducing a regime of security governance. Relief and reconstruction plans were instruments of bargaining for the renegotiation of political authority over the populations. This renegotiation was manifested through varying patterns of displacement and settlement, gaining ownership over reconstruction plans and controlling the social space.

It is evident from these cases that the GWOT regime has changed government-civilian (and also citizen) relations in complex ways. It has also changed the political nature of humanitarian assistance by questioning the meanings of "civilians" and "citizens" and shaking the basic foundations of their immunity and protection.

Notes

1. "Camp" refers to the settlements of the Palestinian refugees in Lebanon since 1948. The common use of the term holds pejorative political meanings as they are in fact high-density urban agglomerations.

2. The group is allegedly held responsible for the bombing of the US embassy in Lebanon in 1983 and is linked to attacks on the Israeli embassy in Buenos Aires in 1992.

3. These representational claims were facilitated by the post-conflict reconciliation pact in 1989 granting Hezbollah the right to armed resistance in the then-occupied south. It was reinforced by the group's continuous sweeping victories in the consociational parliamentary elections and local elections from 1992 onward.

4. Although various Palestinian armed groups were mostly disarmed as a result of the Israeli invasion of Lebanon in 1982, Palestinian groups still have armed control over camps and in a few other areas outside of the camps. The militarization of the camps was based on the Cairo accord of the 1950s, and was later scrapped in the 1980s by the Lebanese parliament (Khalidi and Riskedahl 2007). This legal change was, however, not put in practice until the Nahr al Bared clashes.

5. The Lebanese civil war lasted between 1975 and 1990. The main Palestinian armed groups based in Lebanon joined the National Movement, a coalition of left-wing and Arab Nationalist parties, to fight against the right-wing parties who opposed the Palestinian armed presence in Lebanon. The right-wing armed groups led by the militia of the Lebanese Kataeb Party were implicated in the massacres of Palestinian civilians in the Tal El Zaatar refugee camp in 1976—with the backing of Syria—and later the Sabra and Shatila refugee camps in 1982—with the backing of Israeli forces (El-Khazen 2000; Haddad 2003; Khalili 2005; Sayigh 1993)

6. Despite the general view that the end of hostilities arrived with the end of the civil war, studies show that intermittent violence continued until the present day, including 28 major political assassinations and assassination attempts between 1990 and 2005 (Knudsen and Yassin 2007).

7. In the decade ranging between the end of the civil war (1990) and the withdrawal of the Israeli army from South Lebanon in 2000, Israel launched three military operations against Lebanon in 1993, 1996, and 1999.

8. With reference to the Israeli invasion of Lebanon in 1982 as the "First Lebanon War."

9. The construction of the Lebanese Army as a symbol of national unity was formulated in the post-conflict era after notorious episodes of divisions within the ranks during the civil war.

10. Palestinian refugees are considered by the Lebanese state as temporary residents in view of their eventual returning to their Palestinian homelands. They are deprived of many civilian rights such as the right to vote and to practice 85 professional activities. The "camps," or settlements, are treated as self-governing entities policed by local Palestinian parties and managed by the United Nations Relief and Works Agency for Palestine Refugees in the Near East (UNRWA) in terms of basic social services. They are among the most overpopulated areas characterized by poor-quality housing and extreme deprivation.

11. The degree of this group's direct relation with the war regime is contested. Views range from restrictive definitions of "those who bear weapons" to those who help in producing weapons or indirectly supporting the military networks by breeding and feeding militants (Slim 2003). These debates provided grounds for bombing civilians working in weapons factories.

12. The official response lagged behind the popular outcry and civil society's instant mobilization for humanitarian relief. The role of the local and Arab media was significant in flagging the government's delayed response through minute-by-minute coverage of the deadly attacks. The digital media flourished as it detailed the humanitarian crisis and lobbying for support at the international level.

13. The mainstream media and the majority of civil society organizations played an important role in entrenching these representations. However, some 20 NGOs formed a joint campaign of humanitarian assistance, denouncing such representations of Palestinian civilians.

14. This is not to say that this operation ran without tension. Southerners were framed within unfavorable categories of IDPs, namely as different from and inferior to regular citizens (Brun 2003) and weak and ill (Pupavac 2008). These negative connotations actually increased state and popular mobilization for humanitarian support, while it simultaneously denied them any voice.

15. Relief efforts were mainly handled by Palestinian political groups (including the PLO and Hamas), and Palestinian, Lebanese, and international NGOs. It was coordinated through the "Lebanon Support Network" that was established following the July 2006 war.

16. Although Zetter focuses on formal/legal classifications by European countries, his argument can be extended to include informal classifications that transpire through formal humanitarian assistance policies in non-Western contexts.

17. The government could only negotiate for the compensation payments to be disbursed to and cashed by individual inhabitants, rather than directly transferred to Waad.

12

THE POLITICS OF UGANDA'S ANTI-TERRORISM LAW AND ITS IMPACT ON CIVIL SOCIETY

Joshua B. Rubongoya

Uganda is one of 14 Third World countries that have had anti-terrorism legislation passed with minimal debate in the two years following the 9/11 terrorist attacks on the United States. However, there are at least 13 Third World countries in which similar legislation has been enacted, but only after extensive debate and inordinate controversy. In at least six countries counter-terrorism legislation is pending (Whitaker 2007a). This chapter examines the domestic and international political dynamics that converged to ensure rapid passage of the 2002 Anti-Terrorism Act (ATA) of Uganda and assesses its impact (and potential effect) on civil society organizations. A central claim of this chapter is that the limited and controlled political spaces in Uganda, the atrocities by the rebel group the Lord's Resistance Army (LRA), and pressure from the United States all combined to ease passage of the 2002 ATA. By way of context the chapter explores the reassertion of Uganda as the balancer in the volatile and unstable Great Lakes region and therefore as a key ally for the United States in the global security regime. The chapter concludes by noting the improved relationship between the two countries—Uganda and the United States—albeit it is a relationship that has hitherto been driven by the personality of former US President George Bush and the ideological prerogatives of his Republican Party administration. In the wake of President Barack Obama's election, the code word is "reset," meaning an overall review and re-evaluation of the underpinnings of US foreign policy. The winds of change seem to be pointing toward soft power instruments such as diplomacy and multilateralism and away from the more bellicose, unilateral dispensation with its attendant securitization policies.

The Terrorist Attacks of September 11, 2001

The 9/11 attacks marked a clear volte-face in American foreign policy. President Bush in no uncertain terms defined the way forward as comprising a new form of containment—a strategy that departed from countering communism or Soviet expansionism and confronted terrorism and all extremist elements wherever they might be in the world. Although the Bush rhetoric touted democracy as one of the antidotes with which to fight the War on Terror, it was not lost on keen observers that the United States would prioritize its national security interests above any interest it might have in promoting democracy. The first sign of this was the rapid passage of the Patriot Act that circumscribed civil rights and triggered intense debate among civil liberties groups. Guantanamo Bay was established soon after as a facility for the extra-judicial interrogation and incarceration of suspected terrorists. These developments sent clear signals of the potential expansiveness of anti-terrorism legislation to would-be allies such as Uganda in the new and unfolding global security regime. Indeed, soon after the 9/11 attacks the United States placed two rebel groups in Uganda—the LRA and the Allied Democratic Forces (ADF)—on its list of officially designated terrorist organizations (Privacy International 2004). For its part, Uganda enacted its own "Patriot Act" (that is, the 2002 Anti-Terrorist Act). Furthermore, and closely mimicking the Guantanamo Bay strategy, the National Resistance Movement (NRM) government started using so-called safe houses, or unofficial detention centers, in and around Kampala to unlawfully detain and interrogate terror suspects. It is alleged that some suspects were tortured in safe houses before they were turned over to the courts (Privacy International 2004). Therefore, the post-9/11 security dispensation provided an opportunity for governments such as the NRM regime in Uganda to reorganize security structures and practices. However, internal politics also provided further impetus for major reforms.

Setting the Scene: Significant Political Developments in Uganda (1999–2004)

In the period leading up to and following the 9/11 attacks, counter-terrorism structures in Uganda were introduced in a shifting domestic political context. The NRM scrambled to put in place a plethora of legislation intended to solidify its hold on power. At the same time, Ugandan forces were engaged in a controversial war in the Democratic Republic of the Congo (DRC). The Museveni government argued that the war was motivated by a desire to rout out rebel groups that were destabilizing the country. As shall be argued below, this seemed an unsatisfactory explanation for the actions taken by top military commanders in the DRC. In the meantime there was a noticeable rise in rebel activities inside Uganda. Moreover, the looming 2001 general election and the emergence of opposition political leaders that posed a credible challenge to the continued supremacy of the NRM also provided an impetus for the government to consolidate its power.

The Referendum Act (2000)

The Referendum Act was preceded by the Movement Act in 1997. The latter was passed by Parliament without the two-thirds majority quorum. It legally transformed all Ugandans into members of the NRM, mandated that officials of the ruling NRM[1] be funded by the state through a budget vote, and compromised legislative autonomy, thus freezing any semblance of parliamentary checks on executive power. Furthermore, by superimposing the "party" (the NRM) on the state, the Movement Act signaled a transition of Uganda into a one-party state. This effort by the ruling party to entrench itself was further solidified by the ascension of the Referendum Act of 2000. Based on Article 271 of the 1995 Constitution, Ugandans were to decide, in a referendum, whether to continue with the NRM system of no-party rule or to reintroduce a multiparty political system. The bill to legalize the referendum was tabled in Parliament in August of 1999. As had happened with the passing of the Movement Act, the Referendum bill was passed into law without quorum. The Constitutional Court promptly struck it down, arguing that it was passed unconstitutionally.[2] In response, the NRM-dominated parliament amended, for the first time, the 1995 constitution in order to change the process by which a bill could be passed into law (Bussey 2005). The amendment was introduced in Parliament, debated, passed, and received the presidential assent on the same day, and was then used to give retrospective effect to the Referendum (Political Systems) Act of 2000 (Bussey 2005). However, in 2004 the courts ruled this was unconstitutional because the referendum had already been held in June 2000.[3] Hence the results were upheld by the Court and Uganda continued on the course of no-party rule that the NRM favored.

A close examination of these events reveals four important developments. First, the fact that legislative initiatives that were important to the NRM were failing to muster a quorum in a parliament that it dominated was indicative of serious splits, and therefore weaknesses, within the Movement. Second, there was obvious expansion of executive power and a deliberate policy of skirting constitutional guidelines—a symptom of a weakened Movement. Third, and related to the first development, was a steady decline in legislative authority, most notably its capacity to act as a check and balance on executive power. Finally, most of these struggles took place in the courts with much of the resistance coming from political parties such as the Democratic Party. Because of the heavy legal connotations of these statutes and the restricted political space, there was little opposition from civil society. Indeed it was highly doubtful that civil society could have effectively opposed this legislative juggernaut, considering that the NRM had by then concretized its hegemony. Nonetheless it was in this atmosphere that the Anti-Terrorism bill was tabled in Parliament in 2002.

Military Intervention in the Congo

In 2000 Uganda was beginning to pull out of the western DRC after two years of occupation. The 1998 military intervention took place ostensibly to remove safe havens for anti-Uganda rebels. However, the military—and in particular certain high-ranking members of the Uganda Peoples Defense Forces (UPDF), some of whom were close relatives of the Ugandan president Yoweri Museveni—reportedly looted gold and other valuable minerals out of the DRC.[4] In June 1999, the former DRC President Laurent Kabila accused the Uganda government of territorial aggression and human rights violations and filed a case at the International Court of Justice (ICJ). Congo's complaints to the ICJ were preceded by a suspension of a US$18 million loan (May 1999) by the International Monetary Fund to protest Uganda's military involvement in the DRC. In December 2005, the ICJ ruled that Uganda had violated international law and ordered it to pay the DRC US$10 billion in compensation. Clearly, Uganda's military adventures in the DRC had created a public relations nightmare. It had also damaged Museveni's high status among Western donor states, which considered him to be one of Africa's "new breed of leaders," dedicated to promoting democracy and peaceful interstate relations in Africa. Therefore, as the 2001 elections approached, Museveni's standing among Western donor states had somewhat diminished. Moreover, as shall be extrapolated below, the political events preceding the 2001 elections and its controversial aftermath exacerbated the decline of Museveni's reputation abroad and thus set the stage for his quick acquiescence to Washington's War on Terror and its domestic corollary—namely, passage of an anti-terror law.

Rebel Activities

By 2000, there were at least eight known rebel groups operating inside Uganda and in the border regions of neighboring countries. According to the Human Rights Watch World Report of 2000, the following groups operated in eastern Uganda: the Anti Referendum Army, the Uganda Salvation Army, and the Citizen's Army for Multi-Party Politics. The

Allied Democratic Forces (ADF) operated in western Uganda, mainly in the Ruwenzori Mountains and in eastern Congo. The official explanation for Uganda's invasion of the eastern Congo in 1998 had been the pursuit of members of the ADF. Three groups with rear bases in Sudan operated in the north of the country, including the West Nile Bank Front, the Uganda National Rescue Front, and the LRA. The latter was the most formidable of the three. Also, beginning in the late 1990s, a shadowy group known as the National Army for the Liberation of Uganda carried out bomb attacks in and around Kampala.[5]

It is not the intent of this chapter to explicate the dynamics and raison d'être of these groups. The objective here is to shed light on how contested the political terrain, and in particular NRM rule, was at this time. The various armed groups operating in the east and north of the country and in the capital Kampala were intensely challenging to the authority of the NRM in the run up to the 2001 elections. Indeed, some of the names of these groups suggested resistance against the Referendum Act, the Movement Act, and the basic notion of no-party democracy as promoted by the NRM. Nevertheless, the existence of these groups, and the LRA particularly, provided the Movement with sufficient justification to enact anti-terror legislation. Indeed, LRA atrocities, which included maiming, raping, and killing civilians, received such international condemnation that it was difficult in the Ugandan political climate to oppose the introduction of stiff anti-terrorism legislation. For example, in the conflict-affected districts of Gulu and Kitgum in northern Uganda, the LRA has abducted more than 25,000 and displaced more than 40,000 children since 1986 (Long 2007). Many of these victims have been forced to become sex slaves, child soldiers, or domestic workers. However, the counter-terror response from the Uganda army, whose military operations have been devastating for the civilian population in the north, has served to alienate many northerners from the NRM. A report by Human Rights Focus, a Gulu-based human rights organization, documented attacks by the LRA on "protected villages" of the internally displaced people (IDPs) as well as abuses by the Ugandan security forces administering the camps (Human Rights Watch 2003). As a result, the campaign for the 2001 elections was hotly contested, because the NRM had to win seats in other parts of the country to compensate for its lack of support in the north.

The 2001 Elections

The run-up to the 2001 elections was characterized by several political developments, all of which combined to make for a rather tenuous second (elected) term for President Museveni and the ruling NRM government.

For the first time in his tenure as president, the leadership of Museveni was challenged from within the NRM itself. His erstwhile physician and veteran soldier, Dr. Kizza Besigye, announced in October 2000 that he would contest the 2001 elections and run for president alongside Museveni. This prospect set off a string of intriguing political maneuvers within the NRM and by the president himself.

Because the NRM government had barred parties from legally contesting elections, and because it claimed that all those interested in running for political office could openly do so within the ambit of the NRM, Besigye's candidacy became the litmus test of the no-party system. When the NRM declared Museveni its only possible flag bearer, Besigye abandoned the Movement to form a new political party, the Forum for Democratic Change (FDC). Besigye contested the presidential election under the FDC. His candidacy was met with intimidation and alienation by the Movement government, as was the case with other opposition candidates. Besigye fled the country shortly after the 2001 election, fearing for his life. In the end, his candidacy exposed the hollowness and deceit of the notion of no-party democracy, which was a device to entrench the NRM in power. Indeed, due to the harassment and marginalization of opposition candidates belonging to other political parties, the newly elected parliament was dominated by the NRM. Thus, it is unsurprising that one year later the Anti-Terrorism Bill would pass into law with relative ease, as the ruling party enjoyed a large majority.

The treatment of Kizza Besigye came to symbolize the irregularities that marred the 2001 general elections. The NRM was apprehensive about its prospects at the polls given its limited possibilities for support in the north and the emergence of a formidable challenger in Besigye. Furthermore, demands for a return to multiparty politics were intensifying, and the truth about Uganda's military adventures in the DRC was steadily seeping into the consciousness of voters through radio and print media. Together these factors raised the stakes of the 2001 elections, and, in response, the NRM tightened its grip on the already-constrained space for political discussion. The passage of the Referendum and the Movement Acts was followed by the enactment of the Presidential Election Act (PEA) 2000. Taken together, these laws provided the statutory framework for the 2001 presidential election. Like the Referendum and Movement Acts, the PEA imposed numerous restrictions on the political activities of opposition candidates. These included large fees to be paid by every aspiring candidate, requirements for each candidate to secure signatures from two-thirds of all the districts in Uganda, and limits on campaigning by opposition candidates until nomination time.[6]

These extralegal limitations were combined with intimidation and violence. For example, a peaceful public demonstration by Makerere University students was broken up by the police, who shot into the crowds with live ammunition (Human Rights Watch 2003). Similarly, a UPC party rally was broken up and Jimmy Higenyi, a journalism student covering the rally, was shot dead (Human Rights Watch 2003). Besigye supporters were also prevented from assembling in various venues. Furthermore, a covert gag was slapped on the media, and several columnists of the *New Vision* newspaper were suspended for reportage that was critical of Museveni's government (Mbabazi et al. 2001).

All of these developments further damaged the already-diminished political capital of the NRM. One study found that 42 percent of respondents polled either disagreed or "didn't know" if the NRM government had the "right to make decisions that all people have to abide by." The authors of the study concluded that "the rule of law remains seriously incomplete in Uganda" (Bratton et al. 2000). In the POLITY IV dataset, Uganda earns a regime score of –4, which places it on the autocratic side of a continuum that ranges from –10 for full autocracy and +10 for full democracy. The Freedom House scores of 5 for political rights and 4 for civil liberties mean that Uganda qualifies for a "partly free" designation (Whitaker 2007b). Nonetheless, Museveni won the controversial 2001 poll, which was followed by an even more contentious and violent campaign for Parliament. However, the NRM's tight grip on power continued beyond 2001 and was crucial in helping the government to quickly pass the Anti-Terrorism Act in 2002, as well as legislation that repealed article (105)2 of the constitution, thereby removing limits to presidential terms and paving the way for Museveni's successful bid for a third presidential term in the 2006 election.

Impact of Domestic Politics on Passage of the Anti-terrorism Act

In summary, there is little doubt that both the perception and reality of a terrorist threat in Uganda helped push the Anti-Terrorism bill through Parliament. This chapter focuses on two equally important explanatory factors. This section examines the nature of Uganda's domestic political institutions and the limited influence of domestic constituencies on shaping policy and law.[7]

The legislature was more or less a rubber stamp for executive priorities. The NRM, although weakened by internal cleavages, had an overwhelming majority in the 7th Parliament (2001–2006). Opposition parties such as the Uganda Peoples Congress (UPC), the Democratic Party, and the FDC were weakened by the repressive policies preceding and following the elections. In particular, political parties were constrained by the passage of the Political Parties and Organizations Act (PPOA) in 2000. This law severely circumscribed political party activities. For example,

> sections 18 and 19 restricted political party activity to the national level, and prevented political parties from holding public rallies, from sponsoring candidates for elections to office, and from holding meetings . . . the Act contained provisions making it difficult for political parties to register, since parties had to show that they had founding members in at least one-third of districts in Uganda and to pay a substantial fee. (Bussey 2005)

The NRM was exempt from these provisions, a fact that exposed the Movement's penchant for stifling competition and dissent for its own political advantage.[8]

Civil Society

In Uganda, civil society has been weakened by several factors. These include its inability to find independent sources of funding, and hence its vulnerability to cooptation by both the state and external donors. It is also constrained by various laws that seek to circumscribe the activities it can conduct and the spaces within which it can operate. These limitations have forced civil society organizations (CSOs) to focus on service delivery while abandoning the advocacy function. CSOs in Uganda comprise membership-based and occupational organizations such as trade unions (for example, the National Organization of Trades Unions); professional associations, including the influential Uganda Law Society and the Uganda Journalists Association; and cooperatives. Another category in Ugandan civil society comprises service delivery organizations and groups that carry out development projects. This includes groups such as the Uganda Change Agents Association, CARE, and ACCORD. Groups in this category provide services to communities in the fields of health, education, legal expertise, and social welfare (Thue et al. 2002). Development support and service delivery organizations are considered to be a safe form of political activity because they do not directly confront the state and therefore avoid political persecution. A further category of Ugandan civil society includes community-based organizations (CBOs), which are mostly informal. Advocacy groups are another category that lobbies for civil and political rights. This includes human rights organizations such as the Foundation for Human Rights Initiatives and the Human Rights Networks (HURINET).

These groups face formidable challenges due to the government's ambivalent attitude toward what it considers to be the limits of advocacy, especially when such groups are thought to stray too far into the political arena. The Ugandan government is also suspicious of cultural and faith-based organizations, such as the Buganda Cultural and Development Foundation. These groups lobby for cultural and religious causes albeit they often step into the political sphere, where, in the case of churches, the pulpit is literally used to advance political causes as well as the general social and economic issues affecting their constituencies. As mentioned below, the closure of the Catholic-backed Radio Kyoga Veritas by the government illustrates the government's mistrust of faith groups, which are penalized for becoming involved in political debates.

The media constitutes another category of civil society. It by nature represents different social/political actors and serves broader public interest groups. Although the space for the media to operate in Uganda was relatively open, some media outlets have been targeted by the NRM government, as discussed below.

Although civil society activity is constitutionally protected in Uganda,[9] the politics of the state in Uganda are such that they are seldom given opportunities to influence policy and law. This is particularly true with regard to legislation that has been passed to entrench the power of the ruling regime. In these cases, the government has not tolerated expressions of opposition by civil society. Whether the government tolerates public advocacy by civil society groups depends on how threatening such advocacy may be to the project of regime entrenchment. In the era of the War on Terror, any activity that threatens the political establishment is considered a national security risk and is suppressed in the name of maintaining law and order. The risks are even greater for human rights groups and the media, which are critical of counter-terror policies or speak out on the treatment of terror suspects.

This is fitting a pattern in which political space in Uganda has been constricted progressively over time. The conflation of national security with the political interests of the regime has enabled the regime to solidify its hold on power. The consequence of this on civil society has been that many groups have chosen to maintain a collaborative relationship with the state or limit their activities to service delivery and development support.

Political space for civil society activity was further restricted by two pieces of legislation: the 1989 Non-Governmental Organizations Registration Statute and the proposed Non-Governmental Registration (Amendment) Bill, 2000. The former required that all NGOs be approved and registered by a government-appointed board composed mostly of government officials, including security officials, before they were allowed to operate. Based on the Statute, the board can deny registration of an NGO or impose various conditions before approval. It can also terminate any NGO's registration on vague and arbitrary grounds. Finally, the Statute also imposes fines and jail terms for up to one year for office holders of NGOs who do not pay the fines and who operate without official approval.

The Amendment Bill was submitted to Parliament in December 2000 but was not debated until the 7th parliament was seated in August 2001, when it reappeared as the Non-Governmental Organizations Registration (Amendment) Bill, 2001. The debate concerning the bill would be launched by the Minister for Internal Affairs, the same cabinet member in charge of administering the Anti-Terrorism Act (ATA). Although the precise nature or function of the bill was not defined, it seemed designed to expand government powers and control over NGO activities. It proposed the following new restrictions: first, NGOs would not only have to register with a government-appointed Board, but they would also have to acquire a permit (Art. 1.1). Furthermore, the draft legislation gave the internal affairs minister wide powers of making regulations "prescribing the duration and the form of a permit," in essence giving the minister a "carte blanche" authority to set conditions for permits (Human Rights Watch 2001). Second, the bill had no provisions for including members of NGOs on the board, for transforming it into an independent registration and oversight body, or for subjecting its decisionmaking to judicial oversight and review. In short, the NGO board was to remain firmly under the state's control. Third, the bill sought to punish both the organization and its staff for the same offense committed in the course of their constitutionally recognized roles. Finally, Article 1(4) of the proposed bill stipulated that the board could reject any NGO whose objectives "as specified in its constitution are in contravention of any government policy or plan, or public interest."

On April 7, 2006, after very limited debate, the bill was passed into law. The period between 2001, when the draft amendment bill was tabled, and 2006, when it became law, also coincided with passage of the ATA in 2002. That the latter sailed through Parliament without much opposition is partly explained by the chilling effect of the draft bill on CSOs. A senior advisor at the Africa Division of Human Rights Watch aptly observed that, "the proposed law potentially criminalizes civil society organizations instead of recognizing their enormous contribution to the social, political and economic life in Uganda" (Human Rights Watch 2001). Indeed, since the

NGO Registration Bill of 2006 became law, the effectiveness of civil society has been limited, despite recent efforts to lobby for the repeal of the bill.

Together with the ATA, the NGO Registration Act of 2006 would give the government (through the same ministry) inordinate powers to interfere with and/or terminate legitimate NGO activities such as human rights advocacy. The law has had the effect of seriously threatening the viability of NGO work and CSO activity in general.

Thus with this kind of governmental overreach, and with more and more institutions of government subordinated to the political interests of the NRM ruling regime, it was difficult to envisage any serious opposition to the ATA. It was only in early 2009 that the NGO Registration Act of 2006 was brought back to Parliament for reconsideration. There was a concerted effort by NGOs such as HURINET and the Development Network of Indigenous Voluntary Association to exert pressure on Parliament for changes to the 2006 law. They held meetings and seminars and marched through the streets of Kampala to articulate their concerns about the current law and express their desire for specific changes. Be that as it may, there is no indication that the NRM government will accede to NGO demands or interests. But by this time the government has already achieved its intended objective of weakening civil society by passing the ATA.

Funding

A further factor that contributed to the swift enactment of the ATA relates to the politics of donor funding. The United States was eager to strengthen its relationship with Uganda in a bid to shore up the anti-terror alliance in the Great Lakes and Greater Horn of Africa regions. And for this the United States was willing to increase both development and military aid to Uganda. Consequently, Uganda reasserted its role as a key ally of the United States in the post-9/11 global security regime. This explains why, notwithstanding a stalled transition to democracy, the United States not only provided financial and technical support to the improvement of Uganda's capacity to disrupt terrorist networks and prevent attacks, but also almost tripled its total official development assistance to Kampala (USAID 2009). Together with Djibouti, Eritrea, Ethiopia, Kenya, and Tanzania, Uganda benefits from the US$100 million East African Counterterrorism Initiative launched by the Bush administration in 2003. According to a report by the International Consortium of Investigative Journalists, prior to 9/11 Uganda received no Foreign Military financing dollars; in the years after 2001 it received almost US$2 million (Njau 2007).

Moreover, the United States provides approximately one-fifth of Uganda's foreign assistance in any given year (Whitaker 2007a). It depends on foreign aid for 50 percent of its recurrent expenditures. The legitimacy of an aid-dependent regime such as the NRM is therefore inevitably linked to its ability to keep aid flowing into the country. Considering Uganda's dependence on foreign assistance, and US bilateral aid in particular, it is unsurprising that Uganda closely adheres to US foreign policy interests in the region, including supporting the War on Terror. Clearly Uganda has benefited politically and economically from its partnership with the United States in the War on Terror. In this respect Uganda has become the United States' safety valve in the pressure cooker of the Great Lakes region, and it has thereby become a major actor in the Greater Horn of Africa. Not only has Kampala provided support personnel to back US efforts in Iraq, but it is the only African country (other than Burundi) to contribute peacekeeping troops to Somalia. On the domestic front Uganda has received indirect support from the United States in the passage of the ATA. The prospects of this relationship continuing under the Obama administration are unclear at the moment, given the ongoing review of US foreign policy by the new administration.

The Anti-Terrorism Act (2002)

Before the ATA was passed in 2002, the NRM government had established a Joint Anti-Terrorism Task Force (JATTF) in 1999. It was intended to coordinate efforts among police, the military, and intelligence to respond to domestic terrorist attacks. The JATTF arrested more than 60 individuals for terrorist acts but could only charge them with treason under the existing laws (Whitaker 2007a). Therefore the ATA was intended to add teeth to the JATTF and other anti-terror governmental institutions. A quick review of some prescriptions in the ATA indicates its potential impacts on civil society.

a) *Definition*: The ATA defines terrorism as all or any of the acts listed in the appendix and committed with the "purpose of influencing the Government or intimidating the public or a section of the public and for a political, religious, social or economic aim, indiscriminately without due regard to the safety of others or property" (Anti-Terrorism Act 2002). An examination of the definition itself and the list of activities reveals a wide-ranging breadth and scope, and, not unlike most anti-terror laws, this is the source of the deleterious effects on nongovernmental actors and, most notably, dissidents of the regime. This is because the sweeping definition of "terrorism" in the ATA enables the NRM regime to crack down on a range of political activity and advocacy efforts under the guise of protecting "national security."

Clearly the broader the definition, the less discriminating and more arbitrary is the enforcement. For example, terms such as "influencing the government" and "intimidating the public or a section of the public" highlight how the definition "is so broad that it could be used to prosecute trade unionists involved in an illegal strike or those engaged in civil disobedience ... because it does not specifically exclude legal strikes and protests that do not aim to seriously disrupt an essential service" (Bossa and Mulindwa 2004). The problem of undefined terms raises two other concerns. First, acts of freedom of expression advocating change of public policies, which are totally consistent with international law, would be considered acts of "terrorism." Second, activities that would ordinarily be punishable under regular criminal law would, under the ATA, be punishable as acts of "terrorism," thus attracting much higher sentences that are grossly unfair (Anti-Terrorism Act 2002).

b) *Offenses*: Beyond the definition of "terrorism" itself, the ATA's list of offenses also poses serious concerns regarding prescribed and acceptable conduct. For example, Section 8 specifies that the following constitute "terrorist" offenses: establishing, running, or supporting any institution for a) promoting terrorism, b) publishing and disseminating news or materials that promote terrorism, or c) training or mobilizing any group of persons or recruiting persons for carrying out terrorism or mobilizing funds for the purpose of terrorism. These offenses carry a death sentence upon conviction (Anti-Terrorism Act 2002). Moreover, it is not far-fetched to conceive of a situation in which a member, financier, or supporter of a designated organization could run afoul of the law.

c) *Terrorist organizations*: Part IV, Schedule 2 of the ATA references four prescribed terrorist organizations—the Lord's Resistance Army, The Lord's Resistance Movement, Allied Democratic Forces, and Al-Qaeda. Section 10(5) gives the minister of internal affairs the power to make a statutory instrument "declaring any terrorist organization dissolved" or "providing for the sending up [closing] of the terrorist organization" and "providing for the forfeiture to the State of the property and assets of the terrorist organization" (Anti-Terrorism Act 2002). Section 11(3) applies to those who, though not members of the organization, support or further the activities of the organization in any way. The trouble with this part of the law is that it does not provide any appeal procedure for an organization or individual that is proscribed as a terrorist or terrorist organization under the Act. Yet being a member of such an organization carries a stiff punishment of up to 10 years in prison.

d) *Financial assistance for terrorism*: Any form of financial contribution or assistance toward acts of terrorism is an offense. According to Sections 13 and 14, this includes contributing resources or assistance to terrorist organizations or having retention or control over terrorism funds. One possible implication of this is that any legitimate contribution to an NGO could incur a risk for the individual or charitable foundation making the donation if the state subsequently designates the recipient organization as a "terrorist" group.

e) *Duty to disclose information*: Anyone who suspects or has actual knowledge that another person is providing funding for terrorist purposes has a duty to disclose such information.

f) *Interception of communications and surveillance powers*: Part VII authorizes officers to intercept the communication of any person and otherwise conduct surveillance of terror suspects under the ATA. The ATA limits the scope of interception and surveillance to letters and postal packages, telephone calls, faxes, emails, monitoring meetings of any group of persons, surveillance of the movements and activities of any person, electronic surveillance of any person, access to bank accounts of any person, and searching the housing or business premises of any person suspected of supporting or being a member of a terrorist organization.

g) *Section 17 and Third Schedule*: Authorities are given unlimited stop and search powers of premises specified in a warrant or any person found there, in order to search for articles that could be used in connection with terrorism. However, the law requires that the use of such powers must be given by a magistrate on the application of an investigating officer, and the grounds for such authorization are that the use of such powers must be considered expedient for preventing terrorist acts.

The Impact of the Anti-Terrorism Act

The ATA and related penal code restrictions have had clear impacts on parts of civil society as well as on the space for political debate more generally. This section briefly considers three cases. The first case involves the closure and confiscation of properties of the independent newspaper *The Monitor* in October of 2002. The paper published a story concerning the crash of an army helicopter in the war zone of northern Uganda. The newspaper offices were closed and publication ceased for one week, after which it resumed publication with a front page apology to the government. The army claimed that it took drastic action in reaction to a false report (a reference to the helicopter story) about the War on Terror (Privacy International 2002). The information minister, Basoga Nsadu, accused the paper of promoting crimes by rebel groups. The International Federation of Journalists (IFJ) condemned this action by the government as did the Uganda Journalists Union, which complained of "threats to their impartiality and efforts to report independently" (Privacy International 2002). The closure of *The Monitor* was preceded by a court challenge in which the paper questioned the constitutionality of Section 50 of the penal code that criminalized the publication of "false news likely to cause alarm or disturb the public peace" (Bussey 2005). Following an appeal the Supreme Court ruled in favor of the paper's managing editor Charles Obbo, stating that the government case was "too vague, wide and conjectural to provide the necessary certainty required to impose an acceptable limitation on freedom of expression" (Privacy International 2002).

The closure of Radio Kyoga Veritas referred to above is the second case (Privacy International 2002). The station was accused of running "alarmist" reports on attacks by LRA rebels (Reporters Sans Frontières 2003). News scripts as well as 25 tapes of testimonies given by victims of the fighting that had been aired a few days before were confiscated (Privacy International 2004). Such was the situation in Uganda one year after the passage of the ATA that on World Press Freedom Day (May 3), the Eastern Africa Media Institute organized a conference on press freedom, raising among other issues the threats against journalists contained in the new anti-terrorism law (Human Rights Watch 2003).

Perhaps the most infamous case relating to the misuse of the ATA involves opposition leader and FDC President Kizza Besigye. After fleeing the country in 2001, he was a regular guest on popular call-in radio stations in Uganda, which he used as a platform to accuse the NRM government of graft and vote rigging (Privacy International 2002). In one interview with the Voice of Africa on August 17, 2003, Besigye threatened to resort to "untraditional methods" if his efforts to get fresh elections through constitutional means failed. The government accused Besigye of "inadvertently declaring war on the Government" and brought a case against him under provisions of the ATA. An NRM spokesman stated that anyone who helped Besigye "spread his propaganda . . . comes under suspicion of aiding terrorism and the anti-terrorism law will apply" (Privacy International 2002).

The Besigye saga, however, did not end with this admonition and threat. When he returned from exile in 2005 with the intention of contesting the first multiparty general election in decades, he was immediately thrown in jail with 22 others and charged with offenses of treason, concealment of treason, and rape. These charges were answerable in the High Court. But the additional charges regarding the offenses of terrorism and firearms were to be tried in a military court—the General Court Martial. The Uganda Law Society challenged the constitutionality of trying civilians in military courts. Although the Constitutional Court ruled in favor of the ULS, the treason and terrorism trial of Kizza Besigye and others continued in the General Court Martial. Kathurima M'Inoti, Commissioner of the International Commission of Jurists and trial observer, complained that "the continuation of this trial in clear defiance of a judgment of the Constitutional Court is the latest in a series of attacks on the rule of law in Uganda" (International Commission of Jurists 2006).

Conclusion

This study in one sense confirms Whitaker's (2007a) conclusion, namely that anti-terror laws have been passed quickly and without much resistance in states that are least democratic. For instance, although the terror threat in neighboring Kenya is perhaps greater than that in Uganda, anti-terror legislation was passed swiftly in Uganda, whereas similar legislation was abandoned in Kenya after a concerted campaign by civil society and opposition by parliamentarians, as explained in this book. The 9/11 attacks were a watershed moment with respect to American commitment to promoting democracy in sub-Saharan Africa. As the case of Uganda illustrates, the War on Terror provided an opportunity for the NRM regime to consolidate its hold on power in part through enactment of new counter-terrorism structures. Although these have been used in ways that clearly breach civil and political rights, foreign donors have not objected because of Museveni's unwavering support for Western foreign policy objectives in the Greater Horn of Africa, including the US-backed invasion of Somalia by Ethiopian forces in 2006. Thus, Museveni for a long time skillfully played the terrorism card to target opponents of the "no-party democracy" promoted by his NRM party, without risking a punitive backlash by his foreign backers led by the United States, which requires a strong alliance with states in the Horn to prosecute its War on Terror. Uganda's strategic position in the Great Lakes Region and the Greater Horn of Africa, coupled with Museveni's need for international legitimacy following his intervention in the Congo, provided a perfect confluence of factors for a strengthened United States-Uganda alliance. Uganda was soon the central actor/balancer in central/east Africa in the post-9/11 global security regime.

Following America's lead in passing the Patriot Act, the NRM government responded deftly in enacting its own anti-terror legislation, which gave the state sweeping latitude to prosecute "terrorist offences." The law carried with it equally heavy punitive measures for those convicted of terrorist activities. Unlike in Kenya, there was comparatively little opposition to the ATA. Instead, the limitations on political spaces for civil society to organize and the subordination of institutions such as Parliament, political parties, and, in some cases, the courts to the executive branch, ensured that the ATA passed quickly and unopposed. Consequently a symbiotic relationship of sorts has emerged, and a vicious circle has been created. Although Uganda's stalled democratic transition provided the incubator for the easy passage of the ATA, the government has played the terrorism card to obstruct competitive, multi-party politics and heighten the marginalization of civil society. The cases highlighted above show the thin line that civil society and its backers must walk in order to avoid running afoul of the law. Provisions in the ATA have had a chilling effect on funding to civil society. Indeed, the ATA hangs as a sword of Damocles over civil society, opposition parties, and other institutions that pose a challenge to the NRM. It is a political instrument in the hands of a regime seeking to maintain and consolidate its grip on power. Restrictive legislation enacted to ostensibly protect *national* security in fact extends *regime* security.

Given the atrocities and violence of the LRA, ADF, and other militant groups, passage of the ATA was a politically expedient tool for assuaging the outrage of various anti-terror constituencies at home. It also had the effect of paralyzing CSO activity. Indeed there is no evidence thus far that the law has helped apprehend terrorists. Internationally, the willingness of the NRM regime to acquiesce to Washington's War on Terror earned the government badly needed financial and political backing from the United States. This support is especially important considering that the regime draws its legitimacy from continued aid funding and not from weakened domestic constituencies as such. Development, military, and political support have come Uganda's way at a time when observers would have expected condemnation for the intensifying centralization of power around the presidency. The securitization of aid to Uganda seems to have displaced democracy as the prerequisite for development or military financial assistance.

Notes

1. During this period of time (1999–2004), the political party activities were banned, although political parties themselves remained in existence. What was known as "no-party" democracy referred to the contestation of power within the umbrella of the NRM, which was assumed to be a "Movement" and not a political party.

2. This was in the case *Ssemogerere and Others Vs Attorney General* (Constitutional Petition No.3 of 1999), which was appealed to Supreme Court in Constitutional Appeal No. 1 of 2000.

3. In the case *Ssemogerere and Olum Vs. Attorney General* Constitutional Petition N0. 3 of 2000 (Constitutional Court), decided June 25, 2004. Appealed to the Supreme Court, Appeal decided September, 2004.

4. For a detailed account see Rubongoya (2007).

5. See Simba Kayunga (2000) for a full explanation.

6. See Rubongoya (2007, 149) for details regarding the effect of the PEA on nonincumbent candidates.

7. Whitaker (2007b, 9) argues that weak or less-developed nations comply with the counter-terror regime because of four factors: the perception of a terrorist threat, the availability of funding, the nature of political institutions, and the relative influence of domestic constituencies.

8. In *Ssemogerere and Others Vs Attorney General* (Constitutional Petition No. 5 of 2003) opposition leader Paul Ssemogerere challenged Sections 18 and 19 of the PPOA in the Constitutional Court. On March 21, 2003, the Court declared both sections null and void because they were inconsistent with Section 29 (d) and (e) of the constitution. The Court also ruled that the Movement was a political organization akin to a political party and not a political system.

9. See article 29(1), article 38(2), and article 269 of the constitution.

13

REGIONAL CHALLENGE, LOCAL RESPONSE: CIVIL SOCIETY AND HUMAN RIGHTS IN US–KENYA COUNTER-TERRORISM COOPERATION

Mutuma Ruteere and Mikewa Ogada

The 9/11 attacks on the United States had a far-reaching effect on its foreign policy. Whereas in the 1990s the United States had embraced a measure of multilateralism and rhetorical support for human rights and democracy in its diplomacy, security was now thrust into the center-stage of US foreign policy making. This volte-face in US foreign policy was particularly well-pronounced in Africa, where the US diplomatic rhetoric of democracy and human rights had been most audible in the 1990s. With the 9/11 attacks, the United States was much more interested in forging strategic security links with African countries to counter the terrorist threat associated with Al Qaeda. Directly and indirectly, therefore, the US-led War on Terror regime has resulted in a depreciation of human rights in regions such as East Africa. In this region the nascent human rights and pro-democracy movement had for years found in the United States a keen diplomatic ally (Barkan 2004). Through its development agency, the United States Agency for International Development (USAID), the United States supported human rights groups in countries such as Kenya. The War on Terror introduced a new dynamic with important consequences for human rights in this region. Directly, the War on Terror led to serious violations of international law and human rights by US security officials and cooperating African government officials. In addition, by the United States replacing the diplomatic rhetoric of human rights with that of security cooperation, human rights groups found themselves deprived of a powerful ally in human rights work.

These changed circumstances raise an important question as to the response of human rights groups to the US-led counter-terrorism initiatives.

How would these groups, which had hitherto counted the United States and other Western powers as allies in the human rights struggles in their countries, respond to these new human rights challenges in which their erstwhile allies were culpable?

These questions are important in understanding how civil society groups in Africa have responded to violations spawned by the US-led War on Terror. This is particularly important because most of the existing research on human rights groups in Africa focuses on their activities where the rights violator is the African state, with the Western states as partners to civil society groups in their human rights advocacy. This chapter also contributes to our understanding of the adaptations that human rights groups have undertaken in their advocacy on violations related to state counter-terrorism activities in the US-led War on Terror.

The United States is not the only Western state involved in supporting counter-terrorism activities in East Africa, although it is the most important. Denmark has provided funds to the United Nations Development Program (UNDP) for support to Kenya's counter-terrorism programs. The United Kingdom has also provided limited counter-terrorism funds through the FCO. The focus in this discussion on the United States is based on the fact that it has taken the leading role in this counter-terrorism initiative. Also, given its history of vocal support for democracy and human rights in Kenya, an analysis of the impact of the United States policy is more likely to yield insights into the changing terrain of human rights after 9/11.

Kenya is important, as it has been the epicenter of terrorist attacks in East Africa. It has also been a leading partner of the United States in its prosecution of the global War on Terror in the region. Moreover, Kenya has a vibrant civil society that has in the past received significant diplomatic and financial support from the West and from the United States in particular. The chapter draws on primary data from the work of Kenyan human rights groups, public discourses in Kenya on terrorism and human rights as well as the authors' work as part of the broader Kenyan civil society network.[1]

Global Concerns over Terrorism

Even prior to September 2001, the United Nations had taken up a more robust anti-terrorism agenda. In 1999, the UN Security Council, responding to the Al Qaeda bombing of the US embassies in Kenya and Tanzania in 1998, passed Resolution 1267 under Chapter VII of the Charter imposing mandatory financial and aviation sanctions on members of the Taliban regime in Afghanistan for offering sanctuary to the Al Qaeda leader

Osama Bin Laden and his associates. The Council also established a committee of the Security Council to oversee state implementation of these sanctions.

Following the 9/11 attacks, on September 28, 2001, the Security Council passed Resolution 1373 under Chapter VII requiring states to, among other things, cooperate in combating global terrorist threats, to freeze assets, enact and update their anti-terrorism laws, cooperate in criminal proceedings on terrorism, improve border security, and exchange information with other states on terrorism (Cortright et al. 2004). The Security Council adopted Resolution 1535, establishing a professional directorate to support states in their counter-terrorism measures.

With regard to human rights, analysts believe that although Security Council Resolution 1267 made reference to the Taliban regime's violation of human rights, its monitoring committee has not paid much attention to the human rights consequences of proposed counter-terrorism activities such as the listing of individuals as terrorism suspects (Foot 2007, 496). In 2005, the United Nations independent expert on the protection of human rights and fundamental freedoms while countering terrorism noted that Resolution 1373, "regrettably, contained no comprehensive reference to the duty of States to respect human rights in the design and implementation of such counter-terrorism measures" (Goldman 2005, 6, 21). Resolution 1456 of 2003 tried to remedy this, requiring that states take into account international law and human rights. As far back as 2001, the then UN Secretary General Kofi Annan had tried to warn states of the dangers of sacrificing human rights in the War on Terror through the "Policy Working Group on the United Nations and Terrorism," which in 2002 issued a report emphasizing the centrality of human rights in the UN's counter-terrorism measures.[2]

Both the Organization of African Unity (OAU) and its successor, the African Union (AU) have also called on member states to enact legislation and undertake other measures to counter-terrorism even before the 2001 attacks on the United States. Although efforts toward the development of a multi-lateral counter-terrorism framework precede the events of September 11, 2001, the effect of those attacks was to bring home to the United States the danger that it had previously confronted overseas and to galvanize its response at a global level. The immediate US response to the 9/11 attacks involved a massive mobilization of military, intelligence, financial, and diplomatic resources in a global war against Al Qaeda and its members.[3]

From the outset the administration of the former US President George Bush was clear that the global War on Terror would not be subject to the niceties and restraints of international law and human rights norms. On

September 16, 2001, then Vice President Dick Cheney ominously stated: "We also have to work, though, sort of the dark side, if you wish. We've got to spend time in the shadows . . . so it's going to be vital for us to use any means at our disposal, basically, to achieve our objectives" (quoted in Forsythe 2006, footnote 17). In his testimony to Congress, a former CIA officer Cofer Black stated that: "After 9/11, the gloves came off" (Human Rights Watch 2005b, 9).

East Africa as an Arena for US Counter-terrorism Operations

Kenya in particular has suffered from several incidents of international terrorism. The earliest recorded incident of international terrorism in Kenya was the 1981 New Year's Eve bombing of the Norfolk Hotel in Nairobi. The attack was attributed to the Popular Front for the Liberation of Palestine and resulted in 15 deaths, mainly American and British tourists, with 87 others seriously injured. In 1998 the US embassies in Kenya and Tanzania were bombed by Al Qaeda elements. The bombings in the Nairobi embassy left 224 people dead and 5,000 others injured. In response to these attacks, the US carried out simultaneous missile strikes on what it claimed were Al Qaeda targets in Sudan and Afghanistan. Four years later, in 2002, Al Qaeda-allied suicide bombers killed 15 people and injured 80 others at an Israeli-owned hotel near the coastal town of Mombasa in Kenya. A simultaneous attempt to shoot down an Israeli passenger jet departing from Mombasa airport using surface-to-air missiles narrowly failed. According to the US government, these terrorist attacks, and those of September 11, 2001, heightened the threat of international terrorism in Kenya and the region (Shinn 2004).

The geopolitical importance of East Africa and the Horn increased with the onset of the US-led war against the Taliban regime in Afghanistan in October 2001. This focus was largely informed by US concerns that the perennial instability in Somalia would turn that country into a haven for Al Qaeda and Taliban forces driven out of Afghanistan (Dagne 2002). Although Somalia has not taken a turn in this direction, US intelligence officials have claimed that Al Qaeda has established a footing in the country and in Eritrea, Ethiopia, Tanzania, and Kenya (Dagne 2002). Furthermore, the United States asserts that Al-Itihaad Al-Islamiyya, an influential Somalia-based Islamic charity, and Al-Bakaraat, a vast, Somalia-based money transfer service, are both linked to Al Qaeda (Shinn 2004). Acting on these threats, the US Central Intelligence Agency (CIA) in 2005 channeled funds to Somali warlords who had promised to kill or capture suspected high-level Al Qaeda operatives (Mazzetti 2006a).

The United States was particularly concerned about actors in Somalia, whom it claimed sustain Al Qaeda networks in Kenya (Princeton and Morrison 2004). According to the US intelligence community, Somalia was the launching pad for the November 2002 terrorist attacks against Israeli interests in Kenya and the 1998 bombings of US embassies in Nairobi and Dar es Salaam (USIP 2004). Moreover, Osama Bin Laden had a base in Sudan in the 1990s from which, it is believed, he scouted the targets for the 1998 bombings in Kenya and Tanzania.

Kenya's weak security systems, porous immigration controls, and the pervasive corruption that afflicts the entire public service make the country susceptible to terrorist infiltration. The United States worries that these weaknesses present opportunities to international terrorists to set up clandestine operations and to carry out terrorist attacks against Western interests in Kenya. The Kenyan capital, Nairobi, has many soft targets such as hotels and restaurants frequented by tourists. Additionally, Kenya's relatively advanced financial, communications, and transportation infrastructure provides international terrorists with the logistical capacity they may require to carry out their operations.

US Counter-terrorism Cooperation in East Africa

The US National Security Strategy of 2002 underscores the need for vigorous counter-terrorism assistance to African states. Increasingly, the United States has come to view problems such as conflict, poverty, disease, and corruption, which have long afflicted African societies, through the lens of its national security priorities. Although the US foreign policy on Africa post-9/11 has not totally ignored the long-term goals of development, democracy, and good governance, these have been conceived as a means of enhancing the security of the United States (Hills 2006).

Having identified Kenya as a "frontline state" in the War on Terror, the United States has increased its military assistance to Kenya in the form of grants, International Military Education and Training, Foreign Military Financing, Direct Commercial Sales, and Foreign Military Sales, making Kenya the key beneficiary of the US$100 million East Africa Counter-Terrorism Initiative funds. As the Center for Defense Information (2007) has noted, "In the five years after Sept. 11, Kenya received nearly eight times the amount of military assistance it received in the five years prior to Sept. 11."

The US military and policing agencies have provided training and equipment to over 500 Kenyan security officials in the areas of counter-terrorism and border and coastal security management. These training initiatives partly culminated in the creation by the Kenyan government of the Anti-Terrorism Police Unit in 2003. Some analysts have also suggested

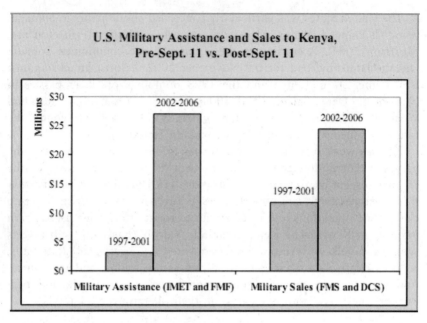

Source: Center for Defense Information (2007)

a US influence in the establishment of the Task Force on Anti-Money Laundering and Combating the Financing of Terrorism, which is coordinated by Kenya's Ministry of Finance.[4] By mid-2008, Kenya had also received US$1.1 million for the improvement of its aviation security systems through the US Safer Skies Program.

In addition, Kenyan security personnel had undergone training in counterterrorism by the Djibouti-based US Combined Joint Task Force—Horn of Africa (CJTF-HOA), whose mission is to identify and neutralize terrorist threats against US interests in the eastern Africa and Horn region (Shinn 2004). Under the framework of this cooperation, the Kenyan Army has stationed two battalions on the Kenyan-Somali border. Moreover, the fact that Kenya is one of two African countries that have signed a military access agreement with the United States means it is likely to play a key role in future exercises or operations undertaken by the newly established US Military Africa Command (AFRICOM).

However, the US–Kenya security relationship is not merely dictated by the United States, nor is it unidirectional. Rather, as in all interstate relationships, it has complex shades and is multifaceted. It also plays out in a context of public discourses in Kenya on governance and human rights, perceived US unilateralism in international relations, and the calculations of economic benefits likely to accrue for Kenya from counter-terrorism cooperation with the United States. That relationship is also prefaced by the difficult diplomatic relationship between Kenya and the United States in the 1990s, which centered on disagreements over human rights and democratization reforms. The US ambassador to Kenya at the time, Smith Hempstone, was the leading diplomatic critic of the leadership of then President Daniel Arap Moi (Hempstone 1997). US–Kenya bilateral relations did not improve until President Moi retired from office in 2002.

However, even in that troubled decade of US–Kenya relations there was still close cooperation between the two countries on security matters. Even then, security concerns often trumped human rights considerations. In 1993 for instance, the United States lowered its criticism of the Kenyan government's record on human rights and democracy at a time when the United States required Kenya's cooperation in support of the US humanitarian mission to Somalia.

With regard to the War on Terror, the United States through its ambassador in Nairobi has attempted to tread a thin line between pledging public support to fighting corruption and promoting better governance in Kenya and cultivating smooth bilateral relations to sustain its regional counter-terrorism campaign. Overall, the United States appears to have been much more measured in its public criticism of the government. For instance, when massive, high-level graft was exposed in President Mwai Kibaki's government in 2004, the reaction of the US ambassador was tepid. Where in the past it would be the United States leading the charge of diplomatic criticism, this time it was Britain that took the lead.[5] Of course US human rights diplomacy at the country level is not always in sync with the preferences of officials in Washington, and on occasion ambassadors have spoken out on Kenyan issues against the cautious advice of their superiors back home (Hempstone 1997).

Another complication in the Kenya–United States relationship was Kenya's reluctance to sign a Bilateral Immunity Agreement (BIA) with the United States following Kenya's ratification of the statute of the International Criminal Court (ICC). Also known as Article 98 agreements, these bilateral security treaties seek to exempt all US nationals, including civil and military officials, from the jurisdiction of the ICC. In a communication to Parliament, the Kenyan government concluded that signing the BIA would undermine international law, a position that was strongly supported by Kenyan and international human rights groups. Kenya eventually faced the wrath of the United States, which struck back by cutting US$13 million worth of military aid in 2005 (Mazzetti 2006b). In 2006, however, US military aid to Kenya was restored to normal levels following a policy shift strongly influenced by the US military's concern that cuts in military aid had weakened counter-terrorism initiatives "where the threat of international terrorism is said to be most acute" (Mazzetti 2006b). The United States has since exempted Kenya from aid cut penalties for not signing an Article 98 agreement.

Since the 1990s Kenyan human rights groups have counted the United States, principally through its embassy in Nairobi, as a reliable ally in their campaigns for promotion of human rights and democracy. Moreover, over the years USAID has generously funded many of these groups. Quite correctly, therefore, many Kenya specialists predicted that human rights in Kenya were likely to be a casualty of the new post-9/11, security-centered US foreign policy (Barkan and Cooke 2001).

Counter-terrorism and the Erosion of Rights in East Africa

Systematic studies on the human rights consequences of the US-led War on Terror are only beginning to emerge.[6] Recent reports by human rights groups and press reports indicate that human rights in East Africa and the Horn have been a casualty of the United States–Kenya counter-terrorism cooperation.[7] At the strategic level, there are clear similarities in the guiding logic behind the War on Terror and that of the Cold War. Throughout the Cold War the United States turned a blind eye to massive human rights violations perpetrated by its allies in Africa, as the imperative to forestall Soviet expansion in Africa and dominate access to vital African energy and mineral resources trumped human rights and good governance considerations.[8] Similarly, the imperatives of the global War on Terror have meant that the US privileges strategic security cooperation with allies who have been widely accused of widespread human rights violations such as Ethiopia, Egypt, and Uganda.[9]

The logic of US security interests has meant that the United States has invested substantially in strengthening the capacities of the security organs of its allies in the region. However, this support has not been accompanied by any measures to ensure accountability and respect for human rights by these security organs. Instead, this US support for regional security appears to have merely reinforced the effectiveness of forces that are deeply implicated in human rights violations in East Africa and the Horn states.[10] Scholars have indeed pointed out that a connection exists between counter-terrorism support to the security organs of these cooperating states and human rights violations. Hills (2006, 637–638) has noted that the "secrecy associated with training and equipping counterterrorism police units increases the chances of repression and unaccountability."

Since September 2001, states in East Africa and elsewhere have been under pressure from both the United States and the United Nations to enact anti-terror legislation without equal regard to human rights, while reports have emerged of the US cooperation with regional states in carrying out extraordinary renditions of terrorism suspects as detailed below.

Post-9/11 Arbitrary Arrests in Kenya

In the post-9/11 period in Kenya, there have been numerous reports of arbitrary arrests of terrorism suspects. For instance, in February 2002 the Kenyan police arrested a total of 966 Somalis in one day on suspicion of being in the country illegally (KHRC 2002). The police were particularly unyielding in their claim that 42 of those arrested in Kenya's North Eastern Province (largely peopled by Kenyan Somalis) had links with Al Qaeda. The Kenya Human Rights Commission (KHRC), an NGO, noted that the arrests were "well-organized operations [by the Kenyan government] . . . to show the world that it too is concerned with ending global terrorism" (KHRC 2002, 32). Most of those arrested were subsequently held in police stations for periods beyond those stipulated by Kenyan law. They were also denied access to legal counsel and barred from receiving visits from their relatives or friends.

Historically treated with suspicion by successive Kenyan governments, the Somali (including Kenyan Somalis) now became regular targets of Kenyan security sweeps based on the suspicion that they might harbor Al Qaeda elements from lawless Somalia. With the renewed violence in Somalia in December 2006, many Somalis fleeing the violence were arrested by the Kenyan authorities on suspicion of terrorism, and some were returned to Somalia in violation of international refugee and Kenyan laws.

Extraordinary Renditions, Torture, and Forced Disappearances

The Nairobi-based Muslim Human Rights Forum (MHRF) and the London-based groups Cageprisoners and Reprieve have collected evidence of extraordinary renditions and disappearances of terrorism suspects by Kenyan security forces working with the United States, Somalia, and Ethiopia since December 2006. Human rights scholars have described this new human rights problem as a "novel . . . hybrid violation" that contravenes at least seven international human rights instruments, including the Universal Declaration of Human Rights, the Convention against Torture, and the Geneva conventions (Weissbrodt and Bergquist 2006).[11] The extraordinary renditions documented by the MHRF in Kenya combine six specific human rights violations: arbitrary arrests, enforced disappearance, forcible transfer, torture, detention without trial, and the denial of access to consular officials (MHRF 2008a). Additionally, arrested persons have been denied visits by their families and medical care. One Kenyan citizen, Mohamed Abdulmalik, who was arrested by Kenyan officials, has already surfaced in the US detention centre at Guantánamo Bay, having been transferred as part of the rendition program.[12]

In the January 2007, at the height of the Ethiopian military operations in Somalia, at least 152 people of 21 different nationalities were arrested by the Kenyan Anti-Terrorism Police Unit and Criminal Investigations Department officers and were subjected to extraordinary renditions.[13] On arrest, the suspects were moved between various police cells in Nairobi, Coast, and Eastern Provinces to avoid the possibility that family members could trace them to police custody. Many of those arrested complained of torture and cruel and degrading treatment during interrogations conducted by Kenyan and US security agents. Where families of arrested terrorism suspects or human rights groups filed habeas corpus writs in Kenyan courts to secure their release, they were secretly put on rendition flights to Somalia and Ethiopia, placing them out of the judicial reach of Kenyan courts (KHRI 2007).

Somali Refugees

In the aftermath of the United States-backed Ethiopian invasion of Somalia in mid-December 2006, the Kenyan government on many occasions turned back Somalis fleeing the conflict in violation of international law. For instance, in January 2007 Kenya turned away 400 Somali refugees, while in the same month Kenyan authorities repatriated 34 Eritrean and Ethiopian refugees to Somalia, where they were placed in the custody of hostile Ethiopian authorities (KHRI 2007). Although it may be argued that Kenya had genuine security concerns with regard to some of the arrested individuals, these security interests could not be said to trump international law prohibiting such expulsions (KHRI 2007).

Civil Society and War on Terror-related Violations

To understand the response of Kenyan human rights groups to the human rights issues associated with the global War on Terror in Kenya, it is important to appreciate these groups' history, composition, and focus. Human rights groups in Kenya were formed as a response to the decades of repressive rule in the country. The most prominent, vocal, and best-resourced Kenyan human rights groups emerged in the 1990s to oppose the government of former President Moi. The bulk of their activities aimed at exposing, shaming, and mobilizing domestic and international opinion against the human rights excesses of the regime. In this regard, the Kenyan human rights movement is made up of the conventional human rights NGOs. The mandate, expertise, and interest of these groups have always been national, with most of their work urban-centered. This identity has persisted over the years. This particular history significantly shaped how these groups responded to the global War on Terror and its attendant violations, the effectiveness of these responses, and the challenges encountered.

Although it took Kenyan human rights groups time to recognize the challenge of the global War on Terror, by 2007 the issue of extraordinary renditions and disappearances of suspects had become a serious concern of human rights groups. Organizations such as the MHRF monitored and documented the fate of terrorism suspects arrested by the Kenyan authorities and their treatment. It published reports on these violations and used them to mobilize public opinion. To a lesser extent, the government's own Kenya National Commission on Human Rights also documented these cases and issued statements denouncing the violations.

The MHRF also moved its advocacy on behalf of terrorism suspects to the courts. From the end of January 2007, MHRF filed a total of 44 habeas corpus applications on behalf of individuals held by the Kenya government.[14] Although in the 44 cases the applications did not lead to the release of the detained, they nevertheless served to bring to public attention the program of arrests, detentions, transfers, and disappearances orchestrated by various governments.

In mid-2008, the Ethiopian authorities began releasing a number of the suspects who had been transferred to Ethiopia. In December 2008, eleven of them—among them eight Kenyans, a Tanzanian woman married to a Kenyan, a Rwandese lawfully resident in Kenya, and a Tanzanian—filed a case at the Kenyan High Court seeking for a declaration that the Kenyan authorities had violated their fundamental rights by unlawfully transferring them to Somalia and Ethiopia.

Kenyan human rights groups have also challenged the government's attempt to introduce legislation on terrorism that has the potential of eroding many constitutionally guaranteed human rights. In 2003, soon after the election of opposition leader Mwai Kibaki as president, the government introduced the Suppression of Terrorism Bill of 2003 in Parliament. This proposed bill became the first ground on which a skirmish between the government and the civil society was played out with respect to counter-terrorism.

The bill was criticized by civil society groups as proposing an imprecise definition of terrorism that would make it particularly difficult to distinguish between "ordinary criminal conduct involving use of firearms (such as robbery or murder) and terrorism."[15] Human rights groups also argued that the bill provided for retroactive criminal offenses and, if passed, it would negate the presumption of innocence principle and shift the burden of proof of innocence to terrorism suspects. Also worrying to human rights groups were the bill's provisions for incommunicado detention of terrorism suspects and its shielding of the police from accountability for injuries or deaths of suspects.

Human rights groups were outraged and perplexed that a government they presumed to be led by reformists and individuals with sterling human rights credentials would publish such a bill.[16] The initial response of these groups organized as Kenya Human Rights Network (K-HURINET) was to reject the bill in its entirety and not to reach out to the government for dialogue.

At the same time, the bill found its way to Parliament's Departmental Committee on Administration of Justice and Legal Affairs, then headed by Paul Muite, a former Law Society of Kenya chair with a long history of human rights advocacy. The Committee, like the human rights groups, expressed its objections to the bill—citing its many encroachments on human rights—and resisted the government's pressure to approve the bill (MHRF 2008b).

The bill stalled in the legislative bureaucracy and did not reach the floor of Parliament for debate by the time the parliamentary session came to a close at the end of 2003. As per the procedures of Parliament, the bill had now lapsed and could only be reintroduced in the following session. The government, which had expressed a willingness to discuss possible amendments with the civil society, did not reintroduce the bill in the subsequent sessions of Parliament.

There were fresh attempts by the government to revive anti-terrorism legislation in 2006, and a bill titled "Anti-terrorism Bill" was drafted. This time, the government tried to reach out to civil society groups on the proposed legislation. A meeting was held with the support of the United Nations Development Programme (UNDP). This time, however, the push for the legislation was led by the Office of the President rather than the Ministry of Justice and Constitutional Affairs, as was the case when the Suppression of Terrorism Bill was introduced. However, human rights groups and parliamentarians criticized the proposed legislation as a rehash of the 2003 bill. The UN Special Rapporteur on the Protection and Promotion of Human Rights while Countering Terrorism addressed a letter to the Kenya government in which he expressed concern over the human rights implications of the broad and imprecise definition of "terrorism" contained in the proposed bill (Human Rights Council 2007, paragraph 37). Yet again the government was forced to shelve the bill.

In 2007, the government attempted to introduce in Parliament the Proceeds of Organized Crimes and Anti-Money Laundering Bill, 2007, which in several provisions resembled the Suppression of Terrorism Bill of 2003. The new bill lifted 22 clauses from the Suppression of Terrorism Bill word for word and incorporated them in the proposed Proceeds of Organized Crimes and Anti-Money Laundering Bill, 2007. The government's efforts were blocked by the parliamentary Departmental Committee on Legal Affairs and Administration of Justice. Its chair at the time, Paul Muite, concluded that the government had tried to "cleverly" reintroduce anti-terrorism legislation masked as the Proceeds of Organized Crime Bill.

Clearly, pressure from human rights groups organized under the K-HURINET umbrella influenced the government's decision to stall the Suppression of Terrorism Bill of 2003. It also helped the cause of the human rights groups that the Departmental Committee on Administration of Justice and Legal Affairs in Parliament denied the government the crucial support it needed to move the bill through Parliament. Moreover, some human rights activists have noted that the minister for justice had bowed to pressure from state security and defense organs to draft the bill.[17]

After the lapse of the bill in 2003, civil society seemed to back away from its efforts to shape the counter-terrorism policy and legal framework. Rather, it resorted to a "fire-fighting" mode, by which it would respond to individual cases of arbitrary arrest and detention of terrorism suspects. A former member of the parliamentary Departmental Committee on Administration of Justice and Legal Affairs has noted that human rights groups' effectiveness is limited by their over-reliance on protests and the neglect of strategic lobbying (MHRF 2008b).[18] For its part, the Kenya government continued to implement various counter-terrorism measures such as the setting up of the ATPU as an administrative unit within the police force.

Lingering Challenges and Persistent Dilemmas

Even though the habeas corpus applications filed by the MHRF certainly embarrassed the government, they largely failed to stop the transfer of individuals to Ethiopia, Somalia, and Guantanamo Bay. Although human rights groups have consistently challenged the Kenyan government over violations related to its counter-terrorism measures, on the balance their approach appears uncoordinated, focused more on individual cases and less targeted at influencing policy-making. This has put a spotlight on both the challenges that counter-terrorism-related human rights violations pose to human rights groups and the impediments that these groups may encounter to effectively address issues raised by the government's counter-terrorism initiatives.

Casualties of the Transition

Counter-terrorism measures by the Kenyan authorities coincided with a period of political transition in the country. As mentioned previously, in 2002 an opposition alliance headed by Mwai Kibaki came to power. The Kibaki regime was elected with significant public support as well as the support of many human rights activists (KHRC 2003). President Moi's exit from the political scene, as well as the defeat of the ruling party KANU, suddenly removed the fixed target of the activities of many human rights groups. The political transition was paralleled by a transition in leadership of most human rights groups. Moreover, a number of human rights activists joined the new administration, opening channels of discussion, hitherto unknown in state-NGO relations in Kenya.

These events had a significant impact on the work of human rights NGOs. The crop of erstwhile human rights campaigners that had led these organizations in titanic confrontations with the state took up leadership positions in the government, compounding the crisis of policy direction already precipitated by the change in political leadership. Many analysts have noted that the civil society lost much of the vibrancy it had in the 1990s following these changes. By 2009, there was little indication that the human rights sector had recovered its footing.

Prisoners of their Mandates

Kenyan human rights groups are essentially focused on human rights within the Kenyan borders. However, counter-terrorism activities involving the rendition of individuals to neighboring countries are transnational in nature. By declaring that the subjects of habeas corpus applications were no longer within the Kenyan jurisdiction, the state was able to render the matter of defending the rights of terror suspects moot. Without corresponding cross-border reach or even concrete collaborations with groups in Ethiopia and Somalia, Kenyan human rights groups found themselves largely without the means of influencing these foreign governments to release the suspects. The executive director of the MHRF notes that his organization was largely helpless when the Kenyan government transferred terrorism suspects to Somalia and Ethiopia. They were able to reach some of them in Ethiopian jails, but that is the most they could do.[19]

The only option left for Kenyan human rights groups working on rendition cases, therefore, was to partner with international human rights groups such as Amnesty International, Human Rights Watch, and Cageprisoners. The MHRF, which was centrally involved in working on behalf of rendition victims, has cultivated close working relations with these groups. Although this partnership was important in providing international visibility and prominence to the plight of the detained individuals, it could not substitute for the influence of a well-organized and mobilized domestic human rights movement.

Islamization of Counter-terrorism Violations

Increasingly, the campaign against violations associated with counter-terrorism measures has increasingly come to be identified with the MHRF. In most cases, whenever incidents of arbitrary arrests and detentions of terrorism suspects have surfaced in the Kenyan media it is the MHRF that has taken the lead on their behalf. On occasions Muslim leaders, particularly through the National Muslim Leaders' Forum, have also added their voices to that of the MHRF. As a result, human rights advocacy around counter-terrorism has acquired a visibly Muslim face. This has increasingly served to solidify the perception that the human rights violations associated with counter-terrorism activities are a "Muslim issue."

As a group working within the Muslim community, the leadership of the MHRF has helped in politically mobilizing the Muslim population to challenge the perceived profiling of Muslims by the security agencies. Unfortunately, it has also served to sideline the issue from the mainstream concerns of the Kenyan human rights movement. One of the Kenyan human rights activists involved in mobilizing against the Suppression of Terrorism Bill in 2003 points out that, from the very beginning, Kenyan human rights groups were alert to the danger of advocacy around counter-terrorism turning into a "Muslim concern."[20] To avoid this human rights groups had decided to set up the *Tetea* Initiative (Advocacy Initiative) as a Kenya Human Rights Network (K-HURINET) initiative to "de-Islamize" the campaign. However, the initiative was aborted due to "leadership problems" as groups competed over control and the potential resources it would attract.[21]

Al-Amin Kimathi, who leads the MHRF that has taken the leading role on the arrests, torture, and renditions of terrorism suspects, is aware of the perception that the violations are a "Muslim issue" but contends that his organization has only taken up the leadership role because other human rights groups were not interested in doing so.[22] The MHRF has forged a working relationship with the Independent Medico-Legal Unit (IMLU), which provides medical assistance to suspects who may have been tortured, as well as with the Kenyan chapter of the International Commission of Jurists, which provides technical support for litigation on behalf of the terrorism suspects. Independently, IMLU is also involved in a joint project with the Copenhagen-based International Council for Rehabilitation of Torture Survivors to share information on state counter-terrorism measures.[23] Nevertheless, a human rights lawyer who has defended many of the terrorism suspects concludes that for most Kenyan human rights groups the issue of violations of the rights of terrorism suspects remains incidental to their work.[24]

Many of the Kenyan human rights activists note that the Muslim leadership has not done a sufficient job of reaching out to the other faiths to take up the matter. However, as one activist noted, "no one needs an invitation to do something about human rights violations."[25] Adding to the marginalization of the violations around counter-terrorism is the fact that a majority of those arrested by Kenyan authorities have been ethnic Somalis—some of them Kenyan citizens and others citizens of Somalia. There is a long background to suspicion of Somalis in Kenya. In the case of the counter-terrorism, it was easy for many Kenyans to see the arrests as a "Muslim" and "Somali" issue. The fact that the majority of Kenyan Somalis are also Muslim has led to the conflation of the problem of religious profiling with that of ethnic profiling.

In addition, Kenyan human rights groups were slow to recognize global counter-terrorism measures as a significant threat to human rights. In Kenya, the public perception has been that the country has only been the unfortunate battleground for "other people's wars"—that the terrorism problem was a peripheral one and largely the business of the United States and Israel, who were the primary targets of the 1998 and the 2002 attacks, respectively. This perception may partly explain why Kenyan human rights groups have been slow to establish programmatic mechanisms to address state counter-terrorism measures.

Taking Terrorism Seriously

For human rights groups, terrorism and counter-terrorism present a new challenge different from the regular human rights concerns they are used to. Like their counterparts elsewhere, Kenyan human rights groups have been quick to denounce the state for human rights violations associated with state counter-terrorism measures, but they have had little to say with regard to victims of terrorist acts. As a result, human rights groups are vulnerable to the criticism that they fail to place equal emphasis on the lives of the victims of terrorism as they do for the rights of terror suspects.

In part this is because, historically, human rights groups have campaigned on actions by states; only recently have they begun to address the human rights violations of nonstate actors.

The failure by human rights groups to seriously confront the question of terrorism has in turn allowed states to define the concept in terms that pose serious challenges to human rights protection and promotion. The shelved Suppression of Terrorism Bill is a case in point. An official of the Kenyan National Commission on Human Rights notes that in 2003 human rights NGOs were reluctant to engage the government on any form of dialogue on the bill and instead insisted that it should be withdrawn.[26] A human rights lawyer who has wide experience on counter-terrorism and human rights in Kenya suggests that human rights groups are reluctant to express any interest in counter-terrorism beyond the human rights consequences of new measures and laws.[27] In his view, although there are valid reasons for human rights groups' distrust of government counter-terrorism measures, the fact that Kenya has been the victim of terrorist attacks in the past is a compelling reason for a statutory framework for counter-terrorism.

Donor Relations and International Politics

As previously noted, in the 1990s Western states were particularly vocal in their support for democratization and human rights in Kenya. Western diplomats were consequently seen by human rights groups as partners in the struggle for human rights, besides being a main source of funding. Consequently, Kenyan human rights groups did not rigorously critique the politics of these international actors and the limits that their national interests may have imposed on the promotion of human rights in Kenya. Under assault from a hostile Kenyan state, pragmatism demanded that the Kenyan human rights movement pay attention to human rights problems in Kenya and not antagonize their international partners.

However, the United States is the key partner of the Kenyan government on issues of counter-terrorism. Media reports and reports by groups such as the MHRF, Human Rights Watch, and Cageprisoners point to the complicity of the United States in the renditions of terrorism suspects from Kenya (Bloomfield 2008; MHRF 2008a; Cageprisoners and Reprieve 2007). Kenyan human rights groups are now expected to challenge the very Western states that have hitherto provided them with crucial diplomatic and financial support. That action requires both a conceptual and policy revolution in the way human rights groups view the world and implement their activities.

That is not to say Kenyan human rights groups are ignorant of the dilemma that this poses to their work. Groups such as IMLU have refused funding from the US government. The executive director of IMLU argued that, "the US strategy in the War on Terrorism is supportive of torture and cruel, degrading and inhuman treatment of terrorism suspects and as such it would be immoral for a human rights group, which views torture as an absolute crime, to accept funding support from any source that supports a policy of the torture and ill-treatment of suspects."[28] Nevertheless, he concedes that the influence of the Kenyan human rights movement on US policies is extremely limited.

Conclusion

The Global War on Terror has added new dimensions to human rights struggles in eastern Africa and the Horn, and in Kenya particularly. State counter-terrorism measures have precipitated a wave of violations that pose new challenges to human rights NGOs. Kenyan human rights groups have found themselves largely unprepared to effectively deal with these challenges.

The challenges are both conceptual and contextual. Conceptual confusion still surrounds the question of terrorism. Human rights groups have spent insufficient resources thinking about the issue of terrorism and therefore have not devised appropriate strategies to address human rights violations in the name of fighting terrorism. How to build popular solidarity for victims of renditions and other state counter-terrorism measures, who in Kenya are stigmatized due to their religious and ethnic backgrounds, is one of the challenges human rights NGOs have to confront.

The contextual problem is one of the environment in which human rights groups implement their advocacy strategies. The context for defending human rights is being transformed by the global War on Terror, which redefines the nature of relationships among states and relationships between Kenyan human rights groups and Western states. To survive that transformation calls for a careful critique of international politics, state interests, and the power of human rights NGOs themselves. Previously, Kenyan human rights groups wielded influence, partly owing to their access to Western corridors of power. Back then the national interests of nations such as the United States converged with the NGO agenda of promoting human rights. However, pursuit of the Global War on Terror has meant that security interests, narrowly defined, now trump the promotion of human rights. The question is whether human rights NGOs can now retool their approaches in light of these changes in the shifting global political context in which they work.

Notes

1. An early version of this chapter was presented in a conference in Nairobi organized by the Centre for Civil Society, London School of Economics, on December 4, 2007. The authors would like to thank the participants for their comments.

2. See *Report of the Policy Working Group on the United Nations and Terrorism*, U.N. G.A. 57th Sess., Item 162, Provisional Agenda, at 2, U.N. Doc. A/57/273-S/2002/875 (2002).

3. Before the 2001 attacks, the United States had been the primary target of terrorist attacks: the 1993 bombing of the World Trade Center in New York, the August 1998 attack on the US embassies in Nairobi and Dar es Salaam, and the 2000 attack in Yemen on the USS *Cole*.

4. The Task Force developed the Proceeds of Crime and Anti-Money Laundering Bill (2007), which was taken to Parliament in 2008 but was rejected by the Parliamentary Departmental Committee on Administration of Justice and Legal Affairs.

5. There are other considerations to take into account in explaining the US reaction to official corruption. The fact that the government of President Kibaki was barely two years old may have convinced the US that it was best not to denounce it publicly. Britain's newfound campaign against corruption in Kenya (after decades of a see-no-evil, hear-no-evil policy toward Kenya) was most surprising, and possibly not altogether free of narrow national interest calculations. There have been unsubstantiated suggestions that Britain was partly unhappy after losing out on lucrative defense contracts that it had traditionally been awarded without competition.

6. For example, see Wilson 2005.

7. See for instance Cageprisoners (2006), Amnesty International (2007), Cageprisoners and Reprieve (2007), MHRF (2008a), and Redress and Reprieve (2009).

8. For instance, Chad's Hissene Habré's extensive program of torture was run by the Chadian state security police, which had been trained in its techniques by US security officials. Furthermore, the United States' legacy of directing the formation of death squads, torture programs, and other mechanisms that operated beyond the rule of law in Latin America during the Cold War is well documented.

9. International human rights law is not the only casualty of the US global War on Terror. The laws governing international armed conflict were contravened in the US-backed Ethiopian invasion of Somalia in December 2006. Neither the UN Security Council nor the Peace and Security Council of the African Union endorsed the military action. For

a lengthier discussion on the implications of this invasion for regional security see KHRI (2007).

10. For example, the UN Special Rapporteur on Extrajudicial, Arbitrary or Summary Executions has documented reports that Kenyan security forces have been involved in human rights violations in 2008 and 2009. Report available online at http://www.reliefweb.int/rw/rwb.nsf/ db900sid/SNAA-7SM9RY?OpenDocument.

11. Other instruments violated by the practice of extraordinary renditions include the International Covenant on Civil and Political Rights, the International Covenant on Economic and Social Rights, the Convention and Protocol Relating to the Status of Refugees, and the Vienna Convention on Consular Relations.

12. See "Letter to the President of Kenya on the Rendition of the Kenyan National, Mohamed Abdulmalik, to Guantanamo Bay," July 21, 2008. Available online at www.redress.org.

13. Some of the nationalities include: Kenyan, American, British, French, Canadian, Swedish, Ethiopian, Eritrean, Tunisian, Omani, Yemeni, Rwandese, Tanzanian, Saudi Arabian, Sudanese, Ugandan, Syrian, Moroccan, and Jordanian.

14. Authors' interview with Al-Amin Kimathi, Coordinator of Muslim Human Rights Forum. Nairobi. January 3, 2007.

15. Authors' interview with Al-Amin Kimathi, Coordinator of Muslim Human Rights Forum. Nairobi. January 3, 2007.

16. Authors' interview with Commissioner Lawrence Mute, Kenya National Commission on Human Rights. Nairobi. January 30, 2009.

17. Authors' interview with Commissioner Lawrence Mute, Kenya National Commission on Human Rights. Nairobi. January 30, 2009.

18. This assessment was made by Amina Abdalla, a member of the Departmental Committee on Administration of Justice and Legal Affairs of the Kenyan National Assembly.

19. Authors' interview with Al-Amin Kimathi, Executive Director, Muslim Human Rights Forum (MHRF). Nairobi. January 3, 2009.

20. Authors' interview with human rights activist Ndung'u Wainaina. Nairobi. January 27, 2009.

21. This view is supported by Al-Amin Kimathi, Coordinator, Muslim Human Rights Forum. Authors' interview. Nairobi. January 3, 2009.

22. Authors' interview with Al-Amin Kimathi, Coordinator, Muslim Human Rights Forum. Nairobi. January 3, 2009.

23. Authors' interview with Sam Muhochi, Executive Director, Independent Medico-Legal Unit (IMLU). Nairobi. March 29, 2009.

24. Authors' interview with human rights lawyer Mbugua Mureithi. Nairobi. March 29, 2009.

25. Authors' interview with Al-Amin Kimathi, Coordinator, Muslim Human Rights Forum. Nairobi. January 3, 2009.

26. Authors' interview with Commissioner Lawrence Mute, Kenya National Commission on Human Rights. Nairobi. January 30, 2009.

27. Authors' interview with human rights lawyer Mbugua Mureithi. Nairobi. March 29, 2009.

28. Authors' interview with Sam Muhochi, Executive Director, Independent Medico-Legal Unit (IMLU). Nairobi. March 29, 2009.

14

CONCLUSION

Jeremy Lind and Jude Howell

There are three legs to the stool of American foreign policy: defense, diplomacy, and development. And we are responsible for two of the three legs. And we will make clear, as we go forward, that diplomacy and development are essential tools in achieving the long-term objectives of the United States. And I will do all that I can, working with you, to make it abundantly clear that robust diplomacy and effective development are the best long-term tools for securing America's future.

—*Hillary Rodham Clinton, remarks to State Department employees, January 22, 2009*

The prosecution of the global War on Terror regime in the aftermath of the 9/11 attacks in the United States indelibly reshaped the terrain for civil society to organize. Although considerable scholarly attention and advocacy efforts have focused on the erosion of civil liberties and threats to human rights resulting from the introduction of new counter-terrorism structures since the 9/11 attacks, the impacts of the global War on Terror regime on the spaces and actors of civil society have been more concealed and obscure, although they are equally crucial to identify and understand. This book set out to examine the effects of the War on Terror regime on civil society in a diversity of contexts. As the chapters in this book demonstrate, civil society is a significant focus of concern in new security frameworks. It is regarded as a central battleground in contemporary conflict, as is evident in its incorporation into counter-insurgency and counter-radicalization initiatives in different settings.

Civil society and security have been linked before. In the Cold War era, Western governments on the one hand used civil society organizations to promote liberal values, while on the other hand they kept a watchful eye on groups they suspected of being communist in orientation or otherwise threatening to the state. However, restrictions on aid to communist states and their allies and on mobility meant that external governments had limited scope for shaping the terrain of civil society in Cold War states and their Third World allies, whether through international development assistance or other means. With the end of the Cold War and the focus on governance and democracy, governments and development agencies began to engage more systematically with civil society. Links between civil society, development, and security in the 1990s were mainly forged in the conflict and post-conflict settings of the so-called New Wars, such as those in Bosnia, Sri Lanka, and Kosovo. In other, more stable aid-recipient contexts, the primary emphasis of donors was on engaging with civil society to promote democracy and/or reduce poverty. The potential links between security and civil society were thus not made—institutionally, operationally, or discursively—in a broad and comprehensive way across development policy. Though there was some attention to security sector reforms, these did not form a major plank of international development policy.

What has changed since 2001 is the expansiveness of these ties, which have become increasingly formalized and institutionalized through new forms of cooperation between states and civil societies, as well as new structures for controlling non-governmental spaces. This book investigated the contradictory treatment of civil society since 2001, identifying the strains that the global War on Terror regime has placed on civil societies in different settings. It explored this through four key themes: the interweaving of the global War on Terror regime with domestic politics; the control and regulation of civil society; the strategic co-option of civil society into the prosecution of the global War on Terror regime; and the deploying of aid and international development policy and the concomitant engagement with civil society for security objectives. In this concluding chapter we return to those themes outlined in the Introduction, considering the significance of the book's findings for understanding the strains placed on civil societies in different political contexts post-9/11.

The Interweaving of Global and Domestic Politics since 2001

Several chapters in the book illustrate how the unfolding of the global War on Terror regime can take on different political dynamics as political leaders manipulate the situation to pursue their own domestic, political objectives. One manifestation of this, as detailed by several contributors, is the appropriation of the discourses of the War on Terror to justify cracking down on opponents and critical voices in civil society. The Museveni regime in Uganda, for example, misused its post-9/11 counter-terrorism law to detain and bring charges against a rival opposition political leader, Dr. Kizza Besigye. It also played the terrorism card to limit critical reporting in the Ugandan press and generally to intimidate Uganda's nascent civil society. Similarly, in India the chief minister, Jayalalitha Layalitha, used state terrorist legislation to detain a political opponent, justifying the action in terms of support for the internationally designated terrorist group the Liberation Tigers of Tamil Eelam (LTTE) in Sri Lanka. Building on over two decades of systematically propagating doubts about the loyalty of Muslims in India to the country, BJP political leaders and related right-wing Hindu groups deftly appropriated the War on Terror discourse to bolster their construction of Muslims as loyal to Pakistan and linked to global jihadist terrorism. The attacks in Mumbai in November 2008 by jihadist terrorists catapulted India onto the stage of international victimhood in the War on Terror. Right-wing nationalist Hindu leaders tried to capitalize on this event to push for counter-terrorist legislation and to reinforce the construction of Muslims as a treacherous and threatening group in Indian society.

Likewise, in Uzbekistan and Kyrgyzstan, Presidents Karimov and Bakiev responded to terrorist threats by curtailing the activities of elements in civil society labeled as destabilizing. However, the climate of fear engendered by these threats and accentuated by the global responses to terrorism provided cover to the governments to cast suspicion more broadly to other groups that were seen as threatening the ruling regimes, including NGOs working on democracy and religious groups. Thus, there has been a clear tendency to conflate the safety of civilian populations in the light of potential terrorist threats with the maintenance of political order and the protection of the political regime. The ways in which the global politics of the War on Terror intersect with a country's domestic politics are therefore not easily predictable.

The case of Lebanon illustrates well the inherent contradictions and tensions that pervade efforts by states to craft a new regime of security governance in the post-9/11 context. Whereas Israel and the United States regard Hezbollah as a terrorist organization, the Lebanese government prioritized the threat from Israel to downplay the tense and complicated relations it had with Hezbollah, allowing Hezbollah to dominate the reconstruction assistance provided to affected populations. In contrast the Lebanese government used the language of terrorism to pursue the Islamic militant group the Fateh Al Islam (FAI), which was responsible for the deaths of several Lebanese soldiers. When the FAI took cover in the Nahr Al Bared Palestinian camp, the Lebanese government invoked the "terrorist" label to rationalize its campaign against militants and to cast suspicion over the residents as complicit in terrorism. In this way it absolved itself of responsibility for the victims of this confrontation, leaving humanitarian assistance to UNWRA and NGOs. Thus these different and expedient approaches to Hezbollah and FAI reflected the contested nature of civil society and citizenship, with implications in turn for deciding who was "worthy" of receiving and giving humanitarian assistance. Ultimately, the need to respond to the threat of terrorism was used by the Lebanese government to pursue its own political priorities and, in doing so, to renege on its responsibility to protect the Palestinian civilian population that was trapped in the fighting.

Another manifestation of the unpredictability of the intersection of global and domestic politics in the War on Terror regime relates to the political inversion of terrorist discourses to challenge US power. The most vivid illustration of this is the case of Uzbekistan, where President Karimov switched from allying with the United States to counter an insurgent, fundamentalist Islamic movement to accusing the United States of fomenting terrorism through its support for protests and pro-democracy groups. The subsequent crackdown on externally funded civil society groups and pro-democracy organizations contrasted with President Karimov's later courting of civil society groups focused on service-delivery. The vacillations in policy toward civil society, swinging from tolerance to intolerance and from selective courting of some groups but not others, make for an uncertain and fragile environment in which civil society groups can operate.

The manipulation of external politics to justify domestic actions affects the maneuverability of civil society and gives legitimacy (or otherwise) to civil society—both in general and to specific parts thereof. The desire of external agents to pursue their own agendas also creates dilemmas for civil society organizations. In the case of Uzbekistan, for example, the US government implied that it was ready to overlook human rights issues to ensure Uzbekistan's alliance in the War on Terror. This then created difficulties for local human rights groups, many of which were funded by Western donors, who had to face the seeming hypocrisy of its external funders.

Similarly, in Kenya human rights groups blossomed under the availability of donor funding during the democracy movement in the 1990s, and such groups contributed to the historic victory of a coalition of opposition political parties in the 2002 election. However, US government support of controversial counter-terrorism measures in the Horn of Africa, including backing proposed anti-terrorism legislation in Kenya and supporting a regional rendition program, has created a dilemma for human rights groups that have relied on US bilateral aid in the past. They became aware that although external funding for human rights work was important, given the difficulties of raising money locally for such political issues, there were also limits on what kind of human rights work could be carried out. Advocacy work that drew attention to the effects of counter-terrorist measures since 2001 was not able to attract external funding.

Control and Regulation of Civil Society

A key thread running throughout this book is how the War on Terror has cast greater suspicion over civil society, fueling the development of tighter legislative and regulatory controls over non-governmental actors. The 9/11 attacks brought firmly to an end the "golden age" for civil society in the 1990s, when donor agencies enthusiastically embraced working with civil society actors both as a way of promoting democracy and of alleviating poverty through service delivery in aid-recipient contexts. Already in the late 1990s concerns had emerged around the transparency and probity of civil society as well as the effectiveness of working around states by channeling aid through non-governmental actors. The attacks of September 11, 2001, marked a turning point in the treatment of civil society in development strategies and the bureaucratic practices of aid agencies. The emphasis on the role of civil society in promoting democracy, human rights, and resolutions to armed conflicts was matched by concern that civil society organizations could also be misused by terrorists, as seen in numerous examples highlighted in this book.

There is of course nothing particularly new about political suspicion of non-governmental actors. The history of relations between states and civil societies is peppered with instances in which political regimes have regarded non-governmental actors as threatening. During the Vietnam War, for example, the US government kept a close eye on peace and solidarity groups and antiwar movements. In South Africa the then apartheid regime harassed and imprisoned anti-apartheid activists. During the Emergency period in India the Congress government, under Indira Gandhi, viewed non-governmental and people's organizations with suspicion, arresting and intimidating activists. What is different about the current situation is the global armory brought to bear on civil society, comprising not only restrictive legislation and regulations but also global discourses casting suspicion over civil society and institutional approaches to civil society. Also distinct is the amorphous and fluid nature of the "enemy," which allegedly hides behind the cover of civil society, thus rendering all parts of civil society suspicious.

A key finding emerging out of the book is that the 9/11 attacks gave added impetus to an emerging drive to strengthen legal, regulatory, and bureaucratic controls over civil society, affecting the spaces for it to organize, raise funds, advocate, and carry out activities. This tightening of controls drew upon a political and media discourse that presented terrorism as exceptional, and therefore requiring extra-ordinary measures. As the chapters on Australia, the United Kingdom, and Palestine showed, the problem was that the discourse of exceptionality was soon used to justify making extra-ordinary legislation permanent. Moreover, exceptional measures and legislation have in several contexts become extended to apply to various types of social and political action, thus undermining the liberal rights of freedom of association and speech.

As the chapters on Palestine, the United States, and the United Kingdom demonstrated, provisions in post-9/11 counter-terrorism laws have imposed burdensome due diligence requirements on non-governmental actors, such as development NGOs working overseas and private grant-making agencies. The global diffusion of anti-money-laundering legislation that draws charities into its ambit, as in India and Kenya, casts suspicion upon the activities of voluntary organizations. New, sector-specific regulations aimed at enhancing accountability, transparency, and audit trails have been motivated not just by public and donor concerns about the legitimacy and probity of charities and community organizations, but also by security concerns around the potential misuse of charities by extremist and terrorist groups.

These developments point to the subsuming of charity regulation into broader security frameworks. In other words, the control and regulation of civil society has merged with security strategies and frameworks in the light of the 9/11 attacks. This convergence is likely to be long-lasting, for it reflects not just the ideological positions of a particular administration, but an outlook of international relations and national and global security players that considers non-governmental actors to be strategic, at once both threatening and vital to stabilization and strengthening security. This leads us to our third and closely inter-related theme of the strategic co-option of civil society.

The Strategic Co-option of Civil Society in the War on Terror

The widespread implementation of new strategies and measures for counter-terrorism since 2001 has involved more than just greater controls and restrictions on the activities of civil society. Indeed, it would be much too simple and empirically incorrect to conclude that the effects of the War on Terror on civil society have been wholly restrictive or negative, or that there has been an unambiguous global clampdown on civil society. Such a conclusion would underestimate the strategic nature of the War on Terror regime. Rather, the War on Terror regime has reaffirmed the strategic relevance of civil society by underlining the importance of its contributions to helping achieve the political objectives of strengthening states and achieving international security. The dual-pronged approach that states have adopted, on the one hand of increasing controls on civil society to limit (ostensibly) its potential misuse by terrorists and on the other hand of cooperating with select parts of civil society, might suggest a contradictory treatment of non-governmental actors. Indeed, this is how in practice it may be felt by civil society.

However, these dualities are not incompatible but are rather complementary, and they reflect the roles and spaces for civil society envisioned in neo-liberal governance. The neoliberal ideal is a minimal state that draws on the inputs of civil society to provide social services and welfare. The rationales for this relate to creating a favorable perception of the state as one that is able to deliver social welfare without excessive intervention in society and to reduce public expenditure. In aid-recipient contexts, such an ideal has also included creating spaces for pro-democratic groups to flourish so as to foster the global spread of liberal democracy. In the post-9/11 context, however, the rationale for incorporating civil society was not just about the effective delivery of social services and the concomitant legitimization of transitional or post-conflict states. It was also not solely about the spread of liberal democratic values. Rather, the War on Terror added to this the rationale of building legitimate and effective states by incorporating the contribution of civil society actors in delivering development and social interventions so as to enhance international security. Civil society thus had a role to play in legitimizing states and making the world a safer place.

The imperative to build legitimacy through delivering development and articulating a clear social policy for the ultimate goal of global security has influenced the political strategies of some states to recruit civil society into participating in state social agendas and counter-terrorism strategies. For example, Jeremy Lind noted in this book how officials in the Palestinian Authority have proposed setting up community social-support organizations in towns and villages in the West Bank to counter-balance the influence of Islamic social welfare groups allied with Hamas. The logic informing these proposals is to strengthen the hand of the Western-backed Palestinian Authority against Hamas by using development as a technique of governance and ideological domination. Governments in Kenya, the United Kingdom, and Spain have sought dialogue with Muslim religious leaders as well as representative bodies for Muslim communities in these countries. These ties are intended ostensibly to give Muslims an outlet for communicating their interests and addressing alienation among sections of Muslim populations in these countries. However, the negligible impacts of these initiatives and doubts over their effectiveness suggest that their ultimate purpose is to boost political support for governments' security regimes in the War on Terror, rather than necessarily seriously addressing the socio-economic condition and human rights situation of Muslims. New programming within bilateral and multilateral aid agencies, arising from international security concerns, has also sought to open up new areas of cooperation with Muslim populations. For example, donor agencies such as USAID have, in aid contexts such as India and Kenya, sought to work with madrassas to develop curricula that promote tolerance and peaceful coexistence of different religious and cultural communities. However, Muslim clerics and other community leaders have expressed reservations over this support and opposed such initiatives in certain contexts.

Aid, Civil Society, and Security

The increased convergence of security, aid, and social policy in the global War on Terror regime has recast the work of non-governmental development actors in a newly politicized light. Cooperation between states and civil societies under the security framework embodied by the global War on Terror regime has seen the further blurring of boundaries between governments and the work of non-governmental actors. This in turn has had an impact upon popular perceptions of civil society as an independent yet political actor. Fast (2006) notes that in the Occupied Palestinian Territories there is an expectation among Palestinians that NGOs will take a stance of solidarity with the Palestinian people against Israeli military aggression and occupation. In other words, there is an expectation that NGOs recognize and articulate a political position.

Yet, donors and the Israeli government insist that NGOs maintain their neutrality and perform rigorous due diligence checks in delivering assistance. In this case, the supposed neutrality of civil society is something privileged in order to preserve existing power relations running through the conflict. Hence, NGOs operating in the Occupied Palestinian Territories must contend with the dilemma of satisfying the expectations of donors (that they remain neutral in a politically charged context) and of the Palestinian populations (that they act in solidarity with them). Thus, they have to reconcile, on the one hand, trying to remain or appearing to remain neutral in a deeply politicized context and carrying out perfunctory due diligence checks on their partners on the ground with, on the other hand, also maintaining their credibility among Palestinians by expressly opposing Israeli military occupation.

The deepening development-security-civil society nexus under the global War on Terror regime has affected not only state-civil society relations but also the ways that militaries intervene in conflict/post-conflict contexts with consequences for development actors. As Mark Duffield (2001) described in detail, militaries began to intervene more systematically in humanitarian relief and development in the context of the New Wars of the 1990s. These trends have deepened and intensified post-September 2001, as militaries have adapted their methods of fighting and models for warfare to the transnational, networked, and hybrid characteristics of militant organizations. Groups such as Hamas in the Occupied Palestinian Territories, Hezbollah in Lebanon, and Lashkar-e-Taiba in Pakistan have armed wings as well as elements that provide social support alongside a compendium of non-governmental actors, including religious schools, social welfare organizations, mosque committees, and other community-based organizations. Just as governments have given greater attention to the "soft" dimensions of security by reaching out to moderate Muslim communities and initiating anti-radicalization programs, so too militaries have engaged more systematically in "hearts and minds" work through the vehicle of development in response to the tactics and structures of extremist groups.

In his chapter on Afghanistan, Stuart Gordon described in detail the expansion of military capabilities in development as part of a stabilization strategy. In Afghanistan, Iraq, and the Horn of Africa, the US military has worked with civilian US government agencies, as well as international aid agencies and local NGOs, to deliver development. What is significant here is the recognition that delivering development is paramount for building the legitimacy of states, defeating extremists, and achieving national and global security. Thus, development and aid are among the techniques governments and militaries are drawing on to strengthen security. Although the belief that "there can be no development without security" has become a truism in international development work, implicit in contemporary counter-terrorism strategy is the thinking that "there can be no security without development."

The four themes explored in this book point to a new politics of civil society that has been forged through the military and political prosecution of the War on Terror regime. This change has put civil society actors under strain. It has saddled non-governmental actors with the pressures of reconciling their cooperation with governments and militaries in strengthening security with their avowed independence and neutrality. Where civil society organizations receive Western donor funds—as has been common, for example, for development NGOs, pro-democracy groups, and human rights groups in aid-recipient contexts—new due diligence requirements reconstitute their relations with their partner organizations, not only burdening them with additional administrative obligations but also veiling those relations with an element of mistrust and suspicion. Human rights groups that have received funding from Western donors as part of a donor agenda to promote democracy are faced with the dilemma as to whether or not to continue to take funds from bilateral donors whose governments are associated with human rights violations in the War on Terror, extraordinary renditions from Kenya being a case in point.

In contexts where government leaders use the War on Terror discourse to create or intensify divisions within civil societies, then civil society organizations come under pressure to reflect on not only how they respond to the negative effects of such discourses on particular civil society actors but also how to respond to government efforts to engage with them. In cases such as Uzbekistan, where government policy toward civil society has vacillated frequently, this in turn creates considerable uncertainty for civil society organizations.

In conflict situations where beneficiary groups expect political solidarity from local civil society groups, then civil society organizations receiving funds from external donors that expect, rather, political neutrality struggle to balance maintaining credibility among their partners and beneficiaries with giving the appearance of neutrality to their donors. Where militaries are engaging in humanitarian relief and development work to stabilize governments, these interventions place strains on humanitarian NGO workers who seek to abide by humanitarian principles of neutrality, independence, and impartiality. These dilemmas have intensified post-9/11, as militaries have committed more strategically to development work as a key element of contemporary warfare and counterinsurgency strategy.

The launch of the War on Terror regime has also placed strains on civil society in terms of how different actors respond to new security measures and the pressures these place on civil society in general, and on selected groups in particular. In many countries civil society groups were slow to respond to the introduction of new counter-terrorism legislation, measures, and practices. This was the case even in so-called advanced liberal democracies, where it might be expected that civil society in general would challenge in a coordinated and coherent way the restrictive measures that might impinge on basic rights and liberties. Whereas the human rights community and Muslim groups have taken the lead in questioning such measures, other parts of civil society, and especially those funded by governments and external donors, have in general been extraordinarily silent about the effects on Muslim organizations and populations and the spaces of civil society, at least until they themselves began to feel the pinch (Howell and Lind 2009).

Recent efforts by advocacy networks in the United States and Europe to resist aspects of charitable regulation, not to mention notable opposition to proposed anti-terrorism laws and practices in newly democratizing states such as Kenya, indicate a gradual awakening of non-governmental actors to the politics of the War on Terror regime of which they are a part. However, at the same time such responses, undertaken as they have been by groups that are most affected by counter-terrorism, underline the divisions within civil society itself, including between secular and religious groups, between organizations working in different sectors, and between dissidents and supporters of governments in power.

There are several possible reasons but no clear explanation for the reticence of much of civil society in response to the global War on Terror regime. It could be that civil society has not adequately comprehended the significance of the War on Terror regime for its own ways of working. It could also indicate a natural reluctance of civil society to engage with issues interpreted as being wholly about security—and therefore lying beyond the social and technical remit that pertains for many organizations and groups. In the United States, many in the voluntary-sector part of civil society were slow to respond because they wrongly concluded that new security laws, measures, and practices would affect only a small fraction of civil society, namely Muslim groups, and thus would not be of concern to the US voluntary sector more broadly (Sidel 2008).

Even if this were the case, it reflects a narrow understanding of "civil society" among mainstream, non-governmental actors. Such a view is blind to the full range of civil society actors that constitute the civil society terrain. In particular it points to an exclusion from predominant understandings of civil society of particular groups representing Muslims, other religious minorities, asylum seekers, and migrant workers. Although it might be argued that counter-terrorism measures and strategies since the 9/11 attacks have affected only a few organizations that are most directly associated with the perceived threat of terrorism, this misses the point that such new structures and practices have demonstrably important effects on and implications for civil society's own ways of working and on public perceptions of civil society.

These are thus the broad contours of a new politics of civil society. Ultimately, the War on Terror highlights the critical importance of civil society's political role, in spite of its reticence to speak out against counter-terrorism measures in some cases. In some contexts the intersection of the War on Terror regime with domestic politics has created an opportunity for civil society to demonstrate its political relevance, such as in Kenya in the new post-Moi democratic setting. In other contexts, too, the War on Terror theoretically throws up an opportunity for civil society to demonstrate its relevance in political debates, particularly at a time when politicians are expressly seeking the assistance of some civil society actors in service delivery—whether to reduce public expenditure, improve state effectiveness, or strengthen the political legitimacy of the state—while simultaneously restricting the spaces for civil society. Given that this strategic focus on service delivery is often matched by a downplaying of the roles of civil society in advocacy and government and market accountability, the need for robust and coherent responses from civil society should be acutely apparent. Civil society is only beginning to understand the implications for its work of the shifting global political context and of its responses to and participation in the political prosecution of the War on Terror.

In his first week in office, President Barack Obama signed executive orders to begin the process of closing the Guantanamo Bay detention facility and banning the use of torture by US intelligence agencies (Priest 2009). The arrival of a new political administration in the United States has prompted a reappraisal of counter-terrorism responses and security strategies. Although the new US administration, like the UK government a few years earlier, has firmly rejected the language of the "War on Terror," the global War on Terror regime still lives on in a spectrum of laws, policies, bureaucratic practices, and institutional linkages. The new strategic ties and networking across government/civil society and military/civil boundaries described in this book will similarly survive the change of political leadership. Although the Obama administration has signaled a clear change in tone in fighting transnational terrorist networks, the incorporation of civil society into legal and institutional structures for counter-terrorism is not being reversed.

The 9/11 attacks and the subsequent War on Terror regime have thus led to a significant reshaping of state–civil society relations as well as a widening and deepening of linkages between civil society, security, and aid. The new politics of state–civil society relations post-9/11 places strains on civil society that have to be acknowledged and dealt with. As security agencies, donor agencies, and governments rethink their approaches to global terrorist threats (and, within that, their strategies toward civil society), this creates an opening for civil society actors to evaluate the effects of this regime on their diverse spaces, values, and operations. It provides a strategic opportunity for civil society actors to critically reflect on how they have responded to the seemingly contradictory state strategy of control and co-option. Perhaps most importantly, it provides an opening for civil society actors to consider how they wish to contribute in the future to the undoing of some of the damaging effects of the War on Terror regime on civil societies, and whether and how to contribute to counter-terrorist strategy in a way that causes the least harm to civil societies.

BIBLIOGRAPHY

24.kg News Agency. 2008a. Special services of Kyrgyzstan has identified over 30 units of religious–extremist organizations within 11 months in 2008. Available at: www.24.kg.

———. 2008b. A law on "State Social Contracting" was adopted in Kyrgyzstan. Available at: www.24.kg.

ABC News Online. 2005. PM denies raids anti-Muslim. November 9. Available at: http://www.abc.net.au/news/newsitems/200511/s1500786.htm.

Adamson, Fiona B. 2006. Crossing borders: International migration and national security. *International Security* 31, no. 1:165–99.

Agier, Michel. 2002a. Between war and city: Towards an urban anthropology of refugee camps. *Ethnography* 3, no. 3:317–41.

———. 2002b. Still stuck between war and city: A response to Bauman and Malkki. *Ethnography* 3, no. 3:361–66.

Agonist.org. 2005. U.S. evicted from air base in Uzbekistan. July 30. Available at: www.agonist.org.

Alam, Md. Muktar. 2004. *Madrasas and terrorism: Myth or reality?* New Delhi: Indian Social Institute.

American Civil Liberties Union. 2007. Comments concerning the Proposed Partner Vetting System. Mimeo. August 27. Available at: http://www.aclu.org/pdfs/privacy/usaid_partnervetting_20070827.pdf.

———. 2008. Court blocks government from designating charity as "terrorist." Press release. October 9.

Amnesty International. 2007. *Horn of Africa: Unlawful transfers in the "War on Terror."* June. London: Amnesty International.

Amnesty International UK, et al. 2008. *The Gaza Strip: A humanitarian implosion.*

Anderson, John. 2000. Creating a framework for civil society in Kyrgyzstan. *Europe-Asia Studies* 52, no. 1:77–93.

Anderson, Mary. 1999. *Do no harm: How aid can support peace—or war.* Boulder, CO: Lynne Rienner Publishers.

———. 2000. *Options for aid in conflict: Lessons from field experience.* Boulder, CO: Lynne Rienner Publishers.

Annan, Kofi. 2001. *Framework for cooperation in peace-building.* New York: United Nations, Secretary General Report to the UN Security Council.

Anti-Terrorism Act. 2002. Available at: http://www.kituochakatiba.co.ug/anti.pdf. Downloaded on January 2, 2008.

Arigita, Elena. 2006. Representing Islam in Spain: Muslim identities and the contestation of leadership. *The Muslim World* 96, no. 2:563–84.

Arulanantham, Ahilan T. 2008. A hungry child knows no politics: A proposal to reform laws governing humanitarian relief and "material support" of terrorism. American Constitution Society. June 25. Available at: http://www.acslaw.org/files/Arulanantham%20Issue%20Brief.pdf.

Associated Press. 2004. Wave of terrorist attacks kill 19 in Uzbekistan. March 30. Available at: www.ap.org.

Australian Government. 2004. *Transnational terrorism: The threat to Australia.* Canberra: Commonwealth of Australia.

Australian Parliamentary Library Website: Terrorism law. 2008. September 8. Available at: http://www.aph.gov.au/library/intguide/law/terrorism.htm#terrstate.

Ayub, Fatima, and Sari Kouvo. 2008. Righting the course? Humanitarian intervention, the war on terror and the future of Afghanistan. *International Affairs* 84, no. 4:641–58.

Babajanian, Babken, Sabine Freizer, and Daniel Stevens. 2005. Introduction: Civil society in Central Asia and the Caucasus. *Central Asian Survey* 24, no. 3:209–24.

Bal, Hartosh Singh. 2006. Image boost for NGOs. *Civil Society* August: 15–19.

Balasingham, Anton. 2004. *War and peace: Armed struggle and peace efforts of Liberation Tigers.* Mitcham: Fairmax.

Barkan, Joel D. 2004. US human rights policy and democratization in Kenya. In *Implementing U.S. human rights policy: Agendas, policies, and practices*, ed. Debra Liang-Fenton. Washington, D.C.: United States Institute of Peace Press.

Barkan, Joel D., and Jennifer G. Cooke. 2001. US policy toward Kenya in the wake of September 11: Can new antiterrorist imperatives be reconciled with enduring US foreign policy goals? *Africa Notes* 4: December.

Barton, Frederick, and Noam Unger. 2009. *Civil-military relations, fostering development, and expanding civilian capacity: A workshop report.* Available at: http://www.csis.org/component/option,com_csis _pubs/task,view/id,5429/.

Bastian, Sunil, ed. 1996. *Sri Lanka: The devolution debate.* Colombo: International Centre for Ethnic Studies.

Bastian, Sunil. 2007. *The politics of foreign aid in Sri Lanka: Promoting markets and supporting peace.* Colombo: International Centre for Ethnic Studies.

Bastian, Sunil, and Robin Luckham, eds. 2003. *Can democracy be designed? The politics of institutional choice in conflict-torn societies.* London: Zed Books.

Bauman, Zygmunt. 2002. In the lowly nowherevilles of liquid modernity: Comments on and around Agier. *Ethnography* 3, no. 3:343–49.

BBC. 2003. Text: Azores Summit statement. Available at: http://news.bbc .co.uk/1/hi/world/middle_east/2855567.stm.

Beall, Jo. 2006. Cities, terrorism and development. *Journal of International Development* 18, no. 1:105–20.

Belloni, Roberto 2008. Civil society in war-to-democracy transitions. In *From war to democracy: Dilemmas of peacebuilding*, ed. Anna K. Jarstad and Timothy D. Sisk. Cambridge: Cambridge University Press.

Beshimov, Erdin. 2004. *Kyrgyzstan's Akayev: The revolution stops here.* Available at: www.eurasianet.org.

Bijoy, C. R. 2003. *The Adivasis of India: A history of discrimination, conflict and resistance.* Core Committee of the All India Coordinating Forum of Adivasis/Indigenous Peoples, PUCL Bulletin, February.

Bingol, Yilmaz. 2004. Nationalism and democracy in post-communist Central Asia. *Asian Ethnicity* 5, no 1:43–60.

Blake, Erica, and David Yonke. 2008. Local charity fights terror allegation: KindHearts seeks day in court. *Toledo Blade.* October 10.

Bloomfield, Steve. 2008. Kenyan men recently released from an Ethiopian jail say US intelligence officials interrogated them. *Newsweek* Web Exclusive, November 19. Available online.

Boletín Económico ICE. 2007. *Veinte años de comercio exterior: El sector exterior en 2006 (Twenty years of foreign trade: The foreign sector in 2006)*. Madrid: Ministerio de Industria, Comercio y Turismo (Spanish Ministry of Industry, Trade and Tourism).

Bossa, S. B. and T. Mulindwa. 2004. The Anti-Terrorism Act, 2002 (Uganda): Human Rights Concerns and Implications. (Paper presented to the International Commission of Jurists.) September 15, 2004. Available at http://www.icj.org/IMG/pdf/Paper_Bossa.pdf.

Boswell, Christina. 2007. Migration control in Europe after 9/11: Explaining the absence of securitization. *Journal of Common Market Studies* 45, no. 3:589–610.

Boutros-Ghali, Boutros. 1992. *An agenda for peace*. New York: United Nations, Secretary General Report to the UN Security Council.

———. 1996. *An agenda for democratization*. New York: United Nations.

Brandon, Ben. 2004. Terrorism, human rights and the rule of law: 120 years of the UK's legal response to terrorism. *Criminal Law Review*: 981–97.

Bratton, Michael, et al. 2000. Democracy, economy and gender in Uganda: Report of a national sample survey. *Afrobarometer Working Paper* No. 4.

Brun, Cathrine. 2003. Local citizens or internally displaced persons? Dilemmas of long term displacement in Sri Lanka. *Journal of Refugee Studies* 16, no. 4:376–97.

Bussey, Erica. 2005. Constitutional dialogue in Uganda. *Journal of African Law* 49, no.1:1–23.

Cabinet Office. 2008. *The national security strategy of the United Kingdom: Security in an interdependent world*. London: Cabinet Office, Cm 7291.

Cageprisoners. 2006. *Inside Africa's War on Terror: War on Terror detentions in the Horn of Africa*. May. London.

Cageprisoners and Reprieve. 2007. *Mass rendition, incommunicado detention, and possible torture of foreign nationals in Kenya, Somalia and Ethiopia*. March 22. London.

Carothers, Thomas. 2003. Promoting Democracy and Fighting Terror. *Foreign Affairs*, January/February. Available at: www.carnegie.org.

———. 2004. *Critical mission: Essays on democracy promotion*. Washington, D.C.: Carnegie Endowment for International Peace.

Carter, Terrance S. 2006. Canadian charities: The forgotten victims of Canada's anti-terrorism legislation. *International Journal of Civil Society* 4: 10–16.

Center for Constitutional Rights. 2009. Court of Appeals affirms: Material support statute, penalizing humanitarian aid, is unconstitutional. Press release. January 9.

Center for Defense Information. 2007. Kenya. Available online.

Central Asian and Southern Caucasian Freedom of Expression Network. 2008. *President of Kyrgyzstan signed the law on assembly.* Available at: www.cascfen.net.

Centre for Just Peace and Democracy. 2006. *Envisioning new trajectories for peace in Sri Lanka.* Luzern: CJPD.

Chan, Janet. 1997. *Changing police culture: Policing in a multicultural society.* Cambridge: Cambridge University Press.

Chandhoke, Neera. 2003. *The conceits of civil society.* Oxford: Oxford University Press.

Charity Commission. 2008. *Counter-terrorism strategy.* July. London: Charity Commission.

———. 2009. *Inquiry report: Palestinians Relief and Development Fund (Interpal).* February. London: Charity Commission.

Chatty, Dawn. 2007. Researching refugee youth in the Middle East: Reflections on the importance of comparative research. *Journal of Refugee Studies* 20, no. 2:265–80.

Chesterman, Simon, Michael Ignatieff, and Ramesh Thakur, eds. 2005. *Making states work: State failure and the crisis of governance.* Tokyo: United Nations University Press.

Chong, Agnes. 2006. Anti-terror laws and the Muslim community: Where does terror end and security begin? *Borderlands*, no. 1.

Chong, Agnes, et al. 2005. *Laws for insecurity? A report on the federal government's proposed counter-terrorism measures.* September 2005. Sydney: Public Interest Advocacy Centre.

Christian Aid. 2004. *The politics of poverty: Aid in the new Cold War.* London, Christian Aid.

Clarke, John. 2008. *Report of the inquiry into the case of Dr Mohamed Haneef (the "Clarke Inquiry").* Canberra: Commonwealth of Australia.

Colás, A. 2004. Geographies of violence and democracy. *Radical Philosophy* no. 126:1–5.

Cole, David. 2004. Constitutional implications of statutes penalizing material support to terrorist organizations. Testimony to the U.S. Senate Committee on the Judiciary. May 5. Available at: http://www.bordc.org/resources/cole-materialsupport.php.

Collier, Paul, et al. 2003. *Breaking the conflict trap: Civil war and development policy.* Oxford: Oxford University Press.

Commission on Integration and Cohesion. 2007. *Our shared future.* June. London: Commission on Integration and Cohesion.

Committee for Rational Development. 1984. *Sri Lanka: The ethnic conflict—Myths, realities and perspectives.* New Delhi: Navrang.

Committee on the Elimination of all forms of Racial Discrimination (CERD). 2005. Concluding observations of the Committee on the elimination of all forms of racial discrimination: Australia. Available at http://www.hreoc.gov.au/legal/submissions/cerd/report.html.

Corbridge, Stuart, et al. 2005. *Seeing the state: Governance and governmentality in India.* Cambridge: Cambridge University Press.

Cornelius, Luke. 2007. A balanced policy response to terror: A police perspective. Paper presented at the Counter-Terrorism International Conference. Melbourne, Australia.

Cortright, David. 2008. Friend not foe: Civil society and the struggle against violent extremism. Fourth Freedom Forum. October. Report to Cordaid from the Fourth Freedom Forum and Kroc Institute for International Peace Studies at the University of Notre Dame.

Cortright, David, et al. 2004. *An agenda for enhancing the United Nations Program on Counter-Terrorism Action Agenda.* An evaluation report of Fourth Freedom Forum and Joan B. Kroc Institute for International Peace Studies. University of Notre Dame. Available online.

Cosgrave, John. 2004. *The impact of the War on Terror on aid flows.* Report for ActionAid.

Dagne, Ted. 2002. *Africa and the War on Terrorism.* Washington, D.C.: Congressional Research Service.

Daly, John C. K., et al. 2006. *Anatomy of a crisis: U.S.–Uzbekistan relations, 2001–2005.* Central Asia-Caucasus Institute & Silk Road Studies Program in Cooperation with the Jamestown Foundation and the United States Institute of Peace. Available at: www.silkroadstudies.org.

Das-Gupta, Indira. 2005. New laws alarm campaign groups. *Third Sector.* August 17.

Dash, Dipak Kumar. 2008. Pak attacked at Eid prayers, subdued celebrations. *Times of India.* December 10.

Demoscopia. 2007. *Estudio de opinión en 2007 entre la comunidad Musulmana de origin emigrante en España (2007 Survey among the Muslim immigrant Community in Spain)*. Madrid: Ministerio del Interior. Available at: http://www.mir.es/EDSE/informe_musulmanes.pdf.

Department for Communities and Local Government. 2007. *Preventing violent extremism—winning hearts and minds*. April. London: DCLG.

De Votta, Neil 2004. *Blowback: Linguistic nationalism, institutional decay, and ethnic conflict in Sri Lanka*. Stanford, CA: Stanford University Press.

DFID. 2004. *Country assistance plan for Palestinians*. July. London: Department for International Development.

———. 2006. *DFID Palestinian Programme interim update*. London: Department for International Development.

Draft Comprehensive Convention on Terrorism. 2002. In report of the Ad Hoc Committee established by General Assembly Resolution 51/210 of 17 December 1996, 57th sess., Supp. no. 37, UN Doc A/57/37, 2002.

Duffield, Mark. 2001. *Global governance and the new wars: the merger of development and security*. London and New York: Zed Books.

Dunn, Alison. 2008. Charities and restrictions on political activities: Developments by the Charity Commission for England and Wales in determining the regulatory barriers. *International Journal of Not-for-Profit Law* 11, no. 1:51–66.

Dyzenhaus, David. The permanence of the temporary: Can emergency powers be normalized? In *The Security of Freedom: Essays on Canada's Anti-Terrorism Bill*, ed. Ronald Daniels, Kent Roach, and Patrick Macklem, 21–37. Toronto; London: Toronto University Press, 2001.

Eade, Deborah. 2000. Preface. In *Development, NGOS, and civil society: Selected essays from development in practice*, introduced by Jenny Pearce. Oxford: Oxfam.

Eaton, Leslie. 2007. U.S. prosecution of Muslim group ends in mistrial. *The New York Times*. October 23.

Edwards, Michael. 2004. *Civil society*. Cambridge: Polity.

Egger, Sandra, and Mark Findlay. The politics of police discretion. In *Understanding Crime and Criminal Justice*, ed. Mark Findlay and Russell Hogg, 209–23. Sydney: Law Book Co., 1988.

Elbayar, Kareem. 2005. NGO laws in selected Arab states. *The International Journal of Not-for-Profit Law*, 7.

El-Khazen, Farid. 2000. *The breakdown of the state in Lebanon, 1967–1976*. Cambridge, MA: Harvard University Press.

El País. 2001. España investiga la presencia en el país de grupos ligados a Bin Laden (Spain investigates the presence of groups linked to Bin Laden), September 18, 2001. Available at: http://www.elpais .com/articulo/espana/Espana/investiga/presencia/pais/grupos/ligados/ Bin/Laden/elpepuesp/20010918elpepunac_2/Tes. Downloaded on June 3, 2008.

————. 2008. El centro islámico pide la regulación de los imames (Islamic Centre requests the regulation of Imams), May 2, 2008. Available at: http://www.elpais.com/articulo/Comunidad/Valenciana/ centro/islamico/pide/regulacion/imames/elpepiespval/20080502elpval _10/Tes/. Downloaded June 5, 2008.

EMHRN. 2003. International rights groups decry increased harassment of monitors. Euro-Mediterranean Human Rights Network, press statement. June 26, 2003. Available online.

————. 2004. Tightened spaces for human rights: a discussion paper on Palestinian NGO work. Euro-Mediterranean Human Rights Network. March 2004.

————. 2008. Appeal to respect the freedom of movement owed to the Al Haq General Director. Euro-Mediterranean Human Rights Network, press statement. May 20, 2008. Available online.

Ethical Corporation. 2005. The EC's NGO Code of Conduct—Unwelcome regulations. November 8. Available at: http://www.ethicalcorp.com/ content.asp?ContentID=3964.

EUMC 2006. *Muslims in the European Union: Discrimination and Islamophobia*. Vienna: European Monitoring Centre on Racism and Xenophobia. Available at: http://fra.europa.eu/fra/material/pub/muslim/ Manifestations_EN.pdf.

Eurasianet. 2008. *Religious freedom under siege in Bishkek*. Available at: www.eurasianet.org.

European Commission. 2005. *Draft recommendations to member states regarding a code of conduct for non-profit organizations to promote transparency and accountability best practices*. JLS/D2/DB/NSK D(2005)8208, July 22.

European Public Health Alliance. 2005. Comments to the Code of Conduct for Non Profit Organizations. September. Available at: http://ec.europa.eu/justice_home/news/consulting_public/code _conduct_npo/contributions/contribution_epha_en.pdf.

Evans, Rob, and Paul Lewis. 2009. "Civil servants attacked for using antiterror laws to spy on public." *The Guardian*. February 28.

Fast, Larissa. 2006. *"Aid in a pressure cooker": Humanitarian action in the Occupied Palestinian Territory.* Humanitarian Agenda 2015 Case Study no. 7. Feinstein International Centre. Tufts University.

Feldman, Ilana. 2007. Difficult distinctions: Refugee law, humanitarian practice, and political identification in Gaza. *Cultural anthropology* 22, no. 1:129–169.

Ferdinands, Tyrol, et al. 2004. *The Sri Lankan peace process at crossroads: Lessons, opportunities and ideas for principled negotiations and conflict transformation.* Colombo: Centre for Policy Alternatives, Foundation for Co-Existence, Initiative for Political and Conflict Transformation, Social Scientists' Association, Berghof Foundation for Conflict Studies Sri Lanka Office.

Finnemore, Martha. 2004. The purpose of intervention: Changing beliefs about the use of force. *International Affairs* 80, no. 2:355–65.

Foot, Rosemary. 2007. The United Nations, counter terrorism, and human rights: Institutional adaptation and embedded ideas. *Human Rights Quarterly* 29: 489–514.

Forsythe, David P. 2006. United States policy toward enemy detainees in the "War on Terrorism." *Human Rights Quarterly* 28, no. 2:465–91.

Forum 18. 2009. *President's signing of restrictive religion law condemned.* Available at: www.forum18.org.

Fowler, Alan. 2005. *Aid architecture: Reflections on NGO futures and the emergence of counter-terrorism.* Occasional Paper Series Number 45. INTRAC.

Freedom House. 2006. *Country report—Kyrgyzstan, accountability and public voice.* Available at: www.freedomhouse.org.

Frydenlund, Iselin. 2005. *The Sangha and its relation to the peace process in Sri Lanka.* PRIO Report. Oslo: International Peace Research Institute, PRIO.

Fuller, William P., and Barnet F. Baron. 2003. How the War on Terror hits charity. *The Christian Science Monitor.* July 29.

Garbutt, Anne, and Simon Heap. 2002. *Growing civil society in Central Asia.* INTRAC Occasional Papers Series no. 39. Available at: www.intrac.org.

Gearty, Conor. 2003. Reflections on civil liberties in an age of counter-terrorism. *Osgoode Hall Law Journal,* 41: 185.

———. 2007. *Civil Liberties* (Clarendon Law Series). Oxford, UK: Oxford University Press.

Gleason, Gregory. 1997. *The Central Asian states: Discovering independence*. Boulder, CO: Westview Press.

Global Security Org. 2009. *Manas International Airport Ganci Air Base Bishkek, Kyrgyzstan*. Available at: www.globalsecurity.org.

Gloger, Dana. 2009. How £100m of your cash goes to fund terror. *Daily Express*. March 16.

Goldberg, Jeffrey. 2006. The forgotten war: The overlooked consequences of Hamas's actions. *The New Yorker*. September 11.

Golder, Ben, and George Williams. 2004. What is "terrorism"? Problems of legal definition. *University of New South Wales Law Journal* 27, no. 2:270–95.

Goldman, Robert K. 2005. *Promotion and protection of human rights: Protection of human rights and fundamental freedoms while countering terrorism*. UN ESCOR, Communication on Human Rights. UN Doc. E/CN.4/2005/103.

Gonsalves, Colin. 2004. *POTA—A movement for its repeal*. Unpublished report, pages 1–2.

Goodhand, Jonathan. 2006. *Aiding peace? The role of NGOs in armed conflict*. Bourton on Dunsmore: ITDG Publishing.

Goodhand, Jonathan, and Bart Klem. 2005. *Aid, conflict and peacebuilding in Sri Lanka*. Colombo, Sri Lanka: The Asia Foundation.

Gooneratne, John. 2007. *Negotiating with the Tigers (LTTE)*. Pannipitiya: Stamford Lake.

Green, Penny, and Tony Ward. *State crime: Governments, violence and corruption*. London: Pluto Press, 2004.

Grugel, Jean. 2002. *Democratization: A critical introduction*. New York: Palgrave Macmillan.

Guardian. 2008. New Plan to Tackle Violent Extremism. June 3.

Guest, Iain. 2003. Commentary: Funding scandal shakes confidence in Palestinian civil society. *Advocacy Net News Bulletin* 3. April 10, 2003. Available online.

———. 2007. *Defending human rights in the Occupied Palestinian Territory—challenges and opportunities. A discussion paper on human rights work in the West Bank and Gaza Strip*. February. Jerusalem: Friedrich Ebert Foundation.

Gunaratne, Rohan. 1990. *Sri Lanka: A lost revolution? The inside story of the JVP*. Colombo: Institute of Fundamental Studies.

Habib, Adam, Imraan Valodia, and Richard Ballard, eds. 2006. *Voices of protest: Social movements in post-Apartheid South Africa.* Durban: University of KwaZulu-Natal Press.

Hacking, Ian. 1986. Making up people. In *Reconstructing individualism: Autonomy, individuality and the self in Western thought,* ed. T.C. Heller, M. Sosna, and D. E. Wellbery. Stanford, California: Stanford University Press.

Haddad, Simon. 2003. *The Palestinian impasse in Lebanon: The politics of refugee integration, studies in peace politics in the Middle East.* Brighton, England and Portland, OR: Sussex Academic Press.

Hajjar, Lisa. 2007. Etats-Unis-Israel: La double guerre contre le terrorisme et la loi humanitaire internationale (The United States and Israel: The double war on terror and international humanitarian law). *Revue d'études palestiniennes*: 32–50.

———. 2008. *Human rights law, executive powers, and torture in the post-9/11 era.* Aldershot, Burlington, VT: Ashgate.

Halabi, Zeina. 2004. Exclusion and identity in Lebanon's Palestinian refugee camps: A story of sustained conflict. *Environment and Urbanization* 16, no. 2:39–48.

Halevi, Ezra 2006. PM Olmert: Enough! Israel will eliminate Hizbullah and Hamas. In *Israel National News.*

Halliday, Fred. 2007. Justice in Madrid: The 11-M verdict. *Open Democracy.* November 5. Available at: http://www.opendemocracy .net/article/globalisation/global_politics/11M.

Hammami, Rema. 2000. Palestinian NGOs since Oslo: From NGO politics to social movements? *Middle East Report,* 214: 16–19, 27, 48.

Harb, Mona, and Reinoud Leenders. 2005. Know thy enemy: Hizbullah, "terrorism" and the politics of perception. *Third World Quarterly* 26, no .1: 173–97.

Haubrich, Dirk. 2003. September 11, anti-terror laws and civil liberties: Britain, France and Germany compared. *Government and Opposition,* 38, no. 1: 3–28.

Hempstone, Smith. 1997. *Rogue ambassador: An African memoir.* Sewanee, TN: University of the South Press.

Herman, Edward. 1993. Terrorism: Misrepresentations of power. In *Violent persuasions: The politics and imagery of terrorism,* ed. David Brown and Robert Merrill. Seattle, WA: Bay Press.

Hills, Alice. 2006. Trojan horses? USAID, counterterrorism and Africa's police. *Third World Quarterly* 27, no. 4:629–43.

Hillyard, Patty. 1993. *Suspect community: People's experience of the Prevention of Terrorism Acts in Britain.* London: Pluto Press.

HM Treasury and Home Office. 2007. *The financial challenge to crime and terrorism.* February. London: HM Treasury.

Hocking, Jenny. 2004. *Terror laws—ASIO, counter-terrorism and the threat to democracy.* Sydney: UNSW Press.

Home Office. 2005. *Improving opportunity, strengthening society: The government's strategy to increase race equality and community cohesion.* January. London: Home Office.

———. 2006. *Countering international terrorism: The United Kingdom's strategy.* London: Home Office, July, Cm 6888.

———. 2009. *The United Kingdom's strategy for countering international terrorism.* March. Cm 7547.

Home Office and HM Treasury. 2007. R*eview of safeguards to protect the charitable sector (England and Wales) from terrorist abuse: A consultation document.* May. London: Home Office.

House of Commons. 2007. *Development assistance and the Occupied Palestinian Territories. International Development Committee.* Fourth Report of Session 2006–2007. January. London.

Houtzager, Peter P., and Adrian Gurza Lavalle. 2009. The paradox of civil society representation. Constructing new forms of democratic legitimacy in Brazil. In *Rethinking popular representation,* ed. O. Törnquist, K. Stokke, and N. Webster. New York: Palgrave Macmillan.

Howard, John. 2005a. Counter-terrorism laws strengthened (Media Release). (September 8, 2005). In *Laws for insecurity? A report on the federal government's proposed counter-terrorism measures.* Chong, Agnes, et al. 2005.

———. 2005b Transcript of the prime minister the Hon John Howard MP interview with Alan Jones. Radio 2GB. November 9. Sydney. Available at: http://pandora.nla.gov.au/pan/10052/20051121–0000/www.pm .gov.au/news/interviews/Interview1667.html.

Howell, Jude. 2006. The global War on Terror, development and civil society. *Journal of International Development* 18: 121–35.

Howell, Jude, and Jeremy Lind. 2008. Changing donor policy and practice on civil society in the post-9/11 aid context. In *NGPA Working*

Paper, ed. J. Howell. London: London School of Economics and Political Science.

———. 2009. *Counter-terrorism, civil society and aid: Before and after the War on Terror.* Palgrave/MacMillan.

Howell, Jude, and Jenny Pearce. 2001. *Civil society and development: A critical exploration.* Boulder, CO: Lynne Rienner Publishers, Inc.

Human Rights and Equal Opportunity Commission (HREOC). 2004. *Ismaε—listen: National consultations on eliminating prejudice against Arab and Muslim Australians.* Sydney: Human Rights and Equal Opportunity Commission.

———. 2008. *Submission of the Human Rights and Equal Opportunity Commission to the Clarke Inquiry on the case of Dr Mohamed Haneef.* Available at: http://www.hreoc.gov.au/legal/submissions/2008/200805 _haneef.html.

Human Rights Council. 2007. *Communications to and from governments: Report of the special rapporteur on the promotion and protection of human rights and fundamental freedoms while countering terrorism (Martin Scheinin).* March 15, 2007. UN Doc. A/HRC/4/26/ Add.1.

Human Rights Watch. 2001. *Uganda: Freedom of association at risk. The proposed NGO Bill and current restrictions on NGOs in Uganda.* Human Rights Watch backgrounder. New York: Human Rights Watch.

———. 2003. *Human Rights Watch world report 2003.* New York: Human Rights Watch.

———. 2005a. *Setting an example? Counter-terrorism measures in Spain.* New York: Human Rights Watch.

———. 2005b. *Getting away with torture? Command responsibility for the U.S. abuse of detainees.* New York: Human Rights Watch.

———. 2006. *Kyrgyzstan: Government takes measures against civil society.* New York: Human Rights Watch.

———. 2007a. *Lebanon: End abuse of Palestinians fleeing refugee camp.* Human Rights Watch (news release). June 12, 2007.

———. 2007b. *UK: Counter the threat or counterproductive? Commentary on proposed counter-terrorism measures.* London: Human Rights Watch.

Huntington, Samuel P. 1992. *The third wave: Democratization in the late twentieth century.* Norman: University of Oklahoma Press.

Humanitarian Policy Group. 2000. The politics of coherence: Humanitarianism and foreign policy in the post-Cold War era. Briefing. July. London: HPG.

Huysmans, Jef. 2000. The European Union and the securitization of migration. *Journal of Common Market Studies* 38, no. 5:751–77.

ICNL (International Center for Non-for-Profit Law). 1996. Kyrgyzstan adopts progressive new NGO laws. Available at: www.icnl.org.

Ilkhamov, Alisher. 2005. The thorny path of civil society in Uzbekistan. *Central Asian Survey* 24, no. 3:297–317.

Informe RAXEN. 2008. *Análisis anual y registro de hechos* (Annual analysis and register of occurrences). Madrid: Movimiento Contra la Intolerancia. Available at: http://www.movimientocontralaintolerancia .com/html/raxen/raxen.asp.

International Commission of Jurists. 2006. Uganda-General Court Martial must respect ruling by Constitutional Court. Press release. February 2. Available at: http://www.icj.org/news.php3?id_article =3859&lang=en.

———. 2009. *Assessing damage, urging action: Report of the Eminent Jurists Panel on Terrorism, Counter-terrorism and Human Rights.* Geneva: International Commission of Jurists.

International Crisis Group. 2001. *Uzbekistan at ten: Repression and instability.* ICG Asia Report 46. Osh/Brussels: International Crisis Group.

———. 2003. *Islamic social welfare activism in the Occupied Palestinian Territories: A legitimate target?* ICG Middle East Report no. 13. Amman/Brussels: International Crisis Group.

———. 2007. *Uzbekistan: Stagnation and uncertainty.* Asia Briefing N°67. Bishkek/Brussels: International Crisis Group. Available at: www .crisigroup.org.

International Media Support (IMS) and Public Association Journalists (PAJ). 2008. *Research project: Political extremism, terrorism and media in Central Asia.* Available at: www.i-m-s.dk.

Islamic Resistance in Lebanon. 2006. The text of the second speech addressed by His Eminence Sayyeh Hassan Nasrallah to the people 16/07/2006 (Nass al nidaa al thani allathi wajjahahu al ameen al "am samahat al sayyed Hassan Nasrallah ila al umma 16–07–2006), edited by Islamic Resistance in Lebanon. Available at: http://www.moqawama .org/essaydetails.php?eid=7807&cid=319.

Izquierdo, Antonio. 1996. *La inmigración inesperada: La población extranjera en España (1991–1995) (Unexpected immigrants: Spain's foreign population (1991–1995).* Madrid: Trotta.

Jacobsen, Karen. 2002. Livelihoods in conflict: The pursuit of livelihoods by refugees and the impact on the human security of host communities. *International Migration* 40 (5): 95–123.

Jahon: Information Agency for the Ministry of Foreign Affairs of Uzbekistan. 2007. Address by President of the Republic of Uzbekistan H.E. Mr. Islam Karimov at the meeting dedicated to the 16th anniversary of adoption of Constitution of Uzbekistan. Available at: www.jahonnews.uz.

Jailobaeva, Kanykey. 2008a. *The state, civil society and the donor development agenda: The case of Kyrgyzstan.* Unpublished PhD research, University of Edinburgh.

———. 2008b. Enhanced government commitment: A key to an effective government-NGO relationship in Kyrgyzstan. Available at: www.src.auca.kg.

———. 2008c. *All the truth about NGO funding in Kyrgyzstan: Numbers and facts.* Available at: www.src.auca.kg.

Jenkins, Rob. 2007a. Civil society versus corruption. *Journal of Democracy* 18, no. 2:55–69.

———. 2007b. NGOs and Indian politics. Pre-publication draft for Niraja Gopal Jayal and Pratap Bhanu Mehta, eds. *The Oxford Companion to Indian Politics.* Oxford: Oxford University Press. pp. 1–35.

Jeong, Ho-Won. 2005. *Peacebuilding in postconflict societies: Strategy and process.* Boulder, CO: Lynne Rienner.

Joffé, George. 2008. The European Union, democracy and counter-terrorism in the Maghreb. *Journal of Common Market Studies* 46, no. 1:147–71.

Jordán, Javier. 2005. El terrorismo islamista en España (Islamist terrorism in Spain). In *Madrid 11-M: Un análsis del mal y sus consecuencias (Madrid 11-M: An analysis of evil and its consequences)*, ed. Andrés Blanco, et al., 79–112. Madrid: Trotta.

Jordán, Javier, and Nicola Horsburgh. 2006. Spain and Islamist terrorism: An analysis of the threat and response 1995–2005. *Mediterranean Politics* 11, no. 2:209–29.

Kaiser, Tania. 2006. Between a camp and a hard place; rights, livelihood and experiences of the local settlement system for long-term refugees in Uganda. *Journal of Modern African Studies* 44 (4): 597–621.

Kaldor, Mary. 1999. *New and old wars: Organised violence in a global era.* Cambridge: Cambridge: Polity Press.

Kandiyoti, Deniz. 2007. Post-Soviet Institutional Design and the Paradoxes of the "Uzbek Path." *Central Asian Survey* 26, no. 1:31–48.

Kearney, Simon. Police alarm on racial profiling. *The Australian*, September 27, 2005.

Kelegama, Saman. 2006. *Development under stress: Sri Lankan economy in transition*. New Delhi: Sage.

Khalidi, Muhammad Ali, and Diane Riskedahl. 2007. The road to Nahr al-Barid: Lebanese political discourse and Palestinian civil rights. *Middle East Report* (244).

Khalili, Laleh. 2005. Places of memory and mourning: Palestinian commemoration in the refugee camps of Lebanon. *Comparative Studies of South Asia, Africa and the Middle East* 25 (1):30–45.

Khamidov, Alisher. 2007. *The power of associations: New trends in Islamic activism in Central Asia*. Available at: www.src.auca.kg.

KHRC. 2002. *Quarterly human rights report* 4(1). Nairobi: Kenya Human Rights Commission.

———. 2003. *Eyes on the prize*. Nairobi: Kenya Human Rights Commission.

KHRI. 2007. *Interventionism and human rights in Somalia: Report of an exploratory forum on the Somalia crisis*. Nairobi: Kenya Human Rights Institute.

Knudsen, Are, and Nasser Yassin. 2007. Political violence in post-war Lebanon 1989–2007. *Chr. Michelsen Institute (CMI) Working Paper* (13):24.

Krikorian, Greg. 2007. Mistrial in Holy Land terrorism financing case. *Los Angeles Times*. October 23.

Lacomba, Joan, and Alejandra Boni. 2008. The role of emigration in foreign aid policies: The case of Spain and Morocco *International Migration* 6, no. 1:123–48.

Lakshmi, Rama. 2008. Lower House of Indian Parliament passes tough new anti-terror laws. *Washington Post*. December 17.

Lamb, Franklin. 2007. "Another Waco in the making": Inside Nahr el-Bared. *Counterpunch*. May 26.

Lang, Anthony F. 2004. Agency and ethics: The politics of military intervention. *International Affairs* [London] 80(2):355–65.

Lasensky, S., and R. Grace. 2006. *Dollars and diplomacy: Foreign aid and the Palestinian question*. USIPeace Briefing. August 2006. Washington, D.C.: United States Institute of Peace.

Laub, Karin. 2007. Abbas shuts Hamas charities in West Bank. *Haaretz*. December 3, 2007.

Leader, Nicholas, and Peter Colenso. *Aid instruments in fragile states*. PRDE Working Paper 5, March 2005, published by DFID.

Lebanese Ministry of Defence. 2007a. Press Release following the end of military operations in Nahr Al Bared. *The Army Magazine (Majallat Al Jaysh)*. October.

———. 2007b. The army's victory is dedicated to its martyrs and people (Intisar Al jaysh mohda ila shouhada'ihi wa l sha'ab). *The Army Magazine (Majallat Al Jaysh)*. July 1.

Le Figaro. 2006. Hezbollah "playing very dangerous game"—Lebanese Druze leader. Available at: http://www.lefigaro.fr/english/20060713 .WWW000000278_hezbollah_playing_very_dangerous_game_lebanese _islamist_leader.html. *Le Figaro*, 13/07/06.

Lewis, David. 2008. The dynamics of regime change: Domestic and international factors in the "Tulip Revolution." *Central Asian Survey* 27, nos. 3–4:265–77.

Liberty. 2004. *The right to protest and section 44*. London: Liberty.

Liyanage, Sumanasiri. 2006. Civil society and the peace process. In *Negotiating peace in Sri Lanka: Efforts, failures and lessons (volume I and II)*, ed. Kumar Rupesinghe. Colombo: The Foundation for Co-Existence.

Lischer, Sarah Kenyon. 2007. Causes and consequences of conflict-induced displacement. *Civil Wars* 9, no. 2:142–55.

Lister, Sarah. 2007. *Understanding state building and local government in Afghanistan*. Crisis States Research Centre. Working Paper no 14. May.

Long, Arika. 2007. A survey of terrorism and human rights in Uganda. In *Review digest: Human rights and the War on Terror—2007 supplement*, ed. Nowakowski, Arianna, et al. Denver, CO: University of Denver, Graduate School of International Studies.

Luce, Edward. 2007. *In spite of the gods: The strange rise of modern India*. New York: Doubleday.

Lutterbeck, Derek. 2006. Policing migration in the Mediterranean. *Mediterranean Politics* 11, no. 1:59–82.

Lynch, Andrew, and George Williams. 2006. *What price security? Taking stock of Australia's anti-terror laws*. Sydney: University of New South Wales Press.

MacGinty, Roger. 2007. Reconstructing post-war Lebanon: A challenge to the liberal peace? *Conflict, Security and Development* 7, no. 3:457–82.

Macrae, Joanna, and Harmer, Adele. 2003. *Humanitarian action and the 'global war on terror': A review of trends and issues.* HPG Report No. 14. Humanitarian Policy Group. London: Overseas Development Institute.

Mair, Vibeka. 2009. Interpal's US terrorism designation blamed for Lloyd's Bank decision. *Charity Finance.* February 25.

Mair, Vibeka, and Tania Mason. 2009. Interpal meets Treasury, while another Islamic charity account it closed. *Charity Finance.* January 14.

Maley, William. 2006. *Rescuing Afghanistan.* London: Hurst and Company.

Malkki, Liisa H. 2002. News from nowhere: Mass displacement and globalized "problems of organization." *Ethnography* 3, no. 3:351–60.

Mander, Harsh. 2004. POTA and its phantom limbs. *Hindustan Times.* September 24.

Manogaran, Chelvadurai, and Bryan Pfaffenberger, eds. 1994. *The Sri Lankan Tamils: Ethnicity and identity.* Boulder, CO: Westview.

Marat, Erica. 2008. Religious authorities in Kyrgyzstan play politics. *Eurasia Daily Monitor* 5, no. 139. Available at: www.jamestown.org.

———. 2009. Kyrgyz government reduces rights of religious groups. *Eurasia Daily Monitor* 5, no. 312. Available at: www.jamestown.org.

March, Andrew. 2003. State ideology and the legitimation of authoritarianism: The case of post-soviet Uzbekistan. *Journal of Political Ideologies* 8, no. 2:209–232.

Mazzetti, Mark. 2006a. Efforts by CIA fail in Somalia, officials charge. *The New York Times,* June 8.

———. 2006b. US cuts in African aid said to hurt War on Terror. *The New York Times,* July 23.

Mbabazi, Pamela, Joshua Mugyenyi, and Timothy Shaw. 2001. Uganda elections 2001: Lesson for/from democratic governance. Paper presented at the 44th Annual African Studies Association (ASA) Conference. Houston, Texas.

McCulloch, Jude. 2002. Counter-terrorism and (in)security: Fallout from the Bali bombing. *Borderlands* 1, no. 1.

———. 2004. Blue armies, khaki police and the cavalry on the new American frontier: Critical criminology for the 21st century. *Critical Criminology* 12: 309–26.

McGreal, Chris. 2006. Israel accuses British-funded Islamic charity of being front for terrorists. *Guardian.* May 31.

McMahon, Joseph. 2007. *Developments in the regulations of NGOs via government counter-terrorism measures and policies*. INTRAC Policy Briefing Paper 11. September.

Meital, Yoram. 2006. *Peace in tatters: Israel, Palestine and the Middle East*. Boulder, CO: Lynne Rienner.

MHRF. 2008a. *Horn of terror: Revised edition*. September. Nairobi: Muslim Human Rights Forum.

———. 2008b. *Civil society responses to counter-terrorism measures in Kenya*. Special Brief. September. Nairobi: Kenya Human Rights Institute.

Miall, Hugh, Oliver Ramsbotham, and Tom Woodhouse. 2005. *Contemporary conflict resolution: The prevention, management and transformations of deadly conflict*. 2nd ed. Cambridge: Polity.

Millar, Alistair, et al. 2009. *Oversight or overlooked? Civil society's role in monitoring and reforming security systems and the practice of counterterrorism*. Fourth Freedom Forum. March. Available at: http://www .fourthfreedom.org/pdf/0903_overlooked.pdf.

Ministry of Defence (MOD). 2005. *The comprehensive approach*. Joint Discussion Note 4.

———. 2009. *The military contribution to peace support operations*. London: MOD.

Molier, G. 2006. Humanitarian intervention and the responsibility to protect after 9/11. *Netherlands International Law Review* LIII (1): 37–62.

Moncrieff, Virginia M. 2008. Potentially lethal: Increased relationship between military and aid. *The Huffington Post*. December 22.

Montclos, Marc-Antoine Perouse de. 2008. Humanitarian aid, war, exodus, and reconstruction of identities: A case study of Somali "minority refugees" in Kenya. *Nationalism and Ethnic Politics* 14, no. 2:289–321.

Moreras, Jordi. 2005 Sermons en la diàspora: La definció del perfil dels imams a Espanya i a Catalunya (Sermons in the diaspora: A definitional profile of the Imams of Spain and Catalonia). In *Imams d'Europa: Les expressions de l'autoritat religiosa Islàmica* (*Imams of Europe: Expressions of Islamic religious authority*), ed. Gema Auberell and Jordi Moreras. Barcelona: Instituto Europeu de la Mediterrània.

Moss, Todd, David Roodman, and Scott Standley. 2005. *The global war on terror and U.S. development assistance: USAID allocation by country, 1998–2005*. Center for Global Development. Washington, D.C.

Nadarajah, Suthaharan, and Dhananjayan Sriskandarajah. 2005. Liberation struggle or terrorism? The politics of naming the LTTE. *Third World Quarterly* 26, no. 1:87–100.

National Commission on Terrorist Attacks upon the US. 2004. Terrorist financing staff monograph, Chapter 6: The Illinois charities case study. 1–27. Available at: www.9-11commission.gov/staff_statements/911 _TerrFin_ch6.pdf.

NGO Monitor. 2005. Analysis of NGO funding: UK Department for International Development (DFID). *NGO Monitor* website. November 15, 2005. Available online.

———. 2007. PNGO continues to advocate boycott of USAID. *NGO Monitor Digest.* January 22, 2007. Available online.

———. 2008. NGO campaigns on Israel's Gaza policy. *NGO Monitor Digest.* January 22, 2008. Available online.

Nixon, Christine. 2006. Forward. In *Police Ethics*, xi–xii, ed. Seumas Miller, John Blackler, and Andrew Alexandra. Sydney: Allen & Unwin, 2006.

Njau, Mutegi. 2007. An incentive to clamp down: With US prodding, 3 East African nations get tough on terrorist suspects—even when evidence is lacking. International Consortium of Investigative Journalists. Available at: http://www.publicintegrity.org/militaryaid/report .aspx?aid=873.

Njeim, Colonel Antoine. 2007. Fateh Al Islam kidnaps the Nahr Al Bared camp and betrays the army (Fateh Al Islam takhtof mukhayyam Nahr Al Bared wa taghdor bil jawsh). *The Army Magazine.*

Njeim, Colonel Antoine, and Nadine Bal'aa. 2007. (Interview with the Commander of the North). *The Army Magazine.*

Norton, Augustus R. 2007. *Hezbollah: A short history.* (Princeton studies in Muslim politics.) Princeton, NJ: Princeton University Press.

Nussbaum, Martha C. 2007. *The clash within: Democracy, religious violence and India's future.* Cambridge, MA: The Belknap Press of Harvard University Press.

OCHA. 2007a. The closure of the Gaza Strip: The economic and humanitarian consequences. *OCHA special focus: Occupied Palestinian territory.* December 2007. United Nations Office for the Coordination of Humanitarian Affairs.

———. 2007b. Increasing need, decreasing access: Humanitarian access to the West Bank. *OCHA Fact Sheet.* September 10, 2007. United Nations Office for the Coordination of Humanitarian Affairs.

Odora, Adong Florence. 2008. Rising from the ashes: The rebirth of civil society in an authoritarian political environment. *International Journal of Not-for-Profit Law* 10, no. 3.

OMB Watch. 2008. *Dangerous partnerships: Humanitarian aid groups and the military*. OMB Report. December. Available at: www .ombwatch.org/node/9546.

OMB Watch and Grantmakers Without Borders. 2008. *Collateral damage: How the War on Terror hurts charities, foundations and the people they serve*. July. Washington, D.C.

Open Kyrgyzstan. 2008. *Interview with Kaipov, the ministry of justice of the Kyrgyz Republic*. Available at: www.open.kg.

Open Society Institute. 2004. *Civil society in Uzbekistan: Status of affairs and international programs*. Unpublished report.

Orjuela, Camilla. 2004. *Civil society in civil war: Peace work and identity politics in Sri Lanka*. Department of Peace and Development Research, Gothenburg University, PhD dissertation.

Owens, Patricia. 2003. Accidents don't just happen: The liberal politics of high-technology "humanitarian" war. *Millennium* 32, no. 3:595–616.

Paffenholz, Thania, and Christoph Spurk. 2006. *Civil society, civic engagement, and peacebuilding*. Washington, D.C.: The World Bank, Social Development Department.

Pannier, Bruce. 2000. Russia: Uzbekistan renews old relations. *RFE/RL Newsline*. May 5. Available at: www.rferl.org.

Paris, Roland. 2004. *At war's end: Building peace after civil conflict*. Cambridge: Cambridge University Press.

Parliamentary Joint Committee on Intelligence and Security (PJCIS). 2006. *Review of security and counter terrorism legislation*. Canberra: Parliament of the Commonwealth of Australia. December.

Patronus Analytical. 2007. Aid worker fatalities pages. Available at: http://www.patronusanalytical.com/aid%20worker%20fatalities/ fatalities%20main%20page.html.

PCHR. 2007. *Silencing the press: A report on Israeli attacks against journalists*. The Palestinian Centre for Human Rights. December.

People's Union for Democratic Rights (PUDR). 2005a. *Why the AFSPA must go. A fact-finding report*. Delhi: PUDR. February.

———. 2005b. *Obsessive pursuit. The Unlawful Activities Prevention Act, 2004. Reinforcing a draconian law*. Delhi: PUDR. January.

Perito, Robert M. 2005. *The US experience with Provincial Reconstruction Teams in Afghanistan: Lessons identified.* Washington, D.C.: The United States Institute of Peace.

Pickering, Sharon, Jude McCulloch, and David Wright-Neville. 2008. *Counter-terrorism policing: Community, policy, and the media.* New York; London: Springer.

Pickering, Sharon, et al. 2007. *Counter-terrorism policing and culturally diverse communities.* Melbourne: Monash University and Victoria Police.

Poynting, Scott, Greg Noble, and Paul Tabar. 2001. Middle Eastern appearance: "Ethnic gangs," moral panic and media framing. *The Australian and New Zealand Journal of Criminology* 34, no. 1:67–90.

Presidency of the Council of Ministers. 2006a. *Lebanon: On the road to reconstruction and recovery. A periodic report published by the Presidency of the Council of Ministers on the post-July 2006 recovery & reconstruction activities, edited by Presidency of the Council of Ministers.* Beirut: Lebanese Government.

―――. 2006b. Official statement by the Lebanese government: Lebanon under siege (Presidency of the Council of Ministers). Available at: http://www.lebanonundersiege.gov.lb/english/F/eNews/NewsArticle.asp?CNewsID=16.

―――. 2006c. Address by the prime minister H. E. Mr. Fuad Siniora in the conference that took place in Rome, July 25, 2006: Lebanon under siege (Presidency of the Council of Ministers). Available at: http://www.rebuildlebanon.gov.lb/english/f/NewsArticle.asp?CNewsID=21.

―――. 2007a. President Siniora presiding a meeting to study the reconstruction of Nahr el-Bared: Rebuild Lebanon (Presidency of the Council of Ministers). Available at: http://www.rebuildlebanon.gov.lb/images_browse/President%20Siniora%20presiding%20a%20meeting%20to%20study%20the%20reconstruction%20of%20Nahr%20el-Bared.mht.

―――. 2007b. The funding needed for relief and reconstruction of Nahr Al Bared and damaged surrounding villages amounts to 382.5 USD: Rebuild Lebanon (presidency of Council of Ministers). Available at: http://www.lebanonundersiege.gov.lb/images_browse/The%20sums%20required%20for%20relief%20&%20reconstruction%20of%20Nahr%20el-Bared.mht.

―――. 2008. Address by H. E. PM Siniora at the launching conference of the master plan for the reconstruction of Nahr El Bared Camp, edited by the Lebanese Palestinian Dialogue Commission. Available at: http://www.lpdc.gov.lb/Uploads/2008-02/Document20_1.pdf.

Press Service of the President of the Republic of Uzbekistan. 2004. *73 International, foreign NGOs registered in Uzbekistan—Justice Minister.* Available at: www.press-service.uz.

Princeton, Lyman N., and J. Stephen Morrison. 2004. The terrorist threat in East Africa. *Foreign Affairs* 83, no.1:75–86.

Privacy International. 2002. *Attacks on the press in 2002.* Committee to Protect Journalists.

———. 2004. Terrorism profile—Uganda. Available at: http://www.privacyinternational.org/article.shtml?cmd[347]=x-347-359656&als [theme]=Anti%20Terrorism.

Priyono, A. E., Willy Purna Samadhi, and Olle Törnquist. 2007. *Making democracy meaningful: Problems and options in Indonesia.* Jakarta: Demos.

Pugliese, Joseph. 2006. Asymmetries of terror: Visual regimes of racial profiling and the shooting of Jean Charles de Menezes in the context of the war in Iraq. *Borderlands*, no. 1.

Pupavac, Vanessa. 2008. Refugee advocacy, traumatic representations and political disenchantment. *Government and opposition* 43, no. 2:270–92.

Quershi, Faiza. 2007. The impact of extended police stop and search powers under the UK Criminal Justice Act 2003. *Policing: An International Journal of Police Strategies and Management* 30, no. 3:466–83.

Quigley, Nolan, and Belinda Pratten. 2007. *Security and civil society: The impact of counter-terrorism measures on civil society organisations.* London: NCVO.

Quinlivan, James T. 1995. Force requirements in stability operations. *Parameters*, Winter: 59–69. Available at the Parameters website.

Radio Free Europe/Radio Liberty. 2003. Commonplaces of spring: Uzbek president bucks trend with attack on hypocrites, pacifists. *Central Asia Report* 3, no. 13. Available at: www.rferl.org.

———. 2005. Message in a courtroom — the Andijon trial. *Central Asia Report* No. 37. Available at: www.rferl.org.

———. 2008. *Kyrgyzstan tightens rules on public assembly.* Available at: www.rferl.org.

————. 2009. *Kyrgyzstan enacts law restricting religious activities.* Available at: www.rferl.org.

Raha, Ashirbad. 2008. Sombre Sunday: City marches for peace. *Times of India.* December.

Rainford, Charan, and Ambika Satkunanathan. 2008. *Mistaking politics for governance: The politics of interim arrangements in Sri Lanka.* Colombo: International Center for Ethnic Studies.

Raman, B., N. Sathiya Moorthy, and Kalpana Chittaranjan, eds. 2006. *Sri Lanka: Peace without process.* Colombo: Vijitha Yapa.

Rapoport, David C. 2001. The fourth wave: September 11 in the history of terrorism *Current History* 100, no. 650:419.

Rashid, Ahmed. 2000. Islamic movement of Uzbekistan's incursion assists the Taliban. *CACI Analyst.* September 13. Available at: www.cacianalyst.org.

Redress and Reprieve. 2009. *Kenya and counter-terrorism: A time for change.* February 2009.

Rein, Lisa, and Josh White. 2009. More groups than thought monitored in police spying. *The Washington Post.* January 4.

Reinares, Fernando. 2005. Mediterráneo y terrorismo internacional: Un nuevo marco para a la cooperación? (The Mediterranean and international terrorism: A new framework for cooperation?). ARI 49: 1–5. Available at: http://www.realinstitutoelcano.org/analisis/860/860_Reinares.pdf.

Reiner, Robert. 1997. Policing and the police. In *The Oxford Handbook of Criminology,* ed. Mike Maguire, Rodney Morgan, and Robert Reiner, 997–1049. New York: Oxford University Press.

Remnick, David. 2006. The democracy game. *The New Yorker.* February 27.

Renwick, James. 2007. The constitutional validity of preventative detention. In *Law and Liberty in the War on Terror,* eds. Andrew Lynch, Edwina MacDonald, and George Williams, 127–135. Sydney: Federation Press.

Reporters sans Frontières. 2003. *Police close radio station.* Available at: www.rsf.or/article.php3?id_article=7414.

Rieff, David. 2002. *A bed for the night: Humanitarianism in crisis.* New York: Simon & Schuster.

Roberts, Adam. 2005. The "war on terror" in historical perspective. *Survival* 47, no. 2:101–30.

Robinson, Glenn. 2007. The fragmentation of Palestine. *Current History,* December 2007: 421–26.

Roth, John, Douglas Greenburg, and Serena Wille. 2004. *National Commission on Terrorist Attacks upon the United States: Monograph on terrorist financing*. Staff report to the Commission. Washington, D.C. Available at: http://www.9–11commission.gov/staff_statements/911_TerrFin_Monograph.pdf.

Roy, Sara. 2000. The transformation of Islamic NGOs in Palestine. *Middle East Report*, 214: 24–26.

Rubin, Barnett, R. 2002. *The fragmentation of Afghanistan*. New Haven and London, Yale University Press.

Rubongoya, Joshua B. 2007. *Regime hegemony in Museveni's Uganda: Pax Musevenica*. New York: Palgrave/Macmillan.

Ruddock, Philip. 2006. "A safe and secure Australia: An update on counter-terrorism." *The Original Law Review* 2, no. 2:40–52.

Rupesinghe, Kumar. 2006. *Negotiating peace in Sri Lanka: Efforts, failures and lessons (volume I and II)*. Colombo: The Foundation for Co-Existence.

Russian and Eurasian Security—Specialized Network for Research on Security Related Developments. 2008. *Kyrgyz rights "worse" than Akaev Era*. Available at: www.rex.ethz.ch.

Sabrang Communications Private Limited. 2002. *The foreign exchange of hate: IDRF and the American funding of Hindutva*. November 20. Sabra Communications Private Limited, 1–88.

Sachar, Rajindar, et al. 2006. *Social, economic and educational status of the Muslim community in India: A report*. Prime Minister's High Level Committee, Cabinet Secretariat, Government of India, November.

Said, Edward. 2001. *The end of the peace process: Oslo and after*. New York: Vintage.

Saikal, Amin. 2006. *Modern Afghanistan: A history of struggle and survival*. London and New York: I.B.Tauris.

Sayigh, Rosemary. 1993. *Too many enemies: The Palestinian experience in Lebanon*. London and Atlantic Highlands, N.J: Zed Books.

Scheinin, Martin. 2006. *Australia: Study on human rights compliance while countering terrorism*.

Security Legislation Review Committee (SLRC). *Report of the Security Legislation Review Committee (Sheller Report)*. June 2006.

Senate Legal and Constitutional References Committee (SLCRC). 2002a. *Australian Security Intelligence Organisation Legislation Amendment*

(Terrorism) Bill 2002 and related matters. Parliament of Australia, December.

———. 2002b. Consideration of legislation referred to the Committee: Security Legislation Amendment (Terrorism) Bill 2002 [No. 2]; Suppression of the Financing of Terrorism Bill 2002; Criminal Code Amendment (Suppression of Terrorist Bombings) Bill 2002; Border Security Legislation Amendment Bill 2002; Telecommunications Interception Legislation Amendment Bill 2002. Parliament of Australia.

———. 2004. *Provisions of the Anti-Terrorism Bill 2004.* Parliament of Australia.

Shanmugaratnam, Nadarajah, and Kristian Stokke. 2008. Development as a precursor to conflict resolution: A critical review of the Fifth Peace Process in Sri Lanka. In *Between war and peace in Sudan and Sri Lanka: Deprivation and livelihood revival,* ed. Nadarajah Shanmugaratnam. Oxford: James Currey.

Shapoo, Rubina Khan. 2008. Malegaon blasts probe findings embarrassing RSS. *NDTV.* October 25, 2008. NDTV.com. Downloaded on March 24, 2009.

Shavit, Ari. 2006. Watching Hamas. *The New Yorker.* February 6, 2006.

Shepherd, Jessica. 2007. The rise and rise of terrorism studies. *The Guardian.* July 3.

Sheth, D. L., and Harsh Sethi. 1991. The NGO sector in India: Historical context and current discourse. *Voluntas,* 2 no. 2.

Shinn, David. 2004. Fighting terrorism in East Africa and the Horn. *Foreign Service Journal.*

Shishkaraeva, Elmira, et al. 2006. *Review of the history of establishment and development of the NGO sector in the Kyrgyz Republic.* Bishkek: Premier Ltd.

Sidel, Mark. 2007. *More secure, less free? Antiterrorism policy and civil liberties after September 11.* Ann Arbor: University of Michigan Press.

———. 2008. Counter-terrorism and the enabling legal and political environment for civil society: A comparative analysis of "War on Terror" states. *International Journal of Not-for-Profit-Law* 10, no. 3:7–49.

Simba Kayunga, Sallie. 2000. The impact of armed opposition on the Movement system in Uganda. In *No-party democracy in Uganda: Myths and realities,* ed. Justus Mugaju and J. Oloka Onyango. Kampala: Fountain Publishers.

Simpson, Ed. 2006. The state of Gujarat and the men without souls. *Critique of Anthropology* 26, no. 3:313–30.

———. 2008. Was there discrimination in the distribution of resources after the earthquake in Gujarat? Imagination, epistemology and the state in western India. *NGPA Research Paper 23*. London: London School of Economics.

Singh, Avtar. 2003. *Contemporary Kyrgyzstan: An overview.* Bishkek: Al Salam.

Singh, Ujjwal Kumar. 2004. State and emerging interlocking legal systems. "Permanence of the temporary." *Economic and Political Weekly* 39, no. 2:149–54.

———. 2007. *The state, democracy and anti-terror laws in India.* New Delhi: Sage Publications.

Siniora, Fouad. 2006. H.E. Prime Minister Fuad Siniora's statement to the Arab foreign ministers: The Presidency of the Council of Ministers.

Slim, Hugo. 2003a. Why protect civilians? Innocence, immunity and enmity in war. *International Affairs* 79, no. 3:481–502.

———. 2003b. Is humanitarianism being politicised? A reply to David Rieff. The Dutch Red Cross Symposium on Ethics in Aid, The Hague. October 8. Available on the Centre for Humanitarian Dialogue website.

———. 2007. *Killing civilians: Method, madness and morality in war.* London: Hurst & Co.

Smith, B. C. 2007a. *Good governance and development.* Houndmills: Palgrave/Macmillan.

Smith, Charles D. 2007b. *Palestine and the Arab-Israeli conflict: A history with documents.* Boston: St. Martin's Press.

Smith, Dan. 2004. *Towards a strategic framework for peacebuilding: Getting their act together.* Oslo: Ministry of Foreign Affairs. Evaluation Report 1/2004.

Snell, Liz. 2008. *Protest, protection, policing: The expansion of police powers and the impact on human rights in NSW.* Sydney: Combined Community Legal Centre's Group (NSW) and Kingsford Legal Centre.

SOS Racismo. 2008. *Informe anual sobre el racismo en el Estado Español (Annual report on racism in the Spanish State).* Madrid: Icaria.

Sriskandarajah, Dhananjayan. 2003. The returns of peace in Sri Lanka: The development cart before the conflict resolution horse? *Journal of Peacebuilding and Development* 2, no. 1:21–35.

Ssemogerere and Others vs. Attorney General (Constitutional Petition No.3 of 1999). Constitutional Appeal No. 1 of 2000.

Stabilisation Unit. 2009a. *Stabilisation quick impact projects handbook*. London: Stabilisation Unit.

——. 2009b. *The stabilisation guide*. London: Stabilisation Unit.

Steinberg, Gerald M. 2005. Terror and the divestment campaign. *The Jerusalem Post*. July 17.

Steinberg, Guido, and Isabelle Werenfels. 2007. Between the "near" and the "far" enemy: Al-Qaeda in the Islamic Maghreb. *Mediterranean Politics* 12, no. 3:407–13.

Stevens, Daniel. 2004. Conceptual travels along the Silk Road: On civil society aid in Uzbekistan. Unpublished PhD dissertation, University of London.

——. 2007. Political society and civil society in Uzbekistan—never the twain shall meet. *Central Asian Survey* 26, no. 1:49–64.

Stokke, Kristian. 1995. Poverty as politics: The Janasaviya Poverty Alleviation Programme in Sri Lanka. *Norwegian Journal of Geography* 49, no. 3:123–35.

——. 1997. Authoritarianism in the age of market liberalism in Sri Lanka. *Antipode* 29, no. 4:437–55.

——. 1998. Sinhalese and Tamil nationalism as postcolonial political projects from "above," 1948–1983. *Political Geography* 17, no. 1:83–113.

——. 2006. Building the Tamil Eelam state: Emerging state institutions and forms of governance in LTTE-controlled areas in Sri Lanka. *Third World Quarterly* 27, no. 6:1021–40.

Stokke, Kristian, and Anne Kirsti Ryntveit. 2000. The struggle for Tamil Eelam in Sri Lanka. *Growth and Change* 31, no. 2:285–304.

Stuntz, William. 2002. Local policing after terror. *Yale Law Journal* 111, no. 8:2137–94.

Swami, Praveen, and Anupama Katakam. 2006. Malegaon: The road to perdition. *The Hindu*. September 9.

Sydney Morning Herald. 2008. Jack Thomas not guilty of taking Al-Qaeda cash. October 23. Available at: http://www.smh.com.au/news/national/thomas-cleared-of-taking-osamas-cash/2008/10/23/1224351422036.html.

Tambiah, Stanley J. 1992. *Buddhism betrayed? Religion, politics and violence in Sri Lanka*. Chicago: University of Chicago Press.

Taulés, Silvia. 2004. *La nueva España Musulmana* (*The New Muslim Spain*). Barcelona: Random House Mondadori.

Telford, John, John Cosgrave, and Rachel Houghton. 2006. *Joint evaluation of the international response to the Indian Ocean tsunami: Synthesis report.* London: Tsunami Evaluation Coalition.

Tessler, Mark. 1994. *A history of the Israeli-Palestinian conflict.* Bloomington: University of Indiana Press.

Tham, Joo-Cheong, and K.D. Ewing. 2007. Limitations of a charter of rights in the age of counter-terrorism. *Melbourne University Law Review* 31, no. 2:462–98.

Thue, Nanna, et al. 2002. *Report on the study of the civil society in Uganda.* Kampala, Uganda: Royal Norwegian Embassy in Uganda.

Törnquist, Olle. 2009. Introduction. The problem is representation! Towards an analytical framework. In *Rethinking popular representation*, ed. Olle Törnquist, Neil Webster, and Kristian Stokke. New York: Palgrave Macmillan.

Törnquist, Olle, Kristian Stokke, and Neil Webster, eds. 2009. *Rethinking popular representation.* New York: Palgrave Macmillan.

Torrente, Nicolas de. 2004. Humanitarian action under attack: Reflections on the Iraq War. *The Harvard Environmental Law Review.* Spring. Available at: http://www.doctorswithoutborders.org/publications/opedsarticles/2004iraq.cfm.

UNCTAD. 2006. *The Palestinian war-torn economy: Aid, development and state formation.* April 2006. New York: United Nations Conference on Trade and Development.

UNFPA. 2008. *State of world population 2008.* Available at: www.unfpa.org

United Nations Development Programme. 1994. *New dimensions of human security: Human development report 1994.* New York: UNDP.

UNRWA. 2007. *Nahr Al Bared Camp emergency appeal progress report September 2007–February 2008.* Beirut: United Nations Relief and Works Agency for Palestine Refugees in the Near East.

———. 2008. *Preliminary master plan and guidelines for the reconstruction of Nahr el-Bared Palestine Refugee Camp.* Beirut: United Nations Relief and Works Agency for Palestine Refugees in the Near East.

USAID. 2009. *The greenbook.* Available at: http://qesdb.usaid.gov/gbk/index.html.

Usher, Graham. 2006. The Hamas triumph. *The Nation.* February 20.

USIP. 2004. *Special report: Terrorism in the Horn of Africa.* Washington, D.C.: United States Institute for Peace.

US State Department. 2004. U.S. re-designates Islamic Movement of Uzbekistan as terrorist group. September 24. Available at: www.state.gov.

———. 2006. Guiding Principles on Non-Governmental Organizations. *International Journal of Not-for-Profit Law,* Volume 9, issue 1, December, p. 1. Available at: www.icnl.org/KNOWLEDGE/IJNL/vol19iss1/art_9.htm.

Uyangoda, Jayadeva. 2001. Sri Lanka's Left: From class and trade unions to civil society and NGOs. In *Sri Lanka: Global challenges and national crises,* ed. Rajan Philips. Colombo: Social Scientists' Association.

———. 2003. The peace process, people and civil society. In *Sri Lanka's peace process 2002: Critical perspectives.* Eds. Jayadeva Uyangoda and Morina Perera. Colombo: Social Scientists' Association.

———, ed. 2005. *Conflict, conflict resolution and peace building.* Colombo: University of Colombo, Department of Political Science and Public Policy.

———. 2009. Sri Lanka: State of research on democracy. *PCD Journal* 1 (1–2).

Uyangoda, Jayadeva, and Morina Perera, eds. 2003. *Sri Lanka's peace process 2002: Critical perspectives.* Colombo: Social Scientists' Association.

Uzbekistan Press Agency. 2008. Uzbek-British cultural cooperation to expand. November 1. Available at: www.uza.uz.

Uzreport.com. 2008. Uzbekistan to set up foundation to back NGOs. December 19. Available at: www.uzreport.uz.

———. 2009. Uzbekistan host conference on fighting intl terrorism. January 16. Available at: www.uzreport.com.

Van Rooy, Alison. 1998. *Civil Society and the aid industry: The politics and promise.* London: Earthscan.

Varadarajan, Siddharth, ed. 2002. *Gujarat: The making of a tragedy.* New Delhi: Penguin Books.

Venugopal, Rajesh. 2008. *The politics of Sri Lanka's Janatha Vimukthi Peramuna (JVP).* Unpublished article manuscript. Oxford: University of Oxford.

Waddington, PAJ. 2005. Slippery slopes and civil libertarian pessimism. *Policing and Society* 15, no 3:353–75.

Waller, Martin. 2008. Net catches Lloyds TSB in charity account row. *The Times (of London)*. November 19. Available at: http://business.timesonline.co.uk/tol/business/columnists/article5182827.ece.

Warde, Ibrahaim. 2007. *The price of fear: The truth behind the financial War on Terror*. Berkeley: University of California Press.

Weissbrodt, David, and Amy Bergquist. 2006. Extraordinary renditions: A human rights analysis. *Harvard Human Rights Journal* 19: 123–60.

Wheeler, Nicholas J. 2002. Dying for "enduring freedom": Accepting responsibility for civilian casualties in the war against terrorism. *International Relations* 16, no. 2:205–25.

Whitaker, Beth Elise. 2007a. Exporting the Patriot Act? Democracy and the "War on Terror" in the Third World. *Third World Quarterly* 28, no. 5:1017–32.

———. 2007b. Compliance among weak states: Africa and the counterterrorism regime. Revised version of paper presented at the 103rd Annual Meeting of the American Political Science Association, August 30–September 2, 2007. Chicago.

White, G. 1994. Civil Society, Democratisation and Development (I): Clearing the Analytical Ground. *Democratisation* 1, no. 3, autumn: 375–390.

White, Jennifer R. 2005. IEEPA's override authority: Potential for a violation of the Geneva conventions' right to access for humanitarian organizations. *Michigan Law Review* 104: 2019–55.

Wickramasinghe, Nira. 2001. *Civil society in Sri Lanka: New circles of power*. New Delhi: Sage.

Wilson, A. J. 2000. *Sri Lankan Tamil nationalism: Its origins and development in the 19th and 20th centuries*. New Delhi: Penguin.

Wilson, Richard Ashby, ed. 2005. *Human rights in the "War on Terror."* New York: Cambridge University Press.

Woods, Ngaire. 2005. The shifting politics of foreign aid. *International Affairs* 81, no. 2:393–409.

World Bank. 2006. *Civil society and peacebuilding: Potential, limitations and critical factors*. Washington, D.C.: The World Bank, Social Development Department.

Zapata-Barrero, Ricard, and Nynke de Witte. 2007. The Spanish governance of border: Normative questions. *Mediterranean Politics* 12, no. 1:85–90.

Zedner, Lucia. 2008. Terrorism, the ticking bomb, and criminal justice values. *Criminal Justice Matters* 73, no. 1:18–19.

Zetter, Roger. 2007. More labels, fewer refugees: Remaking the refugee label in an era of globalization. *Journal of Refugee Studies* 20, no. 2:172–92.

ABOUT THE CONTRIBUTORS

Alejandro Colás teaches international relations at the School of Politics and Sociology, Birkbeck College, University of London, where he directs a postgraduate program on international security and global governance. He is author of *Empire* (Polity, 2007) and *International Civil Society* (Polity, 2002), and co-editor with Richard Saull of *The War on Terror and American Empire after the Cold War* (Routledge, 2005).

Alison Dunn is a senior lecturer in Law at Newcastle University in the UK. She is a member of the Charity Law Association and the Voluntary Sector Studies Network. Her research specializes in the field of charity law and the regulation of civil society, focusing in particular upon legal responses to political participation, organizational advocacy, activism, and policy formation. She has published widely in this field, including (2008) "Demanding Service or Servicing Demand? Charities, Regulation and the Policy Process" in the *Modern Law Review* (71:247–270), and she was editor of *The Voluntary Sector, the State and the Law* (Hart Publishing, 2000). The research for her chapter was completed with the aid of an award from the Arts and Humanities Research Council.

Stuart Gordon is a senior lecturer at the Royal Military Academy. He specializes in the politics of conflict and has written widely on the impact of changing military roles and competences. He has spent much of the past two years conducting research in Afghanistan and has been an adviser to the UK's Stabilisation Unit.

Kay Guinane is the program manager for the Charity and Security Network. She oversees its research and educational work and coordinates policy development and advocacy work aimed at bringing down barriers to legitimate work of nonprofits from ill-advised national security measures.

Prior to that she was director of nonprofit speech rights at OMB Watch, where she wrote and co-authored several reports on related subjects, including *Collateral Damage: How the War on Terror Hurts Charities, Foundations and the People They Serve.* As a public interest lawyer, Ms. Guinane has represented a wide variety of nonprofit organizations.

Jude Howell is professor and director of the Centre for Civil Society at the London School of Economics and Political Science. She has written extensively on civil society, the politics of development, security and civil society, governance, gender, and labor relations. Her recent books include *Counter-Terrorism, Aid and Civil Society: Before and After the War on Terror* (co-authored with Jeremy Lind; 2009, Palgrave Macmillan), *Gender and Civil Society* (co-edited with Diane Mulligan; 2005, Routledge), *Civil Society and Development* (co-authored with Jenny Pearce; 2002, Lynne Rienner, Inc.), *Governance in China* (2004, Rowman and Littlefield Publishers, Inc.), and *In Search of Civil Society: Market Reform and Social Change in Contemporary China* (co-authored with Gordon White and Shang Xiaoyuan; 1996, Clarendon Press, Oxford).

Kanykey Jailobaeva is a doctoral student in sociology at the University of Edinburgh. Her research explores the development of nongovernmental organizations and community-based organizations and their relationship with the state, as well as with international donors. She has recently published a policy brief with the Social Research Center of the American University of Central Asia, on "Enhanced Government Commitment: A Key to An Effective Government-NGO Relationship in Kyrgyzstan."

Jeremy Lind is a research associate at the Centre for Civil Society at the London School of Economics, specializing in conflict and the politics of development in northeast Africa. His main research interests include the links between civil society and violence, the problems of aid delivery in conflict areas, and the role of development in new security frameworks. With Jude Howell, he co-authored *Counter-terrorism, Aid and Civil Society: Before and After the War on Terror* (Palgrave Macmillan, 2009). He was lead editor of *Scarcity and Surfeit: The Ecology of Africa's Conflicts* (Institute for Security Studies, South Africa, 2002).

Nisrine Mansour is a research fellow at the Refugee Studies Centre at the University of Oxford and is affiliated with the Centre for Civil Society at the London School of Economics. She completed her PhD thesis at the

LSE's Social Policy Department, on the "Impact of Family Laws Policy Reforms on Women's Subjectivity and Agency in Post-Conflict Lebanon." Her research interests also include conflict, civilian protection, and humanitarianism, with a focus on the Middle East.

Mikewa Ogada is a human rights specialist with practical and research experience on human rights issues in Africa. He is a co-founder of the Nairobi-based Adili Consulting Group, a human rights and governance consultancy firm. He is the former head of the Research Program at the Kenya Human Rights Commission.

Annie Pettitt is a human rights researcher and consultant in Australia. Annie has extensive experience working as a human rights consultant—in particular, in preparing submissions to United Nations. She has recently completed her doctoral research in counter-terrorism policing and international human rights frameworks, with the Criminology Department at Monash University in Australia. Annie also specializes in economic, social, and cultural rights, focusing in particular on women's rights. She has extensive experience in policy development and working with nongovernmental organizations and civil society.

Joshua B. Rubongoya is a professor of Political Science at Roanoke College in Virginia. Previously he was a journalist in Uganda. He has published widely on democratization in Africa, with a focus on politics in Uganda. His most recent book, *Regime Hegemony in Museveni's Uganda: Pax Musevenica* (Palgrave/Macmillan, 2007), won the Best Book in African Politics award from the African Politics Conference Group of the African Studies Association of the United States.

Mutuma Ruteere is an independent scholar and the managing director of the Nairobi-based Adili Consulting Group, which specializes in governance and human rights. He has published on a diversity of human rights issues in Africa—most recently on violent crime and human rights in Kenya. His current research is on legal orders, security, and human rights in Africa.

Suraj K. Sazawal is the communications/research coordinator for the Charity and Security Network. Prior to that, he worked at OMB Watch and the Campaign Finance Institute. Suraj is a graduate of the University of Virginia and has earned an MA in Public Policy, with a specialization in national security, from George Mason University.

Daniel Stevens trained in political science at the LSE and has a doctorate in development studies from the School of Oriental and African Studies. Based on extensive country experience and work with international donors, his research focuses on the development of civil society in Uzbekistan and its interactions with donors, the state, and the private sector.

Kristian Stokke is a professor of Human Geography at the University of Oslo, specializing in movement politics and democratization in South Africa and conflict transformation and peacebuilding in Sri Lanka. His most recent books include *Rethinking Popular Representation* (edited with Olle Törnquist and Neil Webster; Palgrave, 2009), *Democratising Development: The Politics of Socioeconomic Rights in South Africa* (edited with Peris Jones; Martinus Nijhoff, 2005), and *Politicising Democracy: The New Local Politics of Democratisation* (edited with John Harriss and Olle Törnquist; Palgrave, 2004).

INDEX

Also from Kumarian Press . . .

Civil Society:

Transnational Civil Society: An Introduction
Edited by Srilatha Batliwala and L. David Brown

Nation-Building Unraveled? Aid, Peace and Justice in Afghanistan
Edited by Antonio Donini, Norah Niland and Karin Wermester

CIVICUS Global Survey of the State of Civil Society, Vol. 2: Comparative
Perspectives
Edited by V. Finn Heinrich and Lorenzo Fioramonti

Advocacy for Social Justice: A Global Action and Reflection Guide
David Cohen, Rosa de la Vega and Gabrielle Watson

New and Forthcoming:

From Political Won't to Political Will: Building Support for Participatory
Governance
Edited by Carmen Malena

A Fragile Balance: Re-examining the History of Foreign Aid, Security and
Diplomacy
Louis Picard and Terry Buss

Rights-Based Approaches to Development: Exploring the Potential and Pitfalls
Edited by Diana Mitlin and Sam Hickey

Leadership for Development: What Globalization Demands of Leaders Fighting
for Change
Edited by Dennis A. Rondinelli and John M. Heffron

Visit Kumarian Press at **www.kpbooks.com** or
call **toll-free 800.232.0223** for a complete catalog

Kumarian Press is committed to preserving ancient forests and natural resources. We elected to print this title on 30% post consumer recycled paper, processed chlorine free. As a result, for this printing, we have saved:

4 Trees (40' tall and 6-8" diameter)
2,008 Gallons of Wastewater
1 Million BTU's of Total Energy
122 Pounds of Solid Waste
417 Pounds of Greenhouse Gases

Kumarian Press made this paper choice because our printer, Thomson-Shore, Inc., is a member of Green Press Initiative, a nonprofit program dedicated to supporting authors, publishers, and suppliers in their efforts to reduce their use of fiber obtained from endangered forests.

For more information, visit www.greenpressinitiative.org

Environmental impact estimates were made using the Environmental Defense Paper Calculator. For more information visit: www.papercalculator.org.

 Kumarian Press, located in Sterling, Virginia, is a forward-looking, scholarly press that promotes active international engagement and an awareness of global connectedness.